The Encyclopedia of

TV & Movie Insults

A pop culture guide to put-downs, paybacks and other foul phrases from Television and the Cinema

By J. Alphonse Holst, MSLS

TV Acres Books **Rootstown, Ohio**

Copyright @ 2007 by Jerome Alphonse Holst

All rights reserved. No part of this book may be reproduced, stored in a retrieval system, or transmitted in any form whatsoever without written permission of the copyright owner, except in the case of brief quotations embodied in critical articles and reviews.

TV Acres Books
An Imprint of TVAcres.com
4001 Tallmadge Road
Rootstown, Ohio 44272
330-325-0145
www.tvacres.com

Cover Design: Greg Ricker, Youngstown, Ohio
Layout Design: Jerome A. Holst

ISBN-13: 978-0-9794133-0-8
Library of Congress Control Number: 2007901136

Publishers Cataloging-in-Publication Data

Holst, Jerome A, 1951-
The Encyclopedia of TV and Movie Insults: A pop culture guide to put-downs, paybacks, and other foul phrases from Television and the Cinema. / by J. Alphonse Holst. -- 1st ed. -- Rootstown, OH: TV Acres Books, c2007.
p. 324
Includes index
ISBN-13: 978-0-9794133-0-8 (pbk.)
1. Invective -- Quotations, maxims, etc. 2. Television programs -- United States -- Quotations, maxims, etc. 3. Motion pictures -- Quotations, maxims, etc. 4. Popular Culture -- Dictionaries. I. Title.
PN 1994.9 .H6 2007
791.43

Manufactured in the United States of America

10 9 8 7 6 5 4 3 2 1

CONTENTS

DEDICATION

This book is dedicated to my father, Norman Richard Holst, Sr., and my mother, Mary Louise Rheaume Holst. Married for 60 years, my parents raised nine wonderful children. They leave behind a legacy of love and caring, which even now, continues through their many grandchildren.

ACKNOWLEDGMENTS

The Encyclopedia of TV and Movie Insults would not have been possible if not for the many creative people in Hollywood who dedicated their lives to producing the films and television shows that entertain the masses. Therefore, the author would like to thank the following:

All the TV Networks
All the Movie Studios
All the Technicans (Lighting, Sound, Prop, Art and Scenery)
All the Actors & Actresses
All the Writers, Directors and Producers

INTRODUCTION

Hollywood writers have known for years the impact of a well-written put-down, a glorious payback and the stark effectiveness of a foul phrase or two to make a point and move a story along. Who can forget the final scene of the western *Shane* (1953) when Alan Ladd says, "You're a low down Yankee liar" to Jack Palance; or the legendary "You dirty rat!" attributed to actor James Cagney; and more recently Arnold Schwarzenegger's steely payback of "Hasta la vista, Baby" in the sci-fi classic *Terminator 2: Judgment Day* (1991). These and other phrases (which often become signature trademarks) surely at one time or another made each one of us grimace in disgust or cock our elbows back in delight. As Beavis & Butt-Head might say, "Huh, Huh, Insults rule! Yeah! Yeah!"

With this in mind, I have gathered together a collection of put-downs, paybacks, pejorative nicknames and other foul phrases from classic movies and television. From the bigoted remarks of TV's Archie Bunker, to the menacing paybacks of film land's 'Dirty' Harry Callahan, TV AND MOVIE INSULTS takes the reader on a bumpy ride through the slings and arrows of outrageous affronts. At a glance, one can relive all the anger, bigotry, meanness and hate that Hollywood has to offer.

The phrases in this book were chosen because they make fun of, tease, belittle, degrade, humiliate, hurt, intimidate, mock, mortify, scare, shock or bring disrespect or harm to a person's mental, spiritual or physical well being. For example, racial slurs, sexist remarks (chauvinistic or misogynistic sentiments), pejorative nicknames, belittling put-downs, death threats, etc. In other words, the phrases were selected because they could produce such reactions as "Yuck!" "Ewww!" "Geeze, that isn't very nice." and "Alright! That jerk got what he deserved!"

TV AND MOVIE INSULTS is arranged alphabetically by individual phrase and includes short summaries that describe the situation behind the put-down or insult; the name of the actor and character mouthing the phrase; as well as the source of the phrase, be it from a television program or a motion picture.

Flo: "Well, I've never been so insulted in my life."
Hachenbush: [Looking at his watch] "Well, it's early yet."

– A Day at the Races (1937)

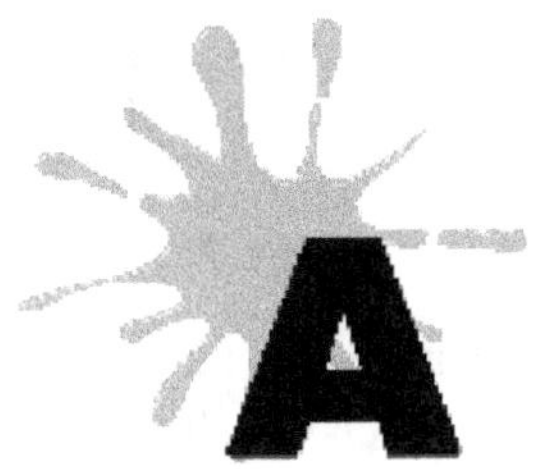

"All dames are all alike" - The sentiments of private eye Rigby Reardon (Steve Martin) in the motion picture *Dead Men Don't Wear Plaid* (1982). His full rant: "All dames are alike. They reach down your throat and they can grab your heart, pull it out and they throw it on the floor, step on it with their high heels, spit on it, shove it in the oven and cook the shit out of it. Then they slice it into little pieces, slam it on a hunk of toast, and serve it to you and then expect you to say, 'Thanks, honey, it was delicious'." Note: In the film *Johnny Dangerously* (1984) Danny Vermin offered this critique: "Dames are put on this earth to weaken us, drain our energy, laugh at us when they see us naked." Jerry Lacy (a Humphrey Bogart double) waxed nostalgic in *Play It Again, Sam* (1972) when he said, "Dames are simple. I never met one that didn't understand a slap in the mouth or a slug from a forty-five." Peter Falk as Abe "Kid Twist" Reles in the 1960 film *Murder, Inc.* did a variation of the phrase when he said, "I'm gonna tell you something about women. I never met one that didn't need a rap in the head, and often." And, in the film *Torrid Zone* (1940), James Cagney as plantation foreman Nick Butler puts down nightclub star Lee Donley (Ann Sheridan) with "The trouble with you dames is you're always building castles in the air and trying to move into them."

"All I need is a little spackling and some napalm to turn it into a really nice mausoleum" - Chevy Chase as Fletch, a Los Angeles reporter mouths disappointment when he first sees the condition of a dilapidated Louisiana home that he inherited in the motion picture *Fletch Lives* (1989). Note: In the film *Beetlejuice* (1988) Catharine O'Hara as Delia Deitz evaluates her new home and says, "A little gasoline...blowtorch...no problem." Delia later tells her husband Charles (Jeffrey Jones), "I will live with you in this hellhole, but I must express myself. If you don't let me gut out this house and make it my own, I will go insane and I will take you with me!"

"All of you! You all killed him! And my brother, and Riff. Not with bullets, or guns, with hate. Well now I can kill, too, because now I have hate!" - Natalie Wood as Maria, a Puerto Rican beauty whose boyfriend Tony (Richard Beymer) gets killed in a gang fight in the motion picture *West Side Story* (1961).

"All the animals come out at night—whores, scum, pussies, buggers, queens, fairies, dopers, junkies. Sick, Venal. Someday a real rain will come and wash all the scum off the street" - Robert De Niro as troubled Vietnam veteran cabbie Travis Bickle narrates the beginning of the motion picture *Taxi Driver* (1976). *See also* "You talkin' to me?"

"All women of the theater were chiselers; parasites—as we called them, gold diggers"- Guy Kibbee as Boston lawyer Faneuil H. Peabody reminisces about his early youth when he trod the primrose path on the Great White Way in the motion picture *Gold Diggers 1933* (1933).

"Alligators have the right idea. They eat their young" - Eve Arden as Ida Corwin offers a morbid quip to friend Mildred Pierce (Joan Crawford) whose troubled daughter Veda Pierce (Ann Blyth) has been bringing her mother untold grief in the motion picture *Mildred Pierce (*1945). When Veda murders Monte Beragan (Zachary Scott) Mildred tells Ida, "You don't know what it's like being a mother, Ida. Veda's a part of me. Maybe she didn't turn out as well as I'd hope she would when she was born, but she's still my daughter and I can't forget that." That is, until Veda makes a play for Mildred's second husband and Mildred threatens to kill her daughter is she doesn't leave her house.

"An artist is someone who is starving in their twenties. I'm thirty-two. I'm a deadbeat" - Joseph Brazil Grasaffi III as Cody in the motion picture *Laughing Boy* (1999).

"An immaculate murder. We've killed for the sake of danger and the sake of killing...How did you feel during it? I felt tremendous, exhilarated" - John Dall as prep-schooler Shaw Brandon expresses elation over the thrill murder of a fellow student that he committed with his partner Philip (Farley Granger) in the motion picture *Rope* (1948). After Professor Rupert Cadell (James Stewart) suspects' foul play from the two boys, he begins a dialog about the theory of murder, saying, "Murder is—or should be—an art, and as such, the privilege of committing it should be reserved for the few who are really superior individuals." Brandon continues the Professor's line of reasoning: "And the victims are inferior, whose lives are unimportant anyway!" Shocked, the Professor quietly replies, "Obviously."

"And don't ever let me catch you guys in America" - Leslie Nielsen as incompetent Lt. Frank Drebin in the motion picture *The Naked Gun* (1988). At the beginning of this film, Lt. Drebin (in a fantasy sequence a la Rambo) crashes into a room filled with all the supposed enemies of America. After kicking their asses, Frank warns, "I'm Lt. Frank Drebin, Police Squad. And don't ever let me catch you in America." Among those beaten to a pulp were Russian Premier Gorbachev, Dictators Idi Amin, Arafat, Khadafi, and Islamic leader Khomeni.

"And I took the butcher knife and put it up to her neck. I said if you want to live to see tomorrow, you better start fryin' them eggs a little bit better than what you a fryin' em—I'm tired of eatin' sloppy, slimy eggs!" - Tap-dancer Jesco White educates his cook about proper food presentation skills in a flashback sequence from the documentary short *The Dancing Outlaw* (1991) produced for West Virginia's public TV "Different Drummer" series.

"And it won't be finished until your dirty little empire is wiped off the face of the earth" - Dana Andrews as U.S. pilot Captain Harvey Ross in the wartime drama *Purple Heart* (1944) who was captured while on a bombing run over Tokyo during WWII.

Condemned to death, Ross explains the indomitable spirit of the American people to his Japanese captors: "No your Excellency. It's true we Americans don't know very much about you Japanese. And we never did. And now I realize you know even less about us. You can kill us. All of us, or part of us. But if you think that's going to put the fear of God into the United States of America, and stop them from sending other flyers to bomb you, you're wrong. Dead wrong. They'll come by night; they'll come by day. Thousands of them. They'll blacken your skies and burn your cities to the ground and make you get down on your knees and beg for mercy. This is your war. You wanted it. You asked for it. You started it. And now, you're going to get it. And it won't be finished until your dirty little empire is wiped off the face of the earth."

"And then he calls me a jerk" - Wisconsin man (David Lomax) reporting an incident to a police officer in the motion picture *Fargo* (1996). Talking to a man shoveling snow, the police officer listens patiently: "So, I'm tendin' bar there at Ecklund and Sedlin's last Tuesday and this little guy's drinkin' and he says, 'So where can a guy find some action? I'm goin' crazy down there at the lake.' And I says, 'What kinda action?' and he says, 'Woman action, what do I look like?' And I says, 'Well, what do 'I' look like, I don't arrange that kinda thing,' So he says, 'So I get it, so you think I'm some kinda jerk for askin,' only he doesn't use the word jerk. And then he calls me a jerk and says the last guy who thought he was a jerk was dead now. So I don't say nothin' and he says, 'What do ya think about that?' So I says, 'Well, that don't sound like too good a deal for him then'."

"And then just a pinch of cyanide" - The makings of a recipe for a deadly cocktail used by Martha Brewster (Jean Adair) in the film *Arsenic and Old Lace* (1944). When Martha's nephew, Mortimer Brewster (Cary Grant) discovers that his loony aunt has been murdering old men and burying them in the basement, he confronts Martha who confides in her method of murder: "For a gallon of elderberry wine, I take one teaspoonful of arsenic, then I add a half a teaspoon of strychnine, and then just a pinch of cyanide." Astonished, at his predicament Mortimer says, "Insanity runs in my family. It practically gallops." In the spirit of poisoning men, the film *Sherlock Holmes* (1970) and the comment of British sleuth Sherlock Holmes (Roberts Stephens) seems appropriate: "Actually, I don't dislike women, I merely distrust them. The twinkle in the eye and the arsenic in the soup."

"And what did that produce? The cuckoo clock" - Orson Welles as black marketer Harry Lime tells novelist Holly Martin (Joseph Cotten) the inadequacies of Switzerland in the motion picture *The Third Man* (1949). His full observation: "In Italy for thirty years under the Borgias, they had warfare, terror, murder, and bloodshed. But they produced Michelangelo, Leonardo da Vinci, and the Renaissance. In Switzerland they had brotherly love, and they had five hundred years of democracy and peace. And what did that produce? The cuckoo clock."

"Angel, ha! She's a female! And all females is poison! They're full of wicked wiles!" - Grumpy (Pinto Colvig), one of the seven dwarfs disagrees with the description of Snow White when she is found sleeping in the dwarfs' forest home in the animated classic *Snow White and the Seven Dwarfs* (1937).

"Anti-wrinkle cream there may be, but anti-fat-bastard cream there is not" - Mark Addy as Dave Althorpe, one of six unemployed steel workers who form a striptease act, critiques his performers in the motion picture *The Full Monty* (1997). Fellow stripper Gerald Arthur Cooper (Tom Wilkinson) put in his two cents and says, "He's fat, you're thin, and you're both fucking ugly."

"Any man I see out there, I'm gonna shoot him" - Widowed gunfighter Will Munny (Clint Eastwood) warns town folks in the western *Unforgiven* (1992). Coming out of retirement to earn money for his children, Will Munny and colleague Ned Logan (Morgan Freeman) take the job of avenging the mutilation of a frontier prostitute. When the town sheriff "Little Bill" Daggett (Gene Hackman) kills Ned, Will comes to avenge his death and tells the sheriff, "That's right, I've killed women and children just about everything that walks or crawls at one time or another. And I'm, here to kill you Little Bill, for what you did to Ned." After a brief fire fight with the townsfolk, Will yells, "All right now, I'm comin' out. Any man I see out there, I'm gonna shoot him. Any son of a bitch takes a shot at me, I'm not only gonna kill him, but I'm gonna kill his wife. All his friends. Burn his damn house down." At the film's conclusion, as Will prepares to ride out of town, he admonishes, "You better bury Ned right, better not cut up nor otherwise harm no whores, or I'll come back and kill every one of you sons of bitches."

"Any man that hates small dogs and children can't be all-bad!" - Surly remark attributed to movie actor W. C. Fields. In reality, the statement is the opinion of Leo Rosten, a writer commenting on Field's comedy persona. Field's is famous for saying "Go away kid, you bother me (or "you draw flies") to child actor Baby Leroy. Field's opinion on children included, "There's no such thing as a tough child. If you parboil them first for seven hours, they always come out tender" and "I believe children should neither be seen nor heard from ever again." *See also* "I'll mow you down"

"Any man who consorts with niggers, deserves to be treated like a nigger" - Spoken by Andrew Duggan in the offbeat post Civil War era comedy film *The Skin Game* (1971). In the film, Duggan plays an angry white southerner preparing to give 50 lashes to a con artist (James Garner) posing as the master of a slave.

"Any of your friends in Tokyo have trouble committing hara-kiri, those boys will be glad to help them out" - Humphrey Bogart as undercover agent Richard Lomas Leland offers a helping hand to Japanese spies in the motion picture *Across the Pacific* (1942).

"Anybody who builds a house today is crazy" - Cary Grant as advertising executive Jim Blanding complains about houses in the motion picture *Mr. Blandings Builds His Dream House* (1948). After he agrees to build a home in the country, Mr. Blanding laments his decision to friend of the family Bill Cole (Melvin Douglas). "Anybody who builds a house today is crazy. The minute you start, they put you on a list—the All-American Sucker list. You start out to build a home and you wind up in the poorhouse. And if it can happen to me, what about the fellas who aren't making $15,000 a year? What about the kids who just got married and want a home of their own? It's a conspiracy, I tell you. A conspiracy against every boy and girl, who were ever in love."

"Anyone connected with drugs deserves to die" - John P. Ryan vents his frustrations with drug dealers (his daughter died from drugs) to urban vigilante Paul Kersey (Charles Bronson) in the motion picture *Death Wish 4: The Crackdown* (1987). Kersey could relate to the father's anger, because his own wife and daughter were attacked and savagely raped by whacked out street punks in the seminal film *Death Wish* (1974).

"Anytime I can embarrass my spouse, it makes me feel better" - Motto of Al Bundy (Ed O'Neill), a frustrated shoe salesman featured on the sitcom MARRIED...WITH CHILDREN/FOX/1987-97. A variation of the motto: "When one Bundy is embarrassed, the rest of us feel good about ourselves." Still another of Al Bundy's credos was "Hooters! Hooters! Yum! Yum! Yum! Hooters! Hooters! On a girl that's dumb!"

"Are there any queers in the theater tonight? Get 'em up against the wall!" - Bob Geldof as 'Pink,' a fictional drug-dependent rock singer in the cult motion picture *Pink Floyd The Wall* (1982). Singing on stage, Mr. Pink looks into the audience and shouts "Are there any queers in the theater tonight? Get 'em up against the wall! That one in the spotlight, he don't look right! Get him up against the wall! And that one looks Jewish...and that one's a coon! Who let all this riff raff into the room? That one's smoking a joint! And that one's got spots! If I had my way, I'd have the lot of you shot!"

"Are you crying? Are you crying? There's no crying in baseball!" - Tom Hanks as baseball coach Jimmy Dugan chastises one of his players on an all-female baseball team about the rules of the sport in the motion picture *A League of Their Own* (1992). Although Jimmy's opinion of girl baseball players changed over time, he initially says, "Ballplayers! I haven't got ballplayers, I've got girls! Girls are what you sleep with after the game, not, not what you coach during the game."

"Are you eating a tomato or is that your nose?" - One of many put-downs expressed by ventriloquist dummy Charlie McCarthy (voice of Edgar Bergen) to comedian W. C. Fields in his role as Larson E. Whipsnade in the movie *You Can't Cheat an Honest Man* (1939). W.C. Fields' comeback to such an insult? "Quiet, or I'll throw a woodpecker at you." Fields also told Charlie "You must come down with me after the show to the lumberyard and ride piggyback on the buzz saw." *See also* "I'll Mow You Down!"

"Are you gonna bark all day, little doggie, or are you gonna bite?" - Michael Madsen as gangster Mr. Blonde goads Mr. White (Harvey Keitel) into fighting in the motion picture *Reservoir Dogs* (1992). When Mr. Blond was asked why he tortured policeman Kirk Baltz (Marvin Nash) he simply replied, "It's amusing to me to torture a cop."

"Are you quitting me?" - Gruff inquiry of Marine Gunnery Sergeant Hartman (R. Lee. Ermey) in the movie *Full Metal Jacket* (1987). As a Marine recruit falters under the pressure of military training, Sgt. Hartman, the drill instructor from hell, lays into the grunt screaming, "Are you quitting on me? Well, are you? Then quit, you slimy fucking walrus-looking piece of shit! Get the fuck off of my obstacle! Get the fuck down off of my obstacle! Now! Move it! I'm going to rip your balls off, so you cannot contaminate the rest of the world! I will motivate you, Private Pyle, if it short-dicks every cannibal on the Congo!" Other Hartman put-downs included "There is no racial bigotry here. I do not look down on niggers, kikes, wops or greasers. Here, you are all equally worthless in my corps."; "Private Pyle I'm gonna give you three seconds, exactly three fuckin' seconds, to wipe that stupid lookin' grin off your face or I will gouge out your eyeballs and skull fuck you!"; and [goading recruit about the Virgin Mary] "Why you little maggot, you make me want to vomit! [Slaps Marine] You goddamned communist heathen, you had best sound off that you love the Virgin Mary, or I'm gonna stomp your guts out!" When one recruit spoke out of turn Hartman exploded, "Who said that? Who the fuck said that? Who's the slimy little communist shit, twinkle-toed cocksucker who just signed his own death warrant?"

"As an actor, no one could touch him. As a human being, no one wanted to touch him" - Walter Matthau as elderly Willy Clark speaks of his former vaudevillian partner Al Lewis (George Burns) in the motion picture *The Sunshine Boys* (1975). Referring to his partner Willy, Al says, "I don't hate him...Can't stand him, but I don't hate him."

"As God is my witness, they're not going to lick me...I'm going to live through this and when it's over I'll never be hungry again. No, nor any of my folks! If I have to lie, steal, cheat, kill—as God is my witness, I'll never be hungry again." - Vivien Leigh as Southern Belle Scarlett O'Hara delivers her defiant pledge to beat adversity in the Civil War motion picture *Gone with the Wind* (1939). *See also* "Frankly, my dear, I don't give a damn"

"As I walk through the valley where there are shadows of death, I will fear no evil, because I am the most evil motherfucker in the valley" - Vicious killer espouses his personal convictions in the motion picture *Killing the Badge* (1999).

"As the cars roar into Pennsylvania, the cradle of liberty, it seems apparent that our citizens are staying off the streets, which may make scoring particularly difficult, even with this year's rule changes" - Carle Benson as a man named Harold narrates the "*Death Race 2000*," a brutal, futuristic cross-country competition that gives points for running down pedestrians in the motion picture *Death Race 2000* (1975). Harold continues explaining the rules: "To recap those revisions: women are still worth 10 points more than men in all age brackets, but teenagers now rack up 40 points, and toddlers under 12 now rate a big 70 points. The big score: anyone, any sex, over 75 years old has been upped to 100 points."

"At first I found it hard to believe that my father was Japanese, and that I was part-Japanese. But that would explain why I've always had these strange, non-American urges to work very hard, save money, and live without credit cards" - John Altamura as The Toxic Avenger, the first superhero from New Jersey discusses his family roots in the motion picture *The Toxic Avenger, Part II* (1989).

"At least he's not a book burner, you Nazi cow!" - Amy Madigan as Annie Kinsella defends the works of 1960s author Terence Mann (James Earl Jones) at a PTA meeting in the motion picture *Field of Dreams* (1989). *See also* "Go Burn the Books"

"At my signal, unleash hell" - Russell Crowe as Maximus, a general commanding the Roman legions against a horde of Germanic barbarians who dare resist the forces of Roman Empire ruled by Marcus Aurelius (Richard Harris) in the film *Gladiator* (2000).

Attila the Nun - Sister Agnes (Priscilla Lopez) is a streetwise nun who works with the poor in a downtown Baltimore mission on the sitcom IN THE BEGINNING/CBS/1978. When Father Daniel McCleary (McLean Stevenson) gets assigned to work with her, their philosophies clash and he soon labels her "Attila the Nun."

"Awful, awful, what do they expect us to do with all this information?" - Holly Hunter as divorcee Judith Mohr reacts to all the bad news on television in the motion picture *Living Out Loud (*1998). She continues, "What am I suppose to do about crack babies? Terrorism?! I can't stand those terrorists, they're so mad at everybody; I wish they'd just get over it! Maybe I should adopt a crack baby, sent it to a good school, get a chance of... Oh shut up! I'm gonna raise an inner city child in this building? I can't stand the people in this building, with their jeeps and their loafers. Their mean, stuck-up private school kids will make fun of my crack baby; my crack baby will have no play dates, poor kid. Awful, what do they expect us to do with all this information? What am I suppose to do with all this information? Awful, awful, awful."

"Awww, go blow your jets!" - Frequent remark directed to the members of the Solar Guard by Cadet Roger Manning (Jan Merlin), a wise cracking radar man assigned to the rocket cruiser *Polaris* on the science fiction adventure TOM CORBETT, SPACE CADET/CBS/ABC/NBC/1950-55. Other catchphrases were, "Now you've done it, Junior!"; "So what happens now, space heroes?"; "By the rings of Saturn!"; "By the craters of Luna!"; "Easy there, don't blast your Jets!" and on a more positive note "Spaceman's Luck!"

"Baby, I wanna..." - The first words of every sexual come-on used by Desperation Lee (Phil Marr), the host of *Funky Walker, Dirty Talker*, a 1970s style talk show skit on Fox network's MAD TV in the 1990s. Sporting an afro-hairdo and flowered disco shirts, Desperation Lee ("Smoother than Ex-Lax and twice as sexy") sweet-talked his female guests with such suggestive overtures as "Baby, I wanna..."

- Open up your liquor cabinet and pour me a stiff one.
- Climb up your turn table and get stuck in your groove."
- Be some kind of astronaut, so I could get caught in your black hole.
- Look at your menu and order some ass cargot.
- Get out my telescope, so I can get a look at Uranus.
- Make like Winnie the Pooh and get my nose stuck up in your honey jar.
- Whip out my hose and water your fresh cut lawn.
- Make like the little Dutch boy and put my finger in your dike.
- Put on one of those miners helmets and do some serious drilling.

The show played "baby making" music and ended with Desperation Lee and his guests doing a "funky walk" as they strutted off camera.

"Bah! Humbug!" - *See* "Humbug!"

"Back off, Mister or these walls will be getting a free paint job" - Joe Senaca as blues harmonica player Willie Brown waves a gun in the motion picture *Crossroads* (1986). Another home improvement idea appeared in the motion picture *Last Action Hero* (1993) when Bridgette Wilson as Whitney shouts, "Lose the guns or I redecorate in brain-matter grey, got it?"

Backseat Becky - College nickname of Miss Rebecca Howe (Kirstie Alley), the manager of a Boston tavern named Cheers on the sitcom CHEERS/NBC/1982-93. Frasier Crane (Kelsey Grammer), a psychiatrist who frequented the bar, discovered that Rebecca Howe—who had gone to the University of Connecticut—was considered a "party girl on campus." Carla (Rhea Perlman), a waitress at Cheers couldn't believe that "Miss Granite Panties" could have ever been that amorous. And Sam Malone (Ted Danson), the head bartender who tried unsuccessfully to bed Miss Howe, comments in disbelief "the one who goes through life with her knees bolted together?" Upon further investigation with an ex-school chum of Rebecca's, Frasier Crane unearthed, the nickname "Backseat Becky." When confronted with the fact that everyone in the bar knew her college nickname, Rebecca told them it was because she was very shy and that the girls in college thought it would be a "real gas" to call her the opposite of what she really was. Seeing that the crowd at Cheers was not buying that story, she then countered with, "I was really aggressive in college. I never took a BACKSEAT to anyone." No, that still didn't convince her friends. Finally, in a quiet moment, she pulled Sam Malone to the side and agreed to tell the real story behind her nickname, if he kept it quiet. With Sam agreeing to her terms, she began:

> "I was living in a women's dorm on campus and one night a fire broke out. Well, I didn't have time to change my cloths, so I had to run out into the parking lot wearing only a teddy...black, but see through. All of a sudden, I was caught in this fire engine's headlights. Well, I didn't know what to do. I looked all around, and suddenly I spotted this open convertible. Well, I climbed in and I slunk down into the back seat. Suddenly, this hulking fireman was standing over me. It was magnificent. I looked in his eyes. I knew what he wanted...and I wanted it, too. When it was over I opened my eyes and I noticed we were not alone. Others had watched and not said a word. And that's why I'm known as 'Backseat Becky'. Satisfied?"

Wiping his now sweaty face with a white bar towel, Sam enters the men's room. Rebecca then walks over to Carla, and says, "Thanks for the story, Carla, here's your ten bucks." To which Carla replies, "Yeah, the twenty dollar one would have killed him."

"Bang, you're dead" - Final words written by professional hit man Arthur Bishop (Charles Bronson) to a younger wannabe assassin Steve McKenna (Jan-Michael Vincent) in the motion picture *The Mechanic* (1972). When Arthur's protégé returned home (after killing Arthur), he sits inside Bishop's car and finds a note: "Steve, if you read this it means I didn't make it back. It also means you've broken a filament to a thirteen-second-delay trigger. End of game. Bang, you're dead." [The car explodes]. Earlier in the film, Arthur justified his career as a hit man by saying, "Murder is only killing without a license and everybody kills...the army...the police..." *See also* "So long, Sport"

Barky - Insulting nickname given to Dana Foster (Staci Keanan) by her stepbrother J. T. Lambert (Brandon Call) on the sitcom STEP BY STEP/ABC/1991-98. J. T. once teased Dana about not being invited to a party by saying, "I'd invite you, but they don't allow dogs!" He also called Dana "Vampira," "Frosty the Step-sister" and "The Undateable." Dana, in turn, called J. T. a "sleazeball" and a "knuckle-dragger", among others quips. Frank's nephew Cody Lambert (Sasha Mitchell), however, thought that Dana was very attractive. He once said, "If she were a prehistoric creature, she'd be a "BABE-ertooth tiger." Dana, however, thought Cody was "a brain-dead idiot." She elaborated by saying "If I had the choice of going out with you or putting out an oil fire with my tongue, I'd be on the first plane to Kuwait."

Bart Simpson Phone Pranks - Bratty little Bart Simpson from THE SIMPSONS/FOX/1990+ had a penchant for pulling pernicious stunts on the folks in his hometown of Springfield. Besides shouting his signature catchphrases, "Eat My Shorts" and "Don't have a cow, man!" Bart especially enjoyed telephoning Moe's Tavern and having Moe the bartender page bogus customers whose names were practical jokes. Some typical exchanges:

Bart: Hello, is Al there?
Moe: Al?
Bart: Yeah, Al. Last name: Coholic.
Moe: Lemme check...Phone call for Al. Al Coholic. Is there an Al Coholic here?

-- "*Some Enchanted Evening*"

Bart: Is Jacques there?
Moe: Who?
Bart: Jacques, last name Strap.
Moe: Uh, hold on. Uh, Jacques... Strap... Hey guys I'm looking for a Jacques Strap.

-- "*Moaning Lisa*"

Bart: Hello, is Homer there?
Moe: Homer who?
Bart: Homer ... Sexual.
Moe: Wait one second, let me check. Uh, Homer Sexual? Hey, come on, one of you guys has got to be Homer Sexual!

-- "*Principal Charming*"

Moe: Hello, Moe's Tavern. Birthplace of the Rob Roy.
Bart: Is Seymour there? Last name Butz.
Moe: Just a sec. Is there a Butz here? A Seymour Butz? Hey, everybody, I wanna Seymour Butz!

-- "*One Fish, Two Fish, Blowfish, Blue Fish*"

Bart: Uh, yes, I'm looking for a friend of mine. Last name Jass. First name Hugh.
Moe: Uh, hold on, I'll check. Hugh Jass! Somebody check the Men's room for a Hugh Jass!

-- "*Flaming Moe's*"

Bart: Uh, yes, I'm looking for a Mrs. O'Problem? First name, Bea.
Moe: Uh, yeah, just a minute, I'll check. Uh, Bea O'Problem? Bea O'Problem! Come on guys, do I have a Bea O'Problem here?

-- "*Burns Verkaufen der Kraftwerk*"

"Basically, I'm fucked!"- Mel Gibson as police detective Martin Riggs talks to his new partner Roger Murtaugh (Danny Glover) in the action adventure *Lethal Weapon* (1987). "Look," says Riggs, "why don't we just cut the shit here? Hey, look friend...We both know why I was transferred. Everyone thinks I'm suicidal, in which case, I'm fucked and nobody wants to work with me. Or they think I'm faking to draw a psycho pension, in which case, I'm fucked and nobody wants to work with me. Basically, I'm fucked."

As Riggs and Murtaugh got closer as partners, Murtaugh begs the question, "Do you want to die?" Riggs reluctantly replies, "Oh, what do you want to hear, man? Do you want to hear that sometimes I think about eating a bullet?...Well, I do...I even got a special one for the occasion with a hollow point. Look...make sure it blows the back of my goddamn head out, do the job right...Every single day I wake up and think of a reason not to do it...This is going to make you laugh...You know why I don't do it?...The job, doing my job—now that's the reason."

"Be advised, I eat concertina wire and piss napalm, I can put a round through a flea's ass at 300 yards" - Clint Eastwood as hell-raising career Marine Sgt. Tom Highway in the motion picture *Heartbreak Ridge* (1986). Highway also told his troops "I've drank more beer, pissed more blood, and banged more quiff than all you numb-nuts put together."

"Beat 'em or burn 'em" - Advice of Pennsylvania policeman Sheriff McClelland (George Kosana) in the cult horror flick *Night of the Living Dead* (1968). Giving tips to the locals on how to kill flesh-eating zombies that are roaming the countryside, McClelland advises, "Well, if you had a gun, shoot 'em in the head. If you didn't, get a torch and burn 'em, they go up pretty easy. Beat 'em or burn 'em." A research scientist (Frank Doak) offered this solution: "Kill the brain and you kill the ghoul." Note: In the film *The Howling* (1980) Dick Miller as a bookstore owner tells how to kill werewolves: "Silver bullets or fire, that's the only way to get rid of the damn things. They're worse than cockroaches."

"Behind every successful man, there's a woman with a big mouth" - Dick Van Dyke as comedy writer Rob Petrie berates his wife, Laura (Mary Tyler Moore) for spilling the beans on an episode of the sitcom THE DICK VAN DYKE SHOW/CBS/1961-66.

"Being miserable and treating other people like dirt is every New Yorker's God-given right" - David Margulies as the Mayor of New York City expresses an unwritten law of the streets in the film *Ghostbusters II* (1989). Later, when a politician ignores Ghostbuster Peter Venkman (Bill Murray), he objects, "Listen, I'm a voter. Aren't you supposed to lie to me and kiss my butt?"

"Better to gas 100,000 Jews than to have a pig like that messing around with my daughter" - Jorg von Liebenfels as Erwin Schneider, a very upset and racist German truck driver longing for better times (the Nazi regime) when he discovers his 14-year-old daughter Hanni Schneider had sex with Franz Bermeier (Harry Baer), a 19-year-old Jewish boy in the made for German television motion picture *Jail Bait aka: Wild Game* (1972)—released in the USA in 1977. The seductive Hanni eventually coaxes Franz into murdering her father. Note: In the film *U Turn* (1997), Sean Penn as wise-guy loser Bobby Cooper says to Darrell (Billy Bob Thornton), "Darrell, 40,000 people die every day. Why aren't you one of them?"

"Billy Blitton couldn't find his butt with both hands" - Gene Hackman shares his opinion of another lawyer to his own assistant Nick Holbrook (Laurence Fishburne) in the motion picture *Class Action* (1991).

"Bite me, pig!" - Bitter retort of cosmetically-challenged secretary Mimi Bobeck (Kathy Kinney) on the situation comedy THE DREW CAREY SHOW/ABC/1995-2004. "Bite me, Pig" is but one of many insults that Mimi hurls at her nemesis, co-worker Drew Carey. Other put-downs include: "Pig!," "Hey, Pig!" and "Bite me Dough Boy!" Mimi even altered Drew's business cards to read: DREW CAREY THE PIG...THE OTHER WHITE MEAT.

"Black guys would rather look good and lose than look bad and win" - Woody Harrelson as Caucasian Billy Hoyle puts down his black partner Sidney Deane (Wesley Snipes) both of whom hustle local neighborhood basketball players for money (which Billy needs to pay off gangsters) in the motion picture *White Men Can't Jump* (1992). *See also* "Your Mama!"

"Blasphemy? Before what God? A God repulsed by the miserable humanity He created in His own image? I will not be shackled by the failures of your God. The only blasphemy is to wallow in insignificance. I have taken the refuse of your God and I have triumphed. There! There is MY creation! - Jeffrey Combs as Herbert West, a mad scientist who revives the dead and steals body parts in the motion picture *Bride of Re-Animator* (1990.

Bond Women - In the James Bond films, many of the female characters are given suggestive, sexist names which help titillate the moviegoers. These names ooze of sexual harassment and disrespect for females, in general. The following is a list of such names with the actresss name and the film in which they appeared:

Character	Actress	Film
Honey Ryder	Ursula Andress	*Dr. No*
Pussy Galore	Honor Blackman	*Goldfinger*
Kissy Suzuki	Mie Hama	*You Only Live Twice*
Plenty O'Toole	Lana Wood	*Diamonds Are Forever*
Mary Goodnight	Britt Ekland	*Man with the Golden Gun*
Holly Goodhead	Lois Chiles	*Moonraker*
Octopussy	Maud Adams	*Octopussy*
Xenia Onatopp	Famke Janssen	*Goldeneye*

As an homage to the James Bond films, the Austin Powers spy films *Austin Powers: International Man of Mystery* (1997) and the sequel *Austin Powers: The Spy Who Shagged Me* (1999) created their own voluptuous females.

Character	Actress	Film
Alotta Fagina	Fabiana Udenio	*International Man of Mystery*
Felicity Shagwell	Heather Graham	*Spy Who Shagged Me*
Ivana Humpalot	Kristen Johnston	*Spy Who Shagged Me*
Robin Spitz Swallows	Gia Carides	*Spy Who Shagged Me*

Note: Another instance of "Bond Women" appeared on the sitcom WINGS/NBC/1990-96 when Casey Davenport (Amy Yasbeck) appeared as the leggy seductress Mounds O'Plenty during a James Bond dream sequence.

Boob Tube - The pejorative term used to describe the television set. It is also called The Idiot Box, The Glass Teat, the Plug-in-Drug, and Bubble Gum for the Eyes (Frank Lloyd Wright's opinion of TV). People who spend many hours watching television are referred to as Vidiots, Couch Potatoes, and TV Junkies.

"The bottom's full of nice people, Albert. Only cream and bastards rise" - Paul Newman as hard-boiled private eye Lew Harper offers his own special view of humanity with Albert Graves (Arthur Hill) in the motion picture *Harper* (1966).

"Boy, just be yourself. If people don't like you for being yourself...*FUCK 'EM!*" - Mac Bernie as Uncle Vester explains the importance of being true to yourself in the motion picture *House Party 3* (1994). He continues his lesson: "Let me tell you something. I scored with a girl when I was about your age. I try to please her poppa all the time; went out my way to please her poppa. I came in one day, I said, 'Nice weather we having.' He said, 'You can't say that. You can't say that; it might rain.' I said, 'Nice tie you got on.' 'You can't say that; wife try to choke me with it.' Point I'm trying to tell you, son, is be yourself. People who don't like ya for being yourself...*FUCK 'EM! FUCK ''EM!* against the wall, with handcuffs on."

"Boy, you better, you tell your boys they better kill me, Bert. They better go all the way with me, 'cause if they just bust me up, I'll put all those pieces back together again, then so help me... So help me God, Bert, I'm gonna come back here and I'm gonna kill you." - Paul Newman as Fast Eddie, a small-time pool hustler at odds with his ruthless and cutthroat manager Bert Gordon (George C. Scott) in the motion picture *The Hustler* (1961)

"Bravely bold Sir Robin, brought forth from Camelot. He was not afraid to die, oh brave Sir Robin. He was not at all afraid to be killed in nasty ways, brave, brave, brave, brave Sir Robin. He was not in the least bit scared to being mashed into a pulp, or to have his eyes carved out, and his elbows broken. To have his knee cut split, and his body burned away, and his limbs all hacked and mangled, brave Sir Robin. His head smashed in and heart cut out, and his liver removed, and his bowels unplugged, and his nostrils ripped and his bottom burned off and his penis" - Neil Innes as a Medieval minstrel sings the praises of Sherwood Forest outlaw Robin Hood (Eric Idle) before being told, "*THAT'S*, that's quite enough, Minstrel" in the motion picture *Monty Python and the Holy Grail* (1975).

"Bring me the big knife, I'm gonna cut my throat" - Nicholas Cage as Ronny Commareri, a brooding Italian baker in the motion picture *Moonstruck* (1987). Having lost his hand in an accident, Johnny gets emotional and occasionally requests one of his coworkers to help him kill himself. When Johnny's brother's fiancée Loretta Castorini (Cher) asks him to put aside past differences and attend their wedding, Johnny shouts, "I'm no friggin' monument to justice! I lost my hand! I lost my bride! Johnny has his hand! Johnny has his bride! You want me to take my heartache, put it away and forget?"

Later, Johnny becomes smitten with Loretta and tells her, "I'm in love with you." A confused Loretta smacks him in the face and yells, "Snap *out* of it!" Professing his love, Johnny educates Loretta to the realities of the world. "But love don't make things nice. It ruins everything. It breaks your heart. It makes things a mess. We aren't here to make things perfect. The snowflakes is perfect. The stars are perfect. Not us. Not us. We are here to ruin ourselves and to break our hearts and love the wrong people and die. The storybooks are *bullshit!* Now I want you to come upstairs with me and *get* in my bed!"

Broccoli - The pejorative nickname of Lt. Reginald Barclay (Dwight Schultz) first heard on episode #69 "Hollow Pursuits" on the science fiction series STAR TREK: THE NEXT GENERATION/SYN/1987-94. It was first spoken by Ensign Crusher (Wil Wheaton) who then explained the play-on-words nickname. After hearing the nickname name, the ship's Captain Picard (Patrick Stewart) made a slip of the tongue and used "Broccoli" instead of Barclay. He was not amused by his mistake, since he made it in a public arena.

"Brother, you better show me some tits or die" - Keenan Ivory Wayans as private eye Shame gets the shock of his life when wakes up next to a friend's transvestite roommate (Corwin Hawkins) in the motion picture *A Low Down Dirty-Shame* (1994).

"Brundle stole my girl, your mother. Got her pregnant. Caused her death. Dissolved my hand and my foot with fly vomit! I had no love for the man. He *bugged* me! As for the *cure* he was working on: he dragged your mother kicking and screaming into that telepod, that they might be fused together in one beautiful body. So your mother blew his brains out with a shotgun. There's your cure. *GO AWAY!"* - John Getz as reclusive Stathis Borans reveals some horrible truths to a scientist's son Martin Brundle (Eric Stoltz) in the sci-fi fantasy film *The Fly II* (1989).

Buddy Sorrell-isms - On the sitcom THE DICK VAN DYKE SHOW/CBS/1961-66 comedy gag writer Buddy Sorrell (Morey Amsterdam) waged a running battle of wits with TV producer Mel Cooley (Richard Deacon). A typical Mel put-down: "Somebody gave him a big mouth and he opened it before Christmas." Buddy's favorite past time is cracking wise about Mel's bald head. Once, when Mel was having a hard time dealing with a pushy quest star, he rushed into the writer's office pleading, "I wish I could hide." Buddy interjects, "Quick, grown some hair!" As Mel leaves, Buddy says, "There he goes, America's greatest emblem–the bald eagle." Another time, Buddy reported that Alan Brady threw a cigar at Mel's head and burned out the whole forest. Adding insult to injury, Buddy says, "Hey, maybe we can get the government to replant." There were sometimes of the year, however, that Buddy swore off insults. As he said, "Never on a holiday!" Note: Alan Brady (Carl Reiner), Mel's boss was also bald. Once, Laura Petrie (Mary Tyler Moore), the wife of Rob Petrie (Dick Van Dyke), the show's head writer accidentally blurted out on a talk show that TV star Alan Brady wore a toupee. Angered that his secret was out to the American public Alan asks Laura, "What do you suggest I do with all these toupees, now!" Laura timidly answers, "Well, Alan. There must be some needy bald person..."

Buffalo-Butt - The insulting nickname given to overweight building superintendent Nathan Bookman (Johnny Brown) by Chicago housing project tenants Willona Woods (Ja'net DuBois) and J. J. Evans (Jimmie Walker) on the sitcom GOOD TIMES/CBS/1974-79. Once, when Bookman's wife threw him out of their apartment, he tried to move in with Willona who quickly refused his proposition with the remark, "Make you home where the buffalo roam!"

"A bullet between the eyes would have been preferable to this charade" - David Duchovny as FBI agent Fox Mulder addresses a secret government panel that has falsely accused him of murder on episode "The Truth, Part II" on the fantasy drama THE X-FILES/FOX/1993-2002. Confronting his accusers, Mulder continues, "But I've learned to pretend over the past nine years—to pretend that my victories matter, only to realize that no one was keeping score; to realize that liars do not fear the truth if there are enough liars. That the devil is just one man with a plan, but evil—true evil—is a collaboration of men. Which is what we have here today. If I am a guilty man, my crime is in daring to believe that the truth will out and that no one lie will live forever. I believe it still. Much as you try to bury it, the truth is out there. Greater than your lies, the truth wants to be known. You will know it. It'll come to you. As it's come to me. Faster than the speed of light. You may believe yourselves rid of your headache now, and maybe you are. But you've only done it by cutting off your own hands."

Bunker-isms - One of the most insulting TV characters to come along in years had to be Archie Bunker (Carroll O'Connor) from the sitcom ALL IN THE FAMILY (ARCHIE BUNKER'S PLACE)/CBS/1971-83. Archie called his wife, Edith, a "Dingbat"; his son-in-law, Mike Stivic, a "Meathead"; and referred to ethnic groups by such pejorative nicknames as 'nigger,' 'wop,' 'chink,' and 'pollack.' Here are a few more examples of Archie's offensive nature:

Archie: Archie Bunker ain't no bigot. I'm the first to say "Look, it ain't your fault you're colored."

(and)

Archie: You are the laziest white boy I ever met.
Mike: You wanna call me lazy, okay. But you don't have to put down a whole race just to do it!
Archie: I wasn't putting down a whole race.
Mike: Yes, you were. You said I was the laziest white boy you ever met.
Archie: That's right. You.
Mike: Meaning that the blacks are even lazier.
Archie: Wait a second wise guy. I didn't say that. You're the one who said that. I never said blacks were lazy. I never said that...of course, their systems is geared a little slower than ours, that's all."

(and)

Archie: Now, no prejudice intended, but I always check with the Bible on these here things. I think that, I mean if God had meant for us to be together he'd a put us together. But look what he done. He put you over in Africa, and put the rest of us in all the white countries.

(and)

Archie: If your spics and your spades want their rightful share of the American dream, let 'em get out there and hustle for it like I done.
Mike: So now you're going to tell me the black man has just as must chance as the white man to get a job?
Archie: More, he has more...I didn't have no million people marchin'and protestin' to get me my job.
Edith: No, his uncle got it for him

"BURN!!!" - The resounding put-down of Michael Kelso (Ashton Kutcher) a vain Wisconsin teenager on the sitcom THAT '70s SHOW/FOX/1998-2006. Kelso loves to use the word "Burn!!!" So, whenever any of his friends get put in their place, Kelso is there to rub salt in the wound. For example, when Kelso finds out that the "not so cool" Fez (Wilmer Valderrama) is dating a former girlfriend of the "ultra-cool" Steven Hyde (Danny Masterson), Kelso barks, "BURN!!!" Kelso calls a burn about a burn a "second degree burn." When Red Forman (Kurtwood Smith) said to his son, Eric (Topher Grace), "So, this is how an engaged high school dumbass with no car, no job, and no money trims the hedges", his friend Hyde says, "That was like, eight burns in one sentence." Eric's girlfriend, Donna Pinciotti (Laura Prepon) adds, "An octo-burn." After Eric and Donna feed their friends laxative-laced brownies as revenge for a prank, Kelso says, "That was a wicked burn. I mean, it had all the elements. You didn't see it coming...parts of it really hurt" Once Hyde said, "Let's face it Forman. You're soft." Then Donna asks, "How soft is he, Hyde?" He replies, "Softer than Liberace at the Playboy mansion." Kelso adds, "Yeah. Because he plays the piano...wait...OOOOH. BURN!!!" When his friends object to Kelso yelling, "BURN!!!" Kelso, just says, "Sorry, I just appreciate a good burn!" On the series finale, Kelso says, "Yeah, things are going great in Chicago. I even taught my baby daughter (Betsy) how to say "Burn." She doesn't use it right though. I get her a lot more than she gets me."

"Burn the town? No. Burn the church" - Dastardly command of a British Officer in the Revolutionary War motion picture *The Patriot* (2000). Frustrated at his attempts to quell the citizens of the American Colonies, Colonel William Tavington (Jason Isaacs) decides to send a message to the colonists not recognizing the power of the Crown by locking a group of men, women and children inside a local church and then burning it to the ground. At the film's conclusion, Tavington meets his match when he is killed by freedom fighter Benjamin Martin (Mel Gibson) who had declared earlier in the fray "Before this war is over, I'm going to kill you."

Butt-Head - Frequently heard put-down used by bully Biff Tannen (Thomas F. Wilson) in the motion picture *Back to the Future* (1985) and its two sequels. At the conclusion of *Back to the Future III* (1990), Michael J. Fox as teenager Marty McFly is challenged to a drag race but declines, saying, "I'm not stupid enough to race that butt-head." Butt-head is also the nickname of Kevin Arnold (Fred Savage) given to him by his obnoxious older brother Wayne Arnold (Jason Hervey) on the sitcom THE WONDER YEARS/ABC/1988-93. Note: On the sitcom THE DREW CAREY SHOW/ABC/1995-2003 Oswald (Diedrich Bader) revealed that he was nicknamed Butt-head by his mother, because "When I was born I came out backwards. I didn't have oxygen for two whole minutes." Butt-head was also the name of a dumb, crude, and thoughtless teenager on the cartoon series BEAVIS AND BUTT-HEAD/MTV/1993-97. *See also* "Chicken"

Butt-knocker - One of many put-downs heard on the 1990s MTV cartoon show BEAVIS & BUTT-HEAD. Beavis and Butt-Head are two pubescent and quite dysfunctional teenagers who watch rock 'n' roll videos from the comfort of their dilapidated couch, and criticize the performers and each other. A typical exchange between B&B follows:

Butt-head: Beavis is like a Chinese food, huh, huh! One hour after he spanks his monkey, he's ready again.
Beavis: No way, dillhole! It's more like ten minutes. Heh, Heh.

(and)

Butt-head: Your mom's a whore.
Beavis: No way. My mom's a slut. She doesn't charge for it.

Some more examples of B&B brain-power:

- Always wear a condominium when doing it to a chick
- Eating makes you go to the bathroom
- Jail dudes get to watch TV all day
- If you have insurance, you can cut off your arm and get like, a million dollars
- Sports are stupid, 'cause they make you exercise.

In an inspired moment, Butt-head shared this bit of information "The butt is the most important part of the body. God gave us the butt so we could, like, have something to talk about...inside the butt there's all this complicated stuff that makes turds happen...the butt rules." B&B's vocabulary included such phrases as Asswipe, Buttmunch, Shut up, Dumb-ass, Bunghole, Butt-brain, Butt-knocker, Dillweed (aka Dillhole), Fartknocker, Fart Recycler (Converts fart gas to fuel for the poor people in the Turd World). Hey, Baby!, Loogie, (Wad of spit), Nads (Testicle), Paranoids (the Pyramids) I'll Kick Your Ass, This Sucks!, Thingies (Boobs), Adjusting the Set, Firing your squirt gun, Knuckling your knob, Spank your monkey, Squeezing out the toothpaste, Tuning the Antenna, and Walking the Log (Euphemisms for Masturbating), Wood (Erection) Wood Fairy (Boing! She makes the Wood), Wuss, (Wimp) and Huh, Huh, We're gonna score!...yeah, yeah. Once, when Beavis drank too much caffeinated coffee at a hip coffee bar, he pulled his shirt over his head, ran around the room drinking from other people's cups and shouted, "I need cappuccino for my bunghole." Note: For a wicked read on these adolescent nin-cum-poops ("Hey, He said, 'Poop!'") read: "Beavis and Butt-Head's Ensucklopedia" by Sam Johnson, Chris Marcil, Guy Maxtone-Graham, Kristofor Brown, David Felton, Glenn Eichler and Mike Judge (MTV Books/Pocket Books, 1994).

"By the authority vested in me by Kaiser William II, I pronounce you husband and wife. Proceed with the execution" - Peter Bull as the Captain of the warship Louisa reads marriage vows to captive saboteurs Charlie Allnut (Humphrey Bogart) and missionary Rose Sayer (Katherine Hepburn) after they attacked the Germans off the coast of Africa during World War One in the motion picture *The African Queen* (1951).

"Cameron's so tight if you stuck a piece of coal up his ass, in two weeks you'd have a diamond" - Matthew Broderick as high school student Ferris Bueller makes a flippant remark about his friend Cameron Frye (Alan Ruck) in the teenage comedy film *Ferris Bueller's Day Off* (1986).

"Can animals marry? You bet! My wife was a dog" - Carol Wayne to Johnny Carson in an 'Art Fern' sketch from THE TONIGHT SHOW STARRING JOHNNY CARSON/NBC/1962-92.

"Cancel the kitchen scraps for lepers and orphans. No more merciful beheadings, and call off Christmas" - Alan Rickman as the evil Sheriff of Nottingham punishes the poor of his realm for helping the outlaw Robin Hood in the motion picture *Robin Hood: Prince of Thieves* (1991). Note: In the film *The Adventures of Robin Hood* (1938) Basil Rathbone as Sir Guy of Gisbourne says, "Our men can't even lay a hot iron in the eyes of a tax dodger without getting a black arrow in the throat. It's an outrage!"

Cancer Man - Sinister government operative featured on the fantasy drama THE X-FILES/FOX/1993-2002. Constantly in a need of cigarette, the Cancer Man (aka "The Cigarette Smoking Man") worked behind the scenes to manipulate secrets which FBI agent Fox "Spooky" Mulder (David Duchovny) tried to bring to the light of day. Cancer Man worked for a secret cabal of anonymous men with names like the Well-Manicured Man (John Neville) and did whatever it took to keep "The Project" shrouded in secrecy. Per Duchovny, "He's like Nietszche's Socrates–he's the rational man, saving the masses from their own imagination." In the heat of anger, Mulder once called Cancer Man, a "black-lunged son of a bitch." Cancer Man first spoke on episode #20 "Tooms." He smokes (Morley Cigarettes) because as he said, "You would too, if you had seen what I have seen." One his more memorable quotes:

> "Life is like a box of chocolates. A cheap, thoughtless, perfunctoral gift that no one ever asks for. Unreturnable because all you get back is another box of chocolates. So, you're stuck with mostly undefinable whipped mint crap, mindlessly wolfed down when there's nothing else to eat while you're watching the game. Sure, once in a while you get a peanut butter cup or an English toffee but it's gone too fast and the taste is fleeting. In the end, you're left with nothing but broken bits filled with hardened jelly and teeth shattering nuts, which if you are desperate enough to eat leaves nothing but an empty box of useless brown paper wrappers."

Note: A survey in *TV Guide* (8/17/1996) found 27.5 % of readers rated "The Cigarette-Smoking Man" (played by William B. Davis) as the nastiest villain on TV. In an interview (*Starlog* No.248 March 1998 p. 50) William B. Davis preferred to be called "Il Fumatore," the Italian translation of CSM. The Cancer Man died on episode "The Truth, Part II" when a black ops helicopter fired a missile into a New Mexico pueblo and disintegrated his body.

Carla-isms - On the sitcom CHEERS/NBC/1982-93, sarcastic waitress Carla Tortelli Le Bec (Rhea Perlman) always insulted her tavern patrons with pejorative nicknames. Here's a list of some: The Stick, Fish-face, Whitey, Answer Geek and Bone Butt (Diane Chambers); Missing Link (Cliff Claven); The Howitzer, Gold Digger (Rebecca Howe); Moonglow (Norm Peterson); Chalk Face (Dr. Lilith Sternin Crane); Festus, Hayseed, Cowpie, Corncob (Woody Tiberius Boyd); and Sigmund Fraud (Dr. Frasier Crane). Note: Carla once said, "Women in my family have no talents, but we make a curse that sticks." Carla's power manifested itself when she asked bartender Sam Malone, "Did you telephone Eddie (her husband) to remember our anniversary?" As Sam denied any involvement, Carla warned if he wasn't telling the truth, she would make his tongue "swell up so big you'll be buying a seat on the plane for it." Seconds later, Sam's speech slurred and he began to stammer and mumble.

The Cheapest Man in the World - This sobering sobriquet goes to none other than veteran vaudevillian, radio, television comedian Jack Benny, the star of THE JACK BENNY SHOW/CBS/1950-65. Reportedly, Benny was so cheap that when a robber accosts him on the street and demands, "Your money or your life?" Jack pauses a long time and then shouts, "I'm thinking!" Jack also had a lock on his refrigerator, a pay telephone in his living room, and, preferred the color "dollar bill green." Being the cheapest man in the world, Jack distrusted banks and consequently, he had a subterranean vault built several hundred feet below his home. The vault was protected by an alligator-filled moat, ear-shattering burglar alarms, a Polar Bear named Carmichael (whose savage roar was provided by Mel Blanc on both radio and TV); and a very lonely guy named Ed, the "Keeper of the Vault" who was surprised to discover the Civil War was over. Jack gains access to his vault be first giving Ed, the password "A fool and his money are soon parted" or "Hair of gold, Eyes of Blue"; and then dialing the vault's combination: Right 45, Left 60, Right 15, and Left 110. In a spoof of Jack Benny's vault, the September 27, 1967 episode of THE LUCY SHOW/CBS/1962-74 featured Lucille Ball as bank secretary, Lucy Carmichael who tried to entice Jack Benny into opening a bank account. For the occasion, Lucy constructs a vault, which is protected by an electronic eye. The vault had a number of wild gadgets and gags to protect the money, including a guillotine, a tribe of tomahawk-tossing Indians, a huge fierce gorilla, a deep stream filled with piranha fish, and a patch of quicksand into which both Lucy and Jack fall prey. Note: Other television cheapskates included grocery store owner Herbert T. Gillis (Frank Faylen) who lived in Central City on the sitcom THE MANY LOVES OF DOBIE GILLIS/CBS/1959-63. Herbert was once voted "The Citizen Most Likely to Hang onto His Last Dollar." Another runner up for this dubious award is Fred Mertz (William Frawley), a tightwad landlord on the sitcom I LOVE LUCY/CBS/1951-57. And finally who could forget apartment manager Mr. Stanley Roper (Norman Fell) on the sitcom THREE'S COMPANY/ABC/1977-84. His tenants called him "The Cheapest Man Alive!" and once reported, "He has every dollar he ever made in his mattress...Maybe that's why he doesn't get romantic (with his wife). He's afraid to wrinkle his money!"

"Check out the headlights on that blonde. How'd you like to play hide the salami with that for a week?" - Ellen Barkin as Amanda Brooks offers up a crude sexist remark to her male escort Walter (Jimmy Smits) in the Blake Edwards comedy film *Switch* (1991). Inside Amanda's gorgeous blonde body is the spirit of Steve Brooks, a murdered philanderer who returned to earth as a woman—against his will. Note: *Switch* is a remake the Vincent Minelli's comedy *Goodbye Charlie* (1964) starring Debbie Reynolds as the reincarnated spirit of womanizing scriptwriter Charlie Sorel. The movie tagline read: "They don't make girls like "Charlie" anymore -- they never did!" Upon seeing his new body, Charlie says, "I don't have to see Bridget Bardot movies anymore. All I have to do is come home and pull down the shades." At the conclusion of the film, Charlie is chased around the room by the lust-crazed director (Walter Mathau), the man who originally killed him. Suddenly, Charlie realizes how it feels to be on the other end of a relationship and shouts, "The punishment *does* fit the crime." Unexpectedly; Charlie is shot by an angry female intruder and falls off the balcony of his bachelor pad into the ocean below. In a final twist of fate, Charlie is again reincarnated but this time into the body of Great Dane dog.

"Cheesy scab-picking, pimple-squeezing finger bandage! Boiled dripping beef fart bubble butt! Hemorrhoidal suck navel! Slug-slimed puked-up sack of rat guts and cat vomit. A week-old maggot burger with everything on it and flies on the side!" - Dante Basco as Rufio, one of the Lost Boys, orders his meal at the dinner table in Never Land in the fantasy film *Hook* (1991).

"Chicken!" - Put-down referring to someone who is a coward. The word chicken plays an intricate part in the motion picture *Back to the Future* (1985) and its sequels *Back to the Future II* (1989) and *Back to the Future III* (1990). In the films, Michael J. Fox plays Marty McFly, a teenager time traveler who zigzags through time (in a DeLorean automobile outfitted with time travel circuitry) from 1985 to the past of the 1950's to the early twenty first century to the Old West of September 2, 1885 and finally back to 1985. Although Marty is a good-hearted person he has one flaw: he despises being called a coward. When called a "chicken" Marty stops dead in his tracks, turns slowly and says, "Nobody calls me chicken!" During his travels through time, Marty finally finds the wisdom to overlook other people's opinion of him and confesses at one point, "It's all my fault, I never should have let Biff get to me" (Biff Tannen being the movie's bully who constantly called Marty a chicken and goaded him into acting against his better nature). Marty was also called "yellow" & "yellow-belly" and a "gutless, yellow turd" by outlaw Buford Tannen while in 1885. One of the funnier lines is when Marty tries to back out of a gunfight and a bystander warns Marty that if he declines people will think that "Clint Eastwood is the biggest yellow belly in the West" (Clint Eastwood is the name Marty adopted while in the Old West). At the conclusion of the final movie when Marty is called "chicken" for not wanting to drag race with some street punks, Marty succumbs to common sense and drives away from his hecklers just in time to avoid a car crash—a crash that would have altered his future for the worse. Note: Another movie using the "chicken" theme is the comedy motion picture *The Ghost and Mr. Chicken* (1966) starring Don Knotts in the role of a nervous, cowardly would-be-reporter (Mr. Chicken of the movie title) whom is challenged to sleep the night in a supposedly haunted mansion.

Chicken Legs - The not-so-affectionate nickname of Marcy Rhodes (Amanda Bearse), a bank employee and feminist next-door neighbor to the Bundy family on the sitcom MARRIED...WITH CHILDREN/FOX/1987-97. When Al Bundy (Ed O'Neill), a frustrated shoe salesman wanted to drive Marcy from his home, he mocked her skinny stature by using quips relating to a chicken, often calling her "Chicken Legs." Once Al said, "Look what's crossed the road. It can't be a chicken; it hasn't got breasts...just nuggets." During an argument, Marcy's husband Steve (David Garrison) told his wife, "You know why you have chicken legs? It's because your mother eats all those eggs." Al calls Marcy a "chicken" for the first time on episode No. 113 "Johnny Be Gone." The dialog follows: Marcy [looking round]: "Al, do you see a fish eye anywhere round here?" Al [looking at her wearing just a towel]: "No, but I see a chicken leg." On episode No. 232 "Kiss of the Coffee Woman," Al puts together a Top Ten List of suggestions to approve Marcy's appearance. It read:

10. Wear traditional Islamic garb covering all but the eyes
9. Feather removing electrolysis
8. Ski mask
7. Sew up holes in ski mask
6. Hire attractive woman to stand in front of you at all times
5. Beak job
4. Put paper bag over ski mask
3. Shave head; tattoo Cindy Crawford's face on back of head; And learn to walk backwards
2. Poke out eyes of every man on Earth
1. Get President to make every day Halloween

Note: On the sitcom I LOVE LUCY/CBS/1951-57 Lucy Ricardo (Lucille Ball) was called "Bird Legs" in grade school.

"Chicolini here may look like an idiot, he may speak like an idiot, but don't let that fool you—he really is an idiot" - Groucho Marx as Prime Minister of Freedonia, Rufus T. Firefly jokingly puts down his brother Chico Marx in the role of Chicolini in the motion picture *Duck Soup* (1933).

Chinzo - During an interview segment of THE TONIGHT SHOW WITH JAY LENO (3/31/98) the jut-jawed Jay Leno revealed that in school the kids gave him the nickname "Chinzo." His guest Denise Richards (*Wild Things*, 1998) informed Jay that she was called "Fish lips" in high school.

The choice is simple: desert or police - The callous statement of Christian Slater as Robert Boyd as he tries to convince his bachelor party buddies how to dispose of a prostitute's body after she accidentally got killed in the motion picture *Very Bad Things* (1998). He continues, "The reality is...you take away the horror of the situation. Take away the tragedy of the death. Take away the moral and ethical implications of all the crap that you've had conditioned and beaten into your head. What are we left with is a

105 pound problem. A105 pound problem, that needs to be moved from point A to point B."

"Christians—are they the one who worship some dead carpenter?" - Robert Taylor as Marcus Vinicius inquires about the Jewish Messiah to fellow Roman Petronius (Leo Genn) in the epic adventure *Quo Vadis?* (1951). "When I have finished with these Christians," barked Emperor Nero (Peter Ustinov), "history will not be sure that they ever existed." Roman citizen Poppaea (Patricia Laffan) questioned the idea of eradicating the Christian movement and says, "It is foolish to kill those you hate, because, once dead, they are beyond pain."

"The cities are full of women...horrible, faded, fat, greedy women" - Joseph Cotton as Uncle Charlie (actually the Merry Widow murderer) gives his opinion of the fairer sex in the motion picture *Shadow of Doubt* (1943). His full observation: "The cities are full of women, middle aged, husbands dead, husbands who've spent their lives making fortunes and then they die and leave their money to their wives. Their silly wives. And what do the wives do, these useless women? You see them in the hotels, the best hotels, every day by the thousands, drinking the money, eating the money, losing the money at bridge, playing all day and all night, smelling of money...Horrible faded, fat, greedy women."

"The closest you'll ever get to a brainstorm is a drizzle" - Michael Caine rains on the parade of his fellow partner in crime (Roger Moore) in the motion picture *Bullseye!* (1991).

"Colonel Dax, you're a disappointment to me. You've spoiled the keenness of your mind by wallowing in sentimentality...You are an idealist —and I pity you as I would the village idiot. We're fighting a war, Dax, a war that we've got to win. Those men didn't fight, so they were shot" - Adolphe Menjou as General Broulard chastises Colonel Dax (Kirk Douglas) in the WWI military adventure *Paths of Glory* (1957).

Colonel Potter-isms - When the veteran army career officer Colonel Sherman Potter (Harry Morgan) got angry at his Korean War troops on the military comedy M*A*S*H/CBS/1972-83 he shouted out borderline profanities. But the power of his put-downs came mostly from his "bark" rather than his bite. The following is a select list of some of his best bluster and bravado: *Buffalo Bagels! Buffalo Chips! Beaver Biscuits! Bull Cookies! Cow Cookies! Geeze Louise! Great Caesar's Ghost! Great Horse Hockey! Mother McCree! Mule Fritters! Pigeon Pellets! Pony Pucks! Road Apples! Sufferin' Sheep dip! Sweet Limburger!* and *What in the Name of Sam Hill!*

"C'mon, suckers, come and get me—what are you waiting for? Didn't think we were here, did you, you dirty rotten rats! We're still here—we'll always be here." - Robert Taylor as WWII army Sgt. Bill Dane surrounded by the dead bodies of his comrades as he frantically shoots his machine gun at the Japanese soldiers rushing his position at the conclusion of the motion picture *Bataan* (1943).

"COME AND GET THEM!" – The defiant cry of King Leonidas (Gerard Butler) to a Persian officer when he demands, "Spartans, lay down your weapons" at the Battle of Thermopylae in 480 B.C. in the motion picture *300* (2006). Advising his warriors, Leonidas demands, "Give them nothing! But take from them everything!" and "This is where we fight. This is where they die." When threatened with a volley of arrows that would blot out the sun, Spartan warrior Stelios (Michael Fassbender) suggests, "Then we will fight in the shade." Descended from Hercules, the Spartans were taught never to retreat, never to surrender. They werer taught that death in the battlefield was the greatest glory a warrior could achieve in his life. In essence, Spartans were the finest soldiers the world has ever known. On the other side of the battlefield, the opposing Persian King Xerxes tells deformed Greek shepherd Ephialtes (Andrew Tiernan), "Cruel Leonidas demanded that you stand. I require only that you kneel" Ephialtes defected to the Persians and revealed to Xerxes the location of a mountain pathway that could be used to outflant the Spartans. Seeing Ephialtes at the head of the Persian hordes, Leonidas curses him with the phrase "May you live forever!" so that he will have to remember for eternity the betrayal of his fellow Spartans.

"Come and take me, mongrels—if you dare! While I have fingers to grasp a sword, and eyes to see your cowardly faces, your treacherous heads will not be safe on your shoulders! For I am Temujin, the Conqueror! No prison can hold me, no army defeat me!" - John Wayne as Temujin (who later becomes the legendary Genghis Khan) shouts defiantly at his enemies in the motion picture *The Conqueror* (1956).

"Come with me into the tormented, haunted, half-lit night of the insane. This is my world. Let me lead you into it. Let me take you into the mind of a woman who is mad. You may not recognize some things in this world, and the faces will look strange to you. For this is a place where there is no love, no hope...in the pulsing, throbbing world of the insane mind, where only nightmares are real, nightmares of the Daughter of Horror!" - The opening narration (Ed McMahon) that sets the stage for a nightmarish events of a woman (Adrienne Barrett) who wakes up in skid-row hotel room in the film noir production *Daughter of Horror* (1955).

"(Comics) They're shiftless, dame-chasing, ambitionless" - Barbara Stanwyck as sassy burlesque performer Dixie Daisy in the motion picture *Lady of Burlesque* (1943). When Dixie's friend Biff Brannigan (Michael O'Shae) asks, "What's the matter with comics?" Dixie says, "I went into show business when I was seven years old. Two days later the first comic I ever met stole my piggy bank in a railroad station in Portland. When I was 11 the comics were looking at my ankles. When I was 14 they were...just looking. When I was 20 I'd been stuck with enough lunch checks to pay for a three-story house. Naw, they're shiftless, dame-chasing, ambitionless..."

Commie - *See* "Red"

Conner the Bomber - On an episode of ROSEANNE/ABC/1988-96, Darlene Conner (Sara Gilbert) bestows this insulting nickname on her sister Becky Conner (Lecy Goranson) after Becky accidentally "cut the cheese" while giving a speech at her school. Sister Darlene adds insult to injury by saying, "the only woman to break the sound barrier without a plane!"

"Consider that a divorce!" - Arnold Schwarzenegger as Doug Quaid seeks closure to a bad relationship in the science fiction movie *Total Recall* (1990). Brainwashed into thinking he is someone else, Quaid shares an abode with wife, Lori Quaid (Sharon Stone). When Doug discovers that his life is a sham and that the woman he loves is actually part of conspiracy to kill him, he seeks escape. When his bogus wife tries to use her feminine wiles to delay him for his pursuers, Doug holds her at gunpoint. "Honey...Sweetheart. You wouldn't hurt me? After all, we're married." Lori then attacks Quaid. Blocking her assault, Doug knocks her to the floor, shoots her in the forehead and says, "Consider that a divorce!" At the end of the film, bad guy Cohaagen (Ronny Cox) boasts to Quaid, "In thirty seconds you'll be dead, and I'll blow this place up and be home in time for Corn Flakes." A few moments later, Cohaagen is sucked into a huge air vent onto the Martian landscape where he suffocates and then explodes in the diminished atmospheric pressure.

Couch Potato - The pejorative term used to describe persons who watch too much television. In essence, they've rooted themselves to their chairs so long they have turned into vegetables. Couch Potatoes are also referred to as Vidiots and TV Junkies.

"Count the years, the months, the hours. Until the day you rot!" - Sam Bowden (Gregory Peck) to criminal Max Cady (Robert Mitchum) in the motion picture *Cape Fear* (1962). In the film, recently released Max Cady slowly begins to stalk the lawyer who put him in prison. "Didn't remember me right off, did you? Well, I guess I've changed a little. Where I've been, if you don't change, they're real disappointed." At the film's climax, Bowden has a chance to shoot Cady, but declines. Instead, he chooses to send his stalker back to jail by saying, "No, No. That would be letting you off too easy, too fast. Your words, do you remember? I do. No. We're gonna take good care of you, gonna nurse you back to health. You're strong Cady. You're going to live a long life. In a cage. That's where you belong and that's where you're going. And this time, for life. Bang your head against the walls. Count the years...the months...the hours. Until the day you rot."

Coward Of Bitter Creek - Pejorative nickname given to cavalry Captain Jason McCord on the western adventure BRANDED/NBC/1965-66. As the series theme song intoned, "What do you do when you're branded (a coward) and you know you're a man." Jason McCord (Chuck Connors) is the lone survivor (knocked unconscious) of an Indian battle of Bitter Creek. Falsely accused of cowardice, he is dishonorably discharged from the Army and forced to wear the brand of a coward throughout the Wyoming frontier where his moniker "The Coward of Bitter Creek" was known by everybody.

Coyote Ugly - Pejorative nickname given to someone who is deemed unattractive. The term was used in the motion picture *Coyote Ugly* (2000) by Lil (Maria Bello) the owner of a New York City nightclub named "Coyote Ugly" where only beautiful women are hired to serve the drinks and drive the largely male crowd crazy. The following script excerpt explains the definition of 'Coyote Ugly' used in the film:

Girl: Can I ask you something?
Lil: What?
Girl: What does Coyote Ugly mean?

Lil: Did you ever wake up sober after a one night stand, and the person you're next to is lying on your arm, and they're so ugly, you'd rather chew off your arm than risk waking 'em? That's coyote ugly.

Girl: My God. Well, why would you name your bar after something like that?

Lil: Oh, 'cause Cheers was taken.

Later, Lil hired an aspiring songwriter named Violet Sanford (Piper Perabo) to be one of her new bar maids. Grateful for the job, but curious as to why Lil hired her, Violet asks, "I don't mean to press my luck, would you mind telling me why you're hiring me?" "Because, said Lil, "the average male is walking around with a toddler inside his pants, a two year old right there inside his dockers. Perplexed, Violet queries, "Men have two year old children in their pants - that's why you're hiring me? Lil replies, "You look like a kindergarten teacher. The kids will love it." The light bulb finally goes on in Violet's brain, and she quickly says, "Sorry I asked." *See also* "Ugly Betty"

"Cram it, Clown!" - According to urban legends, on a live TV broadcast of the BOZO THE CLOWN show produced on the WCVB-TV in Boston, Massachusetts, a local Bozo the Clown host was verbally put-down by an unhappy child who didn't win the prizes he wanted. Apparently, the boy lost his chance at winning big cache of prizes when he failed to toss all three ping pong balls into a barrel (he got two) during the segment of the program called "Bozo's Treasure Chest." After the show's Ringmaster said, "You're never a loser on the Bozo show, you're just an almost winner," he presented the boy with a consolation prize (a towel). The boy looked at the towel, then the Ringmaster and finally Bozo and matter-of-factly registered his disappointment by saying "Cram it, Clown." Bozo quickly replied, "That's a Bozo no-no."

Crazy Eddie - Commercial alter ego of stereo electronics king, Eddie Antar who sold stereos, televisions and the like for the "Crazy Eddie's" electronics stores where prices were "Insaaaaaane!" Antar opened his first store on Kings Highway in Brooklyn when he was 21 years of age. His stores were a success because of their cheap prices, low overhead and aggressive marketing which guaranteed that they would not be undersold–giving customers 30 days to demand a rebate if they found the same merchandise offered at a lower price. When it came time to advertise the Crazy Eddie's stores, Eddie Antar, a small, shy, reclusive businessman instead chose to hire pitchman Jerry Carroll to his on-air persona. Jerry Carroll began live readings of the Crazy Eddie ads in New York on WPIX-FM in the mid 1970s and soon, his maniacal, wild-eyed pitchman style was highly imitated. His characterization was parodied on a HBO comedy skit on NOT NECESSARILY THE NEWS which featured "Crazy Ollie," an Oliver North look alike. Note: In the film *UHF* (1989) John Cadenhead as car salesman Crazy Eddie says, "If nobody comes down here and buys a car in the next hour, I'm gonna club this baby seal. That's right. I'm gonna club this seal to make a better deal. You know I'll do it, to, cause I'm crazy." *See also* "Mad Man Muntz"

Crazy Gun Barney - Barney Fife (Don Knotts) is the bumbling deputy sheriff who lives in the rural town of Mayberry, North Carolina on the sitcom THE ANDY GRIFFITH SHOW/CBS/1960-68. Because the town sheriff Andy Taylor (Andy

Griffith) wouldn't trust Barney with a loaded gun, for fear of accidentally shooting himself or an innocent bystander, Barney never carried a loaded gun, but rather kept one bullet in his left shirt breast pocket. The only time he uses his gun is to start the potato sack races for the annual Mason's picnic. Barney is jokingly called Barney the Beast, Barney the Fierce, Crazy Gun Barney and Fearless Fife by his fellow townsfolk.

"Crooked cops. Do they come in any other way? If I'd been just a little dumber, I could have joined the force myself." - Mel Gibson as Porter, a small time crook shares his thoughts in the motion picture *Payback* (1999). Porter seeks his share of a $140,000 robbery ($70,000) but a couple of crooked cops shadow his movements in hopes of cashing in on the deal. To get them off his case, Porter borrows one of their handguns, commits a murder and then plants the gun at the scene of the crime to implicate them.

"Cross me and you're snail food" - Tony Lo Bianca as hoodlum Leon Coll speaks to 1930s private eye Mike Murphy (Burt Reynolds) in the motion picture *City Heat* (1984).

"Cutting off her nipples with garden shears! You call that normal?" - Elizabeth Taylor as Leonora Penderton refers to Lt. Colonel Langdon's neurotic wife, Alison (Julie Harris) in the motion picture *Reflections in a Golden Eye* (1967).

"Cut off one of his fingers. The little one. Then tell him his thumb's next" - Harvey Keitel as Mr. White, a professional criminal offers advice on how to handle a diamond store heist in the motion picture *Reservoir Dogs* (1992). When fellow criminal, Mr. Orange asks, "What happens if the manager won't give you the diamonds?" Mr. White says, "When you're dealing with a store like this, they're insured up the ass. They're not supposed to give you any resistance whatsoever. If you get a customer, or an employee, who thinks he's Charles Bronson, take the butt of your gun and smash their nose in. Everybody jumps. He falls down screaming, blood squirts out of his nose, nobody says fucking shit after that. You might get some bitch talk shit to you, but give her a look like you're gonna smash her in the face next, watch her shut the fuck up. Now if it's a manager, that's a different story. Managers know better than to fuck around, so if you get one that's giving you static, he probably thinks he's a real cowboy, so you gotta break that son of a bitch in two. If you wanna know something and he won't tell you, cut off one of his fingers. The little one. Then tell him his thumb's next. After that he'll tell you if he wears ladies underwear. I'm hungry. Let's get a taco."

"Daughters! They're a mess no matter how you look at 'em. A headache till they get married—if they get married—and after that they get worse. Either they leave their husbands and come back with four kids and move in your guestroom or the husband loses his job and the whole caboodle comes back. Or else they're so homely that you can't get rid of them at all and they sit around like Spanish moss and shame you into an early grave." - William Demarest as police officer Kockenlocker, the father of two zany unmarried daughters Trudy (Betty Hutton) and Emmy (Diana Lynn) complains about the potential problems of daughters in the motion picture *The Miracle of Morgan's Creek* (1943).

David Letterman's Top 10 List - Each installment of the CBS late night talk show LATE NIGHT WITH DAVID LETTERMAN, features host David Letterman reading his "Top Ten List" prepared from the Home Office in Wahoo, Nebraska (location of the home office changes from time to time). The list's general intent is to lampoon, insult or gently poke fun at persons, places and things (for example: politicians, celebrities, fads and trends). Some top ten list have included Top Ten Bob Dole Excuses (#10 "Shouldn't have taken time away from campaign to father Madonna's baby"...#1 "In retrospect, was a mistake to be cranky old bastard"); Top Ten Elf Pet Peeves (#10 "After too much eggnog, Mrs. Clause is all hands"...#1 "Health plan doesn't cover sleigh rash.")

"The day they lay you away what I do on your grave won't pass for flowers" - Petulant remark of town sheriff (Harry Morgan) upon hearing that legendary gunfighter John Bernard Books (John Wayne) is dying from cancer in the western film *The Shootist* (1976). Later, when Brooks senses that the local undertaker's (John Carradine) offer of a free funeral is bogus, he complains, "You son of a bitch. You aim to do to me what they did to John Wesley Hardin. Lay me out and parade every damn fool in the state past me at a dollar a head, half-price for children, and then stuff me in a gunny sack and shovel me under." Earlier in the film, Brooks shared his philosophy on life to a young Gillom Rogers (Ron Howard), saying, "I won't be wronged, I won't be insulted, and I won't be laid a hand on. I don't do these things to other people and I expect the same from them."

Dean Martin's Friar Club Roast, The - This NBC award show had its origin on THE DEAN MARTIN SHOW/NBC/1965-74 which featured a segment called "Man of the Week Celebrity Roast" telecast in 1973. Seated at a banquet table, one by one the guest of honor was affectionately insulted by his fellow celebrity friends. Some wouldn't consider being insulted much of an award, but it was all done in fun. Don Rickles, a favorite funny man and prankster attended many of these functions. Some of his classic insults included: "Come right in Frank (Sinatra). Make yourself at home...Hit somebody!" Sinatra once said of Rickles, "I like Don Rickles, but that's because I have no taste." As Don Rickles began to say, "It takes many years to be a great comedian," Dean Martin interjects, "Sure does. And you ain't reached that year yet."

"Dear Lord, thank you for this Thanksgiving holiday. And for all the material possessions we have and enjoy. And for letting us white people kill all the Indians and steal their tribal lands. And stuff ourselves like pigs, even though children in Asia are being napalmed" - Christina Ricci as teenager Wendy Hood saying grace at her family's 1973 Thanksgiving dinner in the motion picture *The Ice Storm* (1997). Note: On THE JON STEWART SHOW, TV talk show host Jon Stewart said, "I celebrated Thanksgiving in an old fashioned way. I invited everyone in my neighborhood to my house, we had an enormous feast, and then I killed them and took their land."

"Death is listening and will take the first man that screams!" - Admonishment of Tina Turner as Aunty Entity, the leader of a post-apocalyptic refuge called Bartertown in the science fiction adventure film *Mad Max Beyond Thunderdome* (1985) The Thunderdome was a gladiatorial cage used for settling disputes where (as the rules of the game stated) "Two men enter. One man leaves." When Mad Max, aka "The Man with No Name" (Mel Gibson) challenges a towering figure called The Blaster (Paul Larsson), they both enter the Thunderdome arena to battle to the death. Aunty Entity then cries, "Welcome to another edition of Thunderdome" and warns the players in this deadly endeavor, "Death is listening and will take the first man that screams." The ringmaster of the event, Dr. Dealgood (Edwin Hodgeman) then gleefully says, "Ladies and gentlemen, boys and girls, Dying time's here." After avoiding an onslaught of spears, sledgehammers and chainsaws, Max wins the event but refuses to kill The Blaster when he discovers his opponent is just a retarded boy with the body of a man. For violating the "Two men enter. One man Leaves" rule, (the law says, "Bust a deal. Face the wheel") Max is sentenced to a carnival-like wheel of fortune whose choices included Amputation, Death, Gulag, Hard Labor, and Thunder Dome. Max's wheel stopped on Gulag. He was then unceremoniously bound, thrown onto the top of a horse (backwards) fitted with an oversized Mardi Gras facemask and sent off into the desert wasteland to die. In the end, he survived (found by a band of wild children who thought him a deity) and returned to wreak his revenge on those in Bartertown.

"Death is too easy for you, bitch. I want you to suffer" - Pam Greer as a vigilante who seeks revenge on a drug dealer (Kathryn Loder) for killing her government agent boyfriend in the motion picture *Foxy Brown* (1974). When threatened with the line, "Don't mess with me! I've got a black belt in crime!" Foxy hits her opponent with a chair and says, "I've got a black belt in barstools!" Foxy also said, "The only way to deal with a drug dealer is with a bullet to the gut." Note: The movie poster tagline for *Foxy Brown* read: "Don't mess around with Foxy Brown. She's the meanest chick in town!' She's brown sugar and spice but if you don't treat her right, she'll put you on ice!" In the prequel *Coffy* (1973), Pam Grier played Coffy, a nurse by day, and vigilante by night who conducts a one-woman war on criminal organizations in Los Angeles after her sister becomes addicted to drugs. The movie poster tagline read: "She's the Godmother of them all…the baddest one-chick hit squad that ever hit town."

"Democracy is a dying giant, a sick, sick decaying political concept" - Words of wisdom from conglomerate president Arthur Jensen (Ed Beatty) as he educates network news anchorman Howard Beale (Peter Finch) to the stark realities of the modern world in the motion picture *Network* (1976). His entire diatribe reads: "There are no nations. There are no people. There are no Russians, no Arabs, no Third Worlds, no West, There is only one holistic system of systems. One vast interwoven, interacting multi-varied, multi-national dominion of dollars—petro dollars, electro dollars, Reich marks, rubles, pounds, shekels. That's the atomic and sub-atomic and galactic structure of things today...There is no democracy. There is only IBM, ITT, AT&T, DuPont, Dow, Union Carbide, Exxon—these are the nations of the world today. The world is business, Mr. Beale. Democracy is a dying giant, a sick, sick decaying political concept. It's a nation of two hundred million totally unnecessary human beings as replaceable as piston rods."

"Did ya kill him because he liked ya?" - In the film *Rear Window* (1954) when a woman on a fire escape (Sara Berner) finds her little dog strangled to death, she lashes out at all of her neighbors, sobbing, "You don't know the meaning of the word 'neighbor,' but I can't imagine any of ya bein' so low ya'd kill a helpless, friendly dog, the only thing in the whole neighborhood who likes anybody. Did ya kill him because he liked ya?" The dog, of course, was killed to keep it from digging up evidence that would reveal that one of the neighbors (Raymond Burr) had just killed his wife, chopped her up into pieces and shipped her off in a steamer trunk.

"Did you hear that? They called me a whore! They actually called me a whore!" - Pop singer Madonna in the role of Argentina actress turned political figure Eva Perón in the motion picture adaptation of the stage musical *Evita* (1996). In an attempt to clarify the horrible accusation just thrown into Evita's face, an Italian Admiral says, "But Segnora Perón, it's an easy mistake. I'm still called an admiral, though I gave up the sea long ago."

"Die, Milkface!...Die Gas Pumper!" - Crazed statements of a loony survivalist who indiscriminately targets gas station attendant Navin Johnson (Steve Martin) with rifle fire in the motion picture *The Jerk* (1979). As the bullets whiz pass Navin, they hit cans of oil stacked in front of the gas station. Coming to the wrong conclusion, Navin panics and cries, "He hates these cans! Stay away from the cans!" Navin's boss at the gas station (Jackie Mason) realizes what is actually happening and yells, "We don't have defective cans. We have a defective person out there."

Dingbat - On the sitcom ALL IN THE FAMILY/CBS/1971-83, the blue-collar bigot Archie Bunker (Carroll O'Connor) insultingly refers to his dim-witted, yet sensitive wife, Edith (Jean Stapleton) as a "Dingbat" whenever she expresses an opinion on anything. Archie once inquired, "How long does it take for one dingbat to go twenty-feet for one beer?" The wife counterpart on the British sitcom TILL DEATH US DO PART/BBC/1966-75 that inspired ALL IN THE FAMILY was referred to as a "Silly old moo." Note: According to the dictionary, a Dingbat is an "eccentric, silly or empty-headed person."

Dinghy - Waitress Vera Louise Gorman (Beth Howland) is called "Dinghy" (referring to her lack of intelligence) by her boisterous boss Melvyn Sharples (Vic Tayback) owner of the Mel's roadside diner on the sitcom ALICE/CBS/1976-85. Once, Mel explained to a former Navy buddy the reason why he called Vera a "Dinghy." Simply put, he was the captain of his ship and every ship has a "dinghy" (a dinghy being a small boat, rowboat carried on a warship, yacht or motor cruiser).

"Do I feel lucky? Well, do you, punk?" - Surly question asked by Clint Eastwood in the role of San Francisco police inspector "Dirty" Harry Callahan in the motion picture *Dirty Harry* (1971). In the film, Harry prepares to take a coffee break at a local cafe when a bank robbery occurs across the street. In the ensuing minutes, he pulls out his .44 magnum pistol (Smith & Wesson Model 29 with 8 and 3/8 inch barrel) and dispatches the interlopers. When one of the robbers reaches for a shotgun that had fallen to the ground, Harry looks straight into the man's eyes, points his gun and calmly says, "I know what your thinkin': Did he fire six shots or only five? Well, to tell the truth, I kinda forgot myself in all this excitement. But bein' that this is a .44 magnum, the most powerful handgun in the world, and will blow you head clean off, there's only one question you should ask yourself...Do I fell lucky? Well, do you punk?" The downed bank robber stopped reaching for his fallen shotgun but said to Harry, "I gots to know?" Harry then drew a bead on the man's face and pulled the trigger. Luckily, the chamber was empty. Harry gave the man a wry smile and walked away. At the conclusion of the film, Harry tracked down a psychotic killer (Andy Robinson) and gave him the same "Do I feel Lucky?" speech. The killer decided to go for his gun and Harry blew him away. Note: On the premiere episode of the police drama HUNTER/NBC/1984-91 LAPD Sgt. Rick Hunter (Fred Dryer) confronted a thief who also dropped his gun and in the spirit of Dirty Harry, Hunter said, "Well, punk, you gonna go for it?"

"Do I ice her? Do I marry her? Which one a dese?" - Jack Nicholson as Charlie Partanna, a slow-witted Mafia hit man weighs his options on whether to kill or marry fellow assassin Irene Walker (Kathleen Turner) in the black comedy *Prizzi's Honor* (1985). In the end, Irene snuffs Charlie.

"Do you know how many rich animals I had to fuck to get this?" - When a female animal rights person (Emma Walton) see another woman named Margo (JoBeth William) wearing fur in the movie *Switch* (1991), she shouts, "Do you know how many poor animals had to die for you to get that coat?" Indignant at the intrusive nature of the question, Margo yells back, "Do you know how many rich animals I had to *fuck* to get this?"

"Do you know what I would do if someone did that to me? I would kill him, I wouldn't hesitate. I would stab him 78 times. I would chop off his fingers, slash his throat open, carve numbers in his chest, gouge out his eyes, I swear to God!...But that's me" - Laura Linney as prosecuting attorney Janet Venable speaks her mind concerning a case about a Chicago altar boy accused of murdering a Catholic archbishop who allegedly molested young boys in the motion picture *Primal Fear* (1996).

"Do you know what smoking does to you? It stunts your growth; it yellows your teeth and blackens your lungs. Is that what you want? To be a yellow-toothed midget with lung cancer?" - Chevy Chase as Norman Robberson chastises a friend with a bad habit in the motion picture *Cops and Robbersons* (1994).

"Do you know what's scarier than not believing in God? Believing in Him. I mean, really fucking believing in Him is terrifying because if there is a God, he hates me" - Patricia Arguette as Frankie Paige, whose body suddenly develops mystical stigmata wounds (the wounds of Christ) in the motion picture *Stigmata* (1999).

"Do you mind if my friend sits this one out? She's just dead" - Sean Connery as secret agent James Bond asks a nightclub patron if he wouldn't mind letting his now dead dance partner (Luciana Paluzzi) rest at their table in the motion picture *Thunderball* (1965). Bond had used her body to shield himself from deadly gunfire. Note: In the film *Commando* (1985), John Matrix (Arnold Schwarzenegger) snaps the neck of a mercenary sitting beside him on a plane and then politely asks the stewardess, "and do me a favor. Don't disturb my friend. He's dead tired."

"Do you really think you have the guts to take a bullet, Frank?" - John Malkovich as assassin Mitch Leary goads a secret service agent in the motion picture *In the Line of Fire* (1993). In the film, Leary challenges secret service agent Frank Harrigan (Clint Eastwood) to catch him before he kills the President of the United States. Frank was one of the bodyguards on duty at the Kennedy assassination, and blames himself for not going the extra mile to prevent the President's death. Taunting Harrigan via phone, Leary inquires, "Do you really think you have the guts to take a bullet, Frank?" Frank responds, "I'll be thinking about that when I'm pissin' on your grave."

"Do you really believe I would have a "nigger" run our family business, Randolph?" - Don Ameche as Mortimer Duke, a wealthy businessman responds to his brother, Randolph Duke (Ralph Bellamy) during a restroom conversation in the motion picture *Trading Places* (1983). In the film, Randolph and Mortimer make a bet for $1.00 that they could take a failure off the street and turn him into a successful executive while simultaneously turn an honest, hard-working man into a failure. The brothers select a street hustler named Billy Ray Valentine (Eddie Murphy) to train as an executive and proceed to destroy the life of socialite Louis Winthorpe III (Dan Aykroyd). After Billy Ray proves himself capable, he overhears the Duke Brothers call him a "nigger" and say they would never hire him as the firm's managing director. Betrayed, Billy Ray joins forces with the now down-trodden Louis Winthorpe III to bring the Dukes down and ruin them financially. Armed with secret information that will enable them to corner the market on orange juice (stolen from the Dukes), Louis and Billy Ray both enter the New York Commodities Exchange to do battle. Confident of victory, Louis advises Billy Ray, "Think big, think positive, never show any sign of weakness. Always go for the throat. Buy low, sell high. Fear? That's the other guy's problem. Nothing you have ever experienced will prepare you for the absolute carnage you are about to witness. Super Bowl, World Series - they don't know what pressure is. In this building, it's either kill or be killed. You make no friends in the pits and you take no prisoners. One minute you're up half a million in soybeans and the next, boom, your kids don't go to college and they've repossessed your Bentley. Are you with me?" Exuberant Billy Ray shouts, "Yeah, we got to kill the motherfuckers - we got to kill 'em!"

"Do you want to die now, or in a few minutes?" - Nefarious request uttered by Richard Widmark to Robert Taylor in the western movie *The Law and Jake Wade* (1958). In the film, Richard Widmark played outlaw Clint Hollister who forces his former outlaw buddy turned town Marshall into showing him the location of buried loot ($20,000). As Jake digs up the cache of money, Clint taunts Jake to make an escape and says, "Now there's the chance you've been waiting for, Jake. The only question is. Do you want to die now, or in a few minutes?" Wade, however, gets the better of Clint when he pulls out a gun buried with the money and in a face-to-face gunfight Wade wins the fast draw as Hollister bites the dust.

"Doc, tag 'em and bag 'em" - Sgt. Barnes (Tom Berenger) instructs a medic to load up a dead soldier in the Vietnam War film *Platoon* (1986). Pissed off at the sight, Barnes rebukes his troops, "You all take a good look at this lump of shit. Remember what it looks like. You fuck up in a firefight and I goddamned guarantee you a trip out of the bush—in a body bag! Out here, assholes, you keep the shit wired tight at all times. And that goes for you, shit-for-brains. You don't sleep on no fucking ambush. And the next son of a bitch I catch coppin' Z's in the bush, I personally am gonna take an interest in seeing them suffer. I shit you not. Doc, tag 'em and bag 'em." About the enemy, Sgt Barnes quips, "What's the matter boy? He ain't gonna bite you. That's a good gook; good and dead."

Doctor Death - The somber nickname given to Dr. Jack Kevorkian, a physician who took the limelight in 1990-91 when he advocated helping people to die. He called himself an "obitiatrist," preferring to be known as someone who engaged in "medicide." Dr. Death provided the "means, expertise, counseling and assuredness" to leave this world in peace. Critics, however, called him a "serial mercy killer." The controversy over his tactics in assisting patients with Alzheimer's disease, or other terminal/painful disorders kill themselves made this physician the man of the hour in the media. He made the rounds on the talk show and news magazine circuit defending his position; even appearing as a guest on ABC News NIGHTLINE hosted by news anchor Ted Koppel. Dr. Death's suicide list included an Alzheimer patient whom he helped die in June of 1990; and two Michigan women, a former elementary school teacher who had suffered from a painful genital disorder and a former housewife with Multiple Sclerosis both whom died in a double doctor-assisted suicide on October 23, 1991. Dr. Death wasn't in this for the money, however. He provided his suicide machine at no cost. The machine consisted of three bags of solutions that dripped into an intravenous line attached to the body of the person to die. In the case of a person whose veins were too weak to take an intravenous needle, Dr. Death had a handy, dandy backup system—a face mask attached to a canister of carbon monoxide. Note: In the fall of 1991 the Hemlock Society published their controversial suicide manual entitled "Final Exit."

"Dr. Kevorkian, I presume?" - Clint Eastwood as aging jewel thief Luther Whitney confronts a killer in the motion picture *Absolute Power* (1998). After seeing the President of the United States rough up a woman during sex (which leads to her murder), Luther is tracked down by members of the secret service to keep him quiet. To be sure that all possible leads to the President's involvement in the killing are eliminated, the secret service agents also try to kill Luther's lawyer daughter Kate (Laura Linney). After botching a plan that pushed Kayte's car off a seaside cliff, secret service agent Tim Collin (Dennis Haysbert) enters Kate's hospital room to inject her with a poison. Fortunately, her father intercepts the man, saying, "Dr. Kevorkian, I presume?" and sticks a needle filled with caustic substance into the man's neck. Intimately intertwined, Luther says, "My guess, it should be reaching your carotid artery by now. If I give you the rest of it, it's gonna fry your brain...When you went after my little girl that was entirely unacceptable." As agent Collin begs for mercy, Luther replies, "I'm fresh out" and falls to the floor with the man to finish the job.

Doctor Sphincter - The alter ego of cable celebrity Rich Kornfeld, a former computer programmer who starred in a short series called TIGHTLINE on community public access in Minneapolis in the 1990s. Doctor Sphincter, the host of TIGHTLINE (a parody of ABC News NIGHTLINE) is so tense and repressed that he made Richard Nixon look like Richard Simmons. Dressed in a gray suit with his shirt tightly buttoned about his neck, Dr. Sphincter questions his guests as his forehead sweats and his face strains like a constipated person on a toilet. Dr. Sphincter's worrywart mentality forced him to ponder, "Why people were so sloppy?...so lax?", "Why they don't clean up?" and "Why they don't produce?" His conclusion: "I think the answer is tightness!" He warns his viewers that we "must keep aware at all times of how loose we can become." Kornfeld created the Dr. Sphincter character in college. He continued producing the program with the assistance of his close friends who met weekly at a restaurant to brainstorm for ideas the day before the show was to be recorded. The Dr. Sphincter character appeared on public service announcements and industrial films.

"Don't be so fast to thank me on this, Luger, because you're going to be naked on this one. It's on the line for you. People are going to be watching. Now you blow it, you're going down. You screw up, you're going to be hung out to dry. You drop the ball, you're going to be left twisting in the wind. If you embarrass this department, your pants will be dancing with figs. Is that clear?" - Frank McRae as Los Angeles police Captain Doyle in the motion picture *National Lampoon's Loaded Weapon 1* (1993). Upon hearing the Captain's proposition officer Wes Lugar (Samuel L. Jackson) replies, "Everything except for the dancing with figs part!"

"*Don't* call me, Babe!" - Pamela Lee Anderson expresses her dissatisfaction with being called "Babe" in the motion picture *Barb Wire* (1996). Although, Barb Wire was a Megababe (who sported all sorts of revealing tight-fitting clothes) she treated those who used the word "Babe" with distain. When a street hoodlum used the sexist term, she pulled out her gun and smoked him.

"Don't ever tell anybody they're not free, cause they're gonna get real busy killin' and maimin' just to prove to you that they are" - Jack Nicholson as alcoholic southern lawyer George Hansen shoots the breeze around a campfire with cross-country motorcyclists Wyatt, aka "Captain America" (Peter Fonda) and Billy (Dennis Hopper) in the classic road picture *Easy Rider* (1969). After talking about "killin' and maimin'" to his new pot-smoking biker friends, George and company are attacked by local rednecks. They club George to death and leave Wyatt and Billy badly beaten. The film ends with some hillbilly types in a pickup truck blowing away Wyatt and Billy with a shotgun as they cruise by on their motorcycles.

"Don't ever try to fucking bribe me or I'll have you and Patchett in shit up to your ears." - Russell Crowe as Bud White, a temperamental vigilante on the LA Police force in the early 1950s who warns a prostitute named Lynn Graken (Kim Basinger) to stop interfering in his investigation in the motion picture *L.A. Confidential* (1997). Lynn–the spitting image of actress Veronica Lake–works for a call-girl ring owned by a guy named Pierce Patchett (David Strathairn) that specializes in celebrity look-alike hookers.

"Don't give the enemy a break. Send him to hell" - Military sentiments of Lt. Col. Benjamin Vandervoort (John Wayne) in the WWII adventure film *The Longest Day* (1962).

"Don't fuck with me, fellas. This ain't my first time at the rodeo" - Faye Dunaway as the legendary movie actress Joan Crawford addresses the male boardroom members of the Pepsi Company in the motion picture *Mommie Dearest* (1981). The movie was based on the autobiography of Christina Crawford who reported her mother's tendencies toward child abuse. In the film, Joan Crawford asks her daughter, "Why can't you give me the respect that I'm entitled to? Why can't you treat me like I would be treated by any stranger on the street?" Christina replies, "Because I am *NOT* one of your fans!" The phrase "No wire hangers...*EVER!*" alludes to Crawford's alleged cruelty after she demolishes her daughter's closet by tearing off all of the clothes hung on wire hangers.

"Don't fuck with the Chuck!" – Memorable suggestion of a satanic doll in the horror motion picture sequel *Bride of Chucky* (1998). In the original film C*hild's Play* (1988), a young boy named Andy Barclay (Alex Vincent) receives a red-haired, freckled-faced 'Good Guys' doll (supposedly from Carson's Department Store). At first, the seemingly safe battery-operated talking doll says, "Hi, I'm Chucky. Wanna play?" but eventually the doll murders Andy's Aunt Maggie. Soon after, the police place Andy under observation for his fanciful claim that "Chucky did it." Only when the boy's mother (Catherine Hicks) threatens to burn Chucky in the fireplace does it awaken, bite her arm and flee from her apartment. The doll actually came from a burned out toy store where the spirit of a voodoo practicing serial strangler named Charles "Chucky" Lee Ray (Brad Dourif) transmigrated into a doll after a lightning bolt hit the store as the man was dying. Now animated with revenge, the Chucky doll hunted down the police officer that killed him and then proceeded to possess the body of the young boy who first released him from his box. Andy tries to kill Chucky in a gas fireplace ("This is the end, friend") but the charred doll still wreaks havoc until it gets shot in the heart. In the sequels *Child's Play 2* (1990); *Child's Play 3* (1991), and *Seed of Chucky* (2004) Chucky continues his killing sprees and mouths such memorable quotes as "Nothing like a strangulation to get the circulation going" and "I am Chucky, the killer doll! And I dig it!" When asked, "Why do you kill?" Chucky says, "Umm... hobby, I guess." Note: In the Stephen King film *The Shining* (1980) Danny Lloyd sees the ghosts of two murdered girls garbed in pretty blue dresses that invite him to, "Come play with us...forever...and ever...and ever."

"Don't make me get medieval on your ass, ma'am" - Stern but overzealous warning delivered by Chuck the security guard (Kelly Perine) working for Winford-Louder Department Store on the sitcom THE DREW CAREY SHOW/ABC/1995-2004.

"Don't push it. Don't push it, or I'll give you a war you won't believe. Let it go. Let it go" - Sylvester Stallone as John Rambo, an ex-green Beret veteran wandering the roads of the northwest is harassed by the local constabulary in the motion picture *First Blood* (1982). Unfortunately, the local cops arrest John for vagrancy and brutalize him during his lock up. In retaliation, John breaks free. As the local law enforcement gear up to catch Rambo, his former training officer Colonel Trautman (Richard Crenna) arrives on the scene and warns, "You don't seem to want to accept who you are dealing with. You are dealing with a man who is an expert—with guns, with knives, with his bare hands. A man who's been trained to ignore pain, to ignore weather. To live off the land and eat things that would make a billy goat puke. In Vietnam, his mission was to dispose of enemy personnel. To kill, period. Win by attrition. Well, Rambo was the best." When local Sheriff Will Teasle (Brian Dennehy) doesn't seem to grasp the seriousness of the matter, Trautman warns, "I don't think you understand. I didn't come here to rescue Rambo from you. I came here to rescue you from him." Before Trautman leaves he recommends that if the sheriff goes up against Rambo, he better have "a good supply of body bags."

"Don't torture yourself, Gomez. That's my job." - Dysfunctional words of affection spoken by Morticia Addams (Angelica Huston) to her bizarre husband Gomez (Raul Julia) in the horror film *The Addams Family* (1991). When Wednesday Addams (Christina Ricci) tells her brother Pugsley (Jimmy Workman) to sit in an electric chair, he asks "Why?" Wednesday tells him, "Because we're going to play a game." "What game?" inquires Pugsley. As she straps her brother tightly to the chair Wednesday reveals, "It's called 'Is there a God?'" In the film sequel *Addams Family Values* (1993), Gomez asks, "Children, why do you hate the baby?" Pugsley answers, "We don't hate him. We just wanna play with him." Wednesday adds, "Especially his head."

"Don't touch me!" - Jason Scott Lee as legendary martial arts expert Bruce Lee in the motion picture *Dragon: The Bruce Lee Story* (1993). When a thug accosts Bruce Lee, he tells the creep, "Don't touch me!" The thug threatens, "Or what?" Bruce replies, "Or I'll touch you back."

"Don't touch my knife. That makes me mad. Very, very mad" - In the film *The Night of the Hunter* (1955), Harry Powell, a psychotic religious fanatic (Robert Mitchum) stalks two homeless children for money stolen by their father. When the girl (Sally Jane Bruce) tries to touch the menacing preacher's weapon, he warns her of the consequences of such an act.

"Don't trust whitey" - Racial slur spoken in the comedy film *The Jerk* (1982). In the film, comic Steve Martin plays Naven Johnson, a dim-witted white man who was raised by a family of black sharecroppers. When Naven decides to leave home and search the world for his "special purpose," he is given these three bits of advice by his family: "The Lord loves a working man"; 2) "Don't trust Whitey"; and 3) "See a doctor and get rid of it." Note: In the film *Shaft* (1971), Richard Roundtree as private eye John Shaft informs a friend, "When you lead your revolution, whitey better be standing still because you don't run worth a damn no more." And on a segment of SATURDAY NIGHT LIVE Eddie Murphy played convict Tyrone Green who recites poetry like "C-I-L-L my lanlord" and "I Hate White People Because They Is W-I-T-E" (a takeoff of a black Utah prison convict character originally performed by comedian Garrett Morris on SNL who sang the blues song "I'm gonna get me a shotgun, and kill me all the whiteys I see" during an audition for "The Lifer's Follies" talent show).

"Don't you 'In a minute, Momma' me! Get off your fat little ass or I'll break it for you! I want two soft boiled eggs, white toast, and some of that grape jelly god damn it! And don't burn the toast!" - Anne Ramsey as Momma asks her son Owen (Danny DeVito) for food after he says, "In a minute, Momma" in the motion picture *Throw Momma from the Train* (1987). Note: This movie is a comic homage to Alfred Hitchcock's *Strangers on a Train (1951)* wherein psychotic momma's boy Bruno Anthony (Robert Walker) casually speculates with tennis pro Guy Haines (Farley Granger) about Haines killing Bruno's father in exchange for Bruno killing Haines' wife. Haines takes the conversation as a joke, but Bruno takes the talk serious and sets out to kill. Later, at a dinner gathering Bruno says, "Everyone has somebody that they want to put out of the way. Oh now, surely Madam, you're not going to tell me that there hasn't been a time that you didn't want to dispose of someone. Your husband, for instance."

"Don't you talk back to me! You show me some respect! Without people like me, you're nothing! We're the ones that get you your 40 fuckin' million!" - Robert De Niro as Gil Renard, a dysfunctional baseball fanatic stalks his favorite MVP player Bobby Rayburn (Wesley Snipes) in the motion picture *The Fan* (1996). When Bobby asks, "Look, what do you want?" his crazed admirer tells him, "What do I want? I want everytime they think of you, they're gonna think of me."

"Doorbells should ring once and then electrocute the ringer" - Ilka Chase as Hoppy Grant as he answers the door in the motion picture *No Time for Love* (1943).

"Drop Dead!" - Chuck Norris as Chris Garret has the final word in the motion picture *The Hit Man* (1991). In the film, Seattle detective Chris Garret confronts a number of criminals. One, in particular, is called Hassan (Michael Benyaer), a Persian fanatic. In a final confrontation, Garret get the drop on Hassan who yells, "You! Fuck! Motherfuck!" As Hassan reaches for a pistol in the waistband of his pants, Garret says, "Drop Dead!" and blows Hassan away with a shotgun blast that throws his body through a window. Note: In the film *Terminator 3: Rise of the Machines* (2003), Claire Danes as Kate Brewster, the future wife of John Connor shouts, "Just die, you bitch!" to the female Terminatrix that refuses to die despite repeated attempts to terminate her. *See also* "You bastard! Drop dead!"

"Drop that gun or I'll drill you. I've got a gun here that shoots bullets for twelve miles and throws rocks the rest of the way" - Lou Costello as newspaper photographer Flash Fulton in the motion picture *Hit the Ice* (1943).

"Drugs ain't a black thing, or a white thing. It's a death thing. Death don't give a shit about color" - Judd Nelson as Nick Peretti in the motion picture *New Jack City* (1991).

Dumbass - Frequently used put-down of Red Forman (Kurtwood Smith), a tough, no nonsense father of two and veteran of World War II and the Korean War featured on the sitcom THAT 70s SHOW/FOX/1998-2006. Most of the time, Red uses the term 'Dumbass' to describe the actions of his teenage son Eric (Topher Grace), who often fails to live up to his expectations. As Red once said, "Son, you don't have bad luck. The reason that bad things happen to you is because you're a dumbass." Although Red is reticent to say, he loves his son very much. Red also liked to say, "That kids on dope!" Eric's Mom once in a while uses "Dumbass" when Eric did something extremely stupid, like the time his ex-girlfriend Donna wanted Eric back and he refused because he didn't want to be the rebound guy. Note: Red also tells people that if they get out of line, he will put his foot up their ass. Once, Steven Hyde (Danny Masterson), who lives in the Forman household, said to Eric, "You know, Forman, you ought to write a book 'Things My Dad Threatened To Put Up My Ass'. Chapter One: His Foot". On the series finale, Hyde asks Red, "Did you ever actually do that...with your foot? Red replies, "Once. On Iwo Jima. I can't talk about it." A true patriot, Red believes, "If the US government decides to stick a tracking device up your ass, you say, "Thank You. And God Bless America." *See also* "BURN!!!"

The Dumbest Girl in America - Self-proclaimed title of Kelly Bundy (Christina Applegate), a beautiful blond rock bimbo on the sitcom MARRIED...WITH CHILDREN/FOX/1987-97. At one point, Kelly's greatest aspiration was to get the groupie bragging rights, "I'm with the band!" Kelly did earn the distinction of playing the "Rock Slut" in the Gutter Cats music video. Her popularity with the boys inspired her to say she was "The Beatles of the 1980s." When asked her birth sign, she replies, "I'm an Aquarium." Once Kelly's frustrated father (Ed O'Neill) said, "Pumpkin, when Daddy goes to the chair, would you sit on my lap one last time?" Kelly replies, "I'd be honored." The gorgeous Kelly was later hired (not for her brains) by Channel 83 as the Action News TV Weather Bunny Girl. Note: In the film *The Dentist* (1932) W. C. Fields as the Dentist says, "That kids so dumb he doesn't even know what time it is." When asked, "By the way, what time is it?" by Charley Frobisher (Bud Jamison), the Dentist replies, "I don't know." *See also* "Mr. Empty Pants" and "Spud"

"Dummy!" - Often used word to describe anyone not agreeing with the opinions of Fred Sanford (Redd Foxx), a 65-year-old black junk dealer from Watts on the series SANFORD AND SON/NBC/1972-77. In general, Fred was a curmudgeon. He especially disliked his sister-in-law Ester (La Wanda Page) whom he spent a lifetime abusing. Some typical Esther insults: "I've seen better faces on a can of dog food" and "Two more legs and you could call her Trigger." Esther, in her defense, refers to Fred as an "old fish-eyed fool." One of Fred's biggest attention getters is his fake heart attack scenario. Grasping one hand across his heart and the other one reaching for heaven Fred's cries his signature plea, "Elizabeth, this is the big one...I'm comin', honey (a reference to his deceased wife). His heart condition, of course, is sheer subterfuge to get his son Lamont (Demond Wilson) and others to do things his way. Note: Redd Foxx died of a real heart attack on 10/12/91. He had just begun starring in the sitcom THE

ROYAL FAMILY/CBS/1991-92, about a retired postal carrier from Atlanta. On the 11/27/91 episode of the series, the show's writers gave Foxx's TV character, Al Royal a heart attack while he bowled at the Postman's Bowling Tournament.

"Durwood" - On the sitcom BEWITCHED/ABC/1964-72, Endora the witch (Agnes Moorehead) hated the fact that her daughter Samantha (Elizabeth Montgomery) had lowered herself and married a mortal man, namely, advertising executive Darrin Stephens (Dick York/Dick Sergeant). In an effort to forget this fact or to just intentionally bother Darrin, Endora never pronounced Darrin's name properly. She has called him Durwood, Darwin, Dagwood, Donald, Dennis, Dum-Dum, Dumbo, Derek, Darwood, Durweed, Darius, David and Dobbin (a term also used by his warlock father-in-law, Maurice).

"Dyin' ain't much of a livin'" - In the classic western *The Outlaw—Josey Wales* (1976), Clint Eastwood stars as Josey Wales, a homesteader whose wife was killed by marauding Union soldiers. At the conclusion of the Civil War, Wales is declared an outlaw and a bounty is placed on his head. One such bounty hunter approaches Joey Wales in a frontier tavern and says, "Man's got to make a living" to which Josey replies, "Dyin' ain't much of a livin'." After seeing the death in Josey's eyes, the man leaves the bar but returns saying, "I had to come back. "I know", says Josey. In a face-to-face draw down, Josey won the battle. Later, Josey encounters the man who killed his wife and belly sticks him with a Union saber.

"E-mail is for geeks and pedophiles" - Ryan Phillippe as Sebastian Valmont in the motion picture *Cruel Intentions (1999).*

"Eat My Shorts!" - The bratty retort of Bart Simpson, a dysfunctional 10-year-old juvenile delinquent on the adult animated cartoon THE SIMPSONS/ FOX/1990+. Bart also likes to say "Don't Have a Cow, Man!" He attends fourth grade at Springfield Elementary School, and he can often be seen writing repetitive chalk phrases on the blackboard during detention sessions after school. Some examples:

- I shall not draw naked ladies in class.
- My name is not Dr. Death
- Organ transplants are best left to professionals
- My homework was not stolen by the one-armed man
- I will not Xerox my butt
- I will not do that thing with my tongue.
- I will not belch the national anthem.
- I will not fake rabies
- I will not call my teacher "Hot Cakes"
- I will not make flatulent noises in class
- The Christmas Pageant does not stink
- I will not torment the emotionally frail
- I will not bury the new kid
- I will not call the principal "spud head"
- The Pledge of Allegiance does not end with "Hail Satan!"
- There was no Roman god named "Fartacus"
- I will not hide the teacher's medication
- SpongeBob is not a contraceptive
- Poking a dead raccoon is not research
- A booger is not a bookmark

Note: In the film *Grumpy Old Men* (1993) Walter Matthau as Max Goldman uses Bart Simpson's signature insult "Eat My Shorts!" to put-down his old friend John Gustafson (Jack Lemmon). *See also* "Bart Simpson Phone Pranks"

"Eat it till you choke!" - Spoken by James Caan in the motion picture thriller *Misery* (1990) based on the novel by Stephen King. After successful romance writer Paul Sheldon crashes on a snowy New England road, he is rescued by Annie Wilkes, a reclusive ex-nurse (Kathy Bates) who happens to be his Number One fan.

Unfortunately, she keeps him prisoner in her house and forces him to continue writing the adventures of her favorite character Misery Chastain (whom Paul had recently killed off). Annie disdainfully dubs Paul "Mr. Man" and beats, cripples (ankles snapped with a sledge hammer) and drugs him. Paul then faces his final hurdle–a ritual suicide requested by Annie as he finishes the last chapter of his book. In a last ditch effort to escape, Paul ignites the finished manuscript with lighter fluid and quickly finds himself wrestling on the floor with his demented caretaker. Reaching for a hand-full of ashes from the now burnt book, Paul viciously shoves them down Annie's throat, crying, "Here! You want it! You want it! Eat it till you choke!" Paul delivers a final deathblow to Annie's head with a metal doorstop shaped like a farm pig. *See also* "I wish you were a wishing well..."

"Eddie, you're a born loser" - George C. Scott as Bert Gordon expresses his opinion of pool hustler Eddie Felson (Paul Newman) in the motion picture *The Hustler* (1961). After Bert drives Eddie's sweetheart Sarah Packard (Piper Laurie) to commit suicide, Eddie curses, "You don't know what winnin' is, Bert. You're a loser. 'Cause you're dead inside, and you can't live unless you make everything else dead around you."

Engarde, Bitch! - Surly challenge delivered by Goldie Hawn to Meryl Streep as they pummel each other with shovels in the supernatural black comedy *Death Becomes Her* (1992). After jealous actress Madeline Ashton (Streep) shotguns the belly of Helen Sharp (Goldie Hawn) she calmly says, "These are the moments that make life worth living." Unfortunately, Madeline discovers that Helen (now with a hole in her torso) is still alive, because like Madeline, Helen drank an immortality potion procured from the same mysterious woman (Isabella Rossellini) who warned, "Take care of your self. You and your body will be together a long time. Take care of it." Frustrated at this revelation, the two women began to slam each other with shovels to release their pent up rage. Later, enlisting the aid of Ernest Menville (Bruce Willis), Helen's undertaker fiancé, the two women cover up the damage done to their bodies. Ernest reluctantly agrees to help the ladies because he didn't want to find out "What they do to soft, bald, overweight Republicans in prison?"

"Enough is enough! I have had it with these motherfucking snakes on this motherfucking plane!" - Samuel L. Jackson as Neville Flynn, a black FBI Agent battling a horde of slithering snakes aboard Pacific Air Flight 121 some 30,000 feet above the ocean in the motion picture *Snakes on a Plane* (2006). The 450 poisonous snakes were placed aboard the plane to kill witnesses to a mob murder before they could testify in Los Angeles. Another memorable line was shouted by fellow passenger Bill Leroy (Bill Dallas) when he shrieks, "Someone get this fuckin' snake off my ass!"

"Ever kill anyone? Bet you could tease a man to death without even trying...so stop trying" - Cary Grant as Roger Thornhill clues in the beautiful but deceptive Eve Kendall (Eva Marie Saint) that he knows that she was the one who set him up to be killed by a crop-dusting plane in an Illinois cornfield in the Alfred Hitchcock thriller *North By Northwest* (1959).

"Everybody is insane, everywhere!" - Life-lesson learned by Sheriff Alan Pangborn (Ed Harris) in the Stephen King horror flick *Needful Things* (1993). Trying to break up an argument between his deputy and a villager, Alan interjects, "You know, guys, I moved here and I thought, 'Great! I'm outta the big city and I'm finally in a place where everybody isn't gonna be crawling up everybody's asshole every day! A place where maybe my biggest nightmare is gonna be getting some goddamn cat out of a tree!' But forget that! Everybody is insane, everywhere!"

"Excrement!...That's what I think of Mr. J. Evans Pritchard" - Robin Williams as John Keating, a charismatic English literature professor takes exception to the condescending words of the author of a poetry anthology in the motion picture *The Dead Poet's Society* (1989). Adding to his discontent, John continues, "We're not laying pipe, we're talking about poetry. How can you describe poetry like 'American Bandstand'? 'I'd like Byron, I gave him a 42, but I can't dance to him'...Now, I want you to rip out that page...go on, rip out the entire page...rip it out...I'll tell you what, don't just tear out *that* page, tear out the entire introduction. I want it gone, history, leave nothing of it...Be gone, J. Evans Pritchard."

"Exterminate! Exterminate!" - Popular catchphrase of the Daleks, a mobile army of deadly robot warriors on the science fiction series DOCTOR WHO/BBC/1963-90. Created by Davros, a physically impaired scientist from the planet Skaro (injured in an explosion), the Daleks initially were designed to eliminate a rival race of Thals. Unfortunately, like Frankenstein's monster, these salt & pepper shakers on wheels (genetically altered beings called Kaleds were encased within) became uncontrollable and soon they began their conquest of the galaxy. Those who chose to stand in their way were greeted with a garbled metallic sounding directive "Exterminate!...Exterminate!" The Daleks (created by writer Terry Nation) debuted in the second DOCTOR. WHO adventure "The Dead Planet" (1963) and have appeared in the motion pictures *Dr. Who and the Daleks* (1965) and *Dr. Who: Invasion Earth 2150* (1966). In 2005, the Daleks returned on the continuation of the DOCTOR WHO series starring Christopher Eccleston and later David Tennant as The Doctor.

"Ewwww! I'll harm you!" - The wimpy threat of Stinky (played by pudgy comedian Joe Besser) a bratty little kid dressed in a Little Lord Fauntleroy outfit who terrorized the tenants at Sidney Fields Hollywood Boarding House on the sitcom THE ABBOTT AND COSTELLO SHOW/SYN/1951-53. When Lou Costello tries to discipline the boy, Stinky daintily raises his hand and threatens him with the silly declaration "Ewwww! I'll harm you!" Note: Stinky was also the school nickname of lawyer Crosby Caufield (Peter Krause) on the legal drama THE GREAT DEFENDER/FOX/1995. It seems he had bit of a problem with foot fungus. In the neighborhood of wimpy insults like, "Ewwww! I'll harm you!" Robert Newton as Bill Walker in the movie *Major Barbara* (1941) comes in second with "You leave me alone or I'll do you mischief" while addressing Major Barbara Undershaft of the Salvation Army.

"Face it girls. I'm older and I have more insurance" - Life-lesson taught to punky young women in the motion picture *Fried Green Tomatoes* (1991). While Evelyn (Kathy Bates) positions to pull into a parking spot at a local supermarket, a red Volkswagen convertible zips in to steal it. "Excuse me. I was waiting for that space," Evelyn objected politely. One of the car's two female occupants quips, "Yeah, tough. Face it lady. We're younger and faster." The normally reserved (and now menopausal) Evelyn says, "To Wanda!" and with maniacal glee rams her larger car over and over into the girl's tiny-framed vehicle. "What are you doing," cries the females. "Are you crazy!" With a cool glance Evelyn faces her accusers. "Face it girls. I'm older and I have more insurance." Later, still feeling the rush of power in her new found confidence, Evelyn joyfully confides to her older friend (Jessica Tandy), "After I whip all the punks of the world, I'll take on the wife beaters...and machine gun their genitals. Then Wanda will go on the rampage. I'll put tiny little bombs in *Penthouse* and *Playboy* so they'll explode when you open them. I am gonna ban all fashion models who weigh less that 130 pounds. And I'll give half of the military budget to people over sixty-five and declare wrinkles sexually desirable. To Wanda! Righter of wrongs! Queen beyond compare! Evelyn's friend then inquires, "How many of those hormones you taking, honey?"

Fat Man - The pejorative celebrity nickname of British radio/TV personality Tom Vernon who starred in a series of travelogues sponsored by PBS and Britain's Channel 4 Television as he biked about the world in search of Epicurean delights (Food y'all). In 1987, FAT MAN GOES NORSE visits towns in Norway and eats smoked reindeer. In the 1990s, FAT MAN GOES GAUCHO bicycles a thousand miles and feasts on the Argentinean cowboy delicacy—fried bull's testicles...Gulp! With all of his bicycling bravado, the blimpy brit still weighed in at 250-295 pounds. Another popular TV "Fat Man" appeared on the detective drama JAKE AND THE FAT MAN/CBS/1987-91 that starred the portly William Conrad as Jason Lockinvar McCabe, aka the "Fat Man" (also called "Buster"), a prosecuting District Attorney who chased down criminals in Los Angeles and later Honolulu with the assistance of his partner, Jake Styles (Joe Penny). Brad Runyon (J. Scott) was the star of the radio series "The Fat Man" created by Dashiell Hammett and based on his magazine detective "The Continental Op." In the film *Abbott and Costello Meet Captain Kidd* (1952), Charles Laughton remarks, "I hate fat people!" When reminded of his own girth, he responds, "Hate myself, too!" Note: In military terms, "Fat Man" was the name bestowed on the Atomic Bomb (11 feet long by 5 feet in diameter) dropped onto the Japanese city of Nagasaki August 9th 1945. Reportedly, it was nicknamed after the British politician, Winston Churchill. *See also* "One of these days, Alice...POW, Right in the kisser!"

"The federal government announced today that in an effort to eradicate the national debt, it will be selling the state of Rhode Island to a group of private investors, for a reported $18 billion. The investors plan to enclose the entire state with an all-weather roof, and turn it into the world's largest shopping mall. When asked for comment, a White House spokesperson would only say, "Well, at least we didn't sell it to the fucking Japanese" - Newswoman reports the sale of Rhode Island in the motion picture *Schizopolis* (1996).

"Feed me! Feed me!" - The ravenous cry of an oversized flesh-eating plant in the dark horror classic movie *The Little Shop of Horrors* (1960). In the film, florist wanna-be Seymour Krelboyne (Jonathan Haze) discovers a plant that feeds exclusively on human blood. After Seymour milks all his fingers to nourish the strange plant, he graduates to full-sized corpses to satisfy the plant's huge appetite. Frustrated with the plant's constant cry of "Feed me!", Seymour shouts, "You dirty rat plant, you messed up my whole life!" In the end, the plant eats Seymour to satisfy its hunger. Note: The film featured a very young Jack Nicholson as a patient in a dentist office. When the man confuses Seymour as the dentist, he encourages him to pull his teeth. Reluctantly, Seymour yanks on the man's molars. When the patient shrieks in pain, Seymour immediately stops. But instead of complaining of the pain, the masochistic patient cries, "Oh my God, don't stop now!" In the musical remake *Little Shop of Horrors* (1986) Bill Murray played the role of the masochistic patient Arthur Denton He told his sadistic dentist Orin Scrivello (Steve Martin), "I think I need a root canal. I definitely need a long, slow root canal."

Feminists Against Neanderthal Guys *See* **NO'MA'AM**

Ferg-face - What 14-year-old Clarissa Marie Darling (Melissa Joan Hart) calls her scheming dweeb of a younger brother Ferguson W. Darling (Jason Zimbler) on the sitcom CLARISSA EXPLAINS IT ALL/NIK/1991-94. Clarissa says Ferguson is a "burr on my butt since I was born" and refers to Ferg-Face as a "dork-headed creep they should grind up for puppy puke." She'd rather "eat barf-pie than help her brother." In a tit-for-tat insult fest Clarissa and Ferg-Face could be heard calling each other such choice put-downs as Jerk-wad, Wart-head, Teenage Mutant Ninja Moron, Pip-Squeak, Fungus-face, Little Dictator, Wart-face! and "It's hideous—It looked just like you."

Ferret-face - The insulting but quite appropriate nickname for Major Frank Burns (Larry Linville), a weasel of an army surgeon on the military comedy M*A*S*H/CBS/1972-83. Frank was married but that didn't keep him from fooling around with Nurse Major Margaret "Hot Lips" Houlihan (Loretta Swit) who was stationed at the 4077th Mobile Army Surgical Hospital. Frank always quoted chapter and verse from the Army manual and questioned everyone's patriotism when they didn't do things by the book. When Margaret Houlihan got married later in the series, Frank went bonkers with jealousy, as well as AWOL. While drunk in Tokyo, he accosted a General and his wife in a bathhouse and was place on psychiatric observation. Back at the 4077th, Captain Hawkeye Pierce toasted his departure with a simple "Good-bye, Ferret-Face."

"Fight the *real* enemy" - During the live 10/3/92 broadcast on SATURDAY NIGHT LIVE Irish rock singer Sinead O'Connor rips up a photograph of Pope John Paul II and remarks, "Fight the *real* enemy" as she concludes singing Bob Marley's "War." Reportedly, her action reflected her anger at the Catholic Church and their non-support of women's rights in Ireland. When the program was rerun, NBC censors eliminated the photo-tearing scene.

"A filthy child murderer who killed at least twenty children in the neighborhood...the lawyers got fat and the judge got famous...but somebody forgot to sign the search warrant in the right place and he was freed just like that" - Ronnee Blakley as parent Marge Thompson relates the story behind infamous child killer Freddie Krueger (Robert Englund) to her daughter, Nancy (Heather Langenkamp) in the horror film classic *A Nightmare on Elm Street* (1984). After the trial, however, the people in town—just like a mob scene in a 'Frankenstein' movie—inflicted retribution on Krueger by setting his body on fire. Sadly, the fire killed the body, but it just inflamed Krueger's evil soul to return and haunt the nightmares of the town's children in the sequel films *Nightmare on Elm Street 2 :Freddie's Revenge* (1985); *Nightmare on Elm Street 3: Dream Warriors* (1987); *Nightmare on Elm Street 4: Dream Master* (1988); *Nightmare on Elm Street: The Dream Child* (1989); *Freddie's Dead: The Final Nightmare* (1991); and *Wes Craven's New Nightmare* (1994). Note: The deadly Freddie character also inspired the twisted children's nursery rhyme "One, two, Freddy's coming for you! / Three, four, better lock your door! / Five, six, grab your crucifix! / Seven, eight, better stay up late! / Nine, ten, never sleep again!

"The first one won't kill you" - Robert Shaw as SPECTRE assassin Red Grant in the spy thriller *From Russia with Love* (1963). Instructed to kill British secret agent James Bond (Sean Connery), Grant corners 007 in his train compartment and gleefully taunts, "Keep still. And now get up on your knees. Put your hands in your pocket. Keep 'em there. How does it feel old man?" After Grant reveals his plans for Bond ("I can see the headlines: BRITISH AGENT MURDERS BEAUTIFUL RUSSIAN SPY THEN COMMITS MURDER") Bond sneers, "Tell me. Which lunatic asylum did they get you out of?" Grant replies, "Don't make it tougher on your self. My orders are to kill you and deliver the Lektor (a decoding device). How I do it's my business. It'll be slow and painful. [pointing his gun] The first one won't kill you. Nor the second. Not even the third. Not till you crawl over here and kiss my foot." Bond staying cool as usual, simply says, "How 'bout a cigarette?" Then, luring the killer to open a booby-trapped briefcase, Bond, jumps the man, and in the struggle, stabs the assassin in the shoulder and then uses Grant's own strangle wire to finish him off. Later, when SPECTRE agent Lotte Lenya (Rosa Klebb) tries to jab Bond with a venom-dipped stiletto hidden in the tip of her shoe, Bond's female companion shoots Lotte and Bond quips, "Yes, she's had her kicks." Note: In the film *Sins of the Night* (1993) Miles O'Keeffe as Tony Falcone tells Roxanne Flowers (Deborah Shelton) "I want you to fucking crawl to me. Get on your fucking knees and crawl to me. Crawl to me now. Crawl to me you fucking trash!"

"The first time I saw you, I hated your guts. I think I even hated you before I met you. I hated you on TV. I hated you in Vietnam." - Mickey Rourke as New York cop Stanley White with a dislike for Asians who vents his frustration at TV reporter Ariane (Tracy Tsu) in the motion picture *Year of the Dragon* (1985). He continues his tirade:

"You want to know what's destroying this country? It's not booze. It's not drugs. It's TV. It's media. It's people like you. It's vampires. I hate the way you make your living sticking microphones in people's faces. You lie every night at 6:00. I hate the way you kill real feelings. I hate everything that you stand for. Most of all, I hate rich kids and I hate this place. So why do I want to fuck you so bad?"

"Flowers are the fastest way to a woman's heart. Well, actually, the fastest way is through her rig cage, but flowers are a lot less messy" - Eddie Murphy as Maximillian the vampire offers a few choice bits of courting etiquette in the motion picture *Vampire in Brooklyn* (1995).

Flying Fickle Finger of Fate Award, The - Called the Rigid Digit, the Winged Weenie, Wonderful Wiggler, Friendly Phalange, and the Nifty Knuckle, this weekly satirical award was presented by comedians Dan Rowan and Dick Martin on the weekly comedy variety series ROWAN & MARTIN'S LAUGH-IN/NBC/1968-73 for the dumbest/craziest news item of the week. Gold/Silver in color the award was a "hand" mounted on a trophy base. Its index finger adorned with two small wings rotated in a circular "Whoopee!" motion. Recipients of this "uncoveted" award included then Los Angeles Chief of Police, Ed Davis who suggested that "gallows" be put in all airports for the hijackers, so when they were apprehended, they could be hung on the spot; the City of Cleveland for their Kioga River (It caught fire due to its high pollution levels); and a Wonderful Wiggler went to William F. Buckley for his philosophy "Never clarify tomorrow, what you can obscure today." Top awards went to the Pentagon. They won five times.

"For a nation of pigs, it sure seems funny that you don't eat them! Jesus Christ forgave the bastards, but I can't! I hate! I hate you! I hate your nation! And I hate your people! And I fuck your sons and daughters because they're pigs! You're all pigs!" - Brad Davis as American Billy Hayes lambastes the Turkish court system after his arrest overseas for drug possession in the motion picture *Midnight Express* (1978).

"For Heaven's sake, stop sawing away on that infernal instrument! It was a sad day when Mother gave it to you, a sad day for her, a sad day for you, a sad day for us all...What I cannot understand is why, since you've had that violin with you so long, you never learned to play!" - Robert Morley as Mycroft Holmes irritated at his younger brother Sherlock Holmes' (John Neville) violin playing in the motion picture *A Study in Terror* (1965).

"For me, my family was like, uh, *Dances with Jews*. Oh sure, we had names for our relatives like they had in that movie...Well, we had 'Eats With His Hands,' 'Spits When He Talks,' 'Makes Noise When He Bends,' 'Sweats Like a Pig,' 'Whines In a Cab,' 'Never Buys Retail,' 'Shaves His Back'" - Billy Crystal as aging comic Buddy Young, Jr. recalls his family tree to a reporter (Richard Kind) in the motion picture *Mr. Saturday Night* (1992).

"For me the Internet is just yet another way of being rejected by women" - Steve Zahn as bookstore worker George Pappas in the motion picture *You've Got Mail* (1998).

"For me to POOP on!" - Catchphrase of an insulting Rotweiler hand puppet named Triumph (identified on the show as a Yugoslavian mountain hound) seen on comedy spots on the talk show LATE NIGHT WITH CONAN O'BRIEN/NBC/1993+. This degrading dog (brought to life by puppeteer-writer Robert Smigel) first compliments a person, and then mocks them with his trademark put-down. He "pooped on" such celebrity guests as John Tesh, Pauly Shore, and Fabio. In 1999, Triumph conducted a tour of Hollywood by bus and visited the Hollywood Wax Museum–the sight of many, many stars "for me to POOP on!" While there, he left a turd at the feet of David Hasselhoff's figure and humped the wax displays of Benji and Toto from the *Wizard of Oz*. He also told one of the Asian people on the tour "Do you know how I know you're Chinese?...Because YOU ATE MY DAD!" Note: In the film *Doc Hollywood* (1991) Julie Warner as Lou the ambulance driver says, "Can't poop in this town without everybody knowin' what color it is." *See also* "Krunk"

"Forget it, I quit, I can't do this any more, man. My head's about to explode. My whole life sucks. I don't know what I'm doing, I don't know where I'm going. My dad just died, we just killed Bambi, I'm out here getting my ass kicked and every time I drive down the road I wanna jerk the wheel [shouts] into a goddamned bridge abutment" - Chris Farley as Tommy Callahan III, the son of an Auto Parts distributor who has succumbed to the pressure of running his deceased father's business in the motion picture *Tommy* (1995)

"Frak!" - Swear word used by pilots aboard the gigantic spacecraft *Galactica* on the science fiction series BATTLESTAR GALACTICA/ABC/1978-80. When frustrated or mad Lt. Starbuck (Dirk Benedict) was often heard mouthing this futuristic "cuss" word. Another foul phrase used was "Feldercarp." Note: In the 2004 series remake, the scriptwriters continued to use the word "Frak." It is strange that the word we substitute for "Fuck" is acceptable even though we know that it expresses the same sentiment and meaning. So an actor can safely say, "What the frak" or "Frak you" but he can't say the real "F" word on the air. That's just so "Fraken" hypocritical.

"Frankly, my dear, I don't give a damn" - Clark Gable as Rhett Butler addresses Scarlett O'Hara's (Vivien Leigh) plea, "Oh, my darling, if you go, what shall I do?" in the motion picture adaptation of Margaret Mitchell's *Gone with the Wind* (1939). Before Rhett didn't give a damn about Scarlett, he told her, "I've always thought a good lashing with a buggy whip would benefit you immensely." Note: At the time the movie was produced, the use of the word "damn" was a no-no according to the movie industry's code of ethics board (known as the Hays Office) and consequently, the maker's of GWTW were fined $5,000 for using the 'D' word. Over the years this famous kiss-off line has been a favorite of nightclub impressionists (who sometimes change it slightly to "Frankly, Scarlett, I don't give a damn").

"Fredo, you're nothing to me now. You're not a brother, you're not a friend. I don't want to know you or what you do. I don't want to see you at the hotels; I don't want you near my house. When you see our mother, I want to know a day in advance, so I won't be there. You understand?" - Al Pacino as Mafia Don Michael Corleone renounces his brother Fredo (John Cazale) for his betrayal of the family business in the motion picture *The Godfather: Part II* (1974). *See also* "Kiss of Death"

"Freeze, hombre, or I'll be wearing your asshole for a garter" - Lainie Kazan as saloon owner Marguerite points a gun at some rowdy cowpokes in her Chile Verde, New Mexico saloon in the motion picture *Lust in the Dust* (1985).

"From a distance, you'd almost pass as a man...but up close, you're certainly a disappointment" - Marianna Hill as Callie Travers speaks to the mysterious Stranger (Clint Eastwood) in the western classic *High Plains Drifter* (1972) The Stranger retorts, "And your feet, ma'am, are almost as big as your mouth."

"From Hell's heart I stab at thee!" - Impassioned revenge spoken by Ricardo Montalban as Khan Noonien Singh, a 20th century genetically-engineered Superman featured in the science fiction motion picture *Star Trek II: The Wrath of Khan* (1982). After unsuccessfully trying to kill former foe Admiral James T. Kirk (William Shatner), Khan, in a final act of suicidal revenge, activates the Genesis Device, a terra-forming torpedo whose energy blast would destroy the disabled starship commanded by Kirk. As he awaits the final detonation and a view to his ultimate pay back, the bleeding and burned Khan addresses Kirk with these final words of hate. "To the last I will grapple with thee...No, No. You can't get away from me. From Hell's Heart I stab at thee. For hate sake I spit at thee!" This statement was taken from the classic novel *Moby Dick* written by Herman Melville about the whaling ship Captain Ahab who obsessed over hunting down and killing the great white whale Moby Dick. Earlier in the film, when Khan thought he had abandoned Kirk inside a barren planetoid, he gloats, "I've done far worse than kill you, Admiral. I've hurt you. And I wish to go on hurting you. I shall leave you as you left me, as you left her: marooned for all eternity in the center of a dead planet, buried alive. Buried alive!" Note: The character of Noonien Singh Khan was first introduced in 1967 on the TV science fiction series STAR TREK/NBC/1966-69 episode #24 "Space Seed" when he tries to take over the 23rd century starship USS Enterprise commanded by then Captain James T. Kirk. In the motion picture *Star Trek: First Contact* (1997) when Captain Jean Luc Picard (Patrick Stewart) obsesses over defeating his enemy (The Borg) at any cost, he draws inspiration from Melville's literary classic, saying, "And he piled upon the whale's white hump, the sum of all the rage and hate felt by his whole race. If his chest had been a canon, he would have shot his heart upon it."

"From now on, the rules are off!" - James Cagney as reporter Frank Ross framed for manslaughter and sent to prison in the motion picture *Each Dawn I Die* (1939). Frustrated at the treatment he received while incarcerated, Frank yells, "From now on, the rules are off! I'm gonna talk when I please and do what I like. I'm gonna be as mean and dirty and hard to handle as the worst con in the joint, and I'll skull-drag any rat or screw that gets in my way, do you hear? Now, let me out of here, do you hear-you muddle-headed copper!" Frank continued "When I first came here I believed in justice. I believed that someday, I'd be released. then I began to figure in weeks and months and now I hate the whole world and everybody in it for lettin' me in for this. Buried in a black, filthy hole because I was a good citizen. Because I worked my head off to expose crime. And now I'm a convict! I act like a convict, smell like a convict! I think and hate like a convict! But I'll get out! I'll get out, if I have to kill every screw in the joint." When Frank is asked a question by his parole board (who refused his request for a parole) he responds, "I'd have plenty to say if I could think of anything scummy enough to call you." Even Cagney's girlfriend Joyce Conover (Jane Bryon) got into the act when she calls double-crosser Hood Stacey (George Raft), "a blind, stupid, selfish, contemptible, tinhorn crook."

"Fuck beauty contests. Life is one fucking beauty contest after another. School, then college, then work, Fuck that. And fuck the Air Force Academy. If I want to fly, I'll find a way to fly. You do what you love, and fuck the rest" - Paul Dano as Dwayne, a fanatical follower of Nietzsche, who takes a cross-country trip with his family in a yellow and white VW bus to get his sister to the Little Miss Sunshine contest in far off California in the motion picture *Little Miss Sunshine* (2006)

"Fuck him. He was trash" - Robert Loggia as private eye Sam Ransom gives comfort to attorney Teddy Barnes (Glenn Close) after she is forced to kill her twisted client and former lover (Jeff Bridges) at the end of the motion picture *Jagged Edge* (1985).

"Fuck you, and fuck them, and fuck everybody" - Will Smith as ticked-off police detective Mike Lowery in the film *Bad Boys* (1995). Unburdening himself to fellow partner, Marcus Bennett (Martin Lawrence) Mike explodes, "You know, I'm so sick of this bullshit! Am I supposed to apologize for my family leaving me money? All I ever wanted to do was be a cop. I go out there and take it to the max everyday. I'm the first one there, and the last one to leave, so you know what, fuck you, and fuck them, and fuck everybody that's got a problem with Mike Lowery." Commiserating, Marcus tells his pal, "I love you, man." Mike replies, "Shut up, you slowass driver. You drive like a bitch!" Marcus responds, "Why I gotta be all that? Tell you what. I'll drive off this fuckin' cliff if you keep fuckin' with me. Then it'll be two bitches in the sea. My wife knows I'm no bitch. I'm a bad boy!"

"Fuck you and your self-righteous code of the goddamn streets. Did it pull you out of a 30 year stint in only 5 years? No, it didn't, I did. Did it get you acquitted 4 fucking times? No, it didn't, I did, so fuck you, fuck the streets, your whole goddamn world is this big, and there's only one rule, you save your own ass!" - Sean Penn as lawyer David Kleinfeld talks to his Puerto-Rican ex-con client Carlito Brigante (Al Pacino) in the motion picture *Carlito's Way* (1993).

Fuzz - Derogatory term used for police officers. The word "Fuzz" appears in the motion pictures *Fuzz* (1972) starring Burt Reynolds as a Boston cop on the trail of a bomber killing policemen and vicious pyromaniac punks; *Super Fuzz* (1981) starring Terence Hill as a rookie policeman who develops super powers after being accidentally exposed to radiation; and *Hot Fuzz* (2007) starring Simon Pegg as Sgt. Nicholas Angel, the finest cop in London with an arrest record four hundred percent higher than any other officer, who is transferred to the sleepy little town of Sanford to battle crime. *See also* "Pigs"

"Gee, I wish I had one of them Doomsday Machine things" - George C. Scott as General Buck Turgidson in the cult motion picture *Dr. Strangelove; or How I Learned to Stop Worrying and Love the Bomb* (1964). Explaining his strategic philosophy on nuclear retaliation, Buck informs President Merkin Muffley (Peter Sellers), "I'm not saying we wouldn't get our hair mussed, but I do say that no more than twenty million people killed, tops—depending on the breaks." At the film's conclusion bomber commander Major Kong (Slim Pickens) who earlier in the film said, "Well, boys I reckon this is it—nuclear combat toe to toe with the Russkies," is ordered to drop a nuclear bomb on the Soviet Union. Trying to dislodge a stuck A-bomb from its harness, Kong mounts the nuke like a horse. Unfortunately, the bomb drops. But Kong takes a positive outlook on his predicament and rides the nuke down to ground zero, whirling his hat and hootin' and hollerin' jubilantly despite his imminent destruction.

"Get a life!" - The pointed opinion of Sharon Stone in the motion picture thriller *Sliver* (1993). In the film, Stone plays Carly Norris, a woman seduced into a world of voyeurism by a landlord (William Baldwin) whose hidden surveillance system eavesdrops via video cameras on the lives of all his Manhattan high-rise apartment tenants. When Carly finally breaks away from the morbid obsession, she takes a gun and destroys all the TV monitors and video equipment. Her advice to her now ex-companion: "Get a life!" Note: On a classic episode of NBC's SATURDAY NIGHT LIVE, aired December 20, 1986, William Shatner as himself played a guest speaker at a Star Trek convention. After getting asked a bunch of nit-picky questions from an audience of nerds, Shatner pauses and says, "Before I answer any more questions, there is something I want to say:

> "Get a life, will ya, people! I mean for crying out loud, it was just a show. I mean look at you, look at the way you're dressed. You've turned an enjoyable little job I did as a lark for a few years into a colossal waste of time. I mean, how old are you people? What have you done with yourselves? You–you must be almost 30–have you ever kissed a girl? I didn't think so! Geez. There's a whole world out there! When I was your age, I didn't even watch television. I lived! So move out of your parent's basements, get your own apartments, and grow the hell up! It's just a TV show, dammit! It's just a show!"

Upset at Shatner, the convention organizer chastised him for disrupting the event. In a bit of quick thinking, Kirk returns to the podium and informs his devoted followers that the mean "Get a life!" statement and accompanying remarks were actually the words of the evil Captain Kirk (who appeared on episode #5 "The Enemy Within" when a transporter malfunction split Kirk into two people-one good and meek/one bold and bad). The gullible Trekkies bought the story—hook, line and sinker.

"Get away from her, you bitch!" - Frantic warning directed at an attacking alien creature in the classic sci-fi movie *Aliens* (1986). In the film, Sigourney Weaver starred as Ripley, a female survivor of an alien attack who was asked to return to the scene of the massacre. "You're going out there to destroy them, right? Not to study, not to bring back, but to wipe them out?" inquires Ripley. Unfortunately, her so-called benefactors lied. Their intention all along was to capture an alien and use its potent defenses as a stepping stone for developing newer, deadlier weapons technology on Earth. As Ripley arrives back on the planet where the aliens were last seen, a crew of Marines is dispatched to reconnoiter. One by one the landing party discovers that all personnel sent to the planet to set up a terra-forming station were killed–everyone but a little girl named Newt (Carrie Henn). While leaving the planet, the members of the landing party battle their way through a horde of attacking aliens. When Newt is captured, Ripley rescues her, but not before destroying a nursery of alien eggs. The destruction of the unborn aliens infuriates the queen alien who manages to attach itself to the body of Ripley's rescue craft as the planet below is destroyed by a nuclear blast. Thinking they are safe, Ripley Newt and Bishop (an android) return to the mother ship unaware of the deadly stowaway. As the queen alien again makes her move to kill Newt, Ripley climbs into a loading dock exo-skeleton and lures the alien away from Newt by shouting, "Get away from her, you bitch." In a final battle, Ripley depressurizes an air-lock, and flushes the alien into space.

"Get down off the cross, honey, someone needs the wood" - Irreverent recommendation given by Dr. Shirlee Kenyon (Dolly Parton) to one of her radio callers in the motion picture *Straight Talk* (1992). Shirley's down home country sayings like "I'm busier than a one-legged man in a butt kickin' contest" made her WNDY radio call-in advice program a hit with her many Chicago listeners. Note: In the western film *Gunfight at O.K. Corral* (1957) lady gambler Laura Denbow (Rhonda Fleming) objects to Wyatt Earp's (Burt Lancaster) moralizing and says, "Why don't you buy yourself a new halo? The one you're wearing's too tight."

"Get off my plane!" - The final words spoken to a terrorist (Gary Oldman) who high-jacked the presidential airplane on the political thriller *Air Force One* (1997). As terrorists take over Air Force One, Harrison Ford as the President refuses to leave the plane so he can save the First Lady, his daughter and the hostages left on board. When a majority of the hostages are parachuted off the plane, the lead terrorist forces the President to influence the release of rouge general held in a Russian prison or he will kill his wife and child. After affecting the general's release, the head terrorist uses the President's wife as a shield so that he can parachute from the tail end of the plane. The First lady knocks away his gun allowing the President to battle for control. Wrapping a cargo strap around the terrorist's neck, the President pulls the terrorist's parachute cord and says, "Get off my plane!" The dramatic yank from the billowing parachute snaps the terrorist neck as he is sucked off the plane.

"Get out before I kill you" - The furious proclamation of Mildred Pierce (Joan Crawford) whose troubled daughter Veda Pierce (Ann Blyth) has been bringing her mother untold grief in the motion picture *Mildred Pierce (*1945). When Veda makes a play for her mother's second husband (Zachary Scott), Mildred explodes, "Get out, Veda. Get your things out of this house right now before I throw them into the street and you with them. Get out before I kill you." Note: In the film *Victor/Victoria* (1982) Peter Arne as Labisse shouts, "If you ever come back, I will have you thrown out!" Robert Preston as Toddy answers, "Don't make it sound like such a threat. Being thrown out of a place like this is significantly better than being thrown out of a leper colony."

"Get out, cupcake, unless you want your neck separated from your face" - Harvey Keitel as Alonzo threatening Jack, a womanizer (Robert Downey, Jr.) in the motion picture *The Pick-Up Artist* (1987).

"Get out, go anywhere you want, go to a hotel, go live with her, and don't come back! Because, after 25 years of building a home and raising a family and all the senseless pain that we have inflicted on each other, I'm damned if I'm going to stand here and have you tell me you're in love with somebody else!" - Beatrice Straight as Louise Schumacher, the wife of an unfaithful TV executive (William Holden) throws him out of the house in the motion picture *Network* (1976). Louise continues her rebuke: "Because this isn't a convention weekend with your secretary, is it? Or—or some broad that you picked up after three belts of booze. This is your great winter romance, isn't it? Your last roar of passion before you settle into your emeritus years. Is that what's left for me? Is that my share? She gets the winter passion, and I get the dotage? What am I supposed to do? Am I supposed to sit at home knitting and purling while you slink back like some penitent drunk? I'm your wife, damn it! And, if you can't work up a winter passion for me, the least I require is respect and allegiance! I hurt! Don't you understand that? I hurt badly!"

"Get out of the way, honey, let the nigger pass" - The polite but cruel remark of a white woman who instructs her white child to step aside while Minnie McGhee (Lynn Whitfield) walks toward them in the made for TV movie *The Color of Courage* (1999). The film is based on the landmark Supreme Court case of *Sipes vs. McGhee* argued by Thurgood Marshall about a 1940s black family who move into an all-white neighborhood and then are told by the neighborhood association that they are not wanted there because "their" presence violates an exclusionary "restrictive covenant." Later, when Benjamin Sipes (Bruce Greenwood) denounces the racist claims of the association, one of the members call him a "Nigger lover." In retaliation, Benjamin punches the man in the face and says, "Get you sorry ass out of here" then declares, "I am not going to follow them, their plain wrong."

"Get this through your head you Jew motherfucker, you. You only exist out here because of me. That's the only reason. Without me, you, personally, every fuckin' wise guy skell around'll take a piece of your fuckin' Jew ass. Then where you gonna go? You're fuckin' warned. Don't ever go over my fuckin' head again. You motherfucker, you." - Joe Pesci as Nicky Santoro, a Las Vegas casino operator setting the record straight with colleague Ace Rothstein (Robert De Niro) in the motion picture *Casino* (1995).

"Get your big, fat extra-crispy-bucket-of-chicken, two-liter-Pepsi-Cola drinking ass out of bed." - Denzel Washington as Napoleon Stone, a black lawyer (now deceased) whose heart was transplanted into the body of a police officer in the motion picture *Heart Condition* (1990). Before he died, Napoleon was the nemesis of Jack Moony (Bob Hoskins), a white cop who disliked Stone and his clientele of drug dealers whom he represented in court. But now that Moony hosts Stone's transplanted heart, he must suffer the ghostly presence of his old nemesis who wants Moony to find out who murdered him.

"Get your stinking paws off me, you damn dirty ape!" - In the science fiction film *The Planet of the Apes* (1968), based on Pierre Boulle's novel, Charlton Heston plays Taylor, one of three astronauts who accidentally time warps into the future to find Earth ruled by apes, and the human race now slaves to these hairy masters. When captured, Heston cries, "Get your stinking paws off me, you damn dirty ape!" This vocal rebellion astounds all the apes since humans from the future were not supposed to be able to speak (The apes conveniently lobotomized their captives to keep them quiet and docile). According to the Lawgivers scrolls, the Apes were to "Beware the beast 'man' for he is the devil's pawn. Alone among God's primates, he kills for sport, for lust, for greed. Yea, he will murder his brother to possess his brother's land. Let him not breed in great numbers, for he will make a desert of his home and yours. Shun him; drive him back into his jungle lair, for he is the harbinger of death." At the film's finale, Taylor escapes his captors. Before he leaves, he offers to kiss Dr. Zira (Kim Hunter) a chimpanzee scientist who assisted in his escape. She agrees but admits, "You're so damn ugly." As Taylor travels the coastline, he sees the remains of the Statue of Liberty protruding from a rocky beach and laments, "Oh my God! I'm back. I'm home. All the time. You finally really did it. You maniacs! You've blown it up. God damn you! God damn you all to hell!"

"Ghettoes are the same all over the world. They stink." - Jim Kelly as Williams, a black marital artist from America comments on the Hong Kong harbor poor in the motion picture *Enter the Dragon* (1973). In the film, Williams is invited to an exclusive martial arts tournament on a remote island in the China South Seas. But when he discovers his host, Mr. Han (Kien Shih) is dealing illegal drugs -- drugs which kill many of his black brothers back in the states -- Williams is killed for not joining Mr. Han's organization. Williams is avenged by fellow martial artist (Bruce Lee) who kills Mr. Han in an epic hand-to-hand combat confrontation.

Girly-Man - Put-down spoken by weight training fanatics Hans and Frans who appeared in skits on NBC's SATURDAY NIGHT LIVE in the 1980-90s. Comedians Kevin Nealon and Dana Carvey played these macho fitness trainers with Austrian accents whose mission in life was to "Pump...You Up!" When Hans and Frans observed people who were flabby around the waist and generally out of shape, they referred to such underdeveloped specimens as a "Girly-Man." Their opinion of non-weightlifters included such phrases as "If you don't work out, someone should grab you by your jockstrap and give you the wedgie of your life"; "Maybe someone should take a belt to your buttocks until it is all black and blue and swollen" and "Your body looks like a little pretzel stick. Ja, your name should be Mr. Salty." When they opened up a new gym (The Pumpatorium) in Wayne, New Jersey, the new customers were described as "fat, lazy pigs who should be only dead! You hear me? Dead! Dead! Dead! Dead!" When Hans and Franz's cousin Arnold Schwarzenegger visits, he insults them, saying, "You pathetic losers. I hate the way you talk! Look at your buttocks—soft like marshmallow! You guys are lucky we don't have a campfire here, believe me." On Thanksgiving, Han and Franz declared the holiday was "an excuse to stuff your face like the fat pig loser, you are."

"Glad to meet you, kid. You're a real horse's ass" - Paul Newman as hustler Henry Gondorff when he first meets small time hood Johnny Hooker (Robert Redford) in the motion picture *The Sting* (1973). After Hooker and Luther Coleman (Robert Earl Jones) steal money from an illegal operation controlled by mob Boss Doyle Lonnegan (Robert Shaw), Doyle tells one of his hoods, "Take a good look at that face, Floyd. Because if he ever finds out I can be beat by one lousy grifter, I'll have to kill him and every other hood who wants to muscle in on my Chicago operation. You follow?" During a "sting" operation designed to bilk Doyle of a large sum of money, J. J. Singleton (Ray Walston) one of Gondorff's hired con artists complains, "I don't know what to do with this guy, Henry. He's an Irishman who doesn't drink, doesn't smoke, and doesn't even chase dames." As the con starts to work Johnny tells Henry, "He threatened to kill me." Henry replies glibly, "Hell, kid, they *don't* do that, you know you're not getting to them."

"Go ahead and stare. I'm not ashamed. Go ahead and laugh, get your money's worth. We're not going to hurt you" - Maureen O'Hara as Judy, a young burlesque dancer (with dreams of being a ballerina) gives the men in her audience a lecture they won't soon forget in the motion picture *Dance, Girl Dance* (1940). She continues her speech: "I know you want me to tear my clothes off so you can get you fifty cents worth. Fifty cents for the privilege of staring at a girl the way your wife won't let you. What do you think we think of you up here with your silly smirks your mother would be ashamed of? It's a thing of the moment for the dress suits to come and laugh at us, We'd laugh, too, only we're paid to let you sit there and roll your eyes and make screaming clever remarks. What's it all for? So you can go home and strut before your wives and sweethearts...play at being the stronger sex for a minute! I'm sure they see through you like we do!"

"Go ahead, make my day!" - Welcoming, but deadly put-down spoken by San Francisco police detective "Dirty" Harry Callahan as he dares a crook to shoot his hostage in the movie *Sudden Impact* (1983). Harry approaches the crooks and their hostage and informs them, "We're not just going to let you walk out of here." Confused, one crook barks, "Who's *we,* sucker?" Harry replies, [pulls out his gun] "Smith, and Wesson, and me." Then Harry coolly invites the crook to, "Go ahead, make my day." Note: President Ronald Reagan, a fan of the 'Dirty Harry' movies used the same phrase "Go ahead, make my day" when he threatened a veto and challenged Congress to put a tax increase on his desk.

"Go burn the books!" - Hideous mandate given by buffoonish dictator of Moronica, Moe Hailstone (Moe Howard of the Three Stooges) in the film, *You Nazty Spy!* (1940). When sidekick Curly Pebble (Curly Howard) asks, "Why burn the books? Moe insists, "There are too many bookmakers. The bookies are overrunning the country. These are my orders." Note: Years later, in the film *Indiana Jones and the Last Crusade* (1989)

Sean Connery as Professor Henry Jones tells a Nazi Colonel, "Goose-stepping morons like yourself should try reading books instead of burning them." *See also* "Moronica for Morons"

"Go forth and kill" - The zealot message of Niall Buggy as Zardoz in the science fiction movie *Zardoz* (1973). In the year 2293, two camps run the earth: immortal Eternals living in a protected environment; and wild marauding exterminators who roam the lands outside. The mysterious Zardoz, (aka Arthur Frayne), an immortal bored with his long life, provides the group of outsiders with weapons whom eventually destroy the Eternals inner sanctum. His gospel: "The gun is good...The penis is evil. The penis shoots seeds, and makes new life, and poisons the earth with a plague of men, as once it was. But the gun shoots death, and purifies the earth of the filth of brutals. Go forth and kill!"

"Go on jump!" - Morgan Freeman as high school principal Joe Clark uses reverse psychology on 14-year-old suicidal drug dealer Thomas Sams (Jermaine Hopkins) threatening to jump off the roof of his high school in the motion picture *Lean on Me* (1989). Continuing his mind game with the student, Clark says, "You smoke crack, don't you?...You know what that does to you? It kills you brain cells, son, it kills you brain cells. Now when you destroy your brain cells, you're doing the same thing as killing yourself, you're just doing it slower. Now I say if you want to kill yourself, don't fuck around with it, go ahead and do it expeditiously...Now go ahead and jump. Jump!" Note: In the film *Rebecca* (1940), jealous housekeeper Mrs. Danvers (Judith Anderson) tries to seduce the troubled new Mrs. de Winter (Joan Fontaine) to commit suicide on the rocky coastline below by saying, "You have nothing to stay for. You have nothing to live for, really, have you? Look down there—it's easy, isn't it?" In the film *Lethal Weapon* (1987) Mel Gibson as cop Martin Riggs invites a distraught man to jump off a building. "Do you really want to jump? Riggs taunts. "Do you want to? Well, then that's fine with me!" Riggs then jumps off the building and drags the man along into a waiting rescue net below. And, in the film *Kuffs* (1992) Christian Slater as cop George Kuffs tells a suicidal jumper, "Hey, asshole! Yes, you. Look, if you're gonna jump, jump. Otherwise, use the bridge like everyone else. You're screwin' up traffic down there."

"Go to Hell!" *See* "I'll see you in Hell" and "We'll tear your soul apart"

"God damn it, Gump! You're a God damn genius!" - Screaming drill sergeant (Afemo Omilami) in the motion picture *Forrest Gump.* (1994). When slow-witted Forrest Gump (Tom Hanks) is recruited into the army, he struggles with the rigors of military life. After the drill sergeant asks, "Gump! What's your sole purpose in this army? Gump replies, "To do whatever you tell me, drill sergeant!" Mocking Gump's response, the sergeant yells, "God damn it, Gump! You're a goddamn genius! This is the most outstanding answer I have ever heard. You must have a goddamn I.Q. of 160. You are goddamn gifted, Private Gump."

Golden Pit Awards, The - First bestowed in 1987 the Golden Pit Awards satirized TV programs, commercials and movies that "offend millions of ethnic Americans mostly through negative stereotyping" such as, depicting Blacks stealing bicycles, Jews arguing over prices, Italians involved in crime and Irish drunk in bars. The trophy awarded was a white Styrofoam bust with a peach pit dangling from a blue ribbon. Winners were selected from hundreds of entries by members of the 66 groups belonging to the National Ethnic Coalition of Organizations such as NAACP and the United Farm Workers.

Golden Turkey Award, The - Film award presented on segments of SNEAK PREVIEWS, a PBS movie review program featuring movie critics Jeffrey Lyons and Neil Gabler. Spotlighted on the program were cameo reviews by film critic Michael Medved who with the assistance of his film man, Moose introduced his choice for the worst movies of the week with a warning for the viewers to save their money. The worst movie of the week was given the dreaded "Golden Turkey Award." After Michael Medved replaced Neil Gabler in the fall of 1985, the "Golden Turkey" segments were dropped. Gene Siskel, film critic for the *Chicago Tribune* and Roger Ebert, film critic for the *Chicago Sun-Times* were the original co-hosts of the series when it began on TV station WTTW in 1978. They used a skunk named Aroma as a mascot for the worst film of the week. Siskel and Ebert later co-hosted the syndicated series AT THE MOVIES and SISKEL & EBERT.

Gong Show Awards, The - Zany update of TED MACK'S ORIGINAL AMATEUR HOUR/NBC/ABC/CBS/1948-60. The comedy audience participation program THE GONG SHOW/NBC/SYN/1976-80 featured contestants who performed outrageously bad acts (a woman who whistled through her nose; a man who blew a trumpet through his naval) for a panel of celebrity judges, any of whom could eliminate the act by "Giving them the Gong" (hitting a very large and noisy metallic disk). The winners of this silly talent show received a miniature Golden Gong trophy and a monetary award of $712.05 on the evening program and $516.32 on the daytime version. Chuck Barris, the series co-producer (with Chris Bearde), also hosted the program.

Gooch, The - On the sitcom DIFF'RENT STROKES/NBC/ABC/1978-86 Arnold Jackson (Gary Coleman), an eight-year old black boy was always picked on by a school bully, no matter what grammar school he attended. Arnold referred to this generic school bully as "The Gooch."

"Good luck Captain, you're about to go where everyone has gone before" - Claudia Christina as Commander Ivanova referring to a horny political liaison officer lusting after the body of Captain Sheridan (Bruce Boxleitner) on the syndicated sci-fi television series BABYLON 5/SYN/1994-98.

"Good morning, you fascists" - The beginning of an abusive Arizona roll call of motor cops shouted by Sgt. Ryker (Joe Samsil) in the film *Electra Glide in Blue* (1973). The entire tirade reads: "TEN-HUT! Good morning, you Fascists! You Pigs! You Bigots! You Pinkos! You Fags! You Bastards! Fuzz! This indoctrination of vocal harassment was compiled by our own Juvenile Division in preparation for the concert this weekend." *See also* "Fuzz" and "Pig"

"Gophers are gonna be delivering your mail if you keep that up" - Anna Maria Horsford as Slam Dunk, the prostitute speaks to Boardwalk, her San Francisco pimp (Larry Riley) in the motion picture *Crackers* (1984).

"Grandma was right. Once a shitheel, always a shitheel" - Dinah Manoff as Libby in the motion picture *I Ought to Be in Pictures (*1982). When Libby's friend Herbert (Walter Mathau) asks, "Your grandmother talks like that?" Libby replies, "The words are mine, the wisdom is hers!"

"Grant me revenge!" - Request of warrior Conan the Barbarian (Arnold Schwarzenegger) in the fantasy adventure *Conan the Barbarian*: (1982). After Conan rescues a princess under the spell of religious cult leader Thulsa Doom (James Earl Jones), he must face Doom's henchmen who come to kill him. Before the battle, Conan invokes his God: "Crom, I have never prayed to you before. I have no tongue for it. No one, not even you, will remember if we were good men or bad. Why we fought, and why we died. All that matters, is that today, two stood against many. Valor pleases you, so grant me this one request. Grant me revenge! And if you do not listen, the HELL with you!"

Great Wounder, The - Dennis Farina, who played Lt. Mike Torello on the police drama CRIME STORY/NBC/1986-88 was nicknamed "The Great Wounder" by his fellow police officers when he worked as a policeman in the days before he took up acting as a career. During his eighteen years on the Chicago police force, every time Farina "pulled out his gun to shoot someone, he'd shoot them in the butt or the thumb." (According to *TV Guid*e 2/6/88 interview)

"Greed is good" - The personal philosophy of ruthless Wall Street raider Gordon Gekko (Michael Douglas) in the motion picture *Wall Street* (1987). Addressing a crowd of stockholders, Gekko defends his corporate mission: "I am not a destroyer of companies. I am a liberator of them...The point is ladies and gentlemen, that greed, for the lack of a better word is good. Greed is right. Greed works. Greed clarifies, cuts through and captures the essence of the evolutionary spirit. Greed—in all of its forms—greed for life, for money, for love, for knowledge, has marked the upward surge of mankind, and greed—you mark my words—will not only save Teldar Paper, but that other malfunctioning corporation called the USA. Thank you, very much."

"Gabrewski, if you die, I'm going to shoot myself and come on after you!" -Richard Moll as Coach Horn who isn't quit sure that asthmatic school student Barry Gabrewski (Jonathan Brandis) can handle the exertion of push-ups in gym class in the motion picture *Sidekicks* (1992).

Gringo - Derogatory word used by frontier Mexican settlers in the Old West to describe North Americans moving West across the plains. The term has appeared in a variety of western movies and television programs over the years. The word is derived from the Spanish word "Griego" meaning "Stranger." A popular but supposedly erroneous interpretation of the word comes from the adulteration of a 19th century love song "Green Grow the Lilacs." When the Mexicans heard US Soldiers and settlers singing the tune, they would say "There go the Green Grows" which allegedly gave rise to the ethnic slur "Gringo."

"Guess where you get the first one?" - Question directed to secret agent James Bond (Sean Connery) in the spy adventure *Never Say Never Again* (1983). After sexy villain Fatima Blush (Barbara Carrera) knocks 007 off his motorcycle, she points a handgun and says, "Spread your legs...Guess where you get the first one?" Stalling for time, Bond plays on Fatima's ego by saying what a shame it would be that he wouldn't have the chance to tell the world what a wonderful lover she was. Fatima tosses a piece of paper to Bond and instructs him to write those sentiments down. Bond then reaches into the coat pocket and pulls out a pen (actually a weapon) which launches a miniature dart equipped with an explosive tip. When it hits Fatima, it fizzles but then violently explodes, leaving only a pair of high heels behind.

"A gust of wind to fan my hate..." - Lucille LaVerne as the evil Queen prepares a magic spell to turn herself into an ugly hag so she can deliver a poison apple to Snow white in the classic animated motion picture *Snow White and the Seven Dwarfs* (1937). The full spell reads, "Mummy dust to make me old. To shroud my clothes, the black of night. To disguise my voice, an old hag's cackle. To whiten my hair, a scream of fright. A gust of wind to fan my hate. A thunderbolt to mix it well. And now begin thy magic spell."

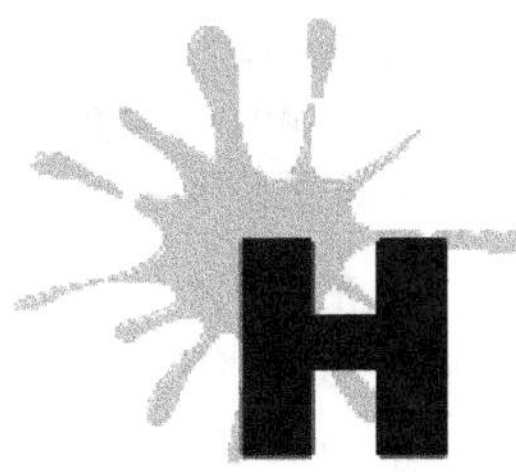

The Hag of Haute Couture - Self proclaimed title of RuPaul, a 6-foot, 7-inch drag queen who hosted VH-1's celebrity chitchat program THE RuPAUL SHOW/VH1/1996-1998. Other credits of this blond bombshell included the "Foxy Lady" album, spokes model for MAC cosmetics and a cameo role as Mrs. Cummings in the film *A Very Brady Sequel* (1996).

"Half the people on this ship are going to die!" - Kate Winslet as Rose Dewitt Bukater explains to her mother Ruth (Frances Fisher) that the freezing waters of the North Atlantic will kill half the passengers because there are not enough lifeboats in the motion picture *Titanic* (1997). Rose's mother, on the other hand, asks, "Will the lifeboats be seated according to class? I hope they aren't too crowded." Upon hearing that "half the people on this ship" will die, Rose's fiancé Caledon "Cal" Haledon (Billy Zahn), coldly quips, "Not the better half." He also says, "You know, it's a pity I didn't keep that drawing. It'll be worth a lot more by morning." To which Rose shouts, "You unimaginable bastard!"

Happy Meals on Legs - The terms refers to the citizens of Sunnydale, California on the cult horror adventure BUFFY THE VAMPIRE SLAYER/WB/1997-2003. The Vampire Spike describes ordinary human beings as "Happy Meals on Legs," fast food for the vampires who are attracted to "Hellmouth," a portal to an evil dimension that rests below the town of Sunnydale.

"Happy Trails, Hans" - In the film *Die Hard* (1988) Bruce Willis plays NYPD detective John McClane who fights off a group of terrorist during his Christmas Eve visit to a Los Angeles high-rise. At the conclusion of the film, McClane comes face-to-face with terrorist Han Gruber (Alan Rickman) who holds McClane's wife, Holly (Bonnie Bedelia) hostage. Feigning surrender, McClane drops his gun in an effort to draw fire from his spouse. As the grinning terrorist draws a bead on McClane, Harry quickly pulls off a handgun that he had taped to his back and shots the terrorist. As the bullet tears into Gruber's chest, John says, "Happy Trails, Hans!" (a reference to McClane's fondness for western star Roy Rogers). As Hans falls to his death from the high-rise building, a police observer below comments, "Gee, I hope that's not a hostage." *See also* "Yippie-Ki-Yay, Motherfucker!"

"Hasta la vista, Baby!" - Payback spoken by Arnold Schwarzenegger in the science fiction movie *Terminator 2: Judgment Day* (1991) when he played a cyborg from the future who returned to the past to protect John Connor (Edward Furlong), the son of Sarah Connor (Linda Hamilton) who would change the face of an apocalyptic future. Pointing a .45 automatic handgun into the face of a more advanced T-1000 cyborg,

Schwarzenegger says, "Hasta la vista, baby" and then pulls the trigger. The bullet shatters the cyborg's body (frozen from liquid nitrogen) into hundreds of little pieces. In the movie's climax, the relentless advanced terminator is finally destroyed when it falls into a boiling cauldron of white hot metal. Earlier in the film, John Connor taught the good Terminator how to act in a social situation saying "No, no, no, no. You gotta listen to the way people talk. You don't say '*affirmative,*' or some shit like that. You say '*no problemo.*' And if someone comes on to you with an attitude you say, '*eat me.*' And if you want to shine them on it's 'H*asta la vista, baby.*' The Terminator repeats the phrase. John continues, "Yeah! Or *'later dickwad.'* And if someone gets upset you say, '*chill out!*' Or you can do combinations." Again the Terminator repeats "Chill out, dickwad." Happy with the Terminator's progress, John shouts, "Great! See, you're getting it!" The Terminator replies, "No problemo." Note: In the film parody *Silence of the Hams* (1994) Antonio Motel (Ezio Greggio) turns things around by saying, "Hasta la baby, vista." *See also* "I'll be back!" and "You're terminated, fucker"

"Have you considered drowning?" - Not-so-well chosen words of Julia Sweeney as sexually ambiguous Pat in the motion picture *It's Pat—The Movie* (1994). Working as a radio talk show host on "Love Chat," Pat advises an irritating call-in show listener, "Well, have you considered drowning? They say it's like God giving you a big wet hug...forever. *STOP CALLING HERE!!!"*

"Have you ever heard the sound a chicken makes when they're wringing off its neck?" - Oliver Reed as Bill Sykes threatening master pick pocket Fagin (Ron Moody) in the musical motion picture *Oliver* (1968) adapted from Charles Dicken's novel *Oliver Twist.*

"Have you noticed that we are being replaced by young men with blank stupid faces...and a dedication to nothing more than efficiency? Keepers of machines, punchers of buttons, hardware men with highly complex toys, and except for language, not an iota of difference between the American model and the Soviet model" - Paul Scofield as Zharkov, a Russian KGB spy laments the changes in the espionage industry to his American CIA counterpart Cross (Burt Lancaster) in the motion picture *Scorpio* (1973).

"He behaved like a swine" - Joseph Cotten as Jedediah Leland in the classic motion picture *Citizen Kane* (1941). In the film, reporters hunt for the significance of the phrase "Rosebud" spoken on the deathbed of millionaire Charles Foster Kane (Orson Welles). Reporter Thompson (William Alland) interviews Kane's now aging friend Jedediah Leland, who offers this perspective on Kane: "I was his oldest friend, and as far as I was concerned he behaved like a swine. Not that Charlie was very brutal; he just did brutal things. Maybe I wasn't his friend, but if I wasn't, he never had one." On the topic of love, Leland summarized, "He (Charlie) just didn't have any to give."

"He called you a 'tin-plated, overbearing dictator with delusions of Godhood!'" - On the classic episode "Trouble with Tribbles" of STAR TREK/NBC/1966-69 Chief Engineer Montgomery Scott (James Doohan) takes shore leave on an orbiting space station. While having a drink in a lounge, he is taunted by a loud-mouthed Klingon. Scotty controls himself nicely as the Klingon calls their Captain Kirk a "tin plated, overbearing dictator with delusions of Godhood." But, when the Klingon denigrates Scotty's ship (The *USS Enterprise*) a fight ensues. Scotty later explains to Captain Kirk (William Shatner) that the Klingons had cast aspersions about the Captain. "And that's when you hit him?" inquires the Captain. "Ah, no, sir," Scotty replies, "We're big enough to take a few insults."

"He can't call me that and get away with it. I'll sock his face so far down into his oxfords, he'll be known as Puss & Boots" - Jim Jordon as Wisful Vista resident Fibber McGee threatens the municipal water commissioner Gildersleeve aka "The Great Gildersleeve" (Harold Peary) in the motion picture *Look Who's Laughing* (1941).

"He disagreed with something that ate him" - Biting pun found on a crumpled piece of paper stuffed into the mouth of newlywed CIA agent Felix Leiter (David Hedison) after he had been thrown to the sharks in the James Bond thriller *License to Kill* (1989). When fellow spy and Best Man, James Bond (Timothy Dalton) discovers Leiter's fate (he lost his left leg below the knee) 007 becomes a rouge agent, forsaking M and the British Secret Service to avenge his longtime friend and Felix's murdered bride, Della Churchill (Priscilla Barnes). Bond hunted down the perpetrator, a ruthless drug runner named Franz Sanchez (Robert Davi) and in a fiery conclusion ignites an engraved gold lighter (given to him by Leiter) and torches Sanchez's gasoline soaked body. *See also* "How 'bout a light?"

"He's got a client who shot his wife in the head six times. Six times, can you imagine it? I mean, even twice would be overdoing it, don't you think?" - Veronica Cartwright as Cathy Brenner, a lawyer's daughter talks about the excessive behavior of a murderer in the classic Alfred Hitchcock motion picture *The Birds* (1963).

"He's a cultural Robin Hood. He steals from the witty and gives to the dull" - Walter Matthau as Pete Seltzer talks about Jimmy Twitchell (René Auberjonais) in the motion picture *Pete 'N' Tillie* (1972). Note: In the film *Deathstalker II* (1987) Monique Gabrielle as Princess Evie asks, "Oh, so you rob from the rich, and give to the poor?" John Terlesky as Deathstalker replies, "No, I rob from the rich, and pretty much keep it for myself."

"He's a hopeless alcoholic" - Philip Terry as Wick Birnam who reaches the conclusion, that his brother Don (Ray Milland) is hopelessly addicted to alcohol in the motion picture *Lost Weekend* (1945). Concerned about Don, Wick talks with Don's girlfriend Helen St. James (Jane Wyman): "Who are we fooling? We've tried everything, haven't we? We've reasoned with him. We've baited him. We've watched him like a hawk. We've tried trusting him. How often have you cried? How often have I beaten him up? Scrape him out of a gutter and pump some kind of self-respect into him and back he falls, back in every time." Worried about Wick's diagnosis, Helen says, "He's a sick person. It's as though there was something wrong with his heart or his lungs. You wouldn't walk out on him if he had an attack. He needs our help." Frustrated, Wick continues, "He won't accept our help. Not Don, he hates us. He wants to be alone with that bottle of his. It's all he gives a hang about. Why kid ourselves? He's a hopeless alcoholic."

"He's a snob of the worst kind. The upside-down variety. Just an ill-bred astronomer who hopes to hitch his present cart to a star and drag it down with him into the mud" - Alec Guinness as Prince Albert refers to Dr. Nicholas Agi (Louis Jourdan) in the motion picture *The Swan* (1956).

"He's an arrogant, egotistical martinet with a God complex" - Charlton Heston as a WWII symphony conductor expresses his opinion of a Nazi General (Maximillian Schell) who captured a group of classical musicians—including Heston—and forces them to put on a private concert for his German officers in the motion picture *Counterpoint* (1968). To make matters worse, the General invites Heston's mistress (Kathryn Hays) to dinner. Boy! Those Nazi's have their nerve.

"He's an unlovely combination of a son of a bitch and a rat's knackers" - Peter O'Toole as the owner of a castle in Ireland gives his opinion about an American named Croesus who holds the mortgage note on the place in the motion picture *High Spirits* (1988).

"He's Hitler with a tail. He's 'The Omen' with whiskers. Even Nostradamus didn't see him coming!" - Nathan Lane as new house owner Ernie Smuntz sizes up a pint size mouse who wreaks havoc in the motion picture *Mouse Hunt* (1997).

"He's like an animal..." - Blanche Dubois (Vivien Leigh) talks to her sister Stella Kowalski (Kim Hunter) about her husband Stanley Kowalski in the classic film *A Streetcar Named Desire* (1951). Stella's full put-down reads: "He's like an animal. He has animal habits. There's even something subhuman about him. Thousands of years have passed him right by and there he is, Stanley Kowalski, survivor of the Stone Age, bearing the raw meat home after the killing, the jungle and you. You! You're waiting for him. Maybe he'll strike you or maybe he'll grunt and kiss you." Later, Stanley vents, "Don't you ever talk that way to me! 'Pig.' 'disgusting,' 'vulgar,' 'greasy,'—those kind of words have been on your tongue and your sister's tongue too much around here. What do you think you are? A pair of queens? Now, just remember what Huey Long said—that everyman is a king—and I'm king around here, and don't you forget" and "Listen, baby when we first met—you and me—you thought I was common. Well, how right you was! I was common as dirt. You showed me a snapshot of the place with the columns, and I pulled you down off them columns, and you loved it! We were having them colored lights going! And wasn't we happy together? Wasn't it okay till she showed up?"

"He's sort of a cross between a Ferris Wheel and a werewolf—but with a loveable streak, if you care to blast for it" - Fredric March as newspaper reporter Wally Cook describes the merits of his dyspeptic editor Oliver Stone (Walter Connelly) for Hazel Flagg (Carole Lombard) in the motion picture *Nothing Sacred* (1937).

"He's the dumbest human being I ever saw. Every time he opens his mouth he subtracts from the sum total of human knowledge" - Warren William as 1930s campaign manager Hal Sampson Blake spouting venom in the motion picture *The Dark Horse* (1932).

"He's the kind of guy that would drink a gallon of gasoline so he could piss in your campfire!" - In the film *Deadly Ground* (1994) Steven Seagal starred as Forrest Taft, a mysterious environmentalist interested in stopping oil refineries from scarring the Alaskan frontier. When he becomes an inconvenience, Michael Jennings (Michael Caine), a ruthless oil executive hires mercenaries to take him out. As a group of bad guy mercenaries prepare to hunt Taft, their leader Stone (R. Lee Ermey) informs his troops, "My guy in D.C. tells me that we are not dealing with a student here, we're dealing with the Professor. Any time the military has an operation that can't fail, they call this guy in to train the troops, OK? He's the kind of guy that would drink a gallon of gasoline so he could piss in your campfire! You could drop this guy off at the Arctic Circle wearing a pair of bikini underwear, without his toothbrush, and tomorrow afternoon he's going to show up at your poolside with a million dollar smile and fist full of pesos. This guy's a professional—you got me? If he reaches this rig, we're all gonna be nothing but a big goddamned hole right in the middle of Alaska. So let's go find him and kill him and get rid of the son of a bitch!" As Taft begins to get the upper hand, one of Jenning's associate asks, "Who the fuck is he?" Jennings replies, "You wanna know who he is? Try this: delve down into the deepest bowels of your soul. Try to imagine the ultimate fucking nightmare. And that won't come close to that son of a bitch, when he gets pissed. In the end, Taft triumphed over the bad guys, saying, "Well, let's see. That's natives 8; oil workers 0."

"He just dropped in for a quick bite" - Roger Moore as secret agent James Bond makes a pun after tossing "Jaws" (Richard Kiel), a huge assassin with sharp metal teeth, off a speeding train in the motion picture *The Spy Who Loved Me* (1977). Note: In the James Bond film *Live and Let Die* (1973), a drug dealer's henchman with a metal-clawed prosthetic arm attacks Bond in his train compartment and 007 tosses him off the train (minus his metal arm). When James' female companion asks what happened, Bond quips, "Just being disarming, darling."

"He says you're a boring, self-centered, insensitive old fool who wouldn't know love if it wore wings, diaper, and shot heart-shaped arrows at your butt" - Matthew Broderick as Alan tells his friend Ed (Brian Kerwin) what professional female impersonator Arnold Beckoff (Harvey Fierstein) thinks of him in the motion picture *Torch Song Trilogy* (1988).

"He was so crooked he could eat soup with a corkscrew" - Annette Benning as sexy con-artist Myra Lantry reminisces with friend, Roy Dillon (John Cusack) about a talented ex-partner named Cole (J. T. Walsh) in the motion picture *The Grifters* (1990).

"He wears a seat belt in the drive-in movie" - Walter Matthau as Oscar Madison belittles the overzealous safety consciousness of his fastidious roommate Felix Unger (Jack Lemmon) in the film *The Odd Couple* (1968).

"He won't kill himself. It'd please too many people" - Roscoe Karns as Owen O'Mailey comments on theatre manager Oscar Jaffe's (John Barrymore) tendency to want to commit suicide in the motion picture *Twentieth Century* (1934). When Oscar threatens, "I could cut my throat" actress Mildred Plotka (Carole Lombard) says, "If you did, grease paint would run out of it."

"He won't take 'Go to Hell!' for an answer..." - In the motion picture *Poltergeist* (1982), Craig T. Nelson plays Steve, a real estate agent who discovers his home was built over a graveyard. After supernatural creatures attack his family, Steve plans to move away from town but not before turning down a lucrative job promotion given in the midst of the poltergeist infestation. Steve's wife, Diane (JoBeth Williams) comments on her husband's boss, "He won't take 'Go to Hell!' for an answer. What are you gonna do?" Steve replies, "Give him directions." (Steve's boss knowingly built a housing development over an old cemetery).

"He'll have you skewed, tattooed and served with an apple in your mouth" - Max Phipps as Ben Pease addresses the Count (Brant Tilly) in the motion picture *Nate and Hayes* (1983).

"Hello. My name is Inigo Montoya. You killed my father. Prepare to die" - Mandy Patinkin as swashbuckler Inigo Montoya challenges Prince Humperdinck (Chris Sarandon) to a sword fight in the motion picture fantasy *The Princess Bride* (1987).

"Hello? What number are you calling? You've dialed the wrong number! Sorry? What good is that? How can you ever repay the last thirty seconds you have stolen from my life? I hate you, your husband, your children, and your relatives!" - Mink Stole as Peggy Gravel chastises an unlucky caller who accidentally phones her in the motion picture *Desperate Living* (1977). Note: On the 1992 episode "The Pitch" on the sitcom SEINFELD/NBC/1990-98, Jerry receives an unwanted phone call from a telemarketer who asks, "Hi, would you be interested in switching to TMI long distance service? Jerry replies, "Oh Gee I can't talk right now, why don't you give me your home number, and I'll call you later. The Telemarker hesitates and says, "Uhh...I'm sorry but we're not allowed to do that." Jerry continues, "Oh I guess you don't want people calling you at home." The Telemarkert says, "No" and Jerry concludes the conversation with "Well now you know how I feel" and hangs up the phone.

"Hello, this is RST Video, customer number 4352, I need to place an order. Okay, I need one each of the following tapes..." - In the film *Clerks* (1994) Randal Graves (Jeff Anderson) is on the phone placing video tape orders when a woman and her child enter the store and request help in finding the children's video *Happy Scrappy Hero Pup*. Randal tells them, "Okay, hang on, I'm on the phone with the distribution house now, lemme make sure we got it. What was it called again?" While the women stands there with her child, Randal orders the following tapes: *Whispers in the Wind; To Each His Own; Put It Where It Doesn't Belong; My Pipes Need Cleaning; All Tit-Fucking Volume 8; I Need Your Cock; Ass-Worshipping Rim-Jobbers; My Cunt Needs Shafts; Cum Clean; Cum-Gargling Naked Sluts; Cum Buns III; Cumming in Socks; Cum On Eileen; Huge Black Cocks and Pearly White Cum; Men Alone II: the KY Connection; Pink Pussy Lips;* and, uh, oh yeah, *All Holes Filled with Hard Cock.* " Finishing his list, Randal looks up from the phone and asks the woman with the child "Uh-huh...yeah...Oh, wait, and, what was that called again?"

"Her mouth shall make an interesting urinal!" - Seamus O'Brien as sadomasochistic theater-of-the-macabre director Master Sardu who tortures and kills women on stage (for real) with the help of his sicko sidekick Ralphus (Luis De Jesus) in the motion picture *Blood Sucking Freaks* (1978).

"Her screams were muffled by the huge candyball. She tried but there was nothing...only sugary sweet death" - Rose McGowan as Courtney Alice Shayne, a Reagan High School student shoved a jawbreaker into the prom queen's mouth to keep her from screaming during a harmless birthday prank (which kills her) in the motion picture *Jawbreaker* (1999). When Courtney says, "We just killed our best friend! Do you realize what this means?" her co-conspirator Marcie Fox (Julie Benz) replies, "That you're a shoo-in for prom queen?"

Herbert - Derogatory term given to starship Captain James T. Kirk (William Shatner) by Dr. Severin (Skip Homeier) and his Hippie-like renegade followers (who renounced modern technology) after Kirk interrupts their pilgrimage to a mythical planet known as Eden on episode #75 "Way To Eden" on the science fiction series STAR TREK/NBC/1966-69. Herbert was a minor government official known for his rigid patterns of thought.

"Here's a finger for you, and one for you..." - On the October 18, 1964 installment of THE ED SULLIVAN SHOW, as comedian Jackie Mason concludes his comedy routine, he notices some off-stage finger gestures from Ed Sullivan indicating that his time is winding down. According to Mason, he jokingly took the moment to comment on the signs by saying, "and here's a finger for you, and one for you" Ed Sullivan thought that the glib finger reference was actually a case of Jackie Mason giving him the "finger" on-the-air. Outraged, Ed Sullivan barred Jackie Mason from any further appearances on his program. The controversy over the "finger" damaged Mason's career. He retaliated with a libel suit in the New York Supreme Court and won. They had viewed his performance and found "nothing offensive." However, the influence that Sullivan possessed relegated Jackie Mason to "show-business-limbo" forcing him to work in outlying Catskill mountain resorts and related second-hand entertainment establishments. Years later, Jackie Mason resurfaced on the successful Broadway Tony Award winning one-man show and in the short lived sitcom CHICKEN SOUP/ABC/1989.

"Herman! This is the last time I'm going to talk to you, and I'm going to tell you you're the worst fraud I've known in my life! If you hear that I'm dead, don't come to my funeral!" - Lena Olin as Masha, a married woman who tries to educate her former lover Herman (Ron Silver) that she doesn't want to see him anymore in the motion picture *Enemies: A Love Story* (1996).

"Herrrreee's Johnny!" - Deadly greeting spoken by Jack Nicholson in Stanley Kubrick's horror classic *The Shining* (1980) based on the novel by Stephen King. In the film, Jack Nicholson plays a writer who takes a job as a handyman at the Overlook mountain resort to maintain the premises until spring arrives. As winter drags on, he slowly goes insane and stalks his wife (Shelley Duvall) with a fireman's ax. In the now famous scene, Jack Nicholson looks for his wife and says, "Come out, Come out wherever you are." When he hears her in the bathroom, he chants, "I'll huff and I'll puff and I'll blow you house in" and then chops a hole through the bathroom door. Twisting his head through the opening, Jack maniacally announces, "Herrrreee's Johnny" (a parody of the late night greeting of TV talk show announcer Ed McMahon from THE TONIGHT SHOW STARRING JOHNNY CARSON/NBC/1962-92.

"Hey, back off! Or I'll rip out your eyes and piss on your brain" - Paul Gleason as security agent Clarence Beeks in the motion picture *Trading Places* (1983). Beeks works for the Duke Brothers, two callous businessmen who hire him to obtain insider trading information that will benefit their personal fortunes. In the end, Beeks plan is thwarted and he ends up dressed in a female gorilla costume and placed in a cage with a very lonely (and real) male gorilla.

"Hey, beautify the neighborhood...stay indoors" - Rodney Dangerfield as Chester Lee, the coach of a girl's soccer team in the motion picture *Ladybugs (*1992). Note: In the film *Good Morning, Vietnam* (1987) Robin Williams as army disk jockey Adrian Cronauer broadcast this humorous news report: "President Johnson today signed a highway beautification bill. Basically, the bill said that his daughters could not drive in a convertible on public highways."

"Hey, I'm not square, you're the one square" - In the dark film *Taxi Driver (1976)* on-the-edge Vietnam war veteran turned New York City cabbie, Travis Bickle (Robert De Niro) makes his point of view clear to a street thug, saying, "Hey, I'm not square, you're the one square. You're full of shit, man. What are you talking about? You walk out with those fuckin' creeps and low-lifes and degenerates out on the streets and you sell your little pussies for nothing, man? For some low-life pimp who stands in the hall? And I'm square? You're the one square, man. I don't go screwing fuck with bunch of killers and junkies like you do. You call that hip? What world are you from?" *See also* "All the animals come out at night" and "You talkin' to me?"

"Hey, we don't serve their kind here!" - Classic put-down spoken by alien bartender as Jedi Master Obi Wan Kenobi (Sir Alec Guinness) and farm boy Luke Skywalker (Mark Hamill) enter a hostile bar on the planet Tatooine in the science fiction film *Star Wars* (1982). "Their Kind" was a reference to the two androids R2-D2 (Kenny Baker) and C3-PO (Anthony Daniels). Note: This phrase has also been used over the years in both TV and movies (especially westerns) to set apart and discriminate against a variety of minorities especially Native American Indians, Chinese or African-Americans. In the movie *The War Wagon* (1967) a frontier bartender says, "We don't serve Indians" to an Indian named Levi (Howard Keel). Levi grabs a bottle of whiskey off the bar, offers John Wayne a drink and asks, "You too good to drink with Indian?" When Wayne responds, "That's right!" he gets punched in the face for his troubles. Levi was actually Wayne's sidekick who forces a fight to create a diversion that gives them both a chance to get out of town. At the end of the film *Heaven Can Wait* (1943) the Devil (Laird Cregar) tells Don Ameche, "I hope you will not consider me inhospitable if I say 'sorry Mr. Van Cleve' we don't cater to your class of people. Please make your reservations somewhere else."

"Hey, you bald-headed prick! Don't you ever get caught on the take. Because if you wind up in any joint I'm in, you'll leave feet first" - Sean Connery as an aging mobster named Jesse makes his point perfectly clear to a law enforcement officer in the motion picture *Family Business* (1989).

"Hey, you bastards! I'm still here" - The parting words of Steve McQueen as Papillon, a brutalized Devil's Island prisoner who floats away to freedom on a makeshift raft at the end of the motion picture *Papillion (*1973).

"Hold it El Guapo! Or I'll fill you so full of lead you'll be using your dick for a pencil!" - Steve Martin as unemployed silent film star Lucky Day threatens a Mexican bandit (Alfonso Arau) in the motion picture *The Three Amigos!* (1986). Lucky later says, "I suppose you could say that everyone has an El Guapo. For some, shyness may be an El Guapo. For others, lack of education may be an El Guapo. But for us, El Guapo is a large ugly man who wants to kill us!"

"Hold it! The next man who makes a move, the nigger gets it" - Mean-spirited but really silly line from the classic comedy western *Blazing Saddles* (1974). To ensure that his claim on a frontier town, crooked politician Hedley LaMarr (Harvey Korman) hires black Sheriff Bart to become law enforcement in Rock Ridge. Unfortunately, the town folks were not expecting a Negro and a rowdy group of townsfolk become surly. Jumping to the bandstand, Sheriff Bart pulls out his gun, points it at himself and threatens, "Hold it. The next man who makes a move, the nigger gets it." Note: As Bart pulls out his acceptance speech from his trousers, he utters the hilariously memorable line "Excuse me, while I whip this out" (a remark alluding to the alleged size of a Black man's penis that sent shivers through the crowd of onlookers). *See also* "Up yours nigger!"

"Home. I have no home. Hunted, despised, living like an animal, the jungle is my home. For 20 years I have lived in this jungle hell" - Bela Lugosi as Dr. Eric Vornoff speaks to Professor Strowski (George Becwar) who was sent to bring Vornoff back to his home land in the motion picture *Bride of the Monster* (1956). Recapping his past, Vornoff informs Storwski: "My dear professor Strowsky, twenty years ago, I was banned from my home land, parted from my wife and son, never to see them again. Why? Because I suggested to use the atom elements, for producing super beings, beings of unthinkable strength and size. I was classed as a madman, a charlatan, outlawed in a world of science which previously honored me as a genius. Now here in this forsaken jungle Hell I have proven that I am alright. No, Professor Strowski, it is no laughing matter." Vornoff concludes "But I will show the world that I can be its master! I will perfect my own race of people. A race of atomic supermen which will CONQUER THE WORLD!!!"

"Homey don't play that!" [SMASH!] - The angry put-down of Homey the Clown (Damon Wayons), a frustrated black ex-convict who performed on the streets to make money on comic skits during IN LIVING COLOR/FOX/1990-94. Homey (his real name is Herman Simpson) sports a clown's grease-painted face, red hair, balding head, and a baggy yellow and orange clown suit with large pompom buttons and over-sized shoes. Working the streets and an occasional party, Homey asks people if they want to see a trick and then demands, "Give me a dollar." This establishment-hating individual has a short temper and often hits people over the head with a stuffed sock. He accompanies his head bashing with the catchphrase "Homey don't play that!" While visiting his parole officer, Homey claims that his file is just a "long list of lies perpetrated by the Man to keep a brother down." During a children's party a child asks, "Why did you become a clown?" Homey answers, "I guess it's because I got so much love to give...and its part of my prison work release program. I got about five more years of this clown crap." He ended the party by singing the Homey the Clown song: "Homey the clown, Don't mess around / Even though the Man, Try to keep him down / One day Homey will break all the chains / Then he'll fly away, but until that day / Homey don't play!"

Honky - Derogatory term used by blacks and other minority groups when referring to a white person. In the motion picture *The Enforcer* (1976) when Inspector 'Dirty' Harry Callahan (Clint Eastwood) asks a black militant leader named Mustapha (Albert Popwell) what he was doing, the man answered, "Waiting for all you white honkys to blow each other up so we can move right in." Note: In the film *Hollywood Shuffle* (1987) a black actor in a "Dirty Larry" spoof mouthed the now classic words, "What you say, honky sucker pig head jive turkey fool?"

"Hope they weren't triplets!" - Sincere wish of an avenging drug agent in *Marked for Death (*1990). In the film, Steven Seagal starred as former DEA agent Hatcher who tries to escape the filth and corruption of the drug trade by returning to his Midwest roots and family. Unfortunately, he discovers that Jamaican drug gangs are infiltrating the quiet and peace of his childhood hometown. During a visit to local nightspot with an old buddy, Hatcher intervenes in a shootout between rival drug gangs and incurs the wrath of one of the Jamaican drug pushers. A few days later, Hatcher's family home is attacked and his sister molested. Taking this personal, he literally cuts off the head of Screwface, a dreadlocked Jamaican mobster. As he dangles the head in front of Screwface's posse (gang), and tells them to leave town, another Screwface (a twin brother) appears and stabs one of Hatcher's friends in the back. Gunfire immediately erupts, and Hatcher chases the double through their warehouse hideout. After a sword fight and fist-pounding struggle, Hatcher picks his opponent up, breaks his back across his knee and throws the man down an elevator shaft. Peering onto the impaled doppelganger, Hatcher sighs, "Hope they weren't triplets."

"Horses are...dumb as fence posts" - Gene Hackman as Captain Frank Ramsey tells a short anecdote to crewman of the nuclear submarine "Alabama" in motion picture *Crimson Tide* (1995). His story goes: "Horses are fascinating animals. Dumb as fence posts, but very intuitive. In that way they're not too different from high school girls: they may not have a brain in their head but they do know all the boys want to fuck 'em." When Ramsey and second-in command Lt. Cmd. Hunter (Denzel Washington) have a disagreement on protocol, Ramsey steps up and says, "Mr. Hunter, I've made a decision. I'm captain of this ship, NOW SHUT THE FUCK UP!" He also added, "All I ask is that you keep up with me. If you can't, then that strange sensation you'll be feeling in the seat of your pants will be my boot in your ass!"

Hot Lips - The sizzling but sarcastic nickname of Major Margaret Houlihan (Loretta Swit), the humorless, career Army nurse on the military comedy M*A*S*H/CBS/1972-83. Margaret earned her nickname because of her passionate, extracurricular activities with married Army Doctor Major Frank Burns (Larry Linville) stationed at the 4077th Mobile Army Surgical Hospital during the Korean War. Note: The nickname originated in the movie *M*A*S*H* (1970) when actress Sally Kellerman as Margaret Houlihan screams, "Oh Frank, my lips are hot...kiss my hot lips." Unfortunately, for both Margaret and Frank (Robert Duvall) their steamy interlude was being broadcast over the camp's loudspeaker via a microphone planted under Margaret's army cot. Henceforth, to her regret, she was known as "Hot Lips." In the movie version when fellow soldiers taunt Margaret by tearing down the shower tent while she is bathing, she runs to her commanding officer wrapped in a towel and shouts, "This isn't a hospital! It's an insane asylum."

"How 'bout a light?" - In the motion picture *The Running Man* (1987) Arnold Schwarzenegger plays Ben Richards, a man framed for murder who is forced to participate in "The Running Man," a futuristic game show that hunts down and kills its contestants. When confronted by a stalker's flamethrower, Schwarzenegger disconnects its fuel line, drenches the stalker's body with fuel, ignites a flare, and asks the burning question, "How 'bout a light?" before tossing it at his opponent [Boom!]. Note: In the action adventure film *Cobra* (1986) Sylvester Stallone as police detective Marian Cobretti says, "You have the right to remain silent" and then tosses a lit match onto the gasoline soaked body of a gunman who tried to kill him. *See also* "He disagreed with something that ate him"

"How about a little fire, Scarecrow?" - Margaret Hamilton as the Wicked Witch of the West speaks perhaps one of the meanest lines in cinema history in the motion picture *The Wizard of Oz* (1939). At the climax of the film, the Wicked Witch of the West corners Dorothy Gale (Judy Garland), and her companions, Scarecrow (Ray Bolger), Tin Man (Jack Haley) and the Cowardly Lion (Bert Lahr) atop her castle. "Well," cackles the witch, "ring around the rosey, pocket of full of spears. Thought you'd be pretty foxy. Well, the last to go will see the first three go before her...and your mangy little dog, too." The witch ignites the straws in her broom, and announces, "How about a little fire, Scarecrow?" When the witch sets the Scarecrow's arm on fire, Dorothy throws a bucket of water to quench the flames but most of the fluid misses and hits the witch. The water 'liquidates' the evil witch into nothingness. As she melts away into the ground, the witch laments, "You cursed brat, look what you done. I'm melting...melting. Oh what a world! What a world! Who could have thought a good little girl like you could destroy my beautiful wickedness. Oh! No! No!...I'm going...Oh!...Oh!"

"How can any race be so stupid?" - The recorded voice of an alien referring to the people of Earth in the low budget cult sci-fi film *Plan 9 from Outer Space* (1959). An alien named Dudley Manlove (Eros) added, "All of you on Earth are idiots!" (Psst! Plan 9 mission: Conquer Earth via resurrecting corpses).

"How could something so small, create so much of something so disgusting?" - Steve Guttenberg as Michael Kellem changes a baby's diaper in the motion picture *Three Men and a Baby* (1987).

"How dare you call Mr. Brooks a thief! Apologize at once. Tell him you're sorry...Mr. Brooks, I'm sorry you're a crook" - Alan Mowbray to Lou Costello in *Abbott and Costello Meet the Killer, Boris Karloff* (1949).

"How do you like children?...Barbecued!" - Goldie Hawn as Toni Simmons gets a W. C. Fields like answer from her acquaintance Harvey Greenfield (Jack Weston) in the motion picture *Cactus Flower (*1969).

"How do you like your stake, bitch?" - Callous inquiry delivered by a vampire slayer (Billy Baldwin) as he impales his prey in John Carpenter's horror flick *Vampires* (1998). Assigned to clear out a nest of the 'undead' in a ramshackle home in the Southwest, slayer Jack Crow (James Woods) and his crew of killers enter their lair and drag them, one by one, kicking and screaming into the daylight and to their doom. "Open up wide, baby," invites Crow as he lets loose an arrow into the chest of a snarling bloodsucker. Perusing the corpse of a slain vampire, Crow quips, "He's not only ugly; he smells bad." As the film concludes, Jack battles the Master vampire, Jan Valik (a product of a botched exorcism performed by the Catholic Church in the 14th century). Piercing Valik's heart with the shaft of a black relic cross and then collapsing the ceiling to introduce sunlight into the darken room, Jack Crow kills the Master (Thomas Ian Griffith) and puts an end to his reign of terror. The catchphrase "Die! Die! You Fucker, Die!" is sprinkled liberally throughout the movie script. Note: In the film, Jack Crow described vampires to a priest as follows: "Well first of all, they're not romantic. It's not like they're a bunch of fags fucking around seducing everyone in rented formal wear. Forget everything you seen in the movies: crosses don't work; they don't turn into bats, and garlic? You stand there with garlic around you neck, they're gonna take a walk up your estrada chocolata while sucking the blood outta ya. If you wanna kill a vampire, you drive a stake right through his heart; sunlight turns 'em into crispy critters."

"How's it going, Dick Tracy?" - Jack Webb as police detective Joe Friday informs a potential recruit what it's like being a cop on the police drama DRAGNET/NCB/1967-70. His full commentary: "It's awkward having a policeman around the house. Friend drops in - a man with a badge answers the door. The temperature drops 20 degrees. You throw a party and that badge gets in the ways. All of the sudden there isn't a straignt man in the crowd. Everybody's a comedian. 'Don't drink too much'. Some body says 'or the man with the badge will run you in.' Or 'How's it going, Dick Tracy? How many jaywalkers did you pinch today.' And then there always the one who wants to know how many apples you stole. All at once, you lost your first name. You're a cop, a flatfoot, a bull, a dick, John Law, you're the fuzz, the heat, you're poison, you're trouble, you're bad news. They call you everything...but never a policeman."

"How would I die when I'm 35?" - Vincent Gallo as Paul Leger offers his slant on how to die in the motion picture *Arizona Dreams* (1993). Paul continues his train of thought: "I'll tell you how I'd die. I'd take off all my clothes and I'd get into a bathtub filled with ice-cold vodka. I'd have a TV in the room with me and I'd be watching 'North by Northwest.' And just when the scene comes with the airplane, I'd pull the TV in the bathtub and I'd shock myself! I hate that film."

"Human beings are a disease, a cancer of this planet, you are a plague, and we are the cure" - Hugo Weaving as Agent Smith in the motion picture *The Matrix* (1999). In the future, artificial intelligence has produced a race of robots that have relegated human beings as an electrical resource. People are grown and implanted with a soothing dream world that makes its host believe they are living a normal life while the robots feed off of their body energy. Those people who somehow find their way out of the computer "Matrix" are hunted down by special Cyber agents. One such Cyber cop, Agent Smith, explains his take on humanity: "I'd like to share a revelation that I've had, during my time here. It came to me when I tried to classify your species. I realized that you're not actually mammals. Every mammal on this planet instinctively develops a natural equilibrium with the surrounding environment, but you humans do not. You move to an area, and you multiply, and multiply, until every natural resource is consumed. The only way you can survive is to spread to another area. There is another organism on this planet that follows the same pattern. A virus. Human beings are a disease, a cancer of this planet, you are a plague, and we are the cure." *See also* "You're the disease and I'm the cure"

"Humbug!" - The grumpy retort of Ebenezer Scrooge in the classic tale *A Christmas Carol* written by Charles Dickens. One of the original meanies, Scrooge says, "Humbug!...If I could work my will, every idiot that goes about with Merry Christmas on his lips should be boiled with his own pudding and buried with a stake of holly through his heart!" When asked for a charitable donation to help the poor, Scrooge responds, "Are there no prisons...work houses?" After hearing that some would rather die than go to these places, Scrooge rebuts, "If they'd rather die, they'd better do it and decrease the surplus population!" These cheery remarks has been uttered in a variety of movie and TV adaptations of *A Christmas Carol* by such performers as Sir Seymour Hicks (1935), Reginald Owens (1938), Alastair Sim (1951), Fredric March (1954), Basil Rathbone (1956), Albert Finney (1970), Henry Winkler (1979), George C. Scott (1984), Bill Murray (1988), Cicely Tyson as Ebonita (1997) and Patrick Stewart (1999). Note: In the film *The Hunchback of Notre Dame* (1939) Count Frollo, a corrupt city official (Cedric Hardwicke) mouthed the scrooge-like opinion "It's not more prison we need; it's more executions."

"Hungry men don't ask—they take" - Kerwin Matthews as Captain Sinbad the sailor observes his crew killing a huge chicken in the fantasy *The 7th Voyage of Sinbad* (1958).

"Husbands should be like Kleenex: soft, strong and disposable" - Madeline Kahn as Mrs. White expresses her feminist views in the motion picture *Clue* (1986).

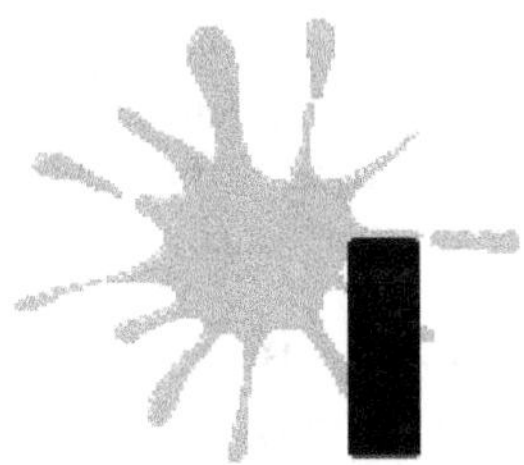

"I aim to kill you in a minute, Ned, or see you hang in Fort Smith at Judge Parker's convenience. Which will it be?" - John Wayne as Marshal Reuben J. "Rooster" Cogburn to outlaw Ned Pepper (Robert Duvall) in the western *True Grit* (1969). Ned answers, "That's bold talk for a one-eyed fat man. Rooster responds, "Fill your hands, you son of a bitch!" and then charges the outlaws with rifle and hand gun blazing. In the last line of film, Rooster tells departing Mattie Ross (Kim Darby) "Well, come see a fat old man sometime!" as he rides away on his horse.

"I'm a ba-a-a-d boy!" - Self-deprecating catchphrase of Lou Costello when he appeared as a trouble-prone, unemployed actor on the sitcom THE ABBOTT AND COSTELLO SHOW/SYN/1951-53.

"I'm an angel. I kill newborns while their mamas watch. I turn cities into salt. And occasionally, when I feel like it, I tear little girls apart. And from now till kingdom come...the only thing you can count on...in your existence...is never understanding why" - Christopher Walken as the heavenly Angel Gabriel in the motion picture *The Prophecy (*1995).

"I'm as mad as hell, and I'm not going to take this anymore!" - Frustrated at the way his network and the world is treating him, aging UBS broadcaster Howard Beale (Peter Finch) from the film *Network* (1976) tells his viewers, "I want you to go to the window, open it, stick your head out and yell, "I'm as mad as hell, and I'm not going to take this anymore!" His passionate message rang a bell with thousands of viewers who screamed their frustrations into the night. Howard's anger was motivated by the fact that he was just fired by the Network. In an attempt to get better rating for his final show, he informs his viewers, "I would like at this moment to announce that I will be retiring from this program in two weeks time because of poor ratings. Since this show is the only thing I had going for me in my life, I've decided to kill myself. I'm going to blow my brains out right on this program a week from today. So tune in next Tuesday. That should give the public relations people a week to promote the show. You ought to get a hell of a rating out of that. Fifty share, easy." To secure the network ratings, a sniper shoots Howard on his final broadcast. The film closes with the narration, "This was the story of Howard Beale, the first known instance of a man who was killed because of lousy ratings."

"I'm calling you a killer. A natural born killer. You always have been, and you always will be. Moving to El Paso. Working in a used record store. Goin' to the movies with Tommy. Clipping coupons. That's you, trying to disguise yourself as a worker bee. That's you tryin' to blend in with the hive. But you're not a worker bee. You're a renegade killer bee. And no matter how much beer you drank or

barbecue you ate or how fat your ass got, nothing in the world would ever change that" - David Carradine as assassin Bill attempts to enlighten Beatrix Kiddo (Uma Thurman), a former assassin - code named "Black Mamba" in the motion picture *Kill Bill Vol. 1 & 2* (2003/2004). A few years earlier, Bill showed up at the church where Beatrix (aka "The Bride") was to be married, and murdered the entire wedding party. After delivering a vicious beating to The Bride, Bill says, "Do you find me sadistic? You know, I bet I could fry an egg on your head right now, if I wanted to. You know, Kiddo, I'd like to believe that you're aware enough even now to know that there's nothing sadistic in my actions. Well, maybe towards those other...jokers, but not you. No Kiddo, at this moment, this is me at my most [cocks pistol] masochistic." Bill shoots The Bride in the head. The Bride's last words: "Bill, it's your baby." When the authorities arrive, they discover that The Bride is still alive. The hospital induces pregnancy and Bill takes possession of the new born girl. Meanwhile, Beatrix lay in the hospital for four years. When she awakes from her coma, Beatrix sets out on a trail of vengeance; first to find her child, then to kill all of her former colleagues who were involved in her wedding massacre, but most of all, Beatrix was determined above all to "Kill Bill." At the conclusion of *Kill Bill Vol 2*, Beatrix kills Bill with a secret martial arts technique called the five-point-palm-exploding-heart technique taught to her by Master Pai Mei. Bill had described the technique years earlier, "Quite simply, the deadliest blow in all of martial arts. He hits you with his fingertips at five different pressure points on your body. And then he lets you walk away. But after you've taken five steps, your heart explodes inside your body, and you fall to the floor, dead."

"I'm chaos, and he's mayhem. We're a double act" - Smart-alecky comeback of Mel Gibson as over-the edge police detective Martin Riggs when a fellow police detective refers to Riggs and his partner Roger Murtaugh (Danny Glover) as "mayhem and chaos" in the action adventure *Lethal Weapon 3* (1992).

"I'm coming looking for you!" - John Candy as Buck Russell in *Uncle Buck* (1989). While babysitting his sister-in-laws three children (as she visits her sick father), Uncle Buck is called upon to visit his young niece's grade school. When her teacher accuses the girl of being a dreamer and a silly heart, Uncle Buck rises to her defense: "I don't think I want to know a six-year-old who isn't a dreamer, or a silly heart. And I sure don't want to know one who takes their student career seriously. I don't have a college degree. I don't even have a job. But I know a good kid when I see one. Because they're ALL good kids, until dried-out, brain-dead skags like you drag them down and convince them they're no good. You so much as scowl at my niece, or any other kid in this school, and I hear about it, and I'm coming looking for you! Take this quarter, go downtown, and have a rat gnaw that thing [her mole] off your face! Good day to you, madam."

"I'm going to cut you into twelve pieces and feed you to this jury" - Spencer Tracy as attorney Adam Bonner striking fear into a suspect in the motion picture *Adam's Rib* (1949).

"I'm going to kick you bowlegged!" - Cary Grant as French army officer Captain Henri Rochard speaks to his new wife WAC Lt. Catherine Gates (Ann Sheridan) in the motion picture *I Was a Male War Bride* (1949). Before they were married, Catherine made it quite clear she could take care of herself: "I may as well warn you, bubble-mouth, that I'm going to carry a revolver and a trench knife and if you so much as lay a finger on me this trip, you're going back to France minus a lot of parts you probably value."

"I'm going to kill them all, sir" - Dutiful statement delivered by TODD 3465, (Kurt Russell) in the science fiction film *Soldier (*1998). Bred from birth as a soldier, by the Adam Project ("Show no mercy. Show no weakness. Weakness is death"), TODD is later replaced by a more advanced version of fighting men (DNA Recombinants) and then unceremoniously left for dead on waste disposal planet, Arcadia 234. When a team of 17 advanced soldiers are let loose on the planet's civilian population of shipwrecked survivors (classified as hostiles), TODD protects his newly adopted world. Asked by a female "What are you going to do" about the approaching soldiers, Todd responds, "I'm going to kill them all, sir." When asked if the others could help fight, Todd says, "No. Soldiers deserve soldiers, sir." Note: In the made-for-cable police drama *Rainbow Drive* (1990) Peter Weller starred as a Hollywood cop who refuses to stop his investigation of a multiple-murder case. He is then told, "Play the game or die." When they kill his girlfriend, the cop says, "I'm gonna kill them. I'm gonna kill them all."

"I am going to make you eat dirt, you soap bubble" - Cutesy put-down delivered by reporter Florence Dempsey (Glenda Farrell) to her news editor boyfriend, Jim (Frank McHugh) in the motion picture *The Mystery of the Wax Museum* (1933).

"I'm gonna get that gun of mine and I'm gonna change you from a rooster to a hen with one shot!" - Dolly Parton as secretary Doralee Rhodes in the corporate comedy film *Nine to Five* (1980). Disgusted at being treated as a sex object, Doralee confronts her "sexist, egotistical, lying, hypocritical bigot" of a boss Frank Hart, Jr. (Dabney Coleman) and discovers disturbing news: "So that's why everyone around here treats me like some dime-store floozy. They all think I'm screwing the boss! And you just love it, don't you? It gives you some kind of cheap thrill like knocking over pencils and picking up papers. I've put up with all of your pinching, poking, staring and chasing me around the desk because I need this job. But this is the last straw! I've got a gun out there in my purse. Up until now I've been forgiving and forgetting because of the way I was brought up, but I'll tell you one thing. If you say another word about me or make another indecent proposal, I'm gonna get that gun of mine and I'm gonna change you from a rooster to a hen with one shot! And don't think I can't do it."

"I'm Gonna Git U Sucka!" - The threatening title of the hip spoof of 70s blaxploitation films, *I'm Gonna Get U Sucka* (1988) starring Keenen Ivory Wayans. The movie follows the adventures of Jack Spade on the avenging trail of those responsible for his brother's death (who died from o. g. - overdose of gold chains). The theme song says it all: "I'm gonna git U sucka, you dirty mother..." (followed by the "Shut your mouth!" put-down from the 1971 movie *Shaft* starring Richard Roundtree).

"I'm gonna kill you if I have to ride all the way to hell to do it." - Sharon Stone as a mysterious female gunfighter threatens to kill the town sheriff in the motion picture *The Quick and the Dead* (1990). In the film, Ellen (aka "The Lady") rides into a dusty prairie town to avenge her father's death. The target of her anger is local sheriff John Herod

(Gene Hackman) who forces Ellen to participate in a gun fighting competition that is rigged in the sheriff's favor. In the end, and with a little help from friends, Ellen blows up the town with dynamite and shots Herod in an old fashioned face-to face drawn down.

"I'm gonna pull the chain on you, pal. And you wanna know why? 'Cause you're fucking up my city. 'Cause you're walking all over people like you own them. And you wanna know the worst part? You're from out of state." - Burt Reynolds as Sgt.Tom Sharky, an Atlanta vice cop talks to a hoodlum in the motion picture *Sharky's Machine* (1981). Previously, Sharky said, "You know Frisco, when we used to flush the toilet upstairs; we always wondered where it came to..."

"I'm gonna suck his eyes out through his nose!" - Mel Gibson as on-the-edge police detective Martin Riggs threatens to siphon some sicko in the motion picture *Lethal Weapon 3* (1992). Note: In the film *Desperate Living* (1977) a policeman gets out of hand while kissing an heiress (Mink Stole) and tells her, "I wish I could stick my whole head in your mouth and have you suck out my eyeballs."

"I'm gonna take you to the bank, Senator Trent—the blood bank" - Steven Seagal as former police officer Mason Storm delivers an Al Bundy like put-down to a corrupt politician in the motion picture *Hard to Kill, aka Seven Year Storm* (1990). In the film, Mason Storm videotapes politician Vernon Trent (William Sadler) making a dirty deal with the mob to finance his bid for the Senate. Unfortunately, the mob's henchmen break into Storm's home to kill him and retrieve the tape. The hoods succeed in killing Storm's wife but don't find the tape nor do they kill Storm but only wound him critically. Tagged as dead, to stop any further mob vendettas, Storm is sequestered in a private hospital. Seven years later Mason awakes from a coma and once again is hot on the trail of the men who hurt him and his family. When Storm recognizes a thug who broke into his house and killed his wife, he kills the man, shouting, "This is for my wife. Fuck you and die!" When Mason breaks through the Senator's private staff of bodyguards, he fires a bullet between the Senator's legs. "I missed! I never miss! They must have been smaller than I thought!" quips Storm. Senator Trent threatens to use all his political power to take Storm down and boasts, "You can take that to the bank!" Mason just snarls and says, "I'm gonna take you to the bank, Senator Trent—to the blood bank!"

"I'm gonna torture him. I'm gonna crucify him. Real bad!" - Threatening statement of boxer Clubber Lang (Mr. T), a lean, mean, killing machine who challenges prizefighter Rocky Balboa (Sylvester Stallone) to a title bout in the classic sports film Rocky *III* (1982). Note: Mr. T (who costarred on the action adventure THE A-TEAM/NBC/1983-87) lampooned his alleged ferocious temperament when he performed an advertising spoof for "Mr. & Mrs. T's Bloody Mary Mix" on a skit for NBC's SATURDAY NIGHT LIVE. Facing the camera, Mr. T. yells, "Now, if anyone tries to tell me he doesn't like Mr. and Mrs. T's Bloody Mary Mix, I say to him, 'Shut up old man! Shut up!' And then I kill him to death. I kill the man who doesn't drink it. But I pity him first. It's a bloody shame. It's Mr. and Mrs. T's Bloody Mary Mix. Buy it, or I'll kill you."

"I'm having an old friend for dinner" - The words of serial killer Dr. Hannibal Lecter to FBI agent Clarice Starling (Jodie Foster) in the movie *Silence of the Lambs* (1990). When Dr. Lecter escapes from custody, he makes a phone call to Clarice to say goodbye. He hangs up before his call can be traced but not before he says, "I do wish we could chat longer but I'm having an old friend for dinner." (The "old friend" refers to prison warden Dr Frederick Chilton played by Anthony Heald). Dr. Lecter, of course, was a cannibal who earlier confessed, "A census taker once tried to test me. I ate his liver with some fava beans and a nice bottle of Chianti...phif-phif-phif-phif-phif." Note: On first meeting Clarice, Lecter observes, "You know what you look like to me, with your good bag and your cheap shoes? You look like a rube. A well scrubbed, hustling rube with a little taste. Good nutrition has given you some length of bone, but you're not more than one generation from poor white trash, are you, Agent Starling? And that accent you've tried so desperately to shed? Pure West Virginia. What's your father, dear? Is he a coal miner? Does he stink of the lamp? You know how quickly the boys found you...all those tedious sticky fumblings in the back seats of cars...while you could only dream of getting out...getting anywhere...getting all the way to the FBI."

"I'm in love with Jeff and he walked out on me. You know why? Because I wanted him to kill you and he couldn't" - Gloria Grahame as Vicki Buckley finally tells the truth about herself and her dirty little affairs as she travels in a train with her hot-tempered husband (Broderick Crawford) in the motion picture *Human Desire* (1954). Continuing her confession, Vicki tells Carl, "You never knew me; you never bothered to figure me out. Well, I'm gonna tell you something. Owens did have something to do with me, but it was because I wanted him to. I wanted that big house he lived in. I wanted him to get rid of that wife of his. But he wasn't quite the fool you are. He knew what I was after. And you know what, I admired him for it. If I'd been a man, I'd of behaved exactly as he did. Now get out of here and let me unpack." Unfortunately, Vicki's painful revelation enrages Carl, who then kills her right there in their private compartment.

"I am just a fat little man, a fat ugly man!" - Self-deprecating admission of Ernest Borgnine as Marty Piletti in the motion picture *Marty* (1955). Marty is a kind-hearted New York City butcher yearning to be loved but lacking self-confidence. He spends most of his time hanging out with his friend Angie (Joe Mantel), both of whom are caught up in the monotonous mantra "What do you want to do tonight?...I don't know what do you want to do tonight?" In a moment of self-loathing, Marty admits to his mother (Esther Minciotti), "I am just a fat, little man, a fat ugly man." After he meets a nice young woman named Clara Snyder (Betsy Blair), Marty finally realizes, "What am I, crazy or something? I got something good here. What am I hanging out with you guys for?" He then tells his friends he's, "gonna beg that girl to marry me" and if "You don't like her? That's too bad."

"I'm just a guy with a one-ton brain who's too nervous to steal and too lazy to work" - Spencer Tracy as "Bugs" Raymond, an ambitious truck driver turned mobster explains why he's involved in the protection rackets for garage owners in the motion picture *Quick Millions* (1931). He continues his rationale: "I do other people's thinking for them and make them like it. I realize that human beings have their weakness and all the man-made laws in the country were made to protect honest people. And how many people will admit that they're honest. Racketeering is just getting what the other guys got in a nice way."

"I'm just gonna shoot him in the leg" - Bruce Willis as oil rig operator Harry Stamper in the motion picture *Armageddon* (1998). When Harry discovers that one of his best oil rig workers A. J. Frost (Ben Affleck) is sleeping with his daughter, Grace (Liv Tyler) he gets overprotective, grabs a gun and proceeds to chase A. J. around the oil rig platform. Coworker Charles "Chick" Chapple (Will Patton) tries to reason with Harry by reminding him that right before AJ's dad died he told you to "take care of his son. I don't think shooting him is taking care of him." Harry counters, "I'm not gonna kill him, I'm just gonna shoot him in the leg. He can still work with one leg. Remember that one guy who worked all those years with one arm?" To which Chick replied, "Yep, but he wasn't very good."

"I'm no white trash piece of shit. I'm better than you all. I can outread you, I can outthink you, and I'm gonna' outlast you" - Robert De Niro as psychopathic ex-con Max Cady stalks the lawyer who put him in prison in the motion picture *Cape Fear* (1991).

"I'm not a roman mum, I'm a kike, a yid, a heebie, a hook-nose, I'm kosher mum, I'm a Red Sea pedestrian, and proud of it!" - Graham Chapman as Brian, a Jewish peasant living in Jerusalem during the time of Jesus Christ offers a variety of ethnic nicknames in the motion picture *Life of Brian* (1979).

"I'm not gonna be ignored, Dan" - Glenn Close as Alex Forrest in the motion picture *Fatal Attraction* (1987). After happily married New York lawyer Dan Gallagher (Michael Douglas) has a quick weekend fling with sexy business partner Alex Forrest, he is unhappily surprised to find out that she won't leave him alone. "I'm not gonna be ignored, Dan…I won't let you treat me like some slut you can bang a couple of times and then throw away like a piece of garbage." Infuriated at being snubbed, Alex goes on a steady trail of vengeance which includes killing the family's pet bunny rabbit and leaving it to stew on the stove in Dan's house. Finally, Alex breaks into the Gallagher's house with murder on her mind. At first, Dan subdues Alex by drowning her in the bathroom tub, but when she emerges screaming from the water, she is finally killed by a handgun shot by Dan's wife, Beth (Anne Archer). Note: In the film *The Best of Everything* (1959) Joan Crawford plays Amanda Farrow, a tough lady editor who tells her inattentive lover (a married man), "I will not be taken for granted. You and your rabbit-faced wife can go to hell."

"I'm not going to put her in a home. I'm going to kill her" - George Segal as Gordon Hocheiser fumes over his mother's (Ruth Gordon) interfering with his love life in the motion picture *Where's Poppa?* (1970).

"I'm not gonna take this. Wormer, he's a dead man!" - John Belushi as John "Bluto" Blutarsky shouts his displeasure in *National Lampoon's Animal House* (1978). Rallying his Delta House fraternity brothers to revenge, Bluto cries, "And it ain't over now. 'Cause when the goin' gets tough...the tough get goin'! Who's with me? Let's go! [no one follows him] "What the fuck happened to the Delta I used to know? Where's the spirit? Where's the guts, huh? 'Ooh, we're afraid to go with you, Bluto, we might get in trouble.' Well just kiss my ass from now on! Not me! I'm not gonna take this. Wormer, he's a dead man! Marmalard, dead! Niedermeyer, Dead!" Concurring with the Bluto's diagnosis, Otter (Judy Jacklin) shouts, "Dead! Bluto's right...Psychotic, but absolutely right. We gotta take these bastards. Now we could do it with conventional weapons that could take years and cost millions of lives. No, I think we have to go all out. I think that this situation absolutely requires a really futile and stupid gesture be done on somebody's part." Jumping back into the conversation Bluto screams, "And we're just the guys to do it....LET'S DO IT!" Bluto later shouts, "No Prisoners!" as he starts to destroy the floats in the college's homecoming parade.

"I am not working here anymore. No, Hinchecliffe has to get himself a new head butcher. I've had ten years of filth and blood. I'm splashed with it, drenched with it! I've had all I can stand! Plenty of it! Take your...killings to Hinchecliffe with my compliments! And tell him to shove it up his..." - Edward G. Robinson as a newspaper editor named Randall who is sick to death over the sensationalist story printed by his publisher Hinchecliffe (Oscar Apfel) that caused the suicide of an elderly couple in the motion picture *Five Star Final* (1931). Note: Years later Randall's "tell him to shove it up his..." sentiments were reflected in a 1970s country song "Take This Job and Shove It" by Johnny Paycheck which inspired the movie of the same name starring Robert Hays.

"I am Pain!" - The ominous revelation of Pinhead, a horrid demon from hell's netherworld in the horror classic *Hellraiser IV: Bloodline* (1996). When two security guards hold Pinhead at gunpoint, he informs them, "Pain has a face. Allow me to show it to you. I am...Pain." Suddenly, out of nowhere, two halves of a metal facemask appears on either side of the confused men. The masks squeeze their faces together, crushing and merging their two skulls into one form. Later, Pinhead is offered the farewell message "Welcome to Oblivion" when he is destroyed in a massive dimensional space explosion.

"I'm pond scum" - Julia Roberts as Julianne "Jules" Potter apologizes to her long-time male friend Michael "Mike" O'Neal (Dermot Mulroney) for interfering with his wedding in the film *My Best Friend's Wedding* (1997). When Jules realizes she still loves Michael, she says, "This is my one chance at happiness. I have to be ruthless!" and then travels to Chicago to break up his impending marriage. A few days into her visit, Jules is ashamed for meddling in her friend's romantic life and confesses, "I was just trying to win you. To win you back. I'm pond scum. Well, lower actually. I'm...like the...the fungus that feeds on pond scum. "Lower," continues Mike (You're) "the pus that infects the mucus, that cruds up the fungus, that feeds on the pond scum. On the other hand, thank you for loving me that much, that way. It's pretty flattering." Jules replies, "Except it makes me fungus."

"I'm sick of you, little boy! And if I have to see you peddling your little wonder dust again, I'm gonna shove my foot so far up your ass, you're going to be sucking my toes 'til graduation" - Famke Janssen as Miss Burke, a beautiful but stern high school teacher who catches a student selling stimulants in the sci-fi motion picture *The Faculty* (1998).

"I am sick to death of straight people" - Comment of Buzz Hauser (Jason Alexander) in the motion picture *Love! Valour! Compassion!* (1997). Sharing his opinion with a group of gay friends while he spends the summer in a secluded home in upstate New York, Buzz laments, "I am sick to death of straight people. Tell the truth, aren't you? There's just too goddamn many of them. I was in a bank the other day; they were everywhere—writing checks, making deposits. Two of them were applying for a mortgage. It's disgusting! They're taking over. No one wants to talk about it, but it's true." Buzz also puts-down movies. For example, "Just once I'd like to see a *West Side Story* where everybody gets it; the Jets and the Sharks, and Officer Krupke; or a *Sound of Music* where the entire Von Trapp family dies in a horrible alpine avalanche; or *A Funny Thing Happened on the Way to the Forum* where nothing happens, and it's not funny." Note: In the film the *Opposite of Sex* (1998) Lisa Kudrow as Lucia Delury confesses to her friend Bill Truitt (Martin Donovan) "That's how I always felt around you too, like the Baroness in *The Sound of Music.* While everybody's just singing and climbing an Alp. And I just wanna *STUFF THAT GUITAR UP THAT NUN'S ASS!* And...ugh!"

"I'm talking to an empty telephone" - Robert De Niro as thief Neil McCauley tells a businessman Roger Van Zant (William Fichtner) that his life is about up in the motion picture *Heat* (1995) In the film, De Niro plays a veteran criminal who likes to score big. After he hits a brinks truck and steals bearer bonds from Van Zant, he turns around and tries to sell them back to the guy. Not amused at being robbed, Van Zant sends hit men to the money drop site to take them out. McCauley anticipates the businessman's move and then kills all the competition. He then phones up Van Zant and says, "Forget the money. I'm talking to an empty telephone. When Van Zandt says, "I don't understand, McCauley replies, "There is a dead man on the end of this fuckin' line." Before leaving town, McCauley kills Van Zant. Then dedicated cop Vincent Hanna (Al Pacino) hunts down McCauley at the airport and mortally wounds him on the runway as he tried to escape justice. Note: Earlier in the film McCauley shared his philosophy about life with Hanna saying, "Guy told me one time. Don't let yourself get attached to anything you are not willing to walk out on in 30 seconds flat, if you feel the heat around the corner."

"I'm the guy that changes the course of your life, man" Derrick O'Connor as Pieter Vorstedt confesses to killing the wife of LAPD detective Martin Riggs (Mel Gibson) in the motion picture *Lethal Weapon 2* (1989). Vorstedt continues his story: "Four years ago, Riggs, when you were a narc off Long Beach, you were getting too close to us so we put a contract out on you. I handled it myself; drove your car right off the fucking road, remember? Now, of course, you weren't driving. You can't imagine the face. I pulled back this moppet of blood-soaked hair to see this woman's face...your wife, right? She didn't die straightaway...took a bit of time." Riggs avenges his wife by activating a loading crane remote control and crushing Vorstedt with a cargo container.

"I'm the Marcia fucking Brady of the Upper East Side and sometimes I want to kill myself for it. So there's your psychoanalysis, Doctor Freud. Now are you in or are you out?" - Sarah Michelle Gellar as Katharine Merteuil makes a bet that her step-brother, Sebastian Valmont (Ryan Phillippe) won't be able to bed a virgin named Annette Hargrove (Reese Witherspoon) in the motion picture *Cruel Intentions* (1999).

"I am the right hand of vengeance and the boot that is gonna kick your sorry ass..." - On the science fiction series BABYLON 5/SYN/1994-98 Lt. Commander Ivanova (Claudia Christian) engages the space fleet sent to attack Babylon 5 forces for refusing to support the (illegal) Earth government. As these two forces converge, the lead Earth ship broadcasts, "This is Captain Jake Thompson of the Advanced Destroyer Group. We have you surrounded. You are ordered to surrender your vessels or be destroyed. I say again. Surrender or be destroyed." Commander Ivanova asks for firing control and then responds, "This is the White Star fleet. Negative on surrender. We will not stand down." Angered, Capt. Thompson yells, "Who is this? Identify yourself." Ivanova answers, "Who am I? I am Susan Ivanova, commander...daughter of Andre and Sophie Ivanov. I am the right hand of vengeance, and the boot that is gonna kick your sorry ass all the way back to Earth, goddammit! I am death incarnate, and the last living thing that you are ever going to see. God sent me." On another occasion, a perturbed Susan advises her crew: "Ivanova is always right. I will listen to Ivanova. I will not ignore Ivanova's recommendations. Ivanova is God. And, if this ever happens again, Ivanova will personally rip your lungs out!"

"I'm the world's first fully functioning homicidal artist" - Jack Nicholson in his role of The Joker, a nefarious Gotham City criminal who ransacks the local art museum in the motion picture *Batman* (1989).

"I'm thinking about taking your head off and shitting in it and then hiding it and see how long it takes you to find it." - Dennis Hopper as police detective Harry 'Nails' Niles responds to a suspect's question, "What are you going to do now, Mr. Pig" in the motion picture *Nails* (1992).

"I'm your worst fuckin' nightmare...a nigger with a badge, man" - Eddie Murphy as Reggie Hammond shouts his now classic catchphrase in the motion picture *48 HRS.* (1982). In the film, Reggie is released from the joint for 48 hours to assist disgruntled cop Jack Cates (Nick Nolte) catch Murphy's former and very disturbed partner. While searching for clues on the man's whereabouts, Reggie enters a redneck bar. When one of its clientele asks "What kind of cop are you?" Reggie replies, "I'm your worst fuckin' nightmare...a nigger with a badge which means I got permission to kick your fuckin' ass whenever I feel like it." Note: In the film *Cop and a Half* (1993) Devon Butler (Norman D. Golden II), a black kid interested in helping solve a crime, tells policeman Nick McKenna (Burt Reynolds), "I'm your worst nightmare...an eight-year-old with a badge." And, in the film *The Santa Clause* North Pole elves rescue Santa Claus from jail. They tell the officer in charge of the lock up "We're your worst nightmare...elves with attitude". Tyrin Turner as Caine in the film *Menace II Society (1993)* offers a variation on the phrase when he refers to his psychopathic friend O-Dog (Larenz Tate) as "America's nightmare—young, black and didn't give a fuck."

"I beat him" - Callous comment of Basil Rathbone as Mr. Murstone in the motion picture *David Copperfield* (1935). Just before Mr. Murstone begins to discipline orphan David Copperfield (Freddie Bartholomew), he tells his step-son how he treats stubborn animals: "David, come here. If I have an obstinate horse or dog to deal with, what do you think I do? I beat him. I make him wince and smart. I say to myself, 'I'll conquer that fellow,' and if it were to cost him all the blood he had—I'd do it." Note: In the film

Friday (1995) John Witherspoon as Los Angeles neighbor Mr. Jones says, "I grab a dog. I choke him and I kick the shit out of him. All day long got my foot up a dog's ass. Just bang, bang, bang up his ass. That's my pleasure."

"I believe in animal attraction. I believe in love at first sight. I believe in *this* [snaps her finger], and I don't feel it with you" - Ellen Barkin as Helen dismisses with the snap of her fingers the possibility that undercover cop Frank Keller (Al Pacino) could possibly have a chance with her in the motion picture *Sea of Love* (1989).

"I bet in one week I can put a bug so far up her ass, she don't know whether to shit or wind her wristwatch" - Jack Nicholson as mental patient R. P. MacMurphy talks to Harding (William Redfield) about Nurse Mildred Ratchitt (Louise Fletcher) in the motion picture *One Flew Over the Cuckoo's Nest* (1975). To avoid being put in prison, MacMurphy convinces his keepers he should be sent to a mental institution, figuring it would be a nicer place. After an initial survey of his fellow patients, MacMurphy concludes, "What do you think you are, for Christ sake, crazy or something? Well, you're not! You're not! You're no crazier than the average assholes out walking around on the streets and that's it!" He later admits, "I must be crazy to be in a loony bin like this." While in the loony bin, MacMurphy comments, "I don't want to break up the meeting, or nothing, but she's (Ratchitt) something of a cunt, isn't she?" Unfortunately, MacMurphy's irreverent attitude pissed off Nurse Ratchitt whom later ordered him lobotomized. Note: In the film *Terms of Endearment* (1983) Jack Nicholson as Garrett Breedlove tells Aurora Greenway (Shirley MacLaine) she needs "a lot of drinks." "To break the ice?" inquires Aurora. "To kill the bug that you have up your ass", concludes Garrett.

"I can't *HEAR* you!" - The abusive catchphrase of Marine Sergeant Vince Carter (Frank Sutton) on the sitcom GOMER PYLE, U. S. M.C./CBS/1964-69. Whenever Sergeant Carter wants to make a point with the Marines under his command, he makes his Second Platoon B Company squad members repeat the acknowledgment of his orders by first shouting out, "I can't *HEAR* you!" On occasion, Carter would single out one Marine and shout the phrase directly in the recruit's ear—usually Private Gomer Pyle (Jim Nabors).

"I certainly had him pegged wrong, didn't I? I thought he was just a rat, but he was a super rat all along—a super rat in rat's clothing" - Audrey Hepburn as jet-setting Holly Golightly who just realizes that her wealthy suitor is actually a married man in the motion picture *Breakfast at Tiffany's* (1961).

"I could easily kill you now, but I'm determined to have your brain" - Donald O'Brian as Dr. Abrera, a mad scientist living on a Molukk island inhabited by cannibals whose past time is harvesting human brains for strange life prolonging experiments in the motion picture *Doctor Butcher, M.D. aka Zombi Holocaust* (1979). The movie's tagline read: "He's a depraved, homicidal killer...and he makes house calls!"

"I could eat a can of Kodak and puke a better film" - Kim Novak as actress Lola Brewster instructs movie director Jason Rudd (Rock Hudson) in the fine art of cinematography in the motion picture *The Mirror Crack'd* (1980).

"I could go on and on about his cock, his bone, his knob, his bishop, wang, thang, rod, hot rod, hump mobile, oscar, dong, dagger, banana, cucumber, salami, sausage, kielbassa, schlong, dink, tool, big ben, Mr. Happy, Peter Pecker, pee-pee, wee-wee, wiener, pisser, pistol, piston joint, hose, horn, middle leg, third leg, meat, stick, joystick, dipstick, one-eyed wonder, junior, little head, little guy, rumple foreskin, tootsie roll, love muscle, skin flute, roto-rooter, snake, hammer, rammer, spammer, bazooka, rubber, chubby, sticky, stubby, schmeck, schmuck, schvantze, ying-yang, yang..." - Jennifer Beals as Angela, a guest at the Mon Signor Hotel in Hollywood on New Year's Eve that can't stop talking about the various names for her friends "huge" penis in the motion picture *Four Rooms* (1995). *See also* "Pussy, pussy, pussy"

"I could peel you like a pear and God himself would call it justice!" - Angry retort of Katharine Hepburn as Eleanor of Aquitane when she learns of her husband's infidelity in the movie *The Lion in Winter* (1968).

"I could shoot you in the middle of Mardi Gras, and they can't touch me" - Ashley Judd as Libby Parsons talks to her philandering husband in the motion picture *Double Jeopardy* (1999). In the film, Libby is sent to prison when her husband fakes his death and points the finger at his wife as the killer. When she discovers her husband is alive, she breaks out of jail, hunts him down, and using the "double jeopardy" feature of the law, forces him to return custody of her child.

"I coulda had class. I coulda been a contender. I coulda been somebody, instead of a bum, which is what I am" - Marlon Brando in the role of boxer Terry Malloy in the classic motion picture *On the Waterfront* (1954). Driving away in a cab, Terry Malloy confronts his brother, Charley (Rod Steiger) whose wheeling and dealing prevented him from having a legitimate shot in the boxing game. Terry reminds Charley, "Remember that night in the Garden you came down to my dressing room and you said, 'Kid, this ain't your night. We're going for the price on Wilson.' You remember that? This ain't your night! My night! I coulda taken Wilson apart! So what happens? He gets the title shot outdoors on the ballpark and what do I get? A one-way ticket to Palooka-ville! You was my brother, Charley, you shoulda looked out for me a little bit. You shoulda taken care of me just a little bit so I wouldn't have to take them dives for the short-end money." Charley rationalizes, "Oh I had some bets down for you. You saw some money." But Terry hits home with the truth: "You don't understand. I coulda had class. I coulda been a contender. I coulda been somebody, instead of a bum, which is what I am, let's face it. It was you, Charley."

"I curse you, Barnabas" - Eternal damnation wished upon Barnabas Collins (Ben Cross) by evil witch Angelique (Lysette Anthony) on the fantasy drama DARK SHADOWS/NBC/1991. When Barnabas declared his love for Josette Dupres (Joanna Going), Angelique casts a love spell to pair Josette with Barnabas' brother Jeremiah Collins thus keeping Barnabas free to marry her. When Barnabas discovered Angelique cast the love spell, he vows he will never love her. Angered, Angelique tries to stab Barnabas with a knife but in the ensuing struggle, she falls on the blade. Dying, she declares, "I curse you, Barnabas. For all eternity, I curse you." Soon after, Barnabas is bitten by a vampire who appears in the image of his love Josette. From the grave

Angelique cries, "Your hell shall take whatever shape I choose." Within a few days Barnabas dies, followed by Josette, who jumped off Widow's Hill five days after her beloved Barnabas expired. Barnabas is resurrected 200 years later only to wander the lonely future pining over the loss of his love Josette. On the original daytime soap opera version of DARK SHADOWS/ABC/1966, Jonathan Frid played the role of Barnabas Collins and Lara Parker appeared as Angelique, the beautiful but wicked witch.

"I do solemnly swear to be a he-man and hate women" - In the motion picture *The Little Rascals* (1994) Stymie (Kevin Jamal Woods) and the rest of the male members of the Little Rascals gang join together to affirm their dislike of girls. Forming the He-Man Women-Haters Club, they proclaim, "I do solemnly swear to be a he-man and hate women, and not play with them, and not touch them unless I have to, and especially never to fall in love, and if I do, may I die slowly and painfully and suffer for hours or until I scream bloody murder."

"I don't care what undercover rock you crawled out from, there's a dress code for detectives in Robbery-Homicide. Section 3-605.10 .20 .22 .24 .26 .50 .70 .80. It specifies: clean shirt, short hair, tie, pressed trousers, sports jacket or suit, and leather shoes, preferably with a high shine on them" - Dan Aykroyd as Los Angeles police Sgt. Joe Friday puts his new partner Pep Streebeck (Tom Hanks) in his place in the motion picture *Dragnet* (1987).

"I don't eat shit. It's against my religion." - Giancarlo Esposito as Tommy Finelli responds to a request in the motion picture *Blue in the Face* (1995). When his friend Pete Maloney (Michael J. Fox) asks, "What religion is that?" Tommy replies, "The religion of sanity, Peter. You should try it some time."

"I don't get married again because I can't find anyone I dislike enough to inflict that kind of torture on" - Roy Scheider as choreographer Joe Gideon talks about his marital status in the motion picture *All That Jazz* (1979).

"I don't get no respect" - The signature catchphrase of veteran stand-up comedian Rodney Dangerfield. Before his death in 2004, Rodney was a frequent visitor to television talk shows like THE TONIGHT SHOW STARRING JOHNNY CARSON and THE TONIGHT SHOW WITH JAY LENO. It was a delight to see the master comedian work his magic as he tugged at his tie and mouthed his jokes. Here are a few of his classic routines:

- "With my dog, I don't get no respect. He keeps barking at the front door. He don't want to go out. He wants me to leave....This morning when I put on my underwear I could hear the Fruit of the Loom guys laughing at me."

- "I tell ya, with my doctor. I don't get no respect. I swallowed a bottle of sleeping pill. He told me to go home, have a few drinks and get some rest."

- "It's not easy being me. When I was born, the doctor told my mother, I done all I could, but he pulled through any way. So that's what I told her today, I got the wrong doctor. You know my doctor, Doctor Vinny Boombots. What a doctor, I told him I want a vasectomy, he said with a face like mine I don't need one…I'm ugly, I tellin' ya, my proctologist, he stuck his finger in my mouth."

- "Once when I was lost, I saw a policeman and asked him to help me find my parents. I said to him, 'Do you think we'll ever find them?' He said, 'I don't know kid. There are so many places they can hide'."

- "I went to see my doctor...Doctor Vinny Boombots. Yeah...I told him once, 'Doctor, every morning when I get up and look in the mirror I feel like throwing up. What's wrong with me?' He said, 'I don't know, but your eyesight is perfect'…I had a lot of pimples, too. One day I fell asleep in a library. I woke up and a blind man was reading my face."

- "I remember I was so depressed I was going to jump out a window on the tenth floor. They sent a priest up to talk to me. He said, 'On your mark'...My psychiatrist told me I'm going crazy. I told him, 'If you don't mind, I'd like a second opinion. He said, 'All right. You're ugly, too!'"

- "I tell ya, when my wife has sex with me there's always a reason for it. One night, she used me to time an egg. I mean at my house, I can't relax. The other night I told my kid, I said someday you'll have children of your own. He said, 'So will you.' I mean that's the story of my life. No respect. I don't get no respect at all. No respect at all."

Note: A posthumous tribute to Rodney Dangerfield appeared in an editorial cartoon drawn by Jeff Stahler for *The Columbus Dispatch*. The sketch depicts Rodney standing in Heaven before a winged St. Peter, whom upon seeing Rodney says, "There goes the Neighborhood." Rodney replies, "Tough Crowd."

"I don't have to show you any stinkin' badges" - When roving Mexican bandits approach gold prospectors in the motion picture *The Treasure of the Sierra Madre* (1948) they claim to be lawmen. Protective of their gold, one of the prospectors hiding behind a rock face (Humphrey Bogart) asks to see a badge to verify their identity. Angered at the request, one of the bandits - referred to as Gold Hat (Alfonso Bedoya) - becomes indignant and growls, "Badges? We ain't got no badges. We don't need no badges...I don't have to show you any stinkin' badges." Over the years, this often parodied phrase has been distilled to "We don't need no stinkin' badges!"

"I don't like crooks. And if I did like 'em, I wouldn't like crooks that are stool pigeons. And if I did like crooks that are stool pigeons, I still wouldn't like you" - Gertrude Short as Marion in the motion picture *The Thin Man* (1934).

"I don't like homosexuals any more than the next man, but—God damn it!—We've got a winning basketball team. Can't we wait and fire them after the season?" - Lorne Allen weighing prejudice against victory concerning a lesbian secretary and a basketball coach/math teacher at Eleanor B. Roosevelt High School in the motion picture *Late Bloomers* (1996).

"I don't like my son spending all this time with a man who carries a gun and goes around whacking people" - Kelly McGillis, as Amish farmer Rachel talks about her young son, Samuel (Lukas Haas) to Philadelphia police detective John Book (Harrison Ford) in the motion picture *Witness* (1985).

"I don't like your kind of people. I don't like to see you come out to this clean country in—oily hair, and dressed up in those silk suits, and try to pass yourselves off as decent Americans...I despise your masquerade—the dishonest way your pose yourself, and your fucking family." - G. D. Spradlin as U. S. Senator Geary shares his utter contempt for Mafia Don Michael Corleone (Al Pacino) for having set him up with a murdered prostitute so that he could be blackmailed in the motion picture *The Godfather, Part II* (1974).

"I don't step on toes, I step on necks" - Chuck Norris as ex-POW Colonel Braddock talks tough as once again he returns to Vietnam—this time to save his wife in the motion picture *Braddock: Missing in Action III* (1988).

"I don't think you'll be needing this anymore" - Miles O'Keeffe as ex-cop Jim Parandine in the motion picture *Silent Hunter* (1995). After a helicopter filled with bank robbers (the same group who killed Jim's wife & child) crashes in a snowy wilderness, the fleeing criminals shoot an old man in a wheel chair and force his grand-daughter to lead them back to civilization. Fortunately, the crooks don't kill her friend, Jim, who promises, "I'm going to kill you" before he is knocked unconscious. When he awakes, Jim sets out on a trail of revenge. One by one, Jim, using his Navy Seal training, kills each of the criminals. When Jim catches the last man, he puts a hand-grenade into the bad guy's jacket and slides him down a rope into a ravine where he unceremoniously explodes. As Jim walks back to the dead body of the only woman crook in the bunch (killed with a hunting arrow) Jim removes a ring from the woman's cold fingers and says, "I don't think you'll be needing this anymore" The 'ring' belonged to Jim's wife. The movie's tagline read: "At 10,000 feet, Silence is deadly!"

"I don't want to know your name. I *don't* want to know your name. Gladiators don't make friends. If we're matched in the arena together, I'll have to kill you" - Woody Strode as Draba, a Nubian gladiator expresses his opinion on friendship to fellow gladiator Spartacus (Kirk Douglas) in the epic motion picture *Spartacus* (1960). This film is filled with blood, gore and violence, including Spartacus drowning a cruel trainer in a boiling pot of soup, and Spartacus getting crucified in the final scenes of the film. During gladiator training, Spartacus tells the gladiator-school owner Batiatus (Peter Ustinov), "I'm not an animal. I'm not an animal." Batiatus replies, "You may not be an animal, Spartacus, but this sorry show gives me very little hope that you'll ever be a man" (Spartacus chivalrously refused a woman given to him for sex).

"I don't want you to love me. I just want out" - Richard Gere as Zack Mayo, a rebellious recruit at the Naval Aviation Officer Candidate School near Puget Sound in Washington state who can't commit to a relationship with mill-worker Paula Pokrifski

(Debra Winger) in the motion picture *An Officer and a Gentleman* (1982). Of course, Zack changes his mind, and visits Paula at her worksite dressed in his finest Navy whites. And, like a knight in shining armor, he sweeps Paula off her feet and carries her away to his magic kingdom where they presumably live happily ever after.

"I drink to your safe return in English ale. I wish that it were English blood" - Kirk Douglas as Einar the Viking drinks a toast to his father Ragnar (Ernest Borgnine) who is setting sail to rape and pillage the English countryside in the motion picture *The Vikings* (1958).

"I expect you to die" - Matter-of-fact remark made by villain Auric Goldfinger (Gert Frobe) to British spy James Bond (Sean Connery) in the espionage thriller *Goldfinger* (1964). Strapped to a table with his legs spread and a laser beam slicing in between them, James Bond coolly inquires of Goldfinger, "Do you expect me to talk?" Goldfinger replies, "No, Mr. Bond. I expect you to die." Goldfinger planned to explode a nuclear device in Fort Knox to irradiate its $15 billion gold reserve and thus wreak havoc on the world's economy. Fortunately, James Bond escapes near death, thwarts the gold contamination plot and lives to see Goldfinger die when a bullet from Goldfinger's gun shatters the window of a private jet, depressurizes the plane's cabin and sucks Goldfinger into the friendly skies. Later, when asked, "Where's Goldfinger" Bond retorts, "Playing his golden harp." Earlier in the film, when Goldfinger's deadly Asian assistant Oddjob crushed a man inside a car at a junkyard, Bond quipped, "As you said...he had a pressing engagement." And after Bond electrocutes Oddjob (Harold Sakata) 007 says, "Oh, he blew a fuse."

"I feel like a country dog in the city. If I stand still they screw me. If I run, they bite my ass" - Burt Reynolds as a small town sheriff expresses his frustration on being stuck in the middle of a hopeless situation in the motion picture *The Best Little Whorehouse in Texas* (1982).

"I flunk English, I'm outta here. I gotta get a job, and you know what that means. That's right, they start me at the drive-up window and I gradually work my way up from shakes to burgers, and then one day my lucky break comes: the French fry guy dies and they offer me the job. But the day I'm supposed to start, some men come by in a black Lincoln Continental and tell me I can make a quick 300 just for driving a van back from Mexico. When I get out of jail I'm 36 years old. Living in a flop house. No job. No home. No upward mobility. Very few teeth. And then one day they find me, face down in the gutter, clutching a bottle of paint thinner and why? Because you wouldn't help me in English!" - John Cusack as college freshman John "Gib" Gibson pleads his case for a better education in the motion picture *The Sure Thing* (1985).

"I get something; you keep something" - The foul request of Nazi interrogator Major Muller (Jurgen Prochnow) in the motion picture *The English Patient* (1996). Handcuffed to a wooden table in a dingy Egyptian basement, a Canadian spy named Caravaggio (Willem Defoe)—codename: Moose—is asked to cooperate with his German captors. "Give me something...a name, a code" asks Muller, "so we can all get out of this room. I'll tell you what I'm going to do. This is your nurse, by the way. She's Muslim, so she'll understand all of this. What's the punishment for adultery? You're married and you were fucking another woman, so that's, uh...Let's leave it at that. Is it the hands that are cut off? Or is that for stealing? Does anyone know?" "Don't cut me!" pleads Caravaggio. The Nazi continues his threats, "Ten fingers. How 'bout this? You give me a name for every finger...Are thumbs fingers?" Suddenly, one of the Nazi soldiers reminds the interrogator of the Geneva Convention rules of behavior in wartime, but he refuses to listen and instructs the nurse to cut off the man's thumbs. Saying anything to stop the butchery, the spy cries, "I'll give you names. How many names did you say? Let me think. Just let me think, I can't think. I know them. Please, let me think. I Promise. Please! Please! No! What names did you say? I know them. I can't think of any names. Not my hands! No! Dear God! Not my hands! No! Dear God! Please don't cut me....No! Please!!!...Aggghh!" A few years later, Caravaggio comes upon a burn-victim (Hungarian Count László Almásy played by Ralph Fiennes) in a crumbling Italian villa and tells the man of his quest for justice. "The man who took my thumbs...I found him eventually. I killed him. The man who took my photograph (pictures that implicated Caravaggio), I found him, too. That took me a year. He's dead. Another man showed the Germans the way to get their spies into Cairo. I've been looking for him." Suspecting the Count as his third target for revenge, the thumbless man discovers that the "English Patient" was a Hungarian cartographer who gave British expedition maps of the region to the Germans for helping him save his lover Katharine Clifton (Kristin Scott Thomas), trapped in the desert. He had only given away the maps after the British refused to help him. Unfortunately, the Count arrived too late to save his lover. She had died alone in the dark of a cave. Upon hearing the Count's rationale for giving away the maps, Caravaggio says, "I thought I would kill you." The dying Almásy says, "You can't kill me I died years ago." The thumbless man finishes, "No, I can't kill you now."

"I get $2,000 a day. I do not do animal acts. I do not do S&M or any variations of that particular bent. No water sports either. I will not shave my pussy. No fist fucking, and absolutely no coming in my face." - Melanie Griffin as porn actress Holly Body rattles off her requirements for working with a producer named Jake (Craig Wasson) in the motion picture *Body Double* (1984). Note: In the film *American Gigolo* (1980) Julian (Richard Gere), a male Beverly Hills prostitute made these work conditions known: "I don't do fags and I don't do couples. I don't do kink." And, in the film *Leaving Las Vegas* (1995) Elizabeth Shue as Sera the prostitute advises her lover, "You can fuck me in the ass. You can cum on my face. Just keep it out of my hair. I just washed it." This line is probably an homage to Bette Davis who said, "I'd like to kiss you, but I just washed my hair" in the motion picture *The Cabin in the Cotton* (1932).

"I go berserk!" - In the film *Billy Jack* (1971) Tom Laughlin starred as Billy Jack, a half breed ex-Green Beret who lived in the Southwest. As Billy Jack enters a local store, he finds children from the nearby reservation covered with flour. Angered, that alleged upright citizens had humiliated the children, Billy Jack says, "They tell me I'm supposed to control my bad temper, but when I see what you've done here...I just go berserk!" Billy proceeds to beat the hell of the uncaring roughnecks. Later, when Billy is surrounded by a group of locals thugs, their racist leader Posner (Bert Freed) says, "You really think those Green Beret karate tricks gonna help you against all these boys?" Billy concedes, "Well it doesn't look to me like I really have any choice, now does it." Offering up his own plan, Bill says, "You know what I think I'm gonna do then?...Just for the hell of it? I'm gonna take this right foot, and I'm gonna whop you on that side of your face [pointing to Posner's left cheek], and you wanna know something? There's not a damn thing you're gonna be able to do about it." And you know…he was right.

"I gotta B-i-i-i-g Mouth!" - What bus driver Ralph Kramden (Jackie Gleason) says when he realizes he's made a fool of himself with his wife or others on the sitcom THE HONEYMOONERS/CBS/1955-56. *See also* "One of these days, Alice...Pow! Right in the kisser!"

"I gotta kill that boy, I just gotta!" - Cry of exasperation uttered by Herbert T. Gillis (Frank Faylen), a Central City grocery store owner on the sitcom THE MANY LOVES OF DOBIE GILLIS/CBS/1959-63. The "Boy" in question was his teenage son, Dobie (Dwayne Hickman) who was always trying to find a girl to "call his own." And in his pursuit of the lovely ladies, Dobie always hit-up poor dad for money to finance his romantic endeavors. Occasionally, Winifred "Winnie" Gillis (Florida Friebus), Herbert's wife would hold him back when he got in that "I gotta kill that boy" frame of mind.

"I've had an epiphany once, Larry. My daddy shot my whole family in the head, and I was the only one to identify the bodies. I was sent to a good Christian school full of good Christian nuns who put my face into their pussies with their crucifixes on for 8 goddamn years!" - Courtney Love as Althae Flynt speaks to her husband Larry Flynt (Woody Harrelson), the publisher of *Hustler* magazine in the motion picture *People vs. Larry Flynt* (1996)

"I hate manure!" - Thomas F. Wilson as Biff Tannen after he falls into a truck load of manure in the sci-fi classic *Back to the Future* (1989). When Marty McFly (Michael J. Fox) travels back in time to the 1950s, he is chased by a bully called Biff Tannen. At the conclusion of a chase scene, Biff crashes his convertible roadster into a truck load of manure and cries, "I hate manure." The Biff character also ate shit in 1885 when Marty McFly met Biff's descendant, outlaw Buford Tannen. At the end of their encounter, Marty knocks Tannen into a cart load of manure with similar results.

"I hate men and I play very dirty" - The top qualifications of lawyer Randi King (Dixie Carter) when she asked to be hired as an attorney for a Los Angeles firm owned by recent divorcée Lynn Holt (Kathleen Quinlan) on the premiere episode of the television drama FAMILY LAW/CBS/1999-2002.

"I hate spunk!" - Ed Asner as newsroom editor Lou Grant growls on the classic THE MARY TYLER MOORE SHOW/CBS/1979-77. When Mary Richards (Mary Tyler Moore) interviews for a position with WJM-TV in Minneapolis, Lou Grant invites her into his office for an interview. After Lou begins to ask some questions that were "technically illegal" (marital status, religion, etc,) Mary stands up for herself. Surprised at Mary's salt, Lou says, "You know...you got spunk!" Mary thinks Lou is complementing her, but in the next instance, Lou barks his now famous line, "I Hate Spunk!" Despite Lou's opinion, he still hired Mary as assistant producer.

"I hate the British" - Intolerant words of Japanese Colonel Saito (Sessue Kayakawa) in the motion picture *The Bridge on the River Kwai* (1957). Responsible for a group of British officers and soldiers captured to help build a bridge, Colonel Saito becomes impatient with the obstinate British officer Colonel Nicholson (Alec Guinness) and lashes out, "I hate the British. You are defeated but you have no shame. You are stubborn but you have no pride. You endure but you had no courage. I hate the British!" In the film's climax, the bridge is destroyed. Surveying the corpse-littered riverbed, Army doctor Major Clipton (James Donald) laments, "Madness. Madness". Note: The motion picture *Fire Over England* (1937) offers additional distain for the British when Raymond Massey as King Phillip II of Spain comments, "I lived a year with Englishmen. I hated every one of them. And how it rained." *See also* "You English..."

"I hate warriors. Too narrow-minded, no subtlety. And worse, they fight for hopeless causes. Honor? Huh! Honor's killed millions of people, it hasn't saved a single one. I'll tell you what I do like though: a killer, a dyed-in-the-wool killer. Cold blooded, clean, methodical and thorough. Now a real killer, when he picked up the ZF-1, would've immediately asked about the little red button on the bottom of the gun." - Gary Oldman as Zorg, a ruthless, profiteering human who sold out Earth to the powers of darkness in the motion picture *The Fifth Element* (1997)

"I hate you more. If hate were people, I'd be China" - Daniel Stern as Phil Berquist illustrates his extreme anger in the motion picture *City Slickers* (1991).

"I hate you so much that I would destroy myself to take you down with me" - Rita Hayworth as Gilda, a sexy, masochistic singer lets her former lover (Glenn Ford) know the depths of her distain in the motion picture *Gilda* (1946).

"I HATE YOUR GUTS ASSHOLE!" - A demented postcard message from an anonymous screenwriter delivered to movie studio executive Griffin Mill (Tim Robbins) in the motion picture *The Player* (1992). David Kahane (Vincent D'Onofrio), another screenwriter insults Griffin by saying, "See you in the next reel, asshole."

"I've been trying to figure something in my head, and maybe you can help me out, yeah? When a person is insane, as you clearly are, do you know that you're insane? Maybe you're just sitting around, reading 'Guns and Ammo,' masturbating in your own feces, do you just stop and go, 'Wow! It is amazing how fucking crazy I really am!?' Yeah. Do you guys do that?" - Brad Pitt as police detective David Mills tests out a theory in the motion picture *Se7en* (1995).

"I've got a gun in my pocket. You open your mouth and you'll be spitting gum out through your forehead" - Joe Pesci as Harry the burglar threatens youngster Kevin McCallister (Macaulay Culkin) in the sequel *Home Alone 2: Lost in New York* (1992). Harry first met Kevin when he tried to break into Kevin's home during Christmas vacation in *Home Alone* (1990). When Kevin defends himself by bombarding Harry with cans, Harry threatens, "You bop me with one more can, kid, and I'll snap off your cojones and boil them in motor oil."

"I have great respect for psychiatry—and great contempt for meddling amateurs who go around practicing it" - Edmund Gwenn as Kris Kringle in the motion picture *The Miracle on 34th Street* (1947). In the film, a jolly bearded man claiming to be the real Santa Claus was hired by Macy's Department Store during the Christmas shopping season. However, when Kris insists that he is actually the one and only, original Santa Claus, he is given a psychiatric interview by Mr. Sawyer (Porter Hall), the store's shrink. When the story of Kris' court case pertaining to his sanity reaches the newspapers, the headlines read: KRIS KRINGLE KRAZY? KOURT KASE COMING; "KALAMITY," KRIES KIDS.

"I have never been able to understand why small children are so disgusting. They're the bane of my life. They're like insects: they should be got rid of as early as possible. Hah, [makes spraying gesture] psst! My idea of a perfect school is one in which there are no children...at all" - Pam Ferris as mean, authoritarian principal Miss Agatha "The" Trunchbull in the motion picture *Matilda* (1996).

"I've never known a better seaman, but as a man, he's a snake. He doesn't punish for discipline. He likes to see men crawl" - Clark Gable as 1st Mate Fletcher Christian critiques Captain William Bligh (Charles Laughlin) in the motion picture *Mutiny on the Bounty* (1935). Fed up with the cruelty of their captain, Fletcher and the crew of the HMS Bounty take over the ship and place Bligh into a longboat. Refusing defeat, Bligh addresses Christian and fellow conspirators "Casting me adrift, not even five hundred miles from a port of call. You're sending me to my doom, eh? Well, you're wrong, Christian! I'll take this boat as she floats to England, if I must. I'll live to see you, all of you hanging from the highest yardarm in the British Fleet!" Good to his word Bligh reaches England and the British Empire hunts down the mutineers. At their trial, the now triumphant Bligh is taken down a notch by captured shipman Byram (Francoise Tone) when he testifies "One man, my lord, would not endure such tyranny. That's why you hounded him. That's why you hate him, hate his friends. And that's why you're beaten. Fletcher Christian's still free." Earlier in the film, Bligh tells Byram, "A seaman's a seaman. A captain's a captain. And a shipman is the lowest form of animal in the British Navy."

"I've seen garbage collectors who are cleaner" - Sidney Poitier as newly hired West Indian teacher Mark Thackeray who can't believe the hygienic habits of his London, England high school students in the motion picture *To Sir with Love* (1967).

"I've seen things you've only seen in your nightmares. Things you can't even imagine. Things you can't even see. There are things that hunt you in the night. Then something screams. Then you hear them eating, and you hope to God that you're not dessert. Afraid? You don't even know what afraid is" - Robin Williams as Allan Parrish who got sucked into a old magic board-game called 'Jumanji' when he was boy and then gets released decades later to explain his ordeal in the motion picture *Jumanji* (1995).

"I have something to give you. I don't want it anymore...thirty hours of pain all at once, all for you!" - Brandon Lee as Eric Draven injects thirty hours of painful memories into the mind a a street thug who was partly responsible for death of his fiancée, Shelly Webster (Sofia Shinas) in the motion picture *The Crow* (1994). On the night before Halloween, Eric is shot and thrown out the window of his apartment by a creep named Top Dollar (Michael Wincott) while Eric's fiancée Shelly is brutally raped by a gang and then dies 30 hours later in a hospital. When Tin Tin (Laurence Mason), one of Top Dollar's thugs is called a murderer, he snarls, "Murderer? Murderer!? Let me tell you a little something about murder. It's fun, it's easy, and you gonna learn all about it. [pulls out two blades] I'd like you to meet two buddies of mine. We never miss." One year later, on Halloween, dark forces return Eric to Earth to seek revenge. ("People used to think that when someone dies, a crow carries their soul to the land of the dead. But sometimes...only sometimes the crow brings that soul back to set the wrong things right.").When Gideon (Jon Polito) another of Top Dollar's thugs first see the Crow, he cries, "Please, I'm beggin' you. Don't kill me." Eric replies, "I'm not going to kill you. Your job will be to tell the rest of them that death is coming for them, tonight. And tell them Eric Draven sends his regards."

"I have this phobia about getting to be 40. I don't know. When you're in your twenties, everybody says 'boy genius!' And then when you're in your thirties, 'Ah, yes! Young man on the way up!' You get to be forty...zip. Nothin'. No more adjectives. Just a man" - Richard Long as magazine publisher Michael Green ponders the lessons of growing old in the motion picture *The Girl Who Came Gift-Wrapped* (1973).

"I have wasted thousands and thousands of kisses on you—kisses that I thought were special because of your lips and your smile and all your color and life. I used to think that was the real you, when you smiled. But now I know you don't mean any of it. You just save it for all your songs. Shame on me for kissing you with my eyes closed so tight." - Liv Tyler as Faye tells off her musician boyfriend James "Jimmy" Mattingly II (Jonathon Schaech) in the motion picture *That Thing You Do! (*1996). Jimmy's contribution to the conversation: "I shoulda dumped you in Pittsburgh!"

"I honestly think you ought to sit down calmly, take a stress pill, and think things over" - The voice of spaceship computer Hal 9000 (Douglas Rain) speaks to astronaut David Bowman (Keir Dullea) who disconnects the allegedly malfunctioning computer in the sci-fi classic film *2001: A Space Odyssey* (1968). As Bowman continued disabling Hal's circuitry, the computer politely protests, "Dave, stop. Stop, will you? Stop Dave. Will you stop, Dave? Dave, my mind is going. I can feel it. I can feel it. My mind is going. There is no question about it." David disconnected Hal because its programming was killing personnel in hibernation modules as well as jettisoning others into outer space.

"I hope it hurts, terribly" - Cold-hearted remark of Pauline Mendelson (Jill Eikenberry), a prim and proper socialite who continues to prune her garden roses while a man named Cyril Rathbone (Roddy McDowall) rolls about her garden lawn in agony as he dies from an allergic reaction to a wasp sting in the film *An Inconvenient Woman* (1991).

"I hope the plane crashes! I don't want him to die. I want her to die...Most of all, I want the Jaguar!" - Shelley Winters as Mrs. Cramer confides to her divorce lawyer (George Segal) about her philandering husband and his mistress in the motion picture *Blume in Love* (1973).

"I hope they burned in hell!" - Impassioned statement of Samuel L. Jackson as blue-collar father Carl Lee Hailey in the racially tense movie *A Time to Kill* (1996). After his 10-year-old daughter Tonya (Rae'ven Kelly) is raped by two low-life, beer-drinking good-old boys, Hailey takes justice into his own hand and shots them down in the Clanton, Mississippi courthouse. Arrested for murder, Carl admits to his lawyer Jake Tyler Burgance (Matthew McConaughey), "I didn't have anything against those boys until they messed with my baby, but I'm not sorry for what I done." At his trial, the prosecutor Rufus Buckley (Kevin Spacey) pushes Carl for an answer to "Did they deserve to die?" The distraught Hailey erupts violently, "Yes, they deserved to die and I hope they burned in hell." Carl's actions were fueled by the fact that a year before, four other white boys raped a young black girl and got off without any jail time. For defending Hailey, his lawyer was called a "Negro loving pig" by a faction of Ku Klux Klan supporters. Freddie Cobb (Kiefer Sutherland) the brother of one of the murdered rapists later contacted the Klan because he wanted to "Kill that nigger." Reminiscing about the good old days, Cobb mused, "10 years ago, that nigger be hanging from a tree with his cock in his mouth."

"I hope you die. I hope you die soon. I'll be waiting for you to die" - Betty Davis as Regina Hubbard Giddens shouts her distain for her ailing husband Horace (Herbert Marshall) in the motion picture *The Little Foxes* (1941). When Horace needs his heart medicine, Regina purposely withholds it from him. This calculated act contributes to his demise. Before he dies, Horace tells Regina, "Maybe it's easier for the dying to be honest. I'm sick of you, Sick of this house. Sick of my unhappy life with you. I'm sick of your brothers and their dirty tricks to make a dime. There must be better ways of getting rich than building sweatshops and pounding the bones of the town to make dividends for you to spend. You'll wreck this town, you and your brothers. You'll wreck this country, you and your kind, if they let you. But not me. I'll die my own way, and I'll do it without making the world any worse. I leave that to you."

"I intend to see to it that any man who sails under a pirate flag or wears a pirate brand gets what he deserves: a short drop and a sudden stop." - Jack Davenport as Norrington, a British Naval officer stationed in the Caribbean who explains that "hanging" is his answer to quelling criminal activities in the motion picture *Pirates of the Caribbean: The Curse of the Black Pearl* (2003).

"I kill myself because you have not loved me, because I haven't loved you. I kill myself because the bonds between us were loose, and to tighten those bonds, I will leave an indelible stain on you" - These words belong to the suicide note left to Lydia (Lena Skerla), the wife of despondent alcoholic Alain Leroy (Maurice Ronet) who quietly finished his latest book project and then shot himself in the heart in the motion picture *The Fire Within* (1964).

"I kill nips with a wave of the hand" - A soldier admits to some disturbing deeds in the film *Hail the Conquering Hero* (1944). In an attempt to be classified as insane, Lafayette Pershing Truesmith (Eddie Bracken) gives an over-the-top performance beginning with, "I'm a great hero. People run when they see me coming. I kill nips with a wave of the hand. I blow them down. Phiff. I shoot them from all angles, backwards, forward, while looking into mirrors. I swim in the water and drown 'em like rats. I pick up a machine gun and brrrt." Upon hearing Truesmith, his sergeant (William Demarest) calls him a "Daffodil from Dopeyville." Note: In the film *Scarface (1983)* a Marielle Cuban named Tony Montana (Al Pacino) confesses, "I kill communists for fun but for a green card, I carve him up real special."

"I killed a girl once. It was no accident. Put the gun right to the back of her head, blew her brains right out the front. I was in love" - Dennis Hopper as a handicapped ex-biker dope dealer named Feck shares "murder" tales with teenager Samson "John" Tollette (Daniel Roebuck) who himself had recently strangled his own girlfriend by accident and left her on the river bank in the motion picture *River's Edge (*1987).

"I killed her, Joey, she talked too much!" - At the conclusion of ABC's FUGITIVE series narrator William Conrad said, "Tuesday, August 29, 1967, the day the running stopped." Richard Kimble (played by actor David Janssen) was a free man, exonerated for the murder of his wife. Later that night on the talk show THE JOEY BISHOP SHOW/ABC/1967-69, there was a live interview with David Janssen who was working in Georgia on a new movie. Bishop asked Janssen whether he had anything to say now that he was a free man and beyond the reach of the law. "Yes," Janssen said. "I killed her, Joey. She talked too much."

"I know exactly where your body is. What I'm looking for is some indication of a brain" - Al Pacino as blind retired Lt. Colonel Frank Slade appraises his new weekend caregiver Charlie Simms (Chris O'Donnell) in the motion picture *Scent of a Woman* (1992). After Frank gets to know Charlie a bit better, he says, "I don't know whether to shoot you or adopt you."

"I like you...I'm going to kill you last" - Arnold Schwarzenegger as retired special forces Col. John Matrix in the motion picture *Commando (*1985). After talking with Sully (David Patrick Kelly), one of the kidnappers who abducted John's young daughter, Matrix promises, "You're a funny guy, Sully. I like you...that's why I'm going to kill you last." Later, John hunts Sully down and dangles him over a cliff to extract information. But after a few seconds of interrogation John tells Sully, "Remember when I promised to kill you last? I lied." John then drops the crook to his doom. When John returns to his car, his companion (Ray Dawn Chong) asks what happened to Sully. John simply tells her, "I let him go." Note: At the climax of the spy thriller *Goldeneye (*1995) James Bond grabs the boot of traitor agent 006 as they dangles precariously from a huge radio telescope. Just as Bond is about to let go of 006, he asks Bond, "For England?" Bond coldly replies, "No...For me."

"I live in a Frat House, right? And these fuckers wanna kick me out for not observing quiet hour! Well, they can SUCK my QUIET COCK!" Lochlyn Munro as a college student named Cliff in the morbid comedy film *Dead Man on Campus* (1998).

"I look upon Brad Allen like any other disease. I had him. It's over. I'm immune to him now" - Doris Day as single decorator Jan Morrow refers to her former beau (Rock Hudson) in the motion picture *Pillow Talk* (1959).

"I met him, fifteen years ago. I was told there was nothing left. No reason, no conscience, no understanding; even the most rudimentary sense of life or death, good or evil, right or wrong. I met this six-year-old child, with this blind, pale, emotionless face and, the blackest eyes...the *Devil's* eyes! I spent eight years trying to reach him, and then another seven trying to keep him locked up for I realized what was living behind that boy's eyes was purely and simply...*EVIL!*" - Donald Pleasance as psychiatrist Dr. Samuel Loomis gives his professional evaluation of Michael Myers in the classic horror film *Halloween* (1978). Institutionalized since the age of six (for killing his sister with a "really big, sharp kitchen knife" on Halloween night in 1963) Michael escapes from his confinement in 1978 and returns to his hometown of Haddonfield to kill again. The masked Michael character went on to wreak havoc in a number of sequels that concluded with the seventh entry *Halloween H20: Twenty Years Later* (1998) wherein Michael's sister Laurie Strode (Jamie Lee Curtis), living under a new identity of Keri Tate chops off Michael's head with an ax and kills him for good. But wait! The man in the mask was not Michael which lead to the next sequel *Halloween Resurrection* (2002) in which Laurie dies in the beginning of the film. Note: On the television sitcom SEINFELD/NBC/1990-98 Jerry Seinfeld once said of his nemesis, postal worker neighbor Newman (Wayne Knight) "I've looked into his eyes...He's pure evil!"

"I never miss!" - Pierce Brosnan as British secret agent James Bond boasts his marksmanship skills in the spy thriller *The World is Not Enough* (1999). When 007 discovers that Electra King (Sophia Marceau) the beautiful daughter of a deceased oil tycoon is behind a plan to explode a nuclear bomb in the Mid-eastern oil fields, he travels to the Caspian Sea to stop her. In an attempt to distract Bond, Electra seductively suggests, "You wouldn't kill me. You'd miss me." James, on the other hand, didn't agree, shot her dead and said, "I never miss." Later, Bond tracks down Electra's partner in crime, psychotic terrorist Viktor Zokas (Robert Carlyle) and impales him with a golden reactor rod to prevent a nuclear melt down on a stolen Soviet submarine. Moments before, Zokas maniacally proclaimed, "Welcome to my nuclear family" as he sent the reactor into critical overload.

"I never trusted Klingons, and I never will" - William Shatner as Admiral James Tiberius Kirk shares his personal opinion on a race of ruthless aliens petitioning to become part of the Federation of Planets in the motion picture *Star Trek VI: The Undiscovered Country* (1991). Dictating into his personal log Kirk confessed "Captain's log, stardate 9522.6: I've never trusted Klingons, and I never will. I could never forgive them for the death of my boy. It seems to me our mission to escort the Chancellor of the Klingon High Council to a peace summit is problematic at best. Spock says this could be an historic occasion, and I'd like to believe him, but how on earth can history get past people like me?" The Klingons had killed Kirk's only son, David (Merritt Butrick) in *Star Trek III: The Search for Spock* (1984).

"I only raped her once" - Sickening admission of WWII American soldier Capt. Aarfy Aardvark (Charles Grodin) after he throws an Italian woman to her death from a window in the motion picture *Catch-22* (1970). When Air Force Capt. John Yasarrian (Alan Arkin) discovers Aardvark cowering in a corner bed of a third floor walk-up, Aardvark rationalizes his violence by telling his friend that he had to kill her because, "I couldn't let her say bad things about me."

"I own you...I brought you, your house, your kid, business...I own a paper on your whole life" - Robert Prosky as Leo, a really pissed mob boss lets a professional thief named Frank (James Caan) know that he owns his soul in the motion picture *Thief* (1981). To make his point crystal clear, Leo threatens, "I'll wipe out your whole family. People will be eatin' 'em for lunch tomorrow in their burgers and not even know it. You're working for me until you are burned out, busted, or dead. Got it?"

"I prayed for an angel of the Lord, and the Devil sent me you" - Victor Mature as legendary Jewish warrior Samson rebukes vixen Delilah (Hedy Lamarr) in the biblical epic *Samson and Delilah* (1949). At the film's climax, after Delilah's betrayal, Samson, now beaten and blind, places his hands on the columns of a pagan temple and brings the massive structure down on his tormentors.

"I recall it's a sign of normalcy in our circle to slaughter anything that moves" - Peter O'Toole as Jack the Ripper in the motion picture *The Ruling Class* (1972).

"I shall kill you tomorrow night" - Claude Rains in his role of the Invisible Man in the science fiction classic *The Invisible Man* (1933). Having the upper hand, now that he is invisible, crazed research scientist Jack Griffin (Raines) promises to kill Kemp (William Harrigan) for betraying him. But since he is otherwise occupied, he tells Kemp, "I've no time now, but believe me, as surely as the moon will set and the sun will rise, I shall kill you tomorrow night. I shall kill you even if you hide in the deepest cave of the earth. At ten o'clock tomorrow night, I shall kill you." Earlier in the film, Griffin, insane with newfound power of invisibility, reveals a murderous plan to Kemp: "The drugs I took seemed to light up my brain. Soon I realized that power I hold—the power to rule...Power to walk into the gold vaults of the nations...into the secrets of kings...into the holy of holies. Power make multitudes run screaming in terror at the touch of my little invisible finger. Even the moon's frightened of me—frightened to death; the whole world is frightened to death...We'll begin with a reign of terror—a few murders of little men, just to show them that we make no distinctions. We might even wreck a train or two—just these fingers round a signalman's throat—that's all." Note: In the film *Theatre of Blood* (1973) Vincent Price as demented actor Edward Lionheart tells a movie critic, "I'll kill you when I am ready—next week, next month, perhaps next year! Oh, I am going to make you suffer as you've made me suffer!"

"I shot Mr. Brady in the head" - Admission of Tom Ewell in the role of Richard Sherman, a paperback novel publisher in the motion picture *The Seven Year Itch* (1955). When Mr. Sherman's wife and child go on summer vacation to escape the heat of the city, he returns to his empty apartment and muses, "It's peaceful with everybody gone. Sure is peaceful. No Howdy Doody. No Captain Video. No smell of cooking. No, 'What happened at the office today, darling?' Daydreaming, he responds, "What happened at the office today? Well, I shot Mr. Brady in the head, made violent love to Ms. Morris and set fire to 300,000 copies of *Little Women.* That's what happened at the office."

"I should go to Paris and jump off of the Eiffel Tower. If I took the Concorde, I could be dead three hours earlier" - Woody Allen as a depressed Joe contemplates suicide after his girlfriend leaves him in the film *Everyone Says I Love You (*1996).

"I should have killed myself when he put it in me...After the first time...before we were married. Ralph promised never again. He promised. And I believed him. But sin never dies. Sin never dies" - Piper Laurie as the religiously fanatic Margaret White, who tells her teenage daughter Carrie White (Sissy Spacek) about the unwanted sexual advances of her husband in the classic horror film *Carrie. (*1976). Later in the film, Carrie's uncontrollable rage over being humiliated at the prom sparks a psychokinetic wave of hatred that burns down the high school gym and eventually Carrie's own home after her mother tries to kill her. Note: In the film *Flowers in the Attic* (1987) Louise Fletcher as the evil grandmother reveals, "Your mother has come home after seventeen years to repent for her sins and for her crime. Not only against your grandfather and me, but against God! Your mother's marriage was unholy! A sacrilege! An abomination in the eyes of the Lord! She did not fall from Grace! She leapt! Into the arms of a man whose veins pulsed with the same blood as hers! Not a stranger, but her own uncle! And you, the children, are the devil's spawn! Evil from the moment of conception!" Grandchild Chris (Jeb Stuart Adams) rebukes his grandmother, saying, "Look at you in your black dress. Your fancy jewels. Your pinched face. We're not afraid of you! We laugh at you! Do you hear that? We laugh!"

"I swear I'll kwill you a mwillion times" - Catchphrase used by Milton Berle on the classic variety program TEXACO STAR THEATER/NBC/1948-59. Berle's other popular phrase was "I'll give you a shot in the head!" Note: In the movie *Let's Make Love* (1960) Milton Berle in a cameo role attempted to teach Ives Montand to be funny by showing him how to properly mouth this popular catchphrase.

"I swear if you existed, I'd divorce you" - Martha (Elizabeth Taylor) puts down her college professor husband, George (Richard Burton) in the dark dramatic film *Who's Afraid of Virginia Woolf?* (1966). George gets in his licks and says, "There isn't any abomination award going that you haven't won."

"I think he got the point" - When a SPECTRE assassin named Vargas attacks secret agent James Bond (Sean Connery) on a tropical island beach in the motion picture *Thunderball* (1965), 007 shoots him with a spear gun. As the steel shaft pins the bad guy to the trunk of a palm tree, Bond quips, "I think he got the point." Note: In the film *Ricochet* (1991) when psychotic killer Earl Talbott Blake (John Lithgow) falls off the Watts Tower and impales himself on a metal rod, assistant district attorney Nick Styles (Denzel Washington) says, "You got the point now, don't you Blake!"

"I think sex is like supermarkets, you know, overrated. Just a lot of pushing and shoving and you still come out with very little at the end" - Pauline Collins as middle-aged Liverpool housewife Shirley Valentine-Bradshaw in the motion picture *Shirley Valentine* (1989).

"I think they were on the way to a funeral" - Sean Connery as secret Agent James Bond reports to a road construction crew member what happened to a hearse filled with bad guys after it plummeted over a cliff, crashed and burned in the motion picture *Dr. No* (1962). The use of a cold-hearted put-down became a running gag in all the Bond film sequels. Once, when Bond (Roger Moore) forced an assassin on a motorcycle off a cliff by running him into a poultry truck he remarked, "All those feathers and he still can't fly!"

"I think you're a selfish, petty egomaniac" - Personal appraisal offered by Maggie Cutler (Bette Davis) of her pompous theatre critic boss Sheridan "Sheri" Whiteside (Monty Woolley) in the movie drama *The Man Who Came to Dinner* (1941). Forced to stay the winter in a Midwestern home filled with zany family members and friends, Maggie let's her guard down and confesses: "I wish I had a laugh left in me. Shall I tell you something Sheri? I think you're a selfish, petty egomaniac who would just as soon see his mother burning at the stake if that was the only way he had of lighting a cigarette. I think you'd sacrifice your best friend without a moment's hesitation if he interrupted the sacred ritual of your self-centered, paltry life. I think you're incapable of any emotion higher up than your stomach and I was a fool of the world for ever trusting you."

"I think you're all fucked in the head" - The first words in a tirade delivered to his family by Clark Griswald (Chevy Chase) as he battles the perils of a cross-country road trip to a theme park called 'Wally World' in the comedy film *National Lampoon's Vacation* (1983). Reaching his breaking point, Clark continues, "We're ten hours from the fucking fun park and you want to bail out. Well, I'll tell you something. This is no longer a vacation. It's a quest. It's a quest for fun. I'm gonna have fun and you're gonna have fun. We're all gonna have so much fucking fun we'll need plastic surgery to remove our goddamn smiles. You'll be whistling 'Zip-A-Dee Doo-Dah' out of your assholes! I gotta be crazy! I'm on a pilgrimage to see a moose. Praise Marty Moose! Holy Shit!"

"I thought Mr. Clutter was a very nice man. He was a real gentleman. I thought so right up to the moment I cut his throat" - Robert Blake as drifter Perry Smith who along with his partner, Dick Hickock (Scott Wilson) rob a wealthy Kansas farmer's home and murder the entire family to avoid identification in the motion picture *In Cold Blood* (1967).

"I Wanna Be a Ho" - On a classic skit on NBC's SATURDAY NIGHT, Eddie Murphy portrayed Velvet Jones, a supposed educator from the Velvet Jones School of Technology. One of the books (and courses) he offered was how to be a prostitute. His sales pitch read: "Are you a female high school dropout, between the ages of sixteen and twenty-five?...Are you tired of lying around in bed all day with nothing to do? Well, you never need get up again, because in six short weeks I can train you to be a high paying Ho...Just think—fifteen hundred dollars a week, without even leaving the comfort of your own bedroom. Sound too good to be true? Just send for my new book, "I Wanna Be a Ho." Velvet Jones follow-up publications included "I Wanna Drive a Pink Cadillac, Wear Diamond Rings and Kick Women in the Butt" (how-to-be-a-pimp guidebook); The Velvet Jones Harlequin Romance series featuring "Velvet Love" and

"Kicked in the Butt by Love." ("I knew in an instant that the three dollars I had spent on wine would not go to waste"); and an exciting new videocassette *The Exercises of Love* marketed with these telling words: "Yes, it's all here: the squatting, the thrusting, the grunting and the groaning. Take it from Velvet, these are exercises you will want to watch again and again."

"I want to be just like you. I figure all I need is a lobotomy and some tights" - Judd Nelson as misunderstood teenager John Bender mocks high school wrestler Andrew Clark (Emilio Estevez) in the motion picture *The Breakfast Club* (1985).

"I want to be the greatest poisoner the world has ever seen" - Hugh O'Conor as the sinister British teenager Graham Young who poisons family members and friends in the motion picture *The Young Poisoner's Handbook (*1995). Graham's step mom Molly (Ruth Sheen) once told him, "You contaminate everything you touch. I'm going to scrub you till you are raw."

"I want to play a game" The voice of a mysterious serial killer in a mask known as the "Jigsaw Killer" (Tobin Bell) heard on a videotape in the horror movie *Saw* (2004). The killer begins, "Hello Amanda. You don't know me, but I know you. I want to play a game. Here's what happens if you lose. The device you are wearing is hooked into your upper and lower jaw. When the timer in the back goes off, your mouth will be permanently ripped open. Think of it like a reverse bear trap. Here, I'll show you. There is only one key to open the device. It's in the stomach of your dead cellmate...Look around Amanda. Know that I'm not lying. Better hurry up. Live or die, make your choice." The Jigsaw Killer never actually kills anyone directly but orchestrates his victims via twisted games to kill themselves, or each other. The killer (aka "John") cuts a piece from his victims. As he says, "The jigsaw piece that I cut from my subjects was only ever meant to be a symbol that that subject was missing something. A vital piece of the human puzzle. The survival instinct." *See also* "Don't fuck with the Chuck!"

"I want you to hold it between your knees" - Sassy remark directed at roadside diner waitress (Lorna Thayer) by oil rig worker Robert Eroica Dupea (Jack Nicholson) in the motion picture *Five Easy Pieces* (1970). In the film, Dupea tries to get some plain toast that's not on the menu (a la carte). It was a simple request, but the waitress gets very rigid, despite Robert's creative ordering. Finally he says, "I'd like an omelet, plain, and a chicken salad sandwich on wheat toast, no mayonnaise, no butter, no lettuce. And a cup of coffee." The waitress repeats his order: "A #2, chicken salad sand. Hold the butter, the lettuce, the mayonnaise, and a cup of coffee. Anything else?" "Yeah", says Dupea "now all you have to do is hold the chicken, bring me the toast, give me a check for the chicken salad sandwich, and you haven't broken any rules." Confused, the waitress asks, "You want me to hold the chicken, huh?" Bobby quickly ends the conversation with "I want you to hold it between your knees." Note: In the film *Dogfight* (1991) Eddie Birdlace (River Phoenix) visits a restaurant with a girl named Rose on the night before going to Vietnam in 1963. When their waiter asks Rose (Lili Taylor), "Are you ready to order?" she answers, "Yes, goddammit. I'm going to have the fucking poached salmon, with the son-of-a-bitching rice, and a dirty bastard salad with a shitload of Roquefort dressing. Thank you. And um, who knows what this asshole wants." Trying to fit in, Eddie says, "Uh. I'll just take a fucking beer"

"I warn you gentlemen, I am not to be trifled with. To pull the tail of a lion is to open the mouth of trouble and reveal the teeth of revenge biting the tongue of deceit" - Victor Spinetti as Duke d'Escargot in the French Revolution spoof film *Start the Revolution without Me* (1970).

"I was trying to get away from a world I had known...and found myself looking up its ass" - Jane Fonda as prostitute Bree Daniels talks to her psychiatrist (Vivian Nathan) about life as a hooker in the motion picture *Klute* (1971).

"I'll be back" - The signature catchphrase used by actor Arnold Schwarzenegger in a number of his films. Much like director Alfred Hitchcock who liked to make a cameo appearance in each of his movies, actor Arnold Schwarzenegger enjoys using the phrase "I'll be back" in each of his films. The most notable "I'll be back" is from his role in the motion picture *The Terminator* (1984) wherein he plays a Terminator, a futuristic killing machine hunting for Sarah Connor (Linda Hamilton). When the Terminator discovers she's being held in police custody, it tells the police officer in charge, "I'll be back." It returns, alright—driving a car through the wall of the police department and killing all the officers in the building as it searches for Sarah Connor. In *Terminator 2: Judgment Day* (1991) Schwarzenegger plays a good Terminator charged with protecting Sarah Connor and her son from a more advanced T-1000 Terminator. In this sequel, Arnold says, "Stay here, I'll be back!" to Sarah's son as he goes to rescue his mother from gunfire. The phrase can also be heard in the following movies: In *Commando* (1985) as John Matrix tells his daughter's kidnapper, "I'll be back, Bennett!"; as Dutch, a Special Forces operative battling an alien hunter in *Predator* (1987); as Ben Richards in *The Running Man* (1987) "Killian! I'll be back!"; as Julius Benedict in *Twins* (1988) "If you're lying, I'll be back!"; Douglas Quaid in *Total Recall* (1990); in *Last Action Hero* (1993) as Jack Slater says, "I'll be back! Ha! You didn't know I was gonna say that, did you?", and in *The Sixth Day* (2000) he says, "Maybe I'll be back." Note: In the film *Ghostbusters II* (1989) the dying words of an evil 17th century Muldavian nobleman Vigo (Wilhelm von Homburg) proclaimed, "Death is but a door, time is but a window...I'll be back!" And, in the film *Heaven's Prisoner* (1996) Alec Baldwin as Dave Robicheaux says, "My wife had to be buried in a closed casket. I want you to think about that for a minute. Now, I'm gonna find those two men, and when I do, I'm gonna squeeze them extra hard, and if your name comes outta either one of their mouths, I'll be back here to feed your sorry fuckin' ass to the shrimp." *See also* "A plague on you!"

"I'll be taking these Huggies, and, uh, whatever cash you got" - Nicholas Cage as thief H. I. McDonnough who kidnaps a baby for his childless wife, and then stops by a convenience store to pick up some needed supplies in the motion picture *Raising Arizona* (1987).

"I'll get you even if I have to crawl back from the grave to do it" - Bette Davis as "clip-joint" hostess Mary Dwight swears revenge (she turns police informer) upon Johnny Vanning (Eduardo Ciannelli), the underworld kingpin responsible for killing her younger sister, Betty Strauber (Jane Bryan) when she refuses a life of prostitution in the motion picture *Marked Woman* (1937).

"I'll get you, my pretty, and your little dog, too" - The threatening words of the Wicked Witch of the West (Margaret Hamilton) to Dorothy Gale (Judy Garland), a young girl from Kansas whose tornado tossed house crushed the Wicked Witch of the East when it lands somewhere over the rainbow in the mystical land of Oz in the motion picture *The Wizard of Oz* (1939). When the Wicked Witch of the West asks, "Who killed my sister? Who killed the Witch of the East? Was it you?" Dorothy cowers and says, "No...No, it was an accident, I didn't mean to kill anybody." "Well, my little pretty, I can cause accidents, too," implies the wicked witch. Just then, Glinda the Good Witch of the North (Billie Burke) affixes the magical ruby slippers of the Wicked Witch of the East onto Dorothy's feet. Covetous of the shoe's powers, the Wicked Witch of the West cackles, "Their gone. The ruby slippers…what have you done with them?" Seeing the shoes on Dorothy's feet, the witch greedily says, "Give them back to me or I'll...Give me back my slippers. I'm the only one that knows how to use them. They're of no use to you. Give them back, give them back." When the wicked witch threatens to "fix" Glinda for meddling in her affairs, Glinda rebukes the evil witch by saying, "Rubbish, you have no power here. Begone! Before somebody drops a house on you." Conceding a temporary defeat, the wicked witch replies, "Very well, "I'll bide my time. And as for you, my fine lady. True, I can't attend to you here and now as I'd like, but just try to stay out of my way. Just try. I'll get you, my pretty, and your little dog, too." Later in the film, the wicked witch tells Dorothy's traveling companions Scarecrow (Ray Bolger) and Tin Man (Jack Haley) not to interfere with her plans to get the ruby slippers or she would "stuff a mattress" with the Scarecrow's insides and turn the Tin Man into "bee hive." When the Wicked Witch of the West sends an army of flying monkeys to capture Dorothy in the haunted forest, they tear Scarecrow to shreds: "They tore my legs off and they threw them over there. Then they took my chest out and they threw it over there." *See also* "How about a little fire, Scarecrow?", "Put 'em up! Put 'em up!" and "Silence Whippersnapper!!

"I'll give you a one way ticket to Harpland" - "Danny DeVito as Ralph, a small-time hood threatens adventurer Jack Colton (Michael Douglas) in the motion picture *The Jewel of the Nile* (1985).

"I'll give you a shot in the head!" - Catchphrase often spoken by Milton Berle on the classic variety program TEXACO STAR THEATER/NBC/1948-59. Another of his popular phrases was "I'll kwill you a mwillion times." Another sketch on the program involved a tiny stagehand with a huge powder puff who delivered a cloudy smack in the face when they yelled "Make-up!" for Berle.

"I'll kill ya" - The simple, clear and easy to understand sentiment delivered by a new recruit called 'Psycho' in the military comedy *Stripes* (1981). "The name's Francis Sawyer," he informs his army colleagues, "but everybody calls me Psycho. Anyone calls me Francis, and I'll kill ya...Also, I don't like no one touching my stuff. If I find any of you guys in my stuff, I'll kill ya. And I don't like no one touching me. Any of you homos touch me, and I'll kill ya." Note: In the film *Lock, Stock and Two Smoking Barrels* (1998) Vas Blackwood as Rory Breaker tells Nick the Greek (Stephen Marcus), "If you hold back anything, I'll kill ya. If you bend the truth or I think you're bending the truth, I'll kill ya. If you forget anything I'll kill ya. In fact, you're gonna have to work very hard to stay alive, Nick. Now do you understand everything I've said? Because if you don't, I'll kill ya."

"I'll knock you so flat, they could play you on a Victrola" - Delmer Daves as Beef Saunders who promises harm in the motion picture *Good News* (1930).

"I'll make him an offer he can't refuse" - The now classic veiled threat of Marlon Brando when he played the Mafia Don Vito Corleone in the Oscar winning movie *The Godfather* (1972) based on the novel by Mario Puzo. When 1940s singer Johnny Fontane (Al Martino) a "good Godson" of Don Corleone expresses a deep interest in starring in a Hollywood war film being produced by movie big shot Jack Woltz (John Marley), the Godfather tells Johnny, "He's a businessman. I'll make him an offer he can't refuse." Don Vito then sends his emissary Tom Hagen (Robert Duvall) to offer the Don's undying friendship, if Woltz could do this favor. But Mr. Woltz, who held a grudge against Johnny Fontane for messing around with one of his starlets, refuses the Godfather's request saying, "Now you listen to me, you smooth talking son-of-a-bitch! Let me lay it on the line for you and your boss, whoever he is. Johnny Fontane will never get that movie! I don't care how many dago guinea wop greaseball goombahs come out of the woodwork!" Soon after, Mr. Woltz wakes one morning to find the decapitated head of his $600,000 race horse (Khartoum) sharing the blood stained satin sheets of his bed. Not surprisingly, Johnny Fontane got a call to report to work on the film. The 'Godfather' movie is filled with extreme examples of graphic violence and retribution as when Santino 'Sonny' Corleone (James Caan) says, "They hit us. So we hit them back." When Vito Corleone sends wiseguy Luca Brasi (Lenny Montana) to snoop around the Tattaglia family, one man impales Luca's left hand onto a tavern countertop while another man chokes him to death with a cord. Later, the Corleone family receives fish bundled in a newspaper. This is the Sicilian message: "Luca Brasi sleeps with the fishes." When Don Corleone is shot in the streets at a neighborhood produce stand, Michael Corleone (Al Pacino) caps a crooked police commissioner in the head with two bullets at an Italian restaurant. And when Sonny Corleone rushes to the home of his sister to protect her from an abusive husband, he is shot to death at a causeway tollbooth by a hail of machine gun bullets. With the death of Vito Corleone, a gruesome list of killings were initiated by the new Godfather Don Michael Corleone who ironically was attending the baptism of his sister's baby, where he answered, "Yes" to the question "Do you renounce the devil?" Throughout the film and its sequels, the Corleone family members made it very clear that their violent actions were "not personal." They were "strictly business."

"I'll mow you down!" - Comic retort of ventriloquist dummy Charlie McCarthy when he got angry at someone—usually comedian W. C. Fields. Ventriloquist Edgar Bergen and his wisecracking wooden dummy Charlie McCarthy were icons of Americana performing on stage, radio, movies and television from the 1920-70s. In 1936, Edgar Bergen had his own radio show on THE CHASE AND SANBORN HOUR. It was at this time that the legendary feud between the brassy Charlie McCarthy and the inebriated comedian/movie star W. C. Fields occurred. A typical on-air exchange:

Fields: Tell me Charlie, is it true your father was a gateleg table?
Charlie: Well, if it is, your father was under it.

Fields: Quiet, you flop house for termites, I'll whittle you down to a coat hanger.
Charlie: [Screaming] I'll mow you down, so help me, I'll Mooowww ya' down.

Another dummy character introduced into Bergen's act included Mortimer Snerd, a chuckling, dimwitted, silly buck-toothed country bumpkin. Once Edgar Bergen appeared on an episode of THE JACK BENNY SHOW/CBS/1950-65 where Jack Benny visited Bergen's home only to find his famous dummies actually walking around like real people. When Jack asked Mortimer Snerd how he got so stupid? Mortimer replied, "Well...er...I got a good deal and I couldn't turn it down."

"I'll never forget the last time you had your picture on the front page. Your mouth was continued on page two" - Lynn Overman as Scoop McPhail talks about Martha Bellows (Martha Raye) after she says, "Gee, I-I'm so cute! I'll bet they put my picture on the front page" in the motion picture *The Big Broadcast of 1938* (1938)

"I'll organize revolt, exact a death for a death, and I'll never rest until every Saxon in this shire can stand up free men and strike a blow for Richard and England....I'm only just beginning. From this night forward I'll use every means in my power to fight you!" - Errol Flynn as Sir Robin of Locksley defies the tyrannical rule of Prince John (Claude Rains) in the motion picture *The Adventures of Robin Hood* (1938). Taking refuge in Sherwood Forest, Robin rallies support for his cause: "I've called you here as freeborn Englishman, loyal to your king. While he reigned over us, we lived in peace. But since Prince John has seized the regency, Guy of Gisbourne and the rest of the traitors have murdered and pillaged. You've all suffered from their cruelty—the ear loppings, the beatings, the blindings with hot irons, the burning of our farms and homes, the mistreatment of our women. It's time we put an end to this! Now, this forest is wide. It can shelter and clothe and feed a band of good determine men—good swordsmen, good archers, good fighters. Men, if you willing to fight for your people. I want you! Are you with me, men?"

"I will personally blow your brains out" - Promise of Lee Marvin in his role of Major Reisman in the military action adventure *The Dirty Dozen* (1967). When Reisman is given twelve murderers/rapists who volunteered for a secret mission behind German lines, he reviews his reluctant troops and says, "You all volunteered for a mission that gives you just three ways to go. Either you can foul up in training and be shipped back here for immediate execution of sentence, or you can foul up in combat, in which case I will personally blow your brains out, or you can do as you're told, in which case you might just get by." An army psychiatrist summarized Reisman's 'Dirty Dozen' crew saying, "Along with these other results, it gives you just the most twisted, antisocial bunch of psychopathic deformities, I have ever run into...You've got one religious maniac, one malignant dwarf, two near idiots, and the rest I don't even want to think about."

"I'll rip your tongue off and slap ya silly with it!" - Lindsay Armstrong Black as Herman Umgar, a German hermit expresses distain in the motion picture *The Worm Eaters* (1977).

"I'll see you in hell" - Jaime Lee Curtis as Laurie Strode says her final goodbye to her brother Michael Myers in the classic horror film *Halloween Resurrection* (2002). In the film, Laurie Strode had been incarcerated in Grace Andersen Sanitarium for chopping off the head of an innocent man (whom Laurie thought was her evil brother, Michael). For three years Laurie waits for the return of her brother. When he arrives, she tries to trap him in an elaborate maze of ropes, but this fails. As they both begin to fall off the roof Michael stabs his sister in the back with a knife. Before she plummets to the ground, Laurie, as a gesture of sisterly love, kisses Michael's rubber mask and says, "I'll see you in hell, Michael" Note: In the film *The Omen* (1976), Patrick Troughton as Father Brennan discovers that the son of businessman Robert Thorn (Gregory Peck) is actually the prophesied Anti-Christ (with 666 on his scalp). When Brennan says, "He must DIE! Mr. Thorn" the boy's father responds, "Now, I've heard you. I want you to hear me: I NEVER want to see you again. Then Father Brennan warns, "You'll see me in HELL, Mr. Thorn. There, we will share out our centuries." In the western film *Unforgiven* (1992) Gene Hackman as Little Bill Daggett, a ruthless frontier sheriff says, "I'll see you in hell, William Munny' just before Munny, a gunslinger called out of retirement, shoots Daggett dead. And in the classic Japanese samurai film *Yojimbo* (1961), a dying gangster named Unosuke the gunfighter (Tatsuya Nakadai) tells his killer, Sanjuro the Samurai (Toshirô Mifune), "The entrance to hell…I'll be waiting there for you." *See also* "I met him fifteen years ago..."

"I'll send you a love letter" - In the film *Blue Velvet* (1986) Kyle MacLachlan plays Jeffrey Beaumont whom recently returned to his hometown only to find a severed ear in a field. His investigation leads to an evil psychotic named Frank Booth (Dennis Hopper) who quickly explains, "Nobody fucks with me." If someone did, Frank would send them a love letter. As he warns a stunned Jeffrey, "I'll send you a love letter! Straight from my heart, fucker! You know what a love letter is? It's a bullet from a fucking gun, fucker! You receive a love letter from me; you're fucked forever! You understand, fuck? I'll send you straight to hell, fucker!" Note: In the spirit of the "don't fuck with me" mentality, Nick Nolte as Mick Brennan said, "You fuck with me, better you piss a kidney stone through your hard on" to Luis Valentin (Luis Guzman) in the motion picture *Q & A* (1990).

"I'll stare the bastard in the face as he screams to God, and I'll laugh harder when he whimpers like a baby. And when his eyes go dead, the hell I send him to will seem like heaven after what I've done to him" - Mickey Rourke as Marv, a tough as nails street fighter who seeks to avenge the murder of a beautiful hooker in the motion picture *Sin City* (2005)

"I'll torture you so slowly you'll think it's a career. I'll kill your friends, your family and the bitch you took to the prom" - Richard E. Grant as Darwin Mayflower threatens wisecracking cat burglar Eddie (Bruce Willis) in the box-office bomb *Hudson Hawk* (1991). Unperturbed, Eddie replies, "Betty Jo Byarsky? I can get you an address on that, if you want."

"I'll turn your balls into earrings" - Not-so-veiled threat of Jack Palance in the western comedy *City Slickers II: The Legend of Curly's Gold* (1994). In the film, Jack Palance plays the twin brother of a now deceased rugged trail boss/guide called Curly.

When spoken to out of turn, Curly's brother barks, "You ever talk to me like that again and I'll turn your balls into earrings." In the first film *City Slickers (1991),* Mitch Robbins (Billy Crystal) a tenderfoot who took part in a trail drive jokingly approaches his gruff trail boss and quips, "Hi, Curly, Kill anybody today?" Curly menacingly replies, "Day ain't over yet." At Curly's eulogy Cookie (Tracey Walter) advises, "Lord, we give you Curly. Try not to piss him off." Note: Instead of turning "balls" into earrings Curly might check out the suggestion of Robert Hays as Buchinski the pimp who tells 'Dirty' Harry Callahan (Clint Eastwood), "You can end up with your balls in spaghetti sauce" in the movie *The Enforcer* (1976). In the film, *Payback* (1999) Kris Kristofferson as Bronson says, "You tell me where he is, and I'll kill you quick. You can die without ever finding out what your left ball tastes like."

"I wish you was a wishing well, so I could tie a bucket to you and sink you" - James Cagney as Prohibition gangster Tom Powers in the motion picture *Public Enemy* (1931). Sitting at breakfast, Tom's blond girlfriend Kitty (Mae Clarke) alludes to whether or not Tom cares for her. Annoyed at her question, Tom recites his now classic "wishing well" put-down and them smashes a grapefruit in her face. One of movie's more memorable lines came from Tommy's female acquaintance Gwen Allen (Jean Harlow) when she said, "You are so different, Tommy, very different. The men I know, and I've known dozens of them. Oh, they're so nice, so polished, so considerate. Most women like that type. I guess they're afraid of the other kind. I thought I was, too. But you're so strong. You don't give; You take. Oh Tommy, I could love you to death." At the end of the film, Tommy gets shot. His dying words: "I ain't so tough."

"I would grab your scrotum, I would stretch it over your head and I would use you as a punching bag" - Rosie O'Donnell as Lucille Toody informs her policeman husband Gunther (David Johansen) what she would do to him if she caught him cheating in the motion picture *Car 54, Where Are You?* (1994).

"I'd like Frank Shirley, my boss, right here tonight" - Holiday wish of Clark W. Griswold (Chevy Chase) in the Yule tide comedy *Christmas Vacation* (1989). When Clark discovers that he is not getting a Christmas bonus from his boss and that his holiday is turning into a disaster, he offers this little tirade to his family members: "Hey! If any of you are looking for any last-minute gift ideas for me, I have one. I'd like Frank Shirley, my boss, right here tonight. I want him brought from his happy holiday slumber over there on Melody Lane with all the other rich people and I want him brought right here, with a big ribbon on his head, and I want to look him straight in the eye and I want to tell him what a cheap, lying, no-good, rotten, four-flushing, low-life, snake-licking, dirt-eating, inbred, overstuffed, ignorant, blood-sucking, dog-kissing, brainless, dickless, hopeless, heartless, fat-ass, bug-eyed, stiff-legged, spotty-lipped, worm-headed sack of monkey shit he is! Hallelujah!"

"I'd like to break her foul, useless little neck" - Farley Granger as Guy Haines yells over the phone to his girlfriend Anne Morton (Ruth Roman) about his unfaithful wife, Miriam (Laura Elliott) who refuses to give him a divorce in the motion picture *Strangers on a Train* (1951).

"I wouldn't..." - This familiar phrase is often used at the beginning of a put-down. The following are samples of some outrageous "I wouldn't" sayings in movie history: "I wouldn't marry you if you were young, which you can't be, if you were honest, but you never were, or if you were about to die tomorrow, which is too much to hope for."—Charlotte Henry in *March of the Wooden Soldiers* (1934); "I wouldn't give you two cents for all your fancy rules if behind them they didn't have a little ordinary everyday human kindness, and a little looking out for the other fella, too" —James Stewart in *Mr. Smith Goes to Washington* (1939); "I wouldn't suck your lousy dick if I was suffocating and there was oxygen in your balls!" —Mink Stole as Taffy in *Female Trouble* (1975); "I wouldn't pee on him if his heart was on fire" —David Strathairn in *Matewan* (1987); "I wouldn't spare a drop of piss on her if she was burnin' to death."; —Tom Berenger in *The Gingerbread Man* (1998); "I wouldn't live with you if the world was flooded with piss and you lived in a tree." —Martha Plimpton in *Parenthood* (1989).

"I'd rather kiss a tarantula" - Gene Kelly as silent movie star Don Lockwood expresses his opinion of costar Lina Lamont (Jean Hagan) in the musical motion picture *Singin' in the Rain* (1952). To prove his point, Don yells, "Hey, Joe...get me a tarantula!"

"I'd rather set my head on fire and have it put out with a sledgehammer" - Nancy Parsons as a nurse who is extremely reluctant to see what's wrong with a looney hospital patient (Dan Aykroyd) in the motion picture *Loose Cannons* (1990).

"If a country goes mad, it has the right to commit every horror within its walls." - Nigel Bruce as Britain's Prince of Wales comments on the French Revolution to noblewoman Marguerite Blakeney (Merle Oberon) in the motion picture *The Scarlet Pimpernel* (1935). Marguerite's husband Percy (Leslie Howard) was in reality a rebel known as 'The Scarlet Pimpernel' whom according to a poem "They seek him here. They seek him there. Those Frenchies seek him everywhere. Is he in Heaven? Is he in Hell? That damned elusive Pimpernel?"

"If brains were birdshit you'd have a clean cage" - Rodrigo Obregón as drug lord Seth Romero in the motion picture *Hard Ticket to Hawaii* (1987).

"If bullshit were poetry, you'd be Shakespeare" - Michael Paré as Robby Durrell, prince of the vice squad in the motion picture *Strip Search* (1997).

"If by accident this door should open during the night, you would be greeted by six bullets—not one of which would miss its mark" - Florence Vidor as the Grand Duchess advises her waiter (Adolphe Menjou) that it wouldn't be healthy to enter her bedroom in the motion picture *The Grand Duchess and the Waiter* (1926). *See also* "That's a Smith & Wesson…"

"If I'm dead, kill him" - Paul Newman as outlaw Butch Cassidy in the western adventure *Butch Cassidy and the Sundance Kid. (1969).* About to enter into knife fight with huge opponent Harvey Logan (Ted Cassidy) for control of the Hole-in-the-Wall Gang, Butch asks for reassurance from his partner the Sundance Kid (Robert Redford), saying, "Listen, I don't mean to be a sore loser but when it's done, if I'm dead, kill

him." Note: In the film *A Low Down Dirty Shame* (1994) Salli Richardson as Angela asks a similar request to friend Shame (Keenan Ivory Wayans): "Shame, just promise me you'll smoke his ass." Shame answers, "Like a motherfucking pack of Kools."

"If I wanted a big brother, I wouldn't have killed mine" - Tom Whiteknight as Texas college football player in the motion picture *Necessary Roughness* (1991).

"If I'd known how much you talked, I'd never have come out of my coma" - Charles Laughton as Sir Wilfrid Robarts complains to his verbose nurse Miss Plimsoll (Elsa Lanchester) in the motion picture *Witness for the Prosecution* (1957). On the subject of 'hats' Sir Wilfrid says, "I'm constantly surprised that women's hats do not provoke more murders."

"If icky girl keep talking that way, big stwong man is going to kick her teeth wight down her thwoat" - Groucho Marx as Professor Wagstaff threatens college student Connie Bailey (Thelma Todd) who tries to use baby talk ("Is great big stwong man going to show little icky baby all about the bad football signals?) to gain access to the opposing team's play book in the motion picture *Horse Feathers* (1932).

"If it turns out there is a God, I don't think He's evil. The worst thing you can say about Him is that He's basically an underachiever" - Woody Allen as devout coward Boris Dimitrovich Gruschenko comments on the Creator in the motion picture *Love and Death* (1975). Note: In the film *Fanny and Alexander* (1983) a Swede named Alexander Ekdahl (Bertil Guve) comments "If there is a God, he is a shit."

"If it was raining hundred dollar bills, you'd be out looking for a dime you lost someplace" - Barbara Stanwyck as newspaper columnist Ann Mitchell lambastes her editor (James Gleason) for not recognizing a good news story in the motion picture *Meet John Doe* (1941). Note: In the film *Buried Alive 2* (1997) Randy Riskin (Stephen Caffrey) says, "It could be raining brains and you wouldn't get wet."

"If only Dad had the guts to knock Mom cold once" - James Dean as Jim, a troubled teenager comments on his father's (Jim Backus) henpecked condition in the motion picture *Rebel Without a Cause* (1955).

"If the international finance-Jewry inside and outside Europe should succeed in plunging the nations into a world war yet again, then the outcome will not be the victory of Jewry, but rather the annihilation of the Jewish race in Europe!" - The opinion of Nazi leader Adolf Hitler in the German documentary film *Der Ewige Jude* aka *The Eternal Jew* (1940). The film depicts Jews as "filthy, evil, corrupt, and intent on world domination."

"If they hadn't shot my dick off in 'Nam, I'd whip it out and piss in your face!" - Samuel L. Jackson as Colonel Ron in the motion picture *The Search for One-eye Jimmy* (1994).

"If this assignment gets blown, I want to go on record right now, that this is the most stupid, dimwitted, idiotic, moronic piece of putrefied garbage that I have ever in my entire professional career, ever had the displeasure of being involved with" - Richard Dreyfus as police detective Chris Lecce expresses his anger to Gina Garrett (Rosie O'Donnell) from the DA's office in the motion picture *Another Stakeout* (1993).

"If the honeymoon doesn't work out, let's not get a divorce, let's kill each other" - Jane Fonda as newly wed Corie Bratter talks to her lawyer husband Paul (Robert Redford) as they plan to spend a romantic six days in New York's Park Plaza hotel in the motion picture *Barefoot in the Park* (1967).

"If you ain't a cowboy, you ain't worth shit" - The personal philosophy of Eddie (Sam Shepard), a broken-down Texas rodeo cowboy with a pick-up truck in the motion picture *Fool for Love* (1985).

"If you ain't any better than a nigger, son, who are you better than?" - Gene Hackman as FBI agent Rupert Anderson remembers his father's words when he poisoned a successful black farmer's mule in the motion picture *Mississippi Burning* (1988). While in the South investigating civil rights violations, Sheriff Ray Stuckey (Gailard Sartain) refutes Anderson's racial equality principles and says, "The rest of America don't mean a damn thing. You in Mississippi now." KKK member Frank Bailey (Michael Rooker) reinforces the sheriff's sentiments by revealing his willingness to kill Negroes with the nasty comment, "I wouldn't give it no more thought than wringing a cat's neck." Note: In the film *Show Boat* (1936) Donald Cook as Steve says to a sheriff, "You wouldn't call a man a white man that had Negro blood in him, would you?" The Sheriff replies, "No, I wouldn't; not in Mississippi. One drop of Negro blood makes you a Negro in these parts!"

"If you dig, I promise you when the time comes I'll shoot you through the back of the head. You don't like that? I can shoot you in the testicles right now and you can bleed to death" - Delroy Lindo as Jackson offering options to Robert (Ewan McGregor) after he refuses to dig a hole for his soon-to-be-dead body in the motion picture *A Life Less Ordinary* (1997). Note: In the film *Men of Respect* (1991) a mobster named Duffy (Peter Boyle) says, "He's history. Tomorrow, he'll be geography."

"If you don't have my money for me, I'll crack your fucking head in front of everyone in the bank. And just about the time I get out of jail, hopefully, you'll be coming out of your coma. But guess what? I'll crack your fucking head again! 'Cause I'm fucking stupid! I don't give a fuck about jail! That's my business. That's what I do" - Joe Pesci as Las Vegas mobster Nicky Santoro in the motion picture *Casino (*1995) Recalling Nicky's method of operation, casino operator Sam "Ace" Rothstein (Robert De Niro) says, "No matter how big a guy was, Nicky would take him on. You beat Nicky with fists, he comes back with a bat; you beat him with a knife, he comes back with a gun; and if you beat him with a gun, you better kill 'em, 'cause he'll be coming back and back, until one of you is dead."

"If you fuck this up, I'm going to take your nuts and tie 'em into a knot and run them through my shredder" - Earl Billings as police Captain Al Giles intimidates detectives Chris Leece (Richard Dreyfus) and Bill Reimers (Emilio Estevez) in the motion picture *Stakeout* (1987).

"If you had gas for brains, you couldn't back a piss-ant out of a pea shell" - Jeff Bridges as Earl Jackson, Jr., a North Carolina moon shiner shares some well chosen words with his competition in the motion picture *The Last American Hero aka Hard Driver* (1973).

"If you had to kill one person to cure cancer, wouldn't you have to do that?" - The foul question posed by Gene Hackman as research scientist Dr. Lawrence Myrick in the motion picture *Extreme Measures* (1996). His associate Dr. Guy Luthan (Hugh Grant) sums up Myrick's personality with "You're quite a creepy person."

"If you look around the table and you can't tell who the sucker is, it's you." - John Turturro as infamous game show contestant Herbie Stempel offers a slice of life observation in the motion picture *Quiz Show* (1994).

"If you say three, Mister, you'll never hear the man count ten" - John Wayne as Sean 'Trooper' Thornton, an ex-boxer from America returns to his family's roots in Ireland and purchases a small house where his family formerly lived in the motion picture *The Quiet Man* (1952). Unfortunately, Sean makes an enemy of local Red Will Danaher (Victor McLaughlin) who had plans of buying the property himself. During a visit to the local pub, Sean tries to make friends with Danaher, but he'd have nothing to do with it. When Will instigates a fight, Sean strongly advises him, "If you say three, Mister, you'll never hear the man count ten." Will had muttered the threat, "He'll regret it to his dying day...if he ever lives that long." Later in the film, Sean marries Will's sister, Mary Kate Danaher (Maureen O'Hara) and Sean and Will come to blows in a rowdy knock-down drag-out fight which goes from one end of the town to the other.

"If you try to eat my face off, or take over my body, you're going to be very sorry, Mister" - Steve Guttenberg as tour boat operator Jack Bonner pathetically trying to ward off Walter (Brian Dennehy) who unmasked his human disguise to reveal he was actually a glowing outer space alien in the motion picture *Cocoon* (1985). Luckily, the aliens were friendly.

"If your gonna run with the big dogs then you better learn to piss on bigger trees" - Malcolm McDowell as jealous husband Roger Everet offers some free advice to his wife's lover, womanizing ad executive Jim Lomax (C. Thomas Howell) in the motion picture *Dangerous Indiscretions* (1994).

"If you'll be kind enough to glance between my shoulder blades, Mr. and Mrs. Gubbins, you'll find there a knife buried to the hilt. On its handle are your initials." - Jack Carson as powerful publicist Matt Libby speaks to Hollywood performers Norman Maine (James Mason) and Esther Blodgett (Judy Garland) in the motion picture *A Star is Born* (1954).

"Imagine you're a deer. You're prancing around. You get thirsty. You spot a little brook. You put your little deer lips down to the clear water - *BAM!* A fuckin' bullet rips off part of your head! Your brains are lying on the ground in little bloody pieces. Now I ask you, do you give a fuck what kind of pants the son-of-a-bitch who shot you was wearing?!" - Marisa Tomei as Mona Lisa Vito gives a fashion lesson in the motion picture *My Cousin Vinny* (1992).

"In a surprise announcement, the Republican National Committee has revealed it is bankrupt. A spokesman for the party said they had plenty of money in their accounts last week, but today they just don't know where the money has gone. But not everybody is going begging. Amnesty International, Greenpeace and the United Negro College Fund announced record earnings this week, due mostly to large, anonymous donations" - TV newscaster heard in the final moments of the motion picture *Sneakers* (1992). The withdrawal of funds was orchestrated by a group of computer hackers who had been manipulated by a sinister government organization to retrieve a valuable computer software program ("THE code breaker") that could literally decrpyt any computer in the world. Hacker Martin Bishop (Robert Redford) explained the consequences of such a program with the simple statement, "No more secrets." The controller of this "black box" could manipulate on a whim the stock markets, the currency markets or the commodities markets of the world. Stunned, his colleague Donald Crease (Sidney Poitier) says, "There isn't a government on this planet that wouldn't kill us all for that thing."

"In the East, the Far East, when a person is sentenced to death, they're sent to a place where they can't escape, never knowing when an executioner may step up behind them, and fire a bullet into the back of their head." - Robert Blake as The Mystery Man talks to Peter Dayton (Bathazar Getty) on the phone in the motion picture *Lost Highway* (1997). Pete made love to Renee Madison (Patricia Arquette) the blond mistress of a ruthless and unforgiving man named Mr. Eddy (Robert Loggia) who calls Pete on the phone and says," I'm really glad to know you're doin good, Pete. Hey, I want you to talk to a friend of mine."

"In Japan, men come first; women come second" - Sexist remark of Japanese espionage leader Tanaka (codename: "Tiger") in the motion picture *You Only Live Twice* (1967). Tanaka tells Bond the above sentiment, just as a bevy of beautiful Asian women prepare to bath and massage the two men. Note: In the Chinese film *Shanghai Triad* aka *Yao a yao yao dao waipo quao* (1995) Baotian Li as gang boss Liu Tang says, "Women's business is nothing but wind. Men's business, no matter how small, is important."

"In NATO, you have to have unanimous approval from all the member nations. It's like getting a troop of horses to piss at the same time" - Lee J. Cobb as Lt. General Henry Steedman explains the ineffectiveness of North Atlantic Treaty Organization in the motion picture *That Lucky Touch* (1975).

"In the old days, I would have raped and tortured you for hours. There's just no time for life's simple pleasures anymore. Oh, well. Goodnight." - Jeff Kober as mercenary Major West waxes nostalgic in the motion picture *Automatic (*1994).

"In the old days they used to put your eyes out with red-hot poker. Any of those bikini bombshells you're always watching worth a red-hot poker?" - Thelma Ritter as nurse Stella telling her patient L. B. 'Jeff' Jeffries (James Stewart)—whose been peeping into the apartment building windows next-door—that maybe he should mind his own business in the Alfred Hitchcock classic motion picture *Rear Window* (1954).

"Intelligence officer. Stupidity officer is more like it. Pentagon wants to open a Stupidity Division, they know who they can get to lead it" - Frank Sinatra as Korean War veteran Major Bennett Marco in the motion picture *The Manchurian Candidate* (1962).

"Into the mud, scum queen!" - In the film *The Man with Two Brains* (1983) brilliant surgeon Michael Hfuhruhurr (Steve Martin) gets pissed at his sadistic sex-crazed wife (Kathleen Turner) and tosses her to the ground. Note: In the film *Big Street* (1942) Gloria Lyons insults a fellow female by saying, "That dame is a lump of mud."

"Is that your nose or did a bus park on your face?" - One of the many self-deprecating remarks fireman C. D. 'Charlie' Bales (Steve Martin) recites to a crowd of tavern patrons in the comedy film *Roxanne* (1987). When a loudmouth customer insults Charlie (called him a "big nose") in a local bar, Charlie bests the man in a dual of wits. The following is a list of Charlie's witticisms:

- *Obvious:* 'Excuse me! Is that your nose or did a bus park on your face?'
- *Meteorological:* 'Everybody take cover, she's going to blow!'
- *Fashionable:* 'You know, you could de-emphasize your nose if you wore something larger...like Wyoming.'
- *Personal:* 'Well! Here we are. Just the three of us.'
- *Punctual:* 'All right, Dillman, your nose was on time, but you were fifteen minutes late.'
- *Envious:* 'Ohhh! I wish I were you. Gosh! To be able to smell your own ear.'
- *Naughty:* 'Pardon me, sir, some of the ladies have asked if you wouldn't mind putting that thing away.'
- *Philosophical:* 'You know it's not the size of a nose that matters, it's what in it.
- *Humorous:* 'Laugh and the world laughs with you; sneeze and its goodbye Seattle.'
- *Commercial:* 'Hi! I'm Carl Shad and I can paint that nose for $39.95.'
- *Polite:* 'Would you mind not bobbing your head, the orchestra keeps changing tempo.' [Singing] "He's got the whole world in his nose."
- *Sympathetic:* 'Ah!!! What happened? Did your parents lose a bet with God?'
- *Complimentary:* 'You must love the little birdies to give them this to perch on.'
- *Scientific:* 'Say! Does that thing influence the tides?'
- *Obscure:* 'I'd hate to see the grindstone.'
- *Inquiry:* 'When you stop and smell the flowers, are they afraid?'
- *French:* ' Say! The pigs have refused to find any more truffles until you leave.'
- *Pornographic:* ' Finally! A man who can satisfy two women at once.'
- *Religious:* 'The Lord giveth, and he just kept on giving it, didn't He?'

- *Disgusting:* 'Say! Who mows your nose hair?'
- *Paranoid:* 'Say! Keep that guy away from my cocaine.'
- *Aromatic:* 'It must be wonderful to wake up in the morning and smell the coffee—in Brazil.'
- *Appreciative:* 'Oh! How original! Most people just have their teeth capped.'
- *Dirty:* 'Your name wouldn't happen to be Dick, would it?'

The above examples were inspired from the play *Cyrano De Bergerac* written by Edmond Rostand (1868-1918). In 1950, Jóse Ferrer portrayed Cyrano in the United Artists film based on the play and magnificently delivers a volley of put-downs from Rostand's classic work (Scene 1.IV).

.

In the film, Vicomte de Valvert (Albert Cavens) tries to insult Cyrano and says, "I'll treat him to…one of my quips! See here! (He goes up to Cyrano, who is watching him, and with a conceited air) "Sir, your nose is...hmm...it is...very big!" In a grave voice, Cyrano replies, "Very…Is that all?" Then Cyrano proceeds to embarrass The Vicomte. Here is Cyrano's (Jose Ferrer) response:

"Ah no! young blade! That was a trifle short! You might have said at least a hundred things. By varying the tone...like this, suppose:

- *Aggressive:* 'Sir, if I had such a nose, I'd amputate it!'
- *Friendly:* 'When you sup, it must annoy you, dipping in your cup; You need a drinking-bowl of special shape!'
- *Descriptive:* 'Tis a rock!...a peak!...a cape! —A cape, forsooth! 'Tis a peninsular!'
- *Curious:* 'How serves that oblong capsular? For scissor-sheath? Or pot to hold your ink?'
- *Gracious:* 'You love the little birds, I think? I see you've managed with a fond research to find their tiny claws a roomy perch!'
- *Truculent:* When you smoke your pipe...suppose That the tobacco-smoke spouts from your nose—Do not the neighbors, as the fumes rise higher, Cry terror-struck: "The chimney is afire"?'
- *Considerate:* 'Take care...your head bowed low by such a weight...lest head o'er heels you go!'
- *Tender:* 'Pray get a small umbrella made, Lest its bright color in the sun should fade!'
- *Pedantic:* 'That beast Aristophanes'
- *Names:* 'Hippocamelelephantoles Must have possessed just such a solid lump Of flesh and bone, beneath his forehead's bump!'
- *Cavalier:* The last fashion, friend, that hook? To hang your hat on? 'Tis a useful crook!'
- *Emphatic:* 'No wind, O majestic nose, Can give THEE cold!—save when the mistral blows!'
- *Dramatic:* 'When it bleeds, what a Red Sea!'
- *Admiring:* Sign for a perfumery!'

- *Lyric:* 'Is this a conch? ... a Triton you?'
- *Simple:* 'When is the monument on view?'
- *Rustic:* 'That thing a nose? Marry-come-up! 'Tis a dwarf pumpkin, or a prize turnip!'
- *Military:* 'Point against cavalry!'
- *Practical:* 'Put it in a lottery! Assuredly 'twould be the biggest prize!' Or...parodying Pyramus' sighs...'Behold the nose that mars the harmony. Of its master's phiz! blushing its treachery!'

"—Such, my dear sir, is what you might have said, Had you of wit or letters the least jot: But, O most lamentable man!—of wit You never had an atom, and of letters. You have three letters only!—they spell Ass! And—had you had the necessary wit, To serve me all the pleasantries I quote Before this noble audience ...e'en so, You would not have been let to utter one—Nay, not the half or quarter of such jest! I take them from myself all in good part, but not from any other man that breathes must have possessed just such a solid lump."

"Is this an ultimatum? Answer me, you ball-busting, castrating, son of a cunt bitch! Is this an ultimatum or not?" - Jack Nicholson as Jonathan Fuerst shows off his extensive vocabulary in the motion picture *Carnal Knowledge* (1971).

"Is this the Cocksucker residence?" - Kathleen Turner as Beverly Sutphin makes a crank call to her nosey neighbor Dottie Hinkle (Mink Stole) in the motion picture *Serial Mom* (1994). Unappreciative of Beverly's intrusive phone calls, Dottie yells, "God damn you! Stop calling here!" But Beverly continues her taunts, "Is this 4215 Pussy Way?" Incensed, Dottie shouts, "You bitch!" Beverly concludes, "Now let me check the zip code. Two-one-two-fuck-you?"

"It's a terrible thing to hate your mother. But I didn't always hate her. When I was a child, I only kind of disliked her" - Laurence Harvey as Medal of Honor winner Staff Sgt. Raymond Shaw whose controlling mother (Angela Lansbury) is behind an assassination attempt on a U. S. Presidential hopeful in the political thriller *The Manchurian Candidate* (1962). Raymond (under the influence of mind control) later shoots his mother in the head with a snipers rifle as she sat on the platform next to a politician during a presidential candidate nomination ceremony.

"It's for sure a white man's world in America" - Ruth Attaway as a poor black senior citizen named Louise frustrated after she sees an addled gardener named Chance (Peter Sellers) posing as an important presidential advisor in the motion picture *Being There* (1979). Pointing to the TV tube Louise shouts, "Look here: I raised that boy since he was the size of a piss ant. And I'll say right now, he never learned to read and write. No, sir. Had no brains at all. Was stuffed with rice pudding between the ears. Shortchanged by the Lord, and dumb as a jackass. Look at him now! Yes, sir, all you've gotta be is white in America, to get whatever you want. Gobbledy-gook!"

"It's I who renounce you. In the name of Satan, I place a curse upon you...my revenge will strike down you and your accursed house...I shall return to torment you and to destroy throughout the nights of time" - Barbara Steele as witch Princess Katia burns at the stake at the direct orders of her brother (Enrico Oliveri) in the horror classic *Black Sunday* (1961). Centuries later, a drop of blood mingles with her bones and her reincarnated body wreaks havoc on the family's descendants. Note: In the movie *American Gothic* (1988) when Rod Steiger loses his family in a tragedy, he cries, "I renounce you, God I renounce you and I give my soul to Satan."

"It's just been revoked" - Detective Roger Murtaugh's (Danny Glover) final remark to a nefarious smuggling kingpin Arjen Rudd (Joss Ackland) in the action film *Lethal Weapon 2* (1989). At the end of a trail of mayhem and murder, Rudd tries to hide behind his diplomatic immunity. But Murtaugh says, "It's just been revoked" and then shoots the man in the line of duty. Earlier in the film, Roger was attacked by a couple of Rudd's hired killers, and survived the encounter by using a portable nail gun as a weapon. "Nailed them both," Roger quips. When Roger's wounded partner Martin Riggs (Mel Gibson) asks did we get "the bad guys" Rogers tells him, "They've been decaffeinated."

"It's lonely being a cannibal. You don't get that many friends" - Jeffrey Jones as Hart, a man living at a remote outpost in the Sierra Nevadas of 1847 in the motion picture *Ravenous (*1999). When a Scottish stranger named Colquhoun (Richard Carlyle) tells a story about wagon train members who had no food, he jokes, "I said no food. I didn't say there was nothing to eat."

"It is no concern of ours how you run your own planet, but if you threaten to extend your violence, this Earth of yours will be reduced to a burned-out cinder. Your choice is simple: join us and live in peace, or pursue your present course and face obliteration. We shall be waiting for your answer. The decision rests with you." Michael Rennie as Klaatu, an emissary from a distant federation of planets who traveled to Earth in a flying saucer to warn the human race of the dangers of their hostile nature in the classic sci-fi motion picture *The Day the Earth Stood Still* (1951), Earlier, Klaatu revealed his people's solution for their violence: "For our policemen, we created a race of robots. Their function is to patrol the planets in spaceships like this one and preserve the peace. In matters of aggression, we have given them absolute power over us. This power cannot be revoked. At the first sign of violence, they act automatically against the aggressor. The penalty for provoking their action is too terrible to risk. The result is, we live in peace, without arms or armies, secure in the knowledge that we are free from aggression and war. Free to pursue more...profitable enterprises."

"It's None of Your Damn Business!" - In the film *The American President* (1996), widowed President Andrew Shepherd (Michael Douglas) becomes infatuated with a beautiful redheaded lobbyist named Sydney Ellen Wade (Annette Benning). When Andrew decides to personally order some flowers for her, one of his aides, Lewis (Michael J. Fox) enters the room and asks, "Who are your calling, sir?" The President who desires a bit of privacy responds, "I'm calling the Organization of the United Brotherhood of It's None of Your Damn Business, Lewis. I'll be with you in a minute." Note: In the film *Mother Night* (1996) Alan Arkin as painter George Kraft says, "The

Brotherhood of the Walking Wounded. It's the largest organization in the world. You don't even know it exists until you're in it. You get your membership card when you lose the one thing that gives your life any meaning, the thing that binds you together. The thing that holds the group in one piece is the fact that the members are absolutely incapable of speaking to one another."

"It's not a pretty face, I grant you, but underneath its flabby exterior is an enormous lack of character" - Oscar Levant as Adam Cook, a sarcastic café piano player in the motion picture *An American in Paris* (1951).

"It's shite being Scottish!" - Opinion of Mark "Rent-boy" Renton (Ewan McGregor) in the movie *Trainspotting* (1996). He continues: "We're the lowest of the fucking low, the scum of the earth, the most wretched, servile, miserable, pathetic trash that was ever shat into civilization. Some people hate the English. I don't. They're just wankers. We, on the other hand, are colonized by wankers. We can't even pick a decent culture to be colonized by. We are ruled by effete assholes. It's a shite state of affairs and all the fresh air in the world won't make any fucking difference."

"It's stupid to just sit here and admire that little red haired girl from a distance. It's stupid not to get up and go over and talk to her. It's really stupid! It's just plain stupid; so why I don't I go over and talk to her?...Because I'm stupid" - Charlie Brown, the perennial loser created by cartoonist Charles M. Schulz tries to gather enough courage to speak to the girl of his dreams in the TV special *You're in Love, Charlie Brown* (1967).

"It's the kind of face that you want to throw a brick at" - Alec Guinness as eccentric painter Gulley Jimsen offers personal platitudes in the motion picture *The Horse's Mouth* (1958).

"It's time to die!" - Chuck Norris as Matt Hunter, a former CIA agent delivers a message to a terrorist in the motion picture *Invasion U.S.A.* (1985). In the film, a Russian terrorist plans to attack America ("18 hours from now, America will be a different place"), but Matt Hunter intervenes and kills a number of Rostov's mercenaries. During an interview directed towards Rostov, Hunter says, "One night you'll close your eyes, and when they open I'll be there. It'll be time to die." Later, Hunter puts an active grenade into the hands of a terrorist and says, "If you live though this, tell Rostov 'It's time to die'." During another encounter with a terrorist, Matt picks up a bomb and says, "Did you lose this?" then throws it at the bad guys who get blown away.

"It's times like this I think of my father's last words" - The comment of a psychotic criminal named Chains (Lance Henriksen) in the action crime drama *Stone Cold* (1991). Taken to court for multiple extortion offenses, Chains arranges his escape by smuggling guns into the courtroom. After his Mississippi biker accomplices spray the room with machine gun fire, Chains points his weapon at a man and says, "It's times like this I think of my father's last words." The innocent bystander asks, "What were they?" Chains answers, "Don't son, that gun is loaded!" He then proceeds to kill the man and others in the area. When undercover cop John Stone (Brian Bosworth) arrives on the scene, Chains says, "Welcome to my slaughterhouse." Battling marauding bikers who screech their motorcycles through the marble hallways of the courthouse, Stone finally subdues Chains. In a moment of ultimate payback, Stone points a gun at Chain's forehead and advises, "Imagine the future, Chains. 'Cause you're not in it." Stone pulls the trigger, but the chamber is empty. His psych-out makes Chains faint. Later, in custody, Chains, unwilling to be caught, grabs a handgun from a cop's holster. But before he can shoot, he is shot dead by Stone's partner (Sam McMurray).

"It's true, she's a cannibal. She would drink the blood of her children from the skull of her lover, and not feel so much as a stomach-ache" - Mandy Patinkin as Alfred de Musset replies to an editor (Ian Marshall de Marnier) who just said about a memoir, "No! It's, it's about her childhood. I expect you come in later, after she chews up her husband, and about a hundred other fellows" in the motion picture *Impromptu* (1991).

"It takes all kinds of critters to make Farmer Vincent's fritters" - The demented tagline from the cult horror movie *Motel Hell* (1982) wherein Rory Calhoun as Farmer Vincent waylays unsuspecting travelers and kills them for a food source. What's Farmer Vincent's secret sausage recipe? First, take a person, bury them in the ground up to their neck, force feed them until they get plump and juicy, slaughter them, smoke their carcasses and then grind their body parts into sausage. Next time you're in town, don't forget to stop by Farmer Vincent's roadside stand and get a heapin' helpin' of the best sausage in the county. Yum, Yum, eat 'em up!

"It was easy" - The ice-cold parting words of private eye Mike Hammer (Biff Elliot) as he fatally shoots a sexy murderess at the end of the motion picture *I, the Jury* (1953). Mike's victim, Charlotte Manning (Peggie Castle) was trying to seduce him into keeping silent about her crimes by stripping down to her naked body. Her last words: "How could you?"

"It was nothing like that, penis breath!" - In the film *E. T.: the Extraterrestrial* (1982) youngster Elliot (Henry Thomas) sees a marooned alien botanist in his family's tool shed. When he tells what he's just seen, his older brother Michael (Robert MacNaughton) taunts him and says, "Maybe an elf or a leprechaun." Elliot responds with his now classic "penis breath!" put-down.

"It would've been a blood bath." - Woody Allen as Mickey, a hypochondriac TV producer in the motion picture *Hannah and Her Sisters* (1986). After a Thanksgiving Day party Mickey reveals, "A week ago I bought a rifle, I went to the store...I bought a rifle! I was gonna, you know, if they told me I had a tumor, I was gonna kill myself. The only thing that might've stopped me—might've—is that my parents would be devastated. I would have to shoot them also, first. And then I have an aunt and uncle - you know - it would've been a blood bath."

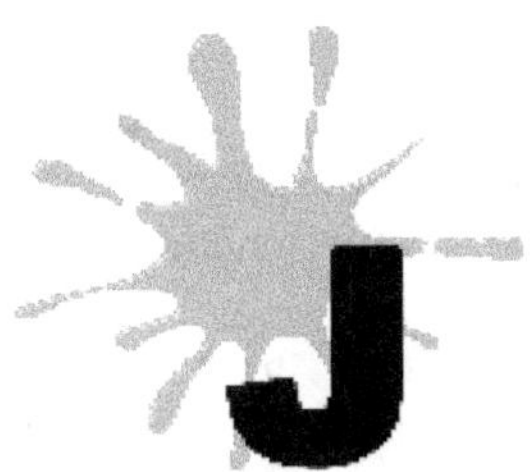

J. Fred Muggs Awards - *TV Guide* magazine's annual award honoring the bleeps, blunders and monkey business seen on television. As they put it, "Here is our salute to the foot-in-the-mouth utterances and other minor disturbances of the past TV season." Named after J. Fred Muggs the chimpanzee that shared the morning spotlight with newscaster/host Dave Garroway on NBC's TODAY SHOW in the 1950s, this in-print booby prize premiered in the 1/9-15/82 issue of *TV Guide*. The award (pictured as a "golden banana") was discontinued and replaced by the Annual Zap Awards introduced in January 6, 1990. The award, named the 'Zapper' (aka: the remote control), was the video equivalent of "thumbs down."

"Jane, you ignorant slut!" - On the "Point-Counterpoint" segment of the SATURDAY NIGHT LIVE program in the late 1970s, Dan Aykroyd responds with insults when he answers his weekend news partner, Jane Curtin. For example, when Jane supported diplomatic relationships with China, Dan supported Taiwan and countered, "Jane, you ignorant slut...I suppose you'd like to conduct our foreign policy the way you conduct your private life! Hopping from bed to bed with anyone that can do you some good. Then what do you have? An old dried-out scuz that no decent man would be seen with. Is that what you want for America! It's too late for you. Jane, but our country still has some dignity left." Jane simply closed with "Good night and have a pleasant tomorrow."

"Jerk! Jerk! Jerk!" - Popular catchphrase chanted by the rowdy audience members of the controversial 1980s syndicated talk show HOT SEAT starring Wally George (the father of actress Rebecca De Mornay). At the beginning of each show, the camera panned the audience which cheered on their ultra-conservative talk show host by yelling, "Wal-lee! Wal-lee! Wal-lee!" As the show continued, Wally read letters sent to the show with such sentiments as "You and your show both STINK!!" Before Wally could finish reading such a letter, the audience began chanting "Jerk! Jerk! Jerk! To keep the audience in a frenzy, Wally regularly featured guests who advocated abortion, homosexuality, and nude dancing. Wally once ejected a guest off the show who said, "The Bible was the work of the Devil"; and when an ex-Marine who opposed the U.S. invasion of Grenada got under Wally's skin, he shouted, "Get the hell out of my studio!" The man promptly overturned Wally's desk and left the set. Of course, the audience went wild, shouting, "Jerk! Jerk! Jerk!"

"Jethro...you head is emptier than last year's bird nest. If your head was filled with dynamite, you wouldn't know how to blow your nose" - Cloris Leachman as Granny Clampett puts down her goofy nephew Jethro Bodine (Diedrich Bader) in the motion picture *The Beverly Hillbillies* (1993). In the original TV series, THE BEVERLY HILLBILLIES/CBS/1962-1971, Jethro's uncle Jed Clampett (Buddy Ebsen) said of his nephew, "If brains were lard, his wouldn't grease too big a pan." And commenting on the attractiveness of a female Jed remarked, "You could throw her into the pond and skim ugly for a month." Note: In the film *American Grafitti* (1973) Mackenzie Phillips as Carol said to her friend, "If brains were dynamite you couldn't blow your nose."

"Jonathan, before a man gets married, he's a—he's a tree in the forest. He—he stands there independent, an entity unto himself. And then he gets chopped down" - Rock Hudson as bachelor Brad Allen explains to associate Jonathan Forbes (Tony Randall) how a man loses his standing in life when he commits to marriage in the motion picture *Pillow Talk* (1959). Brad continues his analogy: "His branches are cut off, and he's stripped of his bark, and he's thrown into the river with the rest of the logs. Then the tree is taken to the mill. Now, when it comes out, it's no longer a tree. It's a vanity table, a breakfast nook, a baby crib and the newspaper that lines the family garbage can."

"Just because my grandfather didn't rape the environment and exploit the workers doesn't make me a peasant. And it's not that he didn't want to rape the environment and exploit the workers, I'm sure he did. It's just that as a barber, he didn't have that much opportunity!" - Steve Martin as lawyer Roger Cobb speaks to millionaire Edwina Cutwater (Lily Tomlin) in the motion picture *All of Me* (1984).

"K-Mart sucks" - Corporate put-down mentioned in the motion picture *Rain Man* (1988). We first hear about K-Mart when Dustin Hoffman in the role of autistic savant named Raymond Babbitt tells his brother, Charlie (Tom Cruise), "I buy my boxer shorts at K-Mart in Cincinnati." Later, Charlie tells Raymond, "I'll let you in on a little secret, Ray. K-Mart Sucks." At the end of the film, when Raymond is returned to his special home, Dr. Bruner (Gerald R. Molen) asks, "Do you feel more relaxed in your favorite K-Mart clothes? Charlie looks at Ray and says, "Tell him, Ray." Ray responds, "K-Mart sucks" Surprised, Charlie's doctor says, "I see." Note: In the film *Baby's Day Out* (1994) Joe Mantegna as Eddie the kidnapper advises "If you want to shoplift, go to J.C. Penney."

"Keep it up and you'll be carrying your face home in a doggy bag" - Charlie Sheen as Air Force pilot Sean "Topper" Harley sports with Kent Gregory (Cary Elwes) in the motion picture *Hot Shots!* (1991).

"Keep on ridin' me, they're gonna be pickin' iron out of your liver" - Elisha Cook, Jr. as neurotic gun-totting crook Wilmer Cook warns private investigator Sam Spade (Humphrey Bogart) to lay off with the criticism in the motion picture *The Maltese Falcon* (1941). Note: In the movie *The Cheap Detective* (1978) Paul Williams as Boy says to Lou Peckinpaugh (Peter Falk), "Keep riding me, Mack, and they'll bury you in 42 different cemeteries."

"Keep shooting, you scum! You'll get a chance yet to die with your boots on!" - Brian Donlevy as the sadistic Sgt. Markoff shouts to his French legionnaire troopers who are defending an isolated desert fort against attacking desert tribesmen in the motion picture *Beau Geste* (1939). When Markoff met his new recruits, he said, "I am Sergeant Markoff. I make soldiers out of scum like you, and I don't do it gently. You're the sloppiest looking lot I've ever seen. It's up to me to prevent you from becoming a disgrace to the Regiment. And I will prevent that if I have to kill half of you with work. But the half that lives will be soldiers. I promise you!" Before escaping the fort with his brother John Geste (Ray Milland), Digby Geste (Robert Preston) carries the bodies of his slain brother Beau (Gary Cooper) as well as Markoff (killed by John) into the barracks. Placing Beau on a bed, Digby prepares a funeral fire in the style of a Viking funeral. Placing the body of Markoff at the base of the fire, Digby fulfills the Viking funeral custom of placing a "dog" at the foot of a slain warrior. Then Digby ignites the funeral pyre and flees the fiery fort.

"The kid who tells on another kid is a dead kid" - Matt Dillon as Richie, a 14-year-old rebel living in a planned suburban community who reminds his gang members of the time honored code of the street that favors killing snitches in the motion picture *Over the Edge* (1979). Note: In the film *Dead End* (1937) street kid Spit (Leo Gorcey) says, "I pity the guy who snitched. *See also* "You know what I do to squealers?"

"The kids today don't have the patience for vampires. They want to see some weird slasher running around and chopping off heads" - Roddy McDowall as Peter Vincent, a TV horror movie host (and part-time vampire hunter) laments for the good old days when sucking someone's blood and impaling the living dead was considered cool in the motion picture *Fright Night* (1985).

"Kill everyone now! Condone first degree murder! Advocate cannibalism! Eat shit! Filth is my politics! Filth is my life!" - Divine as Babs Johnson, an obese, incestuous, transvestite, slut tenderizes steaks between her thighs and revels in her notoriety as "the filthiest person alive" in the cult film *Pink Flamingos* (1972).

"Kill for the love of killing" - The fanatic cry of Guru (Eduardo Ciannelli), a Kali cult leader in the motion picture *Gunga Din* (1939). Stirring up his band of religious followers, Guru cries, "Rise, our new-made brothers. Rise and kill. Kill as you'll be killed yourselves. Kill for the love of killing. Kill for the love of Kali. Kill! Kill! Kill!" Before his rabble are defeated by British troops, the Guru jumps into a pit of deadly snakes rather than surrender ("see them down there, coiling and wiggling, sticking their pretty tongues out").

"Kill! [laughs] Me? I am immortal, child. I am the eater of worlds, and of children. And you are next....I'm every nightmare you've ever had. I'm your worst dream come true. I'm everything you ever were afraid of" - The boast of a demonic creature named Pennywise the Clown (Tim Curry) who lures children into the sewers in the Stephen King horror thriller *It* (1990).

"Kill more Japs get more guns" - Cold-hearted but practical suggestion spoken by John Wayne in his role of Colonel Madden, an American soldier leading the Filipino resistance in the war movie *Back to Bataan* (1945). Note: In the movie *The Best Years of Our Lives* (1946) Frederic March as returning WWII veteran comments, "Last year, it was kill Japs and this year it's make money."

"Kill, then love! When you have known that, you have known ecstasy!" - The personal philosophy of mad Russian Count Zaroff (Leslie Banks) as he prepares to hunt down human prey Bob Rainsford (Joel McCrea) on a remote island in the motion picture *The Most Dangerous Game* (1932). Bored of hunting the usual big game, the Count tells his shipwrecked guest, "I have invented a new sensation." Giving his human prey a head start, the Count cries, "First the hunt...then the revels" as he begins his hunt with snarling dogs and bow and arrow. Unfortunately, for the Count, his prey becomes the hunter and as the Count admits defeat ("Yes...yes I insist you have beaten me.") Rainsford stabs him to death. Note: In the film *Flesh for Frankenstein* (1974) Udo Kier as Baron Frankenstein says, "To know death, Otto, you must first fuck life in the gall bladder!"

"Killin' is my business people, and business is gooood!" - Damon Wayans as discharged Marine Major Benson Winifred Payne becomes the commanding officer of a local school's JROTC program where he teaches with the aide of live grenades and real bullets in the motion picture *Major Payne* (1995).

"Killing generals could get to be a habit with me!" - Spoken by Charles Bronson at the conclusion of the military drama *The Dirty Dozen* (1967). In the film, Bronson plays Joseph Wladislaw, a U. S. Army soldier convicted of murder who is given a chance to redeem himself by joining a suicide squad known as 'The Dirty Dozen.' After successfully killing a number of high ranking German officers, Joseph recuperates in a hospital from wounds received in the operation. One of his visitors, (an American general who had nothing but insults for him and his outfit before the operation) compliments him on his actions. Wladislaw then turns to his roommate Major Reisman (Lee Marvin) and says, "Boy-oh-boy-oh-boy, Killing General's could get to be a habit with me!"

"Kiss my ass!" - Emilio Estevez as frontier outlaw, William H. Bonney in the western motion picture *Young Guns* (1988). Upon discovering his worth as a wanted fugitive, Bonney jots down a few thoughts to the governor: "Dear Governor Axtell. I've heard that you will give 200 dollars for my head. Perhaps we should meet and talk. I am at the Juarez village at the border. Send 3 men, and instruct them *not* to shoot, as I am unarmed. In short, Sir: I surrender. Your obedient servant. William H. Bonney. PS: I changed my mind. Kiss my ass!" *See also* "Pucker up and kiss my ass!" and "You can kiss my ass!"

"Kiss my grits!" - Popular repartee of Florence Jean 'Flo' Castleberry (Polly Holliday), the sassy waitress working at Arizona roadside diner on the situation comedy ALICE/CBS/1976-85. Her insults were usually directed at Mel Sharples (Vic Tayback), the cafe owner. She continued her "Kiss my grits" comebacks on the spin-off series FLO/CBS/1980-81 where she opened her own restaurant in Cowtown, Texas.

Kiss of Death - The traditional Mafia (aka "Cosa Nostra") method of informing an opponent that his days were numbered. The kiss on the lips was both a warning to get something done (i.e., pay your debts or else) or a disingenuous means of informing someone that their life would soon end. Reportedly, mob leader Vito Genovese gave Joe Valachi a simple "kiss of affection" while both were serving time in a Federal penitentiary in Atlanta. Valachi, thinking his death was imminent, became an informer to the FBI to gain protection from the underworld. The motion picture *The Valachi Papers* (1972) from the book by Peter Maas told the story of Mafia life as seen through the eyes of famed informer Joseph Valachi (played by Charles Bronson). In the movie *The Godfather Part II* (1974) Mafia Don Michael Corleone (Al Pacino) cups his hand around the face of his brother Fredo, firmly plants a kiss on his lips and says, "I know it was you Fredo. You broke my heart. You broke my heart." Michael then waited until his mother died (in respect for her feelings) and had Fredo killed for betraying the family business. Note: According to the *Mafia Encyclopedia,* in 1931 mobster Lucky Luciano "ordered the act (of kissing) stopped even as a form of greeting when Mafiosi met. Such public acts...might strike terror in the hearts of Sicilian peasants but were counterproductive in the United States."

Klingon Insults - The science fiction series STAR TREK and it spin-off sequels feature an alien race called the Klingons. This gross, barbaric race of warriors was by human standards extremely rude. Their in-the-face conversation style put many on the alert for potential fistfights and bar brawls. The following examples of the Klingon language appear in *The Klingon Dictionary: the Official Guide to Klingon Words and Phrases* by Marc Okrand:

- Face me if you dare! - Qab jiH nagil
- Shut up! - bljatlh 'e' ylmev
- Surrender or Die! - bljeghbe'chugh vaj blHegh
- Your ship is a garbage scow! - veQDuj 'oH Dujllj'e'
- You're very ugly! - blmoHqu

"A knave, a rascal, an eater of broken meats; a base, proud, shallow, beggarly, three-suited, hundred-pound, filthy worsted-stocking knave; a lily-livered, action-taking, whoreson, glass-gazing, super-serviceable, finical rogue; one-trunk-inheriting slave; one that wouldst be a bawd in way of good service, and art nothing but the composition of a knave, beggar, coward, pander, and the son and heir of a mongrel bitch; one whom I will beat into clamorous whining if thou deny'st the least syllable of thy addition" - Colin Blakely as Kent speaks of Oswald (Geoffrey Bateman) in the British made-for-TV movie adaptation of Shakespeare's *King Lear* (1984).

Krunk - A swear word first used in 1994 on the late night talk show LATE NIGHT WITH CONAN O'BRIEN/NBC/1993+. According to its creator, Conan O'Brien, Krunk was "America's newest swear word...so new that the networks don't know whether to censor it or not!" Phrases like "What the krunk do you want?" and "It's none of your krunking business!" were exchanged by both guests and the host of the show. *See also* "Frak"

"Lady, you take my picture with that thing, and I'm gonna rip your brassiere off, and I'm gonna strangle you with it. You get that?" - Harrison Ford as John Book, a Philadelphia police detective living undercover as an Amish farmer who tells a female tourist to back off after she asks, "Would you mind if I took your picture" in the motion picture *Witness* (1985). When a loudmouthed punk smears an ice cream cone on the nose of one of the pacifist farmers, John angrily approaches him. An elder Amish man tries to counsel John to ignore the brutality by saying, "It's not our way." But John concludes, "It's my way" and punches the offending tourist in the face.

"Larkin, you're gonna get 30 days for that killin'...Then we're gonna hang you" - George "Gabby" Hayes informs his prisoner (Harry Woods) that first he's going to do some time in jail and then he's *really* gonna do some time in eternity in the western motion picture *Trail Street* (1947).

"The law sucks" - Philosophy of Greg Germann as Richard Fish, the senior partner at Fish and Associates, a law firm in Boston on the television series ALLY MCBEAL/FOX/1997-2002. Greg once explained his reason why he became a lawyer: "Let me tell you something. I didn't become a lawyer because I like the law; the law sucks. It's boring, but it can also be used as a weapon. You want to bankrupt somebody? Cost him everything he's worked for? Make his wife leave him, even make his kids cry? Yeah, we can do that."

"Lawyers should never marry other lawyers. This is called 'inbreeding,' from which comes idiot children and more lawyers" - David Wayne as Kip Lurie in the motion picture *Adam's Rib (*1940). Some other lawyer put-downs: "If there is ever to be law and order in the West, the first thing we have got to do is take all the lawyers out and shoot 'em down like dogs"—Henry Hull in *Jesse James* (1939); "What do you got in place of a conscience? Don't answer. I know...a lawyer."—Kirk Douglas in *Detective Story* (1951); "There's only one thing more devious than a Philadelphia lawyer, and that's an Irish lawyer." —James Stewart in *Anatomy of a Murder* (1959); "Some men are heterosexual, some men are bisexual, some men don't think about sex at all they become lawyers"—Woody Allen in *Love and Death* (1975); "The justice system moves swiftly, now that they've abolished all the lawyers."—Christopher Lloyd in *Back to the Future* Part II (1989); "What's 500 lawyers at the bottom of the ocean?...A start!"—Danny De Vito in *The War of the Roses* (1989); "You got it backwards, pal, first you go to law school, then you become a sleazeball with no respect for anyone."—*True Colors* (1991); "Scientists are now using lawyers instead of rats for their experiments. There are two reasons for this. The scientists don't become attached to the lawyers; and there are some things rats won't do."—Robin Williams in *Hook* (1991); "Lawyers are like nuclear warheads. I have them because the other guy has them, but the first time you use them it fucks everything up"—Danny DeVito in *Other People's Money* (1991); and "What's the difference between a lawyer and a hooker? A hooker'll stop screwing you when you're dead"—Matt Damon in *The Rainmaker* (1997).

"Leave him be. A dead man is a dead man, and nobody cares" - Gene Evans as army Sgt. Zack tells his troops not to bother with the dead body of an American soldier (it's booby-trapped) in the motion picture *The Steel Helmet* (1951).

"Let me give you a little inside information about God" - Al Pacino as powerful lawyer John Milton (the Devil in disguise) explains the Creator to a new associate, Kevin Lomax (Keanu Reeves) in the motion picture *The Devil's Advocate* (1997). Milton continues his observation: "God likes to watch. He's a prankster. Think about it. He gives man INSTINCTS! He gives you this extraordinary gift, and then what does He do, I swear for His own amusement, his own private cosmic gag reel. He sets the rules in opposition. It's the goof of all time. Look but don't touch. Touch, but don't taste! Taste, don't swallow. Ahaha! And when you're jumpin' from one foot to the next, what is he doing? He's laughin' His sick, fuckin' ass off. He's a tight-ass! He's a sadist! He's an absentee landlord. Worship THAT? *NEVER!*"

"Let me tell you something, Jack. If shit was worth something, poor people would be born with no hole in their ass" - Eddie Murphy as Reggie Hammond, a prisoner on temporary release in the motion picture *Another 48 HRS.* (1990).

"Let me tell you something you already know. The world ain't all sunshine and rainbows. It is a very mean and nasty place and it will beat you to your knees and keep you there permanently if you let it. You, me, or nobody is gonna hit as hard as life. But it ain't how hard you hit; it's about how hard you can get hit, and keep moving forward. How much you can take, and keep moving forward. That's how winning is done. Now, if you know what you're worth, then go out and get what you're worth. But you gotta be willing to take the hit, and not pointing fingers saying you ain't where you are because of him, or her, or anybody. Cowards do that and that ain't you. You're better than that!" - Sylvester Stallone as heavyweight prizefighter Rock Balboa sets his grown son Rocky, Jr. (Milo Ventimiglia) straight about life in the motion picture *Rocky Balboa* (2006). Earlier, Rocky Jr. told his father that he "Cast a big shadow" - implying that all of his personal problems was his father's fault.

"Let me tell you the story of right hand, left hand" - Bill Nunn as Radio Raheem explains the significance of his two sets of brass knuckles in the motion picture *Do the Right Thing* (1989). In the film, Rahemm owns a set of brass knuckles displaying the words love and hate. He informs homey Mookie (Spike Lee), "Let me tell you the story of right hand, left hand, It's a tale of good and evil. Hate—it was with this hand that Cain iced his brother. Love—these five fingers, they go straight to the soul of man: the right hand, the hand of love." At the film's conclusion, a riot ensued; the neighborhood burns and a local pizza store goes up in flames because a proud Italian guy refuses to put up a few pictures of black celebrities in his store to reflect the neighborhood's changing culture. Note: The 'left hand/right hand" premise was inspired by an earlier film *Night* *of the Hunter* (1955) starring Robert Mitch as psychotic preacher Reverend Harry Powell who chases down two homeless children for money stolen by their father. Along the way, he reveals the tale behind the tattoos on his hands. "Ah, little lad, you're staring at my fingers. Would you like me to tell you the little story of the right hand, left hand? The story of good and evil? H-A-T-E. It was with this left hand that older brother Cain struck the blow that laid his brother low. L-O-V-E. You see these fingers, dear hearts? These fingers has veins that run straight to the soul of man—the right hand, friends, the hand of love. Now watch, and I'll show you the story of life. Those fingers, dear hearts, is always a-warring and a-tugging, one against the other. Now watch 'em! Old brother left hand, left hand he's a fighting, and it looks like love's a goner. But wait a minute! Hot dog, love's a winning! Yessirree! It's love that's won, and old left hand hate is down for the count!"

"Let me warn you. I say what I think. I'm a complete individualist. I'm against communism, capitalism, fascism, nazism. I'm against everything and everybody. I hate my fellow man and he hates me" - Burgess Meredith as Sebastian, a malcontent pianist speaks his mind about a multitude of topics in the motion picture *That Uncertain Feeling* (1942).

"Let the mayhem begin" - The insane words of evil media tycoon Elliot Carver (Jonathan Pryce) who kills all the sailors onboard a British submarine in the South China Sea and threatens global war to get a headline to launch his new worldwide satellite network in the spy thriller *Tomorrow Never Dies* (1997). When his henchmen subdue secret agent James Bond (Pierce Brosnan) Carver advises one of them, "When you remove Mr. Bond's heart, there should just be enough time for him to watch it stop beating." Bond, however, like all good heroes, escapes his torturers and in a final confrontation with Carver says, "I may have some breaking news for you, Elliot! [Bond attacks him] You forgot the first rule of mass media, Elliot: 'Give the people what they want.'"[Carver falls to his death into a printing press].

"Let's play!" - The breathy pay back of Antonio Banderas in the movie *Desperado* (1995). When a Mexican drug lord kills his girlfriend, a guitar-toting gunman vows revenge. As he battles the men responsible for her death, Banderas pulls out a gun and says, "Let's play!"

"Life's a bitch, now so am I" - Catwoman's revelation in the motion picture *Batman Returns* (1992). Thrown out of a high-rise, secretary Selina Kyle (Michelle Pfeiffer) is reincarnated as the catty criminal Catwoman. When crime fighter Batman first meets Catwoman, she says, "Life's a bitch, now so am I." When Bruce Wayne (Michael Keaton) meets Catwoman in the guise of Selina, he comments, "You have kind of a dark side, don't you?" She responds, "No darker than yours, Bruce." Catwoman also had words with fellow criminal The Penguin (Danny DeVito). When he makes a sexual overture, ("You're just the kind of pussy I've been looking for") she yawns, "Oh, please. I wouldn't touch you to scratch you." Penguin later tells Catwoman, "You lousy minx, I ought to have you spayed." Note: In the film *Dolores Claiborne* (1995) Kathy Bates as Dolores Claiborne says, "Sometimes being a bitch is all a woman has to hold on to."

"Life is as brief as a butterfly's fart, but death is something that you have forever. From now on, you will march until you drop, and when you have dropped, you will crawl. Some may consider that I am excessively cruel, but there is a reason for this cruelty: I enjoy it!" - Peter Ustinov as the sadistic French Legionnaire commander in the motion picture spoof *The Last Remake of Beau Geste* (1977).

"Life is like a box of crap. It smells funny and looks like crap in a box"- Kenny Sullivan as Bob Joe in the motion picture *Bob* (1999). Note: The expression is a spoof of a phrase from the film *Forrest Gump* (1994) where Forrest Gump's mother (Sally Field) says, "Life's a box of chocolates, Forrest. You never know what you're gonna get." *See also* "Cancer Man"

"Lincoln said, 'With malice toward none, with charity to all.' Nowadays they say, 'Think the way I do, or I'll bomb the daylights out of you'" - Lionel Barrymore as Martin Vanderhoff shares his philosophy on the modern world in the motion picture *You Can't Take It with You* (1938).

"Listen before I met you I disliked you intensely. When I met you I disliked you intensely. Even now I dislike you intensely. That was the sensible, sane portion of me. But there's an insane portion of me that gets a little violent every time I think of you." - Henry Fonda as newspaperman Peter Ames lets it all hang out concerning his opinion of dizzy débutante Melsa Manton (Barbara Stanwyck) in the motion picture *The Mad Miss Manton* (1938). He follows up with, "You're a nasty creature. But, in time, I'll beat it out of you."

"Listen kid, I'm not gonna bullshit you, all right? I don't give a good fuck what you know, or don't know, but I'm gonna torture you anyway, regardless. Not to get information. It's amusing, to me, to torture a cop. You can say anything you want cause I've heard it all before. All you can do is pray for a quick death, which you ain't gonna get." - Michael Madsen as Mr. Blonde, a trigger-happy killer about to slice up a cop with a razor blade in the motion picture *Reservoir Dogs* (1992). Before cutting the cop, Mr. Blonde nonchalantly asks, "You ever listen to K-Billy's 'Super Sounds of the Seventies' weekend? It's my personal favorite." Mr Blonde is later killed by Mr. Orange (Tim Roth).

"Listen, Lady. I generally never sock a dame. But I'm inclined to make an exception of you" - Edmund Lowe as Duke Sheldon in the motion picture *I Love You Again* (1940). Note: In the film *Masterminds (1997)* Patrick Stewart as Raif Bentley says, "You know, I'm not a violent man but I really do think I'm going to have to kill someone here."

"Listen to me, Cooney! If you put me and my men in a wringer—if you send us out there and let us hang—I swear, I swear by all that's holy, I'll come back. I'll come back and take this grenade and shove it down your throat and pull the pin!" - Jack Palance as National Guard Infantry Company Lt. Joe Costa threatens Captain Erskine Cooney (Eddie Albert) in the World War II war film *Attack!* (1956).

"Listen to me you hicks!" - Defiant words spoken by Broderick Crawford as politician Willie Stark in the motion picture *All the King's Men* (1949). In a bid to win the election, Willie delivers these sentiments to a crowd of potential voters: "Now, shut up! Shut up, all of you. Now, listen to me, you hicks. Yeah, you're hicks too, and they fooled you a thousand times, just like they fooled me. But this time, I'm going to fool somebody. I'm going to stay in the race. I'm on my own and I'm out for blood. Listen to me, you hicks..." In a conversation with political consultant Jack Burden (John Ireland), Willie is advised, "Make them cry. Make them laugh. Make them mad, even mad at you. Stir them up and they'll love it, and come back for more, but for heaven sake, don't try to improve their minds."

"Listen, you crummy, flat-footed copper" - Edward G. Robinson as gangster Caesar Enrico Banderelli in the motion picture *Little Caesar* (1930). In the film, Rico murders his way up the ladder of success but eventually begins his decline. While talking to Sergeant Flaherty over the phone, Rico explodes when he is not taken seriously: "This is Rico speaking. Rico R-I-C-O! Rico. Little Caesar, that's who! Listen you crummy flat-footed copper, I'll show you whether I've lost my nerve and my brains" Rico continues taunting the cops, saying, "You want me, you're going to have to come and get me! At the film's conclusion, the police gun Rico down. His dying words: "Mother of Mercy! Is this the end of Rico?"

"Listen, you little piece of scum, you...You can go back to that sweet-smelling family of yours back of the railroad tracks in Passaic!" - Wallace Berry as entrepreneur Dan Packard threatens his wife, Kitty (Jean Harlow) with poverty if she doesn't come around to his way of thinking in the motion picture *Dinner at Eight* (1933). To drive his point home, Dan says, "And get this—if that sniveling, money grubbing, whining old mother or yours comes fooling around my office anymore, I'm going to give orders to have her thrown down those sixty flights of stairs, so help me."

"Listen, you little spazoids! I know where you live and I've seen where you sleep. I swear that your mothers will cry when they see what I've done to you!" - Julie Warner as Michelle Brock in the motion picture *Tommy Boy* (1995).

"Listen. you snot-nose little shit, I was takin' shrapnel in Khe Sanh when you were crappin' in your hands and rubbin' it on your face" - Gary Busey as veteran FBI agent Angelo Pappas yells at his new partner, Johnny Utah (Keanu Reeves) in the motion picture *Point Break* (1991).

"Live or die, asshole, your choice" - Mark Harmon as police detective Jay Austin draws down on a felon who stole an officer's hand gun in the police station in the motion picture *The Presidio* (1988).

"Living with a Sicilian is like cooking pasta and pissing olive oil 24 hours a day" - Sean Connery as Jessie McMullen, an Irish career criminal reminisces with his grown son, Vito McMullen (Dustin Hoffman) about his marriage to an Sicilian woman (Vito's mom) in the motion picture *Family Business* (1989).

"Look at that cheap squirt, passin' up and down...For a nickel, I'd grab him, stick both thumbs in his eyes, hang on till he drops dead." - Richard Widmark as crazed criminal Tommy Udo wishes no good to a prison guard in the motion picture *Kiss of Death* (1947). *See also* "You know what I do to squealers?"

"Look at us, C'mon look at us. See? A couple of bums" - Jack Lemmon as an alcoholic named Joe looks into a mirror with wife, Kirsten (Lee Remmick) and realizes the toll that drinking alcohol has taken on them both in the motion picture *Days of Wine and Roses* (1962). Joe first came to this conclusion when as he said, "I walked by the Union Square Bar, I was going to go in. Then I saw myself—my reflection in the window—and I thought, 'I wonder who that bum is.' And then I saw it was me. You're a bum. Look at you."

"Look out, Hitler! The niggers is coming to get your ass!" - David Alan Grier as black Corporal Cobb prepares to travel overseas to Europe in the WWII motion picture *A Soldier's Story* (1984). Fellow soldier Corporal Ellis (Robert Townsend) offered this opinion: "They're finally going to give us Negroes a chance to fight. Hitler ain't got a chance now. And, after what Joe Louis did to Max Schmeling."

"Look, you fools. You're in danger. Can't you see? They're after you. They're after all of us. Our wives, our children, everyone...You're next!" - The crazed ramblings of Miles Bennel (Kevin McCarthy), a small town doctor who discovers that alien pods are taking over the bodies and minds of all the residents Santa Mira, California in the sci-fi classic film *Invasion of the Body Snatchers* (1956).

Lord of the Idiots - Nickname of George Costanza (Jason Alexander) on the sitcom SEINFELD/NBC/1990-1998 mentioned on episode #10 "The Apartment" (4/4/91). George once said, "I'm disturbed. I'm depressed. I'm inadequate...I've got it all!" George's friend Jerry Seinfeld called George 'Biff,' a reference to the character Biff Loman "The biggest loser in the history of American Literature" in Arthur Miller's play *Death of a Salesman* (1949).

Lousy Awards, The - Humorous awards presented on the comedy variety series THE STEVE ALLEN SHOW/NBC/ABC/1956-61. The Lousy Awards picked fun at lousy persons, places or things. *See also* "David Letterman's Top Ten List"

"Lousy Japs, they lost the war, now they send us their junk!" - Walter Mathau as retired vaudevillian Willy Clark pissed off with his malfunctioning TV set in the motion picture *The Sunshine Boys* (1975).

Lovable Lush, The – Nowadays, with the influence of MADD (Mothers Against Drunk Drivers) so prominent in our society, alcoholism is taken seriously but a few decades ago, alcoholism was more of a joke. Comedian Foster Brooks, made alcoholism his trademark by creating a lovable but blitzed drunk known as 'The Lovable Lush' who stuttered, stammered and belched his way through a conversation. He once explained his "Favorite Hangover Cures" on an installment of the variety program THE BOOK OF LISTS/CBS/1982. His drunken routine was a recurring skit on the comedy variety program THE DEAN MARTIN SHOW/NBC/1965-74.

"Lower your flags and march straight back to England, stopping at every home to beg forgiveness for a hundred years of theft, rape, and murder. Do this, and your men shall live. Do it not, and every one of you will die today" - Mel Gibson as William Wallace tells the leaders of apparently superior invading English forces that he will permit them safe passage through Scotland back to England in the motion picture *Braveheart* (1995). Confident of victory, the British refuse Wallace's offer. A few moments later, Wallace tells his soldiers, "I AM William Wallace! And I see a whole army of my country men, here, in defiance of tyranny. You've come to fight as free men, and free men you are. What will you do with that freedom? Will you fight? A soldier responds, "Against that? No, we'll run, and we'll live." Wallace continues, "Aye, fight and you may die, run, and you'll live...at least for a while. And dying in your beds, many years from now, would you be willin' to trade ALL the days, from this day to that, for one chance, just one chance, to come back here and tell our enemies that they may take our lives, but they'll never take...OUR FREEDOM!" The word "Freedom" was the last word spoken by Wallace who was betrayed, captured and tortured by his enemies for his alleged treasonous actions against England.

"Lucky it's not a bull-shit detector or no one would get in" - Sean Young as Susan Atwell, a sexy politician's mistress comments on the metal detector checking all incoming guests to a presidential inaugural celebration in the motion picture *No Way Out* (1987). Note: In the film *Die Hard 2* (1990) police detective John McClane (Bruce Willis) says, "Hey, Carmine, let me ask you something. What sets off the metal detectors first? The lead in your ass, or the shit in your brain?"

Lumpy - Nickname of Clarence Rutherford (Frank Bank), the friend of Wally Cleaver (Tony Dow) on the sitcom LEAVE IT TO BEAVER/CBS/ABC/1957-63. Originally, Clarence was a bully who picked on the Cleaver kids on the way home from school. Lumpy got his nickname from the kids of the neighborhood whom he also bullied—possibly a reference to the 'lumps' he gave them when he caught them. However, there were also references about his hulking body and stupid facial expression that concluded that he looked like a 'Lumpy.' Once, the Cleaver boys, Wally and his younger brother, Beaver (Jerry Mathers) placed barrel hoops on the driveway of Lumpy's house hoping to trip him when he ran after them. Unfortunately, the hoops caught Lumpy's father, Fred Rutherford (Richard Deacon) instead. When Lumpy's father discovered the reason why the kids pulled their prank, he disciplined Clarence for being a bully. Later, Lumpy became friends with Wally Cleaver and appeared as a regular on the revival series STILL THE BEAVER/DIS/1985-86 and THE NEW LEAVE IT TO BEAVER/TBS/1986-89. Note: In the film *Scrooged* (1988) Bill Murray played Mr. Cross, an insensitive, venal television executive who long ago lost the spirit of Christmas. In his more innocent days, his girlfriend (Karen Allen) called him 'Lumpy.' *See also* "Humbug!"

Madman Muntz - Used car king Earl William 'Madman' Muntz became famous for introducing an affordable TV set in Chicago in 1949. The TV set featured a built-in antenna, one knob picture control, and a low price that helped bring down the price of televisions nationwide. Owning 72 stores, Muntz sold over $20 million sets by 1950. He was forced to sell his TV business when a plan to sell an automobile (The Muntz Jet) failed in 1953-54. He later went into the stereo business and created the Muntz stereo chain. The concept for 'Madman' originated when Earl Muntz was selling cars. He wanted an advertising gimmick that would really get people's attention, and so he hired artist Mike Shore to come up with an idea. He designed a caricature of Muntz dressed in long red flannel underwear and sporting a Napoleon hat. Muntz was born in Elgin, Illinois in 1914. *See also* "Crazy Eddie"

Madonna on LETTERMAN - On the 2/13/95 episode of CBS's LATE NIGHT WITH DAVID LETTERMAN, pop songstress Madonna, dressed in a tight black dress came bearing gifts of candy and roses to wish David Letterman a Happy Valentine's Day. "I'm a changed woman since I met you," said the pop diva "and I'm not going to say 'Fuck' anymore." Madonna's statement referred to her March 31, 1994 guest appearance when she uttered the word 'Fuck' 13 times during her short visit to the show. Note: In 1981 comedian Charles Rocket got fired after accidentally saying 'Fuck' on NBC's SATURDAY NIGHT LIVE. On April 12, 1997, Norm MacDonald let the word 'Fuck' slip out while doing the SNL "Weekend Update" segment. He apologized to NBC and promised not to say it again—and he wasn't fired. In an interview with *Entertainment Weekly* magazine MacDonald revealed, "I'm surprised it doesn't happen all the time because *"that"* word is always on my mind. I find it's an excellent word because that way you don't need a large vocabulary." Reportedly, the first time the word 'fuck' was heard in the cinema occurred in the film *I'll Never Forget What's 'is Name* (1967) when Marianne Faithful as Josie says, "Get out of here, you fucking bastard!"

"Mama says, 'Stupid is as stupid does'" - Response of a slow-witted boy named Forrest Gump (Michael Connor Humphreys) when he is called stupid in the motion picture *Forrest Gump* (1994). Tom Hanks later repeated the same phrase in his role as a grown Forrest Gump.

"Man is like a banana. Strong and firm, bright and phallic, and he's protected by his all-important shield..." - The beginning of a tirade against women spoken by aspiring screenwriter Barry McMullen (Edward Burns) in the motion picture *The Brothers McMullen* (1995). Barry continues [holding a banana] "But, when a woman comes along, you know, she sees this bright phallic beast and she wants it. So, she starts peeling away your all-important shield. [peels the banana] First, she wants to see your romantic side, then she wants to see your passionate side, finally she wants to see your soft, caring, feminine side. She keeps peeling and peeling until your left there buck naked, totally exposed with your balls blowing in the wind. And that's when she gets her knife, and she cuts away your manhood piece by piece until she's having your cock in her corn flakes."

"Man's got to know his limitations!" - Payback line of Inspector 'Dirty' Harry Callahan in the motion picture *Magnum Force* (1973). After Harry exposes a vigilante division of the San Francisco Police Department that executes people who defeated the legal system on technicalities, he is confronted by crooked Police Lieutenant Neill Briggs (Hal Holbrook) who swears he will frame Harry for the murder of three rogue policeman. As Briggs holds Harry at gunpoint, Harry manages to activate a bomb sitting in the front seat of the automobile that Briggs is about to use for a get-away. As Briggs drives away, the car explodes and Harry wryly smiles and says, "Man's got to know his limitations." Earlier in the film, Briggs bragged that he never pulled a gun on anyone, to which Harry said, "You're a good man and a good man always knows his limitation." Harry had his own beliefs. One of them: "Nothing wrong with shooting as long as the right people get shot."

Marx-isms - The comedy troupe of the Marx Brothers (Groucho, Chico, and Harpo) appeared in a number of zany films in the 1920s and 30s. Among the brothers, Groucho had the most biting wit. The following are samples of some of his wickeder one-line zingers: "You're the most beautiful woman I've ever seen, which doesn't say much for you."—*Animal Crackers* (1930); "I've got a mind to join a club and beat you over the head with it."—*Duck Soup* (1933); "Say, the next time I see you, remind me not to talk to you, will you?"—*The Cocoanuts* (1929); "Why don't you bore a hole in yourself and let the sap run out."; "I married your mother because I wanted children. Imagine my disappointment when you arrived."—*Horse Feathers* (1932); "Why don't you trade in your head for a bowling ball?"—*At the Circus* (1939); and "I'll bet your father spent the first year of your life throwing rocks at the stork." —*At the Circus* (1939). *See also* "Why I'll murder ya!"

"May a weird holy man..." - Johnny Carson of THE TONIGHT SHOW STARRING JOHNNY CARSON/NBC/1962-92 created a bumbling telepath-in-a-turban called 'Carnac The Magnificent' (first seen in 1964) who could divine answers to questions sealed in envelopes. If the audience booed one of Carnac's responses, he'd fight back by saying something like:

- May a weird Holy man use a Black & Decker tool on your only sister
- May a love-starved fruit fly molest your sister's nectarines
- May a nearsighted sand flea suck syrup off your short stack
- May a camel with a weak kidney condition find your Hope Chest
- May a desert weirdo lower his figs into your mother's soup
- May the Shah of Iran seek refuge under your sister's skirt
- May a diseased yak squat in your hot tub
- May you get your first French kiss from a diseased camel
- May your prize bull hate cows

- May a crazy Holy man set fire to your nose hair
- May your Perrier water be secretly bottled in Tijuana
- May your only daughter take up with a yak of another faith
- May a crazed lizard unravel your underwear
- May a desert nomad do a desert no-no to your sister
- May the winds of the Sahara blow a scorpion up your sister's caftan
- May a diseased Holy man soil your shelf paper
- May your platform shoes fail you in a camel pasture
- May a weird Holy man with a rash play with your face
- May a queasy camel freshen up your mother's evening bath
- May a sick yak leave a gift in your sock drawer
- May Orca the whale relieve himself on your carpet

A typical skit opened with announcer Ed McMahon saying, "I have in my hand an envelope, a child of four can plainly see these envelopes are hermetically sealed. They've been kept since noon today in a mayonnaise jar on Funk & Wagnalls' porch. No one—but one!—knows the contents. In his mystical and borderline way; Carnac will now ascertain the answers having never heard the questions." Carnac then placed the white envelopes on his turban to sense the answers to the questions within. The following are some examples of answer/question exchanges:

Answer: The Moonies
Question: Name the religion that drops its pants?

Answer: Sis Boom Baa!
Question: Describe the sound you hear when a sheep blows up?

Answer: A pair of Jordache jeans and a bread box
Question: Name two places where you stuff your buns?

Answer: Fondue
Question: What do you get on your Fon if you leave it out all night?

When the announcer said, "I hold in my hand...the last envelope." The audience usually cheered, as if to say "Thank God this skit is almost over."

Meanest Dog in the USA, The - White dog featured on the live (later taped) comedy series THE SOUPY SALES SHOW starring comedian Soupy Sales (Milton Hines). During each program, a hairy white paw would jut in front of the television camera followed by growling sounds, which only Soupy Sales seemed to understand. This was White Fang, the "Biggest and Meanest Dog in the USA." Black Tooth, the "Kindest Dog in the USA" was the counterpart to White Fang. Frank Nastasi supplied the dog sounds. Clyde Adler manipulated their furry paws from off camera. These silly off screen canines were not beneath throwing cream pies into Soupy's face.

Meathead - Archie Bunker (Carroll O'Connor) called his unemployed son-in-law Mike Stivic (Rob Reiner) a 'Meathead' on a regular basis on the sitcom ALL IN THE FAMILY/CBS/1971-83. While Mike was going to college, he stayed with his in-laws. The cramped quarters and the volatile tempers of both Mike and Archie often put them at odds with each other which resulted in Archie calling Mike a 'Meathead.' The term was once explained to mean "dead from the neck up." During one of their disagreements, Archie tells Mike, "Sticks and stone may break my bones, but you are one dumb Pollack!" Archie once commented to his wife (Jean Stapleton), "We lost a daughter, Edith, but we gained a Meathead." Archie also called Mike a 'Knucklehead!' Ironically, in high school Archie was known as 'Meathead.' During the 1982-83 TV season Mike Stivic divorced his wife, and ran off to a commune with a flower child thus fulfilling Archie's opinion of him. Note: The son-in-law counterpart on the British sitcom TILL DEATH US DO PART/BBC/1966-75 that inspired ALL IN THE FAMILY was referred to as a 'git.' *See also* "Shoebootie"

"Men aren't true to anything. They will have sex with a tree" - Rita Wilson as Catherine O'Shaughnessy offers solace to a member of a Venice, California suicide help line in the motion picture *Mixed Nuts* (1994).

"Men are such cock suckers aren't they? You don't have to answer that. It's true. They're scared. Their dicks get limp when confronted by a woman of obvious power and what do they do about it? Call them witches, burn them, torture them, until every woman is afraid. Afraid of herself...afraid of men...and all for what? Fear of losing their hard-on" - Jack Nicholson as Daryl van Horne (the Devil in disguise) expresses his opinion on men in the motion picture *The Witches of Eastwick* (1987). Note: In the film *The Big Chill* (1983) Mary Kay Place as Meg offers this rant on men: "They're either married or gay. And if they're not gay, they've just broken up with the most wonderful woman in the world, or they've just broken up with a bitch who looks exactly like me. They're in transition from a monogamous relationship and they need more space. Or they're tired of space, but they just can't commit. Or they want to commit, but they're afraid to get close. They want to get close; you don't want to get near them."

"Men! Can't live with 'em, can't shoot 'em" - Personal opinion expressed by Wendy (Mare Winningham) to her friend Julie (Ally Sheedy) in the film *St. Elmo's Fire* (1985). Variations of this same sentiment have appeared in the films *Night on Earth* (1991) when Winona Ryder as Corky says, "Boys! Can't live with 'em, can't shoot 'em"; in *Grumpy Old Men* (1993) when Burgess Meredith as Grandpa Gustafson says, "Kids! Can't live with 'em, can't shoot 'em." in *True Lies* (1994) when Tom Arnold as Gibs says, "Women! Can't live with 'em, can't kill 'em"; and on the detective dramedy MOONLIGHTING/ABC/1985-89 private eye David Addison (Bruce Willis) remarks, "Women: Can't live with 'em, can't leave 'em on the curb when you're done with them." Peg Bundy (Katey Sagal) on the FOX sitcom MARRIED...WITH CHILDREN stated, "Men, God Love 'em. They're just children with a paycheck." Peg's neighbor Marcy Darcy once said, "I hate men. They're stupid ignorant animals with stupid ignorant hobbies."

"Men die all the time, and pigs live on and on when you'd think that their own smell would kill them" - Joan Crawford as Julie expresses her opinion on men and animals in the motion picture *Strange Cargo* (1940).
Merchant of Venom *See* "Mr. Warmth"

Mickey Pants - Nickname of Bob Barsky (Sam Freed), the sportscaster featured on the sitcom KATE AND ALLIE/CBS/1984-89. When Bob played baseball as a little leaguer (he was eight-years-old), a small mouse got into his pants while he was on the field. As he dropped his pants to catch the mouse, everyone laughed and he reluctantly earned the moniker, 'Mickey Pants.'

"Might I remind you OO7, you are licensed to kill, not to break the traffic laws" - Weapons designer "Q" (Desmond Llewelyn) chastises British secret agent James Bond (Pierce Brosnan) as he reveals the latest features on Bond's new BMW sports car—equipped with stinger missiles mounted behind the headlights—in the motion picture *Goldeneye* (1995).

"The missiles are flying, Hallelujah!" - Crazed jubilation of Martin Sheen in the role of presidential hopeful Greg Stillson in motion picture *The Dead Zone* (1983). In the film, Christopher Walken starred as Johnny Smith, the recipient of clairvoyant powers bestowed on him by a freak lightning accident. When Johnny shakes the hand of Greg Stillson at a political rally, he receives a psychic vision that if Stillson wins the presidential election, he will be responsible for firing nuclear weapons that cause world destruction. To prevent the vision from occurring, Johnny stalks Stillson, and shoots him. Unfortunately, security guards also kill Johnny. Drawing his last breath, Johnny touches Stillson's body and senses the future is now safe.

Mr. Beer Belly - Just one of many names given to Mr. Lynn Belvedere (Christopher Hewitt) by a scatterbrained teenage cheerleader named Angela on the sitcom MR. BELVEDERE/ABC/1985-90. Angela (Michele Matheson) was the best friend of Heather Owens (Tracy Wells) whose family employed a British manservant named Mr. Belvedere. Whenever Angela visited the Owens household, she incorrectly called Mr. Belvedere by such ignominious misnomers as Mister Beer Belly, Mr. Bumper Sticker, Mr. Beaver Dam or Mr. Bell Ringer. Once, Angela entered and won the Miss Beaver Falls Beauty Pageant. Her talent: a ventriloquism act with a dummy resembling Mr. Belvedere.

"Mr. Brady died of AIDS" - Ethan Hawke as Troy Dyer in the motion picture *Reality Bites* (1994). In the film, newly graduated high school student Lelaina Pierce (Winona Ryder) ponders, "I just don't understand why things can't just go back to normal at the end of the half hour, like on 'The Brady Bunch' or something." Her friend Troy bluntly tells her, "Well, 'cause Mr. Brady died of AIDS."

Mr. Empty Pants - A cartoon character created by Peg Bundy (Katey Sagal) on the sitcom MARRIED...WITH CHILDREN/FOX/1987-97. After Peg pick-pocketed her husband's wallet, Al warns, "Never leave me with empty pants again!" The expression inspired the cartoon character called "Mr. Empty Pants" that Peg developed into a comic feature for *Modern Gal* magazine about "a hapless loser" of a man (actually her husband

Al). The name Mr. Empty Pants was a sexual put-down for Al's lack of manhood. "If you had what other men have, Peggy said, "I wouldn't need batteries." After *Playgirl* magazine wanted Al as a centerfold (with bikini-clad babes), a jealous Peggy kills-off Mr. Empty Pants and says, "I couldn't handle your happiness, so I killed you." (with a lady's shoe-shaped meteorite). "Did I suffer?" asked Al? "Sure!" quipped Peggy.

"Mister, if you don't shut up I'm gonna kick one hundred percent of your ass" - Judge Reinhold as Brad Hamilton talks back to a customer (Sonny Carl Davis) who said, "It says one hundred percent guaranteed, you moron!" in the motion picture *Fast Times at Ridgemont High* (1982).

"Mr. Madison, what you've just said is one of the most insanely idiotic things I have ever heard. At no point in your rambling, incoherent response were you even close to anything that could be considered a rational thought. Everyone in this room is now dumber for having listened to it. I award you no points, and may God have mercy on your soul" - James Downey as a grade school Principal speaks to Billy Madison (Adam Sadler), lazy son of a millionaire who goes back to grades 1-12 in order to inherit his father's hotel empire in the motion picture *Billy Madison* (1995).

Mr. Nude - What Red Forman (Kurtwood Smith) from the sitcom THAT '70S SHOW/FOX/1998-2006 called his teenage son, Eric (Topher Grace) after he came out of his bedroom one night wrapped only in a sheet. The next morning in the kitchen, Red repeated his mean-spirited moniker ("Well, if it isn't Mr. Nude") in front of their visiting next-door neighbor Bob Pinciotti (Don Stark) who informed everyone, "Hey! That was my nickname in college." Curious, his daughter, Donna (Laura Prepon) says, "Dad, you didn't go to college." To which her father replies, "Didn't stop me getting a nickname." The next night, Eric's father stood outside of his son's bedroom banging pot and ladle and yelling "FIRE!" When Eric appears wrapped in a sheet, his father tells him "we're doing this every night until you put on some pants."

"Mr. Powers, I would never have sex with you, ever! If you were the last man on earth and I was the last woman on earth, and the future of the human race depended on our having sex, simply for procreation, I still would not have sex with you" - Miss Vanessa Kensington (Elizabeth Hurley) fighting off the sexual advances of world famous spy Austin Powers (Mike Myers) in the motion picture *Austin Powers: International Man of Mystery (*1997).

Mr. Warmth - Insult comedian Don Rickles was sarcastically nicknamed "Mr. Warmth" by his show business buddies because of his verbal barbs that showed no mercy. Be you Black, Asian, Irish, Italian, whatever, Rickles jokingly incorporated ethnic slurs and bigotry into his act. If you were Asian, he might mention slanty-eyes, buck teeth and Pearl Harbor; if you were Black, the topic of watermelon might be brought up; if you were Irish, drunkenness would be implied; and if you were Italian, talk of the Mafia would surely arise. The unique thing about his comedy is that when he finished shooting his slings and arrow of outrageous insults, he announced to the audience that "It was all in fun." Rickles once said, "I've got a sixth sense that releases a trip-hammer in my mind–warning me when I go too far. The presence of anger in an insult destroys the humor." His philosophy is that if you can get people to laugh at bigotry, stereotypes, etc., you can help them see how foolish it all is. Richard Lewis, Rickles' costar on the sitcom DADDY DEAREST/FOX/1993 said of Rickles, "He insults everybody, he takes no prisoners, but he is a man with a golden heart. His type of ethnic humor will upset some people. But if you look at the total package, this guy's message is that we should all laugh at ourselves." A sample insult: [to an Arab] "Hey, 7-Eleven called...Your camels are blocking the aisles." Don Rickles was a frequent guest on NBC's THE TONIGHT SHOW and starred in three short-lived comedy series including, THE DON RICKLES SHOW/ABC/1968-69 (comedy/variety); THE DON RICKLES SHOW/CBS/1972 (sitcom); and C.P.O. SHARKEY/NBC/1976-78 (military comedy). Also known as the "Merchant of Venom," Don Rickles co-hosted FOUL-UPS, BLEEPS AND BLUNDERS/ABC/1984.

"Mr. West, not every situation requires your patented approach of shoot first, shoot later, shoot some more and then when everybody's dead try to ask a question or two" - Kevin Kline as President Ulysses S. Grant offers some criticism to his secret service agent James T. West (Will Smith) in the western adventure film *Wild Wild West* (1999).

Mistress Bitch - Book title mentioned in episode "The One with Mrs. Bing" on the twentysomething sitcom FRIENDS/NBC/1994-2004. Mistress Bitch was written by romance novelist Nora Bing (Morgan Fairchild), the mother of Chandler Bing (Matthew Perry). Chandler's friend Rachel Green (Jennifer Aniston) thought his mom's books were cool and says, "I got to tell you, I love your mom's books...I can't get on a plane without one." Chandler responds, "Yeah, well, It's not so cool when you're eleven and all your friends are passing around page seventy-nine of *Mistress Bitch.*"

"Mitch is 'The Man,' I'm the idiot, you're the screw-up, and we're all losers" - Curt assessment by Joe (Anthony LaPaglia), an independent record store worker in the motion picture *Empire Records* (1995). When a customer is discovered shoplifting, an eagle-eyed clerk named Gina (Renée Zellweger) makes the announcement: "Attention Rex Manning fans! To your left you will notice a shoplifter being chased by night manager Lucas (Rory Cochrane), this young man will be caught, deep fried in hot oil and served to our first hundred customers. Just another tasty treat from the gang at Empire Records!" Note: In the film *That Thing You Do!* (1996) Tom Hanks as rock music promoter Mr. White says, "You know, Horace was right about you, Guy; you are the smart one. Lenny is the fool, Jimmy is the...talent, and Faye is...well, now, Faye is special, isn't she? And you are the smart one. That's what I think, anyway."

"The mob is full of thieving, cheating, psychopaths...*We* work for the President of the United States" - Trey Wilson as Regional Director Franklin explains the subtleties between the thugs in the Mafia and the supposed shiny white knights in the Federal Bureau of Investigation in the motion picture *Married to the Mob* (1988).

"Mom always liked you best!" - The classic sound of sibling rivalry humorously shouted by Tommy Smothers (guitar player) to his brother Dick Smothers (bass player) on the musical variety program THE SMOTHERS BROTHERS COMEDY HOUR/CBS/ABC/NBC/1967-75. Their eighth album "Mom Always Liked You Best" (Mercury Records, 1965) features a five minute track where Tom and Dick argue about their relationship with their mother. According to an interview in the *PortFolio Weekly* by Jim Newsom (11/01/2005) 'Mom liked you best' came out of frustration; it was just an adlib. I had totally demeaned him (Tom)," said Dick Smothers, "told him everything that was wrong with him, that he wasn't even fit to live. 'Oh yeh? Mom always liked you best!'...hammered the last nail in the coffin of his self-esteem." A selection of "Mom liked you best" themed merchandise can be purchased at the Smothers Brothers Winery gift shop located on Highway 12 and Warm Springs Road in Kenwood, California.

"Money! I hate, loathe, despise and abominate money" - Lucille Bremer as Rose Smith shares her opinion on wealth in the motion picture *Meet Me in St. Louis* (1944). Her father, Alonzo Smith (Leon Ames) was quick to point out, however, "You also spend it."

Monty Python's Flying Circus Insults - On the British comedy MONTY PYTHON'S FLYING CIRCUS/BBC/1969-74, a group of five zany Oxford/Cambridge graduates (Graham Chapman, John Cleese, Eric Idle, Terry Jones, Michael Palin) and American artist, Terry Gilliam created a comedy program (a continuation of the craziness typical of the British 1950s classic radio series THE GOON SHOW) filled with blackouts, surreal skits, and irreverent humor which targeted virtually anyone in any position of power. Amidst the utter confusion and insanity of their skits ("And now for something completely different...") came a multitude of verbose put-downs and insults espoused by John Cleese. Some of his greatest insults: "You stupid, furry Bucktoothed gits!"; "You excrement! You lousy hypocritical whining toadies with your lousy color TV sets and your Tony Jacklin golf clubs"; and "I unclog my nose in your direction...I wave my private parts at your aunties, you cheesy-lover, second-hand-election donkey-bottom-biters!" On the skit entitled "In Search of an Argument" we hear Cleese say, "Shut your festering gob, you tit! Your type makes me puke! You vacuous stuffy-nosed malodorous pervert!!!" In the film *Monty Python and the Holy Grail* (1975) we hear a French sentry (John Cleese) insulting King Arthur with "I fart in your general direction. Your mother was a hamster and your father smelt of elderberries!"

"Moronica for Morons" - The national motto of a Nazi-like country in the comedy spoof *You Nazty Spy!* (1940). During an attempt to rouse the citizenry, Moe Hailstone, the dictator of Moronica (Moe Howard doing a spoof of Adolph Hitler) gives the following speech: "My good people of Moronica. I'm very happy to see this little gathering. We must throw off the yoke of monarchy and make our country safe for hypocrisy. Our motto shall be: 'Moronica for Morons.' We will have less work and more play. Every Thursday, you will receive hamburgers and eggs. Moronica must expand. We must extend our neighbors a helping hand. We will extend them two helping hands and help ourselves to our neighbors." In *Half-Wits Holiday* (1947), one of the many black & white episodes of THE THREE STOOGES comedy shorts produced in Hollywood from the 1930-50s, Moe Howard reveals, "We are members of the Morons' Union, local 6 and 7/8! Their official song went, "We are Morons, through and through, let us sing our song for you (followed by grimacing and silly moaning)." Other Stooge insults included the phrase "Why, I'll murder ya!" and the application of 81-C ("No, Not 81-C!") a two-handed eye-poke designed to take out two people at once. Note: In the 1940s, a popular series of moron jokes circulated in the form of questions and answer. For example, Question: "Why did the little moron throw the clock out the window?" Answer: "He wanted to see time fly." DUH! *See also* "Why I'll murder ya!"

"Mortals are weak" - Rex Ingram as a Persian genie speaks to Abu the Thief (Sabu) who releases the genie from its bottle in the motion picture *The Thief of Bagdad* (1940). His full statement: "You're a clever little man, little master of the universe, but mortals are weak and frail. If their stomach speaks, they forget their brain. If their brain speaks, they forget their hearts. And if their hearts speak [laughing boldly]—if their hearts speak, they forget everything!"

"Move boys, unless you want to look like boxes of Cheerios" - Robert Forster as private eye 'Hollywood' Harry warns the bad guys to step aside in the motion picture *Hollywood Harry* (1985). Note: In the film *Running Scared* (1986) Gregory Hines as Ray Hughes says, "Listen, Snake, here's the situation: I have this gun here. Now I am going to take the gun out and I am going to shoot a lot of holes in the door. If you are standing if front of the door, what can I tell ya? Some of the holes are gonna be in you. Ya catching my drift, Snake?"

"Música! and make it sweet, goddammit, or I'll shoot the band!" - Boothe Powers as drug lord Cash Bailey strikes up the band in the motion picture *Extreme Prejudice* (1987).

"My brother wouldn't touch your titties with a ten foot pole. He likes his women bad, Lenora, not cheap" - Ricki Lake as Pepper to her friend Lenora (Kim Webb) in the motion picture *Cry Baby* (1990).

"My contribution to birth control" - Sylvester Stallone as police detective Ray Tango as he stuffs a hand-grenade down a bad guy's pants in the motion picture *Tango & Cash* (1989). Note: In the film, *Roman Scandals* (1933), Eddie Cantor says "It wouldn't only be murder, it would be birth control" to a plan to send him back in time to be killed by Roman soldiers.

"My cousin was a weird guy" - Jason Lee as Brodie Bruce in the motion picture *Mallrats* (1995). Just to pass the time, Brodie tells his suburban high school friend: "One time my cousin Walter got this cat stuck in his ass. True story. He bought it at the local mall, so the whole fiasco wound up on the news. It was embarrassing for my relatives and all. But the next week, he did it again. Different cat, same results, complete with a trip to the emergency room. Then, last week, I saw him in the pet store. He was buying another cat! I said, 'Walt, what the hell are you doing, you know you're just gonna get this cat stuck up your ass too, why don't you knock it off?' And he says to me, 'Brodie, how the hell else am I supposed to get the gerbil out?' My cousin was a weird guy." Note: Comedy skits on THE STEVE ALLEN SHOW in the 1950s featured an Army Sergeant (played by Wally Cox) whose hookline catchphrase was "What a crazy guy!" And, in the film *The Doom Generation* (1995) James Duval as Jordon White says, "I feel like a gerbil spinning around in Richard Gere's butt."

"My dear girl, don't flatter yourself. What I did this evening was for King and country. You don't think it gave me any pleasure, do you?" - Sean Connery as secret agent James Bond deflates the ego of female enemy Fiona Volpe (Luciana Paluzzi) to whom he just made love in the motion picture *Thunderball* (1965).

"My dog's bigger than your dog!" - Ad slogan for Ken'l Ration dog food used in a series of memorable TV commercials in the 1960s. Based on the song "My Dog's Bigger Than Yours" (written by Tom Paxton), the commercials featured the voices of two children in a shouting match as they try to convince the other that their own dog is better. The lyrics began:

Kid #1:	My dog's faster than your dog.
Kid #2:	My dog's bigger than yours.
Both Kids:	My dog's better 'cause he gets Ken-L Ration. / My dog's better than yours.
Kid #1:	My dog's prettier.
Kid #2:	Smarter.
Kid #1:	Taller.
Both Kids:	My dog's better than yours.

"My great Aunt Jennifer ate a box of chocolates every day of her life. She lived to be a hundred and two, and when she had been dead three days, she looked better than you do now" - Monty Woolley as smart-alecky patient Sheridan Whiteside insults his long-suffering private nurse Miss Preen (Mary Wickes) in the motion picture *The Man Who Came to Dinner* (1941).

"My home is hell" - George C. Scott as Dr. Herbert Bock expresses an opinion about his family life in the medical drama *The Hospital* (1971). He continues, "We've got a 23-year-old boy, I threw him out of the house last year. Shaggy haired Maoist! I don't know where he is—presumably building bombs in basements as an expression of his universal brotherhood. We've got a 17-year-old daughter who's had two abortions in two years. Got arrested last week at a rock festival for pushing drugs. They let her go. A typical affluent American family. I don't mean to be facile about this. I blame myself for those two useless young people. I never exercised parental authority. I'm no good at that." Note: Family problems continue in the film *Carbon Copy* (1981) when George Segal as a disgruntled corporate executive complains, "I'm Jewish, my son is black (illegitimate 17-year-old son) and my lawyer smokes pot. Don't tell me I'm not in trouble."

"My job is to teach these natives the meaning of democracy, and they're going to learn democracy if I have to shoot every one of them." - Paul Ford as frustrated Colonel Purdy who is stationed on the American occupied Island of Okinawa after World War II and trying to teach its inhabitants about United States values in the motion picture *The Teahouse of the August Moon* (1956).

"My life is like death, my children are the spawn of Hell and you are the Devil" - In the film *Overboard* (1987) Goldie Hawn starred as Joanna, a spoiled rich bitch heiress who falls off her yacht, bumps her head on a garbage scow and gets amnesia while cruising the waters near a small Oregon town of Elk Cove. Dean Proffitt, a local carpenter (Kurt Russell) with a bunch of motherless kids comes forward to claims Joanna as his wife and then takes her to a broken-down home filled with loud, feuding children. When Dean leaves the woman (now called Annie) alone with the children, he returns to find her babbling, "My life is like death, my children are the spawn of Hell and you are the Devil." After Annie regains her memory, she decides to stay with her new family and the man she previously called "This missing link person."

"My mom called me a bum-magnet. If there was a bum within a fifty-mile radius, I was completely attracted to him." - Julia Roberts as prostitute Vivian Ward shares her personal history with wealthy client Edward Lewis (Richard Gere) in the motion picture *Pretty Woman* (1990).

"My mother always told me that violence doesn't solve anything...Really. I wonder what the city founders of Hiroshima would have to say about that" - Dina Meyer as starship trooper Dizzy Flores talks to fellow soldier Jean Rasczak (Michael Ironside) in the sci-fi motion picture *Starship Troopers* (1997). Trooper Carmen Ibanez (Denise Richards) interjects, "They wouldn't say anything. Hiroshima was destroyed. Rasczek concludes, "Correct. Violence has resolved more conflicts than anything else. The contrary opinion that violence doesn't solve anything is merely wishful thinking at its worst!"

"My mother says the world's a garbage dump and we're just flies it attracts" - Natalie Wood as singing teenage movie star Daisy Clover shares her mother's (Ruth Gordon) opinion of life in the motion picture *Inside Daisy Clover* (1966).

"My name is Karl Glocken and this is a ship of fools! I am a fool. You'll meet more fools as we go along. This tub is packed with them. Emancipated ladies and ballplayers. Lovers. Dog lovers. Ladies of joy. Tolerant Jews, Dwarfs. All kinds. And who knows—if you look closely enough, you may even find yourself on board" - Michael Dunn as Glocken narrates the beginning of the motion picture *Ship of Fools* (1965) about the ocean liner Grand Hotel cruising from Vera Cruz to Bremerhaven in the pre-Nazi days of 1931. The passengers are tagged as fools because of their inability to see the foreshadowing of the holocaust and the reign of terror of the Nazi Regime soon to come. Note: In the film *The Addams Family (1991)* Raul Julia as Gomez Addams says to a court judge, "They say a man who represents himself has a fool for a client. Well, as God as my witness. I am that fool!"

"My name is Maximus Decimus Meridius, commander of the Armies of the North, General of the Felix Legions, loyal servant to the true emperor, Marcus Aurelius. Father to a murdered son, husband to a murdered wife. And I will have my vengeance, in this life or the next" - Russell Crowe as Roman General Maximus Decimus Meridius confronts Commodus (Joaquin Phoenix), the usurper of the Roman throne in the historical epic *Gladiator* (2000). As Marcus Aurelius was to appoint Maximus the new leader of the Empire, the emperor's treacherous son, Commodus suffocates his father, orders Maximus killed and his family murdered. Maximus eludes death but is sold into slavery and becomes a seasoned Gladiator who eventually finds his way to Rome and back in the presence of the man who destroyed his life. In a final battle in the Colloseum, Maximus defeats and kills Commodus. Now mortally wounded, Maximus dies but not before he orders the release of unjustly imprisoned Romans and gives the glory of what was Rome back to its rightful heirs.

"My wife is a witch!" - When newlywed advertising executive Darrin Stephens on the sitcom BEWITCHED/ABC/1964-72 complained to a man at a local bar that his wife was a witch, the man responded, "You should meet MY wife!" Darrin, of course, is actually referring to the fact that he just discovered he got married to an honest to goodness, broom-carrying, cauldron-stirring witch named Samantha (Elizabeth Montgomery). *See also* "Durwood"

"My wife will be home soon. Can you say, 'bitch'?" - Eddie Murphy as Mr. Robinson as he portrays a ghetto version of Mr. Fred Rogers in comedy sketches on the late night NBC program SATURDAY NIGHT LIVE! Murphy once began the skit with a corrupted version of Mr. Roger's theme song which began "It's a hell of a day in the neighborhood...I hope I get to move into your neighborhood. But the problem is, when I move in, you all move away!"

Nature's Revenge on Pepping Toms - The pejorative nickname of Ms. Duffy (Pattee Chapman), the unmarried (but desperate to be married) daughter of the proprietor of a New York City neighborhood tavern on the sitcom DUFFY'S TAVERN/NBC/1954. The character was based on the successful radio program of the same name that aired from 1941-51. *See also* "The Peeper"

"Nazis! I hate those guys!" - Harrison Ford as archeology professor Indiana Jones expresses dissatisfaction upon discovering his father Dr. Henry Jones (Sean Connery) had been taken prisoner by German soldiers in the motion picture *Indiana Jones and the Last Crusade* (1989). Indy had his fill of Nazi bad guys in his first encounter *Raiders of the Lost Ark* (1984) when we learn Indy "hates snakes."

Nerd - Derogatory term used to describe someone who is unsophisticated or inept in the social skills, (i.e. someone who can't get a date, wears pocket protectors, and is a "dues" paying member of the *Star Trek* Fan Club). Note: In the film *Hype!* (1996) Van Conner as an interviewee offered this explanation of a nerd "We were the guy in high school who people used to beat up and we couldn't even talk to the pretty girls. I mean, we couldn't...we're nerds, goddammit!" The motion picture Revenge *of the Nerds* (1984) and its sequel *Revenge of the Nerds II: Nerds in Paradise* (1987) followed the adventures of a group of "geeky" college freshmen who matched wits with campus jocks and snobby coeds who looked down on the brainy newcomers. Robert Carradine played the head nerd in both movies. In the late 1970s on NBC's SATURDAY NIGHT LIVE, Gilda Radner and Bill Murray played Lisa Loopner and Todd DiLaMuca on a skit entitled "The Nerds." On one episode Lisa and Todd promoted their rock album "Trying Desperately to be Liked" on a local radio station. The album included such songs as "I'll Give You My Lunch Money," "I Can't Help It If I Have Egg Salad Sandwich on My Retainer" and "Let My Head Up Out of the John and I'll Give You Tomorrow's Lunch Money." As Lisa said, "We're young, we're gifted and we're Nerds." The album had no takers (even free copies). Other television series to explore the "nerd" phenomenon included DWEEBS/CBS/1995 (about ultra nerdy computer techs at Cyberbyte Software); FREAKS AND GEEKS/NBC/1999 (about the nerdy students at a 1980s Michigan high school.); and BEAUTY AND THE GEEK/WB/CW/2005 (MENSA-worthy "geeks" pair with gorgeous women)

"The nerve of some people. Well I'll teach him a lesson" - Angela DiMeglio as Sheila Tidepool seeking revenge in the sci-fi film *Walkin' on Sunshine: The Movie* (1997). Elaborating on her plan, Sheila threatens, "I will go back in time and sabotage his coordinates so that when he tries to go back in time to the Poobah's promotion, he will go to the future instead! Er...no, I will go back in time and sabotage the coordinates so that when he tried to go back in time to the Poobah's promotion he did go to the future instead. Right. That egomaniacal voyeur will look like an idiot in front of the Poobah! No wait, he already did look like an idiot in front of the Poobah. The English language is sorely lacking a verb tense for this situation. At any rate, I'll show him whose boss. At any rate, I showed him whose boss."

"Never, EVER, fuck with an antique dealer!" - The angry cry directed to a vampire as the protégé of Van Helsing impales his attacker in the film *Dracula 2000* (2000). After a group of high-tech crooks break into an established antique store in London, they discover a silver casket in a subterranean vault that they think is filled with a fortune of some kind. Transporting their booty via airplane, the contents of the coffin escapes and reveals itself to be the historical Dracula, who it turns out is actually the condemned spirit of Judas Escariot, the betrayer of Jesus Christ. At the end of the film, Van Helsing's daughter wraps a wire around Dracula's neck, tosses him off a building and hangs his body just as the sunrise bursts his body into flames.

"Never give a sucker an even break" - When a conniving patent-medicine salesman Professor Eustace McGargle (W. C. Fields) parts company with an heiress named Poppy (Rochelle Hudson) in the motion picture *Poppy* (1936) he leaves her with this advice: "Let me give you one word of fatherly advice—Never give a sucker an even break." Earlier in the film, Oulietta Hemoglobin (Susan Miller) sees McGargle's large nose and asks her mother (Margaret Dumont), "Do you think he drinks?" Mama replies, "He didn't get that nose from playing ping-pong." Note: In the film *You Can't Cheat an Honest Man* (1939) W. C. Fields as Larsen E. Whipsnade says, "As my dear old grandfather Litvak said (just before they swung the trap), he said, 'You can't cheat an honest man. Never give a sucker an even break or smarten up a chump'."

"Never, never, interrupt me, okay? - Jack Nicholson as cranky New York City novelist Melvin Udall berates his gay artist neighbor Simon Bishop (Greg Kinnear) in the motion picture *As Good As It Gets* (1997). To make his point crystal clear, Melvin continues, "Not if there's a fire, not even if you hear the sound of a thud from my home and one week later there's a smell coming from there that can only be a decaying human body and you have to hold a hanky to your face because the stench is so thick that you think you're going to faint. Even then, don't come knocking. Or, if it's election night, and you're excited and you wanna celebrate because some fudgepacker that you date has been elected the first queer president of the United States and he's going to have you down to Camp David, and you want someone to share the moment with. Even then, don't knock. Not on this door. Not for ANY reason. Do you get me, sweetheart?"

"Next person who says Merry Christmas to me, I'll kill them" - Myrna Loy as Nora Charles speaks to her husband Nick Charles (William Powell) in the motion picture *The Thin Man* (1934).

"Next time I see you I'm gonna hit you so hard I'm gonna knock you back to the Stone Age where you come from" - Burt Reynolds as 1930s private eye Mike Murphy lets police Lt. Speer (Clint Eastwood) know just where their relationship stands in the motion picture *City Heat* (1984). Note: In the film *Diner* (1982) Timothy Daly as temporarily incarcerated Billy tells a cellmate, "I'll hit you so hard, I'll kill your whole family." And, in the film *Tank Girl* (1995) Lori Petty as Tank Girl threatens, "I'm gonna hit you so hard, your children will be born bruised!"

"Nice day for a murder" - Mean-spirited suggestion spoken by gangster Rocky Sullivan (James Cagney) to a mug named Mac Keefer (George Bancroft) in the motion picture *Angels With Dirty Faces* (1938). Rocky Sullivan grew up tough on the means streets of New York City. His growing influence over the neighborhood kids - who idolize the thug - get the attention of local priest, Jerry Connelly (Pat O'Brien), Rocky's former childhood friend. After Rocky is arrested for murder and sentenced to death, Father Jerry asks Rocky to act afraid as he is dragged to the electric chair so the kids will reject Rocky's deeds and lifestyle. Rocky refuses the request, but at the last minute he begins to cry and struggle ("crawl on his belly") with the guards who took him to his doom. The next day, the newspaper headline read: ROCKY DIES YELLOW...KILLER COWARD AT END.

"Nice tie. Did they have a sale at Tie City?" - Stacy Keach as private eye Mike Hammer insults a police detective in the television series MICKEY SPILLANE'S MIKE HAMMER/CBS/1984-87. Note: In the film *End of Days* (1999) Satan returns to earth just prior to the New Year's Millennium celebration to father a child and usher in an apocalyptic future. As he walks the streets of New York City, he bumps into a teenager. Looking at the kid's shirt, the Prince of Darkness sees the message *Satan Rules* and says, "Nice shirt." The rude youth, however, "Dis's" the Devil and crosses the street. In retaliation, the Devil distracts the kid just enough so that he gets hit by a transit bus.

"Nigger is just another word for guilty" - Esther Rolle as Aunt Sarah, a black woman who lived in the 1923 Florida town of Rosewood that a white racist lynch mob burned to the ground in the motion picture *Rosewood* (1997).

"Nigger, you ain't nothin' but the white man's dog!" - Denzel Washington as Trip, a Negro Civil War soldier disenchanted with fellow Negro John Rawlins (Morgan Freeman) in the motion picture *Glory* (1989). In the film, Rawlins takes exception to Trip's accusation that he is "hollerin and orderin; everybody around" because the white man "give you some stripes", and slaps Trip in the face. He then says, "And who are you? So full of hate that you have to fight everybody, because you've been whipped and chased by hounds. Well that might not be living, but it sure as hell ain't dying. And dying's been what these white boys have been doing for going on three years now, dying by the thousands, dying for you, fool. And all this time I keep askin' myself, when, O Lord, when gonna be our time? Gonna come a time when we all gonna hafta ante up and kick in like men, LIKE MEN! You watch who you callin' nigger! If there's any niggers around here, it's YOU, just a stupid-ass, swamp-runnin' nigger! And if you not careful, that's all you ever gonna be!"

"The niggers, the niggers are gettin' all da money. Why work, tell me, why the fuck work, when you can screw, have babies, an' get paid for it?" - Peter Boyle as hard-hat bigot Joe Curran expresses racist sentiments in the motion picture *Joe* (1970). Another Joe-ism: "Thirty-two percent of all liberals are queer, that's a fact. The Wallace people did a poll."

"Nine killed you, nine shall die!" - The blood oath of Dr. Anton Phibes in the horror film *The Abominable Dr. Phibes* (1971). Blaming the death of his wife, Victoria on nine people involved in her unsuccessful surgery, Dr. Phibes (Vincent Price) swears revenge. Chanting "Nine killed you. Nine shall die. Nine times, nine! Nine killed you! Nine shall die! Nine eternities in DOOM!", Phibes prepares to kill off his enemies one by one in a series of spectacular and extremely cruel executions based on the ten Hebrew curses placed on the Egyptian Pharaohs during Exodus. Phibes method of extermination, includes attack by killer bats; a party mask that slowly crushes its wearers skull; draining all the blood from a victim while still alive; freezing a man to death with a minus 100 degree zero hail storm; placing rats in a plane cockpit to force a crash; a brass statue of a unicorn impaling man's chest; dropping locust onto the face of a sleeping nurse which eat away her flesh; and forcing Dr. Vesalius, the surgeon who operated on Phibe's wife, to use his surgical skills to save his son's life who was strapped on a gurney underneath an acid bath (a key sewn inside the boy's body had to be removed within six-minutes to unlock the restraining collar holding him to the table). Dr. Phibes continued his revenge in *The Return of the Abominable Dr. Phibes* (1972).

Nip, The - Nickname of Elaine Benes (Julia Louis-Dreyfus) heard on the sitcom SEINFELD/NBC/1990-98. For the holiday season, Elaine wanted to send a Christmas card with her photograph and so she got her friend Cosmo Kramer (Michael Richards) to take a snapshot. Unfortunately, Elaine (and Kramer) didn't realize her blouse was not fully buttoned and that her breast nipple was exposed to the camera lens. When Elaine first saw the mistake, she cried, "Oh my God that's my nipple!" For this little photo faux pas, she was nicknamed "The Nip" by her coworkers at Pendant Publishing.

NO MA'AM - The woman hating fraternal organization featured on the dysfunctional situation comedy MARRIED...WITH CHILDREN/FOX/1987-97. The chief member and advocate of NO MA'AM was Al Bundy (Ed O'Neill), a henpecked husband with two children and a dog who worked as a shoe salesman in a Chicago mall. Each member of the all-male group proudly wore a white T-shirt bearing the initials NO MA'AM on the front of the shirt. On the reverse side of the shirt, the full name of the group (National Organization of Men Against Amazonian Masterhood) ran vertically down the back. Marcy Rhodes/D'Arcy (Amanda Bearse), Al's women's libber next-door neighbor (whom he called "Chicken Legs") was the group's chief nemesis who headed a group called "Feminists Against Neanderthal Guys" (FANG). Marcy managed to destroy Al's hopes of getting the group tax free status on episode "Reverend Al" when Al Bundy and his NO MA'AM cronies tried to form the "Church of NO MA'AM" to avoid paying beer tax. At first, the movement gained momentum and Al became a televangelist who preached the NO MA'AM way of life. Unfortunately, Marcy exposed him as a fraud when she presents photographic evidence of Al wining and dining his wife (being nice to one's spouse definitely violated the group's philosophy). Al once mentioned NO MA'AM also stood for "Numb Old Men Anxiously Awaiting Morticians" just after having sex with his wife, Peggy. On episode "Legend of Ironhead Haynes" Al Bundy is forced to stop insulting his customers when a fat woman complains to his boss. Disgusted with political correctness, and his nuisance of a neighbor, Marcy, Al Bundy and his NO MA'AM cronies seek out the advice of the macho legend Ironhead Haynes. Ironhead passes on the following Ten Commandments:

- Rule 1. It is OK to call hooters 'knockers' and sometimes 'snack trays'
- Rule 2. It is wrong to be French
- Rule 3. It is OK to put all bad people in a giant meat grinder
- Rule 4. Lawyers, see Rule 3
- Rule 5. It is OK to drive a gas guzzler if it helps you get babes
- Rule 6. Everyone should car pool but me
- Rule 7. Bring back the word 'stewardesses'
- Rule 8. Synchronized swimming is not a sport
- Rule 9. Mud wrestling is a sport
- Rule 10. Err..., that's it.

"No more foreplay" - In the James Bond film *Goldeneye* (1995) Agent 007 (Pierce Brosnan) makes love in a steam bath to a Russian woman named Xenia Onatopp (Famke Janssen). In the midst of their romantic encounter, Onatopp wraps her legs about Bond and tries to crack his spine like a walnut. To escape her deadly embrace, Bond body-slams her against the wall, grabs his gun then firmly announces, "No more foreplay." When Bond first pointed the gun, Onatopp said, "You don't need a gun commander." Bond replied, "That depends on your definition of safe sex." In the film's climax, Bond shots down a helicopter that consequently yanks Onatopp repelling line through the air and mortally slams her into the tree. To which Bond coolly quips, "She always did enjoy a good squeeze." Note: Daryl Hannah played a rogue android who squeezed men to death with her thighs in the science fiction film *Blade Runner* (1982) loosely based on the novel "Do Androids Dream of Electric Sheep?" by Phillip K. Dick.

"No niggers allowed in there" - Racist words spoken by Eddie Murphy as black Detroit cop Axel Foley in the box office hit *Beverly Hills Cop* (1984). Posing as a writer in town to do an article on singer Michael Jackson, Axel tries to scam his way into a posh Beverly Hills hotel. To intimidate the desk clerk, Axel pulls out the race card and starts shouting, "Don't you think I realize what's going on here, Miss? Who do you think I am, huh? Don't you think I know that if I was some hotshot from out of town that pulled inside here and you guys made a reservation mistake, I'd be the first one to get a room and I'd be upstairs relaxing right now. But I'm not some hotshot from out of town, I'm a small reporter from *Rolling Stone* magazine that's in town to do an exclusive interview with Michael Jackson that's gonna be picked up by every major magazine in the country. I was gonna call the article 'Michael Jackson Is Sitting On Top of the World,' but now I think I might as well just call it 'Michael Jackson Can Sit On Top of the World Just As Long As He Doesn't Sit in the Beverly Palm Hotel 'Cause There's No Niggers Allowed in There!'" Of course, Axel got his room.

"No priest died during the potato famine" - Richard Harris as "Bull" McCabe, a 1930s Irish farmer expresses his contempt for men of the cloth in the motion picture *The Field* (1990). In the film, McCabe had nurtured a small piece of land for years until the widow who owned the property decides to sell it at auction. Unfortunately, McCabe's plans to buy the land are thwarted by an outsider American who buys the property to build a highway. While trying to convince the man to sell the land back to him, McCabe kills the American.

"No sequel for you!" - Arnold Schwarzenegger revokes a comic book villain's franchise in the action adventure *Last Action Hero* (1993). In the film, young Danny Madigan (Austin O'Brien) is given a magic ticket by Nick the Projectionist to the new Jack Slater action adventure film. Danny has seen all of Slater's film and can't wait to see his latest (4th) film. While watching the movie, Danny is miraculously transported into Slater's movie world (dynamite comes out of the movie screen and blows Danny into the movie itself). Unfortunately, movie hit man Benedict (Charles Dance) steals the ticket and enters Danny's world. Realizing the bad guys in Danny's reality can actually win, Benedict sets out to kill the actor who plays Jack Slater. During one encounter Benedict threatens to feed Jack Slater to guard dogs: "I snap my fingers and sometime tomorrow you emerge from several canine rectums." In a final confrontation Jack Slater (from the movie world) kills Benedict, but not before saying, "No sequel for you!" During one of Jack Slater's movie trailers [Jack Slater as Hamlet] intones, "Hey Claudius, You killed my father! Big Mistake!" The narrator interjects, "Something is rotten in the state of Denmark, and Hamlet is taking out the Trash." Jack Slater concludes, "To be or not to be?...Not to be!"

"No soup for you!" *See* - **Soup Nazi**

"Nobody beats me in the kitchen!" - Steven Seagal as Casey Ryback, a former Special Forces trained soldier turned cook kills a terrorist in the food galley of a train in the motion picture *Under Siege 2: Dark Territory* (1995).

"Nobody hurts my horse" – Viggo Mortenson as Frank T. Hopkins in the motion picture *Hildago* (2004). In the film, Hopkins, considered in his day to be one of the best riders in the American west, partakes in a desert horse race called the Ocean of Fire, a sixty-eight day, life-endangering 3,000-mile trek across the Arabian Desert. Along the way, nefarious Bedouins dig holes in the sand and camouflage the tops of each with bamboo to catch and debilitate oncoming riders in the race. When Hopkins and his horse, Hildago, a half-wild Spanish mustang fall into one of the traps, the horse's hind quarter is impaled on a lethally-pointed wooden shaft set in the bottom of the pit. Quickly, Hopkins pulls out the wooden spike by cutting into the horse's hide, and pulls his horse out of the hole so he they can continue on with the race. When Hopkins comes upon one of the men responsible for the trap, he whispers "Nobody hurts my horse" and then kills the man. Earlier in the film, Hopkins rebukes a stranger, saying, "Mister...you can say anything you want about me. I'm gonna have to ask you not to talk about my horse that way."

"No one fucks with the union!" - Dock worker boss Tony Two Toes (Joe Viterelli) expresses his dissatisfaction with a bunch of rouge agents transporting arms - without the union's permission - in the motion picture *Erased* (1996). When Tony calls the intruders "Those dirty commies!" his learned sidekick Mikey says, "They're not commies any more. They're a federation of independent liberated states." Tony Two Toes snarls "Don't make me hurt you, Mikey."

"Nobody has ever escaped from Stalag 17. Not alive, anyway" - Otto Preminger as German POW camp commander Oberst Von Scherbach addresses his Allied prisoners in the WWII motion picture *Stalag 17 (*1953). Another Nazi nugget of information:

"Always remember just because the Krauts are dumb doesn't mean they're stupid." When Sefton (William Holden) reluctantly exits the escape tunnel to rescue a fellow prisoner, he says, "Just one more word. If I ever run into any of you on the street corner, just let's pretend we never met before."

"Not everybody in the world is interested in your magnificent body, lady" - In the film *The Goodbye Girl* (1977) Richard Dreyfuss as young actor Elliot Garfield reluctantly shares a NYC apartment with single parent divorcée Paula McFadden (Marsha Mason). When she suspects, that her roommate may be coveting her pulchritude, Elliott vents his displeasure at the accusation, and says, "Not everybody in the world is interested in your magnificent body, lady. In the first place, it's not so magnificent. It's fair, but it ain't keepin' me up nights, ya know? I don't even think you're very pretty. Maybe, if you smiled once in a while, okay, but I don't want to do anything against your religion...I don't want to jump on your bones. I don't even want to see you in the morning."

"Not in my movie!" - The final words in the Wes Craven film *Scream* (1996). Standing over the body of a subdued serial killer, Sydney (Neve Campbell) is counseled, "Careful this is the part when the killer comes back to life." As he does, she pulls the trigger, shots him in the head and says, "Not in my movie!" Earlier in the film, the killer's partner told Sydney he once had a "thing" for her. To express her appreciation, Sydney toppled a TV set onto his head and said, "In your dreams!"

"Not only don't you have the scruples, you don't have any brains" - Ann Savage as a femme fatale named Vera insults hitchhiker Al Roberts (Tom Neal) in the motion picture *Detour* (1945).

"Now cut that out!" - Familiar yell of comedian Jack Benny (aka, the "Cheapest Man in the World") when he got frustrated with someone on episodes of THE JACK BENNY SHOW/CBS/1950-65. An exasperating "Well!" and a questioning "Hmmmm" were his other favorite expressions. *See also* "The Cheapest Man in the World"

"Now, get this, you double-crossing chimpanzee: There ain't going to be any interview and there ain't going to be any story. And that certified check of yours is leaving with me in twenty minutes. I wouldn't cover the burning of Rome for you if they were just lighting it up. If I ever lay my two eyes on you again, I'm gonna walk right up to you and hammer on that monkeyed skull of yours 'til it rings like a Chinese gong!" - Rosalind Russell as ace-reporter Hildy Johnson speaks on the phone to her ex-husband Walter Burns (Cary Grant) in the motion picture *His Girl Friday* (1940).

"Now, I ask you, Duarto, who's supposed to wear that? Some anorexic teenager? Some fetus? It's a conspiracy, I know it is! I've had enough. I'm leading a protest. I'm not buying another article of clothing until these designers come to their senses!" - Bette Midler as ex-wife Brenda Morelli Cushman expresses her hostility upon seeing a slinky dress (which she'll never fit into) in the motion picture *The First Wives Club* (1996).

"Now if you write any more cracks about Lois Underwood I'll cut off your ears and mail them to your father." - James Cagney as Dan Quigley threatens a movie critic with bodily harm if he doesn't lay off writing bad reviews about his actress girlfriend Lois Underwood (Margaret Lindsay) in the motion picture *Lady Killer* (1933). To drive home his point, Dan literally makes the critic eat his own words, by force feeding him his article, and then shoves the man's head into the toilet and flushes it.

"Now, if you're lucky you can hack through your ankle in five minutes!" - Instruction given to motorcycle punk in the Australian post-apocalyptic adventure film *Mad Max* (1979) starring Mel Gibson. After a band of crazed cyclists kill his wife and child, a police officer named Max embarks on a trail of high-speed vengeance. When he finds one of them looting an accident victim by the side of the road, he drags the punk to a nearby auto wreck, and instructs the creep to handcuff his ankle to the car. Max then proceeds to collect dripping gasoline from a broken fuel line and places it by an approaching flame. The frightened motorcyclist cries, "Hey listen I'm not a bad man. I'm sick, see. Sick. What do you call it? Psychopathic. You know. Personality disorder. The judge, man, he says so! You can't kill me...What are you doing? I want to know what your doing?" Max obliges and says, "The chain in those handcuffs is high tensile steel. It'd take you ten minutes to hack through them with this [Max throws a shard of glass on the ground near the man]. Now, if you're lucky you can hack through your ankle in five minutes." As the young man screams, "Come back...don't do this to me!" Max drives away. In a matter of moments, the fire from the auto wreck touches the spilled gasoline. Boom! No more bad guy.

"Now listen to me you benighted muckers. We're going to teach you soldiering. The world's noblest profession. When we're done with you, you'll be able to slaughter your enemies like civilized men" - Sean Connery as Daniel Dravot, an ex-solider from British-ruled India explains the soldier's trade to new recruits in the motion picture *The Man Who Would Be King* (1975). He further advises: "You are going to become soldiers. A soldier does not think. He only obeys. Do you really think that if a soldier thought twice he'd give his life for queen and country? Not bloody likely." Daniel and his partner Peachy Carnahan (Michael Caine) had traveled to Kafiristan in search of their destiny. Daniel stategized their plan: "In any place where they fight, a man who knows how to drill men can always be a King. In those parts say to any King we find 'D'you want to vanquish your foes?' and we will show him how to drill men; for that we know better than anything else. Then we will subvert that King and seize his Throne and establish a Dynasty."

"Now listen, you queer!" - During the coverage of the 1968 Democratic Convention (8/28/68) for ABC, Gore Vidal called William Buckley a "Crypto-Nazi." Buckley replied, "Now listen, you queer, stop calling me a Crypto-Nazi or I'll sock you in your Goddamn face and you'll stay plastered." Meanwhile on NBC, John Chancellor was manhandled on the convention floor by several members of the Chicago Police Department. "This is John Chancellor reporting from somewhere in custody."

"Now look here, you stupid little broad, do you know who I am? Do you think I let dames talk that way to me?" - James Cagney as gangster Martin "The Gimp" Snyder puts singer Ruth Etting (Doris Day) in her place for showing him disrespect in the motion picture *Love Me or Leave Me* (1955).

"Now the first time you kill somebody, that's the hardest. I don't give a shit if you're fuckin' Wyatt Earp or Jack the Ripper" - James Gandolfini as a gangster named Virgil explains the finer points of killing in the motion picture *True Romance* (1993). Continuing his lesson, Virgil says, "Remember that guy in Texas? The guy up in that fuckin' tower that killed all them people? I'll bet you green money that first little black dot he took a bead on, that was the bitch of the bunch. First one is tough, no fuckin' foolin'. The second one...the second one ain't no fuckin' Mardis Gras either, but it's better than the first one 'cause you still feel the same thing, you know...except it's more diluted, you know it's...it's better. I threw up on the first one, you believe that? Then the third one... the third one is easy, you level right off. It's no problem. Now...shit...now I do it just to watch their fuckin' expression change."

"Now they will know why they are afraid of the dark" - Ominous statement of religious cult leader Thulsa Doom (James Earl Jones) in the adventure fantasy film *Conan the Barbarian* (1982) based on the stories of Robert E. Howard. Thulsa Doom had massacred the village of Conan the Barbarian. Years later Conan infiltrates a fortress and rescues a princess held under the spell of Doom's snake cult. As Conan races away into the night Doom proclaims "Infidels of violence. They should all drown in lakes of blood. Now they will know why they are afraid of the dark. Now they will learn why they fear the night." Doom then sent his best warriors to kill Conan, but they were defeated. In a final confrontation, Conan cuts off Thulsa Doom's head and throws it down the steps of the Snake Temple. *See also* "Grant me revenge"

"Now you listen to me, you gutter-mouth punk!" - The stern voice of LAPD Sgt. Joe Friday (Jack Webb) putting a criminal in his place on a 1969 episode of the classic police drama DRAGNET/NBC/1967-70. Normally, Joe Friday was interested in "Just the Facts" but occasionally, some low-life got his dandruff up and he laid into them with the fervor of preacher delivering a fire-and brimstone sermon on Sunday. On this occasion, Joe growls, "Now you listen to me, you gutter-mouth punk! I've dealt with you before, and every time I did, it took me a month to wash off the filth. I'll tell you what you did to that four-year old girl out in Westlake Park: you staked out a bench like you've always done. You bought a sack of penny candy; you waited until the right little girl came along...You got her in your car. She started to cry; you hit her across the mouth twice. You cut her lip with your ring. Knocked out three of her teeth. And then you know what you did to her... Now, I didn't say that, Rockwell, you did. That's exactly what you told those officers who arrested you. They advised you of your constitutional rights before you opened your mouth. Now you're trying to tell us you didn't understand. Well, you're a liar... Like every hoodlum since Cain up through Capone, you've learned to hide behind some quirk in the law. And mister, you are a two-bit hoodlum. You've fallen twice for ADW Burglary, three times. Twice for forcible rape; I tagged you for those. And now you've graduated—you've moved to the sewer. You're a child molester."

"Now you sure you wanna have a fight?" - Sean Connery as Lt. Colonel Alan Caldwell in the motion picture *The Presidio* (1988). While Caldwell sat drinking coffee at a small diner, he asks his police officer companion Jay Austin (Mark Harmon) what his intentions were towards his daughter, Donna Caldwell (Meg Ryan). As the two continued to speak, a burly loudmouth customer in a red flannel shirt begins to taunt Caldwell who politely ignores the man. After Caldwell advises the man to "Let it alone, boy," the creep continues to refer to Caldwell as "Major" and then puts a lit cigar out in Caldwell's coffee. Having exhausted his patience, Caldwell asks "Now, you sure you wanna have a fight? Because I'm only gonna use my thumb....My right thumb. The left one's much too powerful for you." Caldwell then hits various pressure points on the man's body and beats him into submission. Finally, placing his thumb on the man's jugular vein, Caldwell concludes, "You see these little oak leaves. They're silver. That means I'm a Lt. Colonel. If they were gold, then I'd be a Major. You understand? ...That's good because the next time you see an officer of the Army, you'll be able to recognize his rank and he won't get ticked off and accidentally hurt you. You understand?" The thug says, "Yes, sir" and the Lieutenant Colonel gives him one more thumb jab to the stomach that knocks him to the ground. As Caldwell leaves the diner, Officer Austin cautiously says, "About your daughter, sir, I want you to know my intentions are strictly honorable." Note: In the film *The Lords of Discipline* (1983) Rick Rossovich as "Pig" shares what he learned at Carolina Military Institute: "Listen, you know what I learned this summer? How to kill usin' just my thumbs."

"Nurses are just like husbands. You can abuse them, insult them, work 'em to death, jump all over 'em. They'll take it. But give 'em a bad cup of coffee and you got a revolution on your hands." - Philosophic comment of Alma Kruger as Nurse Molly Byrd in the medical drama *Dr. Kildare's Strange Case* (1940).

"Nuts to you, dope" - Fred MacMurray as Richard Myles insults a Nazi soldier who salutes "Heil Hitler!" in the WWII action film *Above Suspicion* (1943). Note: In the film *Battle of the Bulge (1965)* a note from General McAuliffe simply states, "Nuts" to Nazi's who want his surrounded troops to surrender.

"NYPD means, I will Nock Yo Punkass Down!" - Will Smith as James Eduards, a hot-shot police officer turned alien fighter in the motion picture *Men in Black (*1997). Note: In the film *Smashing the Rackets* (1938) Frances Mercer as Susan "Pat" Lane asks, "What does F.B.I. stand for? Feeling Brutally Inclined?"

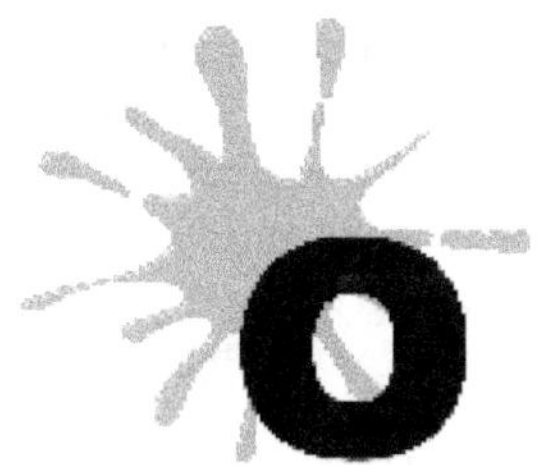

"Off with their heads!" - The imperial command issued by the looney Queen of Hearts who lived in Wonderland in the classic children's tale *Alice's Adventures in Wonderland* and *Through the Looking Glass and What Alice Found There* written by Lewis Carroll. The Queen of Hearts was quick to lop off the heads of anyone who didn't agree with her or didn't carry out their work assignments properly—like painting the roses in her garden. The Queen of Hearts character has been played by a variety of actresses in motion pictures, including *Alice in Wonderland (*1931) with Vie Quinn; *Alice in Wonderland* (1933) with Alec B. Francis; *Alice in Wonderland* (1950) with Pamela Brown; *Alice's Adventures in Wonde*rland (1972) with Flora Robson); *Alice in Wonderland* (1983) with Eve Arden; *Alice in Wonderland* (1985) with Jayne Meadows; and *Alice in Wonderland* (1999) with Miranda Richardson. Verna Felton provided the voice of the Queen of Hearts in the Disney's 1951 animated version of the story. Note: In the film *The Man in the Iron Mask* (1998) Louis XIV, the King of France (Leonardo DiCaprio) shouts, "Bring me the heads of Athos, Porthos, and Aramis, or I will have yours. And as for you, back to the prison you will go. And into the mask you hate. Wear it 'til you love it! And die in it."

"Oh, cut the bleeding heart crap, will ya? We've all got our switches, lights, and knobs to deal with, Striker. I mean, down here there are literally hundreds and thousands of blinking, beeping, and flashing lights, blinking and beeping and flashing—they're *flashing* and they're *beeping*. I can't stand it anymore! They're *blinking* and *beeping* and *flashing*! Why doesn't somebody pull the plug!" - William Shatner as Buck Murdock talks to pilot Ted Striker (Robert Hays) in the motion picture *Airplane II: The Sequel* (1982).

"Oh Fuck!" - "THE word, the big one, the queen-mother of dirty words, the 'F-dash-dash-dash' word" accidentally uttered by young Ralphie Parker (Peter Billingsley) while helping his dad change a tire in the film *A Christmas Story* (1983). Shocked at what came out of his son's mouth, Mr. Parker (Darrin McGavin) inquires, "WHAT did you say? Ralphie stammers, "Uh, um..." Disappointed, Mr. Parker says, "That's...what I thought you said. Get in the car. Go on!" Fearing for his life, Ralphie mournfully muses, "It was all over–I was dead. What would it be? The guillotine? Hanging? The chair? The rack? The Chinese water torture? Hmmph. Mere child's play compared to what surely awaited me." For his punishment, Ralphie had to stick a bar of soap in his mouth until his mother decided he had learned his lesson. As he sat gagging on the soap, the adult Ralphie narrating the story reflected, "Over the years I got to be quite a connoisseur of soap. Though my personal preference was for Lux, I found that Palmolive had a nice, piquant after-dinner flavor - heavy, but with a touch of mellow smoothness. Lifebuoy, on the other hand...YECCHH!" Note: Raphie's father (Darrin

McGavin) was a master of vulgarity and could cuss up a storm of obscenity. Of course, the audience is only allowed to hear bits and pieces of his tirades. Ralphie as an adult reminisced "Now, I had heard that word at least ten times a day from my old man. He worked in profanity the way other artists might work in oils or clay. It was his true medium; a master." The consequences of his father's bouts with curse words culminates when Ralphie gets into a heated fight with the neighborhood bully and let's loose a volley of punches and just about every word he's ever heard his father utter. This act shocks and delights the youthful onlookers at the event.

"Oh, God, we pass onto you the body and soul of this nameless peckerhead" - Lee Marvin as Beb Rumson offers a eulogy over the body of a farmer who died along the journey to the gold fields in the motion picture *Paint Your Wagon* (1969) He continued his eulogy: "Well, at least he went quick, and he ain't going to have to suffer the scurvy, the dysentery, the spotted fever, the cholera, not to mention those other maladies contracted in consorting with low women."

"Oh Great! Terrific! He decides to keep the zoo open so you kill him!" - John Cleese as zookeeper Rollo Lee upset over Bugsy (Michael Palin) accidentally shooting tycoon Rod McCain (Kevin Kline) in the motion picture *Fierce Creatures* (1997). Rollo continues his rant: "Brilliant! Well done, thank you so much! Especially for shooting him right between the eyes so that it doesn't look like an accident...because the people at Octopus will know that he was coming here to close us down so there's our motive for murdering him. Stunning! Well, Mr. Brain of Britain, what are we going to tell the police, who are, of course, already on there way here?!...Another example of the thoroughness of your plan. Go on, I'm all ears, what do you suggest we do with the dead body of the incredibly famous man, who you have just... ASSASSINATED!!! Sorry, I didn't...quite catch it...What? What was that?...Pop him in the blender?"

"Oh, I know your type—I've seen hundreds of them" - Laird Cregar as twisted cop Ed Cornell taunts promoter Frankie Christopher (Victor Mature) for a crime he didn't commit in the motion picture *I Wake Up Screaming* (1942). As Cornell continues his macabre interview, he says, "I don't scare you enough to commit suicide, but I worry you just the same. And when the day comes, they all are different. Some scream, a few faint, some light a cigarette and try a wisecrack, but it sticks in their throats—especially when they're hung."

"Oh, I am so sick of this shit, it's not NORMAL! It's not NORMAL the three of us LIVING TOGETHER! I am so sick of falling for guys who don't give a fuck about me! I need help! I need a facial! I need to go on a diet! I need money! I need new shoes! Oh, God, just do something!" - Laura Flynn Boyle as Alex complains about her dormitory living arrangements in the motion picture *Threesome* (1994). In the film, Alex (a female) is mistakenly assigned a room with two young men named Eddy and Stuart. Soon, however, Alex falls for Eddy and Stuart lusts after Alex. But wait! Eddy soon realizes that he is gay and attracted to Stuart. What a mess!

"Oh Joanna! My new dress! How could you do a thing like that? Just when I was going to give you coffee!" - Paula Prentiss as Bobbie Markowe robotically puts-down a fellow housewife in the motion picture *The Stepford Wives* (1975). In the film, Joanna

Eberhart (Katherine Ross) has just moved with her husband to an exclusive community in Stepford, Connecticut. Slowly, Joanna discovers, to her horror, that all of the women in the community have been methodically replaced by perfectly behaved androids (gynoids) who obey the every wish of their husbands. When Joanna suspects that her friend Bobbie has been replaced, she stabs her with a knife which causes a short in the imposter's circuitry. The counterfeit Bobbie continues, "How could you do a thing like that? I thought we were friends! Just when I was going to...how could you do a thing like that...just when I was going to give you coffee! Oh Joanna...I thought we were friends...I thought we were friends...friends...coffee...how could you do a thing like that? Like that? Like that? Like that? Friends...friends..." Note: The film was based on the 1972 feminist science fiction novel "The Stepford Wives" by Ira Levin. The updated version of the original film starring Nicole Kidman as Joanna Eberhart was released to theaters in 2004. In 1998, a teenage version of the "Stepford Wives" entitled *Disturbing Behavior* chronicled a small town whose solution to rebellious teens involved the reprogramming of its teen poulation into polite, well-behaved zombies.

"Oh my God! They killed Kenny!" - Popular catchphrase from the animated cartoon SOUTH PARK/COM/1997+ featuring the adventures of four foul-mouthed third graders Kyle, Stan, Cartman and Kenny who attend South Park Elementary School. Kenny is the little boy in an orange parka and hood that mumbles under the cover of his winter clothes. Unfortunately, during nearly every episode, the viewers hear Stan screams, "Oh my God! They killed Kenny!" Then Kyle shouts, "You Bastards!" When asked why they kept killing off this little kid, the series co-creator Matt Stone confessed, "We just like to kill him...And we really like the line "Oh my God! They killed Kenny!" Note: The killing theme in the cartoon stems from a film short made by Trey Parker and Matt Stone at the University of Colorado at Boulder about four little boys trying to stop a snowman on a killing spree. This later inspired their *The Spirit of Christmas* (1991) cartoon short which spawned the phrase "Oh my God! Frosty killed Kenny!" To make Kenny's blood for his death scenes, animators use an ink dot from a Sharpie red marker they scan into the computer.

"Oh, that's silly. No woman could ever run for President. She'd have to admit she's over 35" - Katharine Hepburn as Mary Matthews, the wife of an aircraft tycoon (Spencer Tracy) courted by the Republican Party as a candidate for the U.S. Presidency in the motion picture *State of the Union* (1948).

"Oh, You English. You're so fucking superior, aren't you?" - Kevin Kline as Otto, a dim-witted crook expresses ethnic issues in the motion picture *A Fish Called Wanda* (1988). Angered at the very, very British attitude of Ms. Wendy Leach (Maria Aitken), Otto initiates an anti-Brit diatribe: "Oh, you English. You're so fucking superior, aren't you? Well, would you like to know where you'd be without us, the old U. S. of A., to protect you? I'll tell you—the smallest *fucking* province in the Russian Empire." When Otto gets mad at lawyer Archibald "Archie" Leech (John Cleese) he shouts, "You pompous, stuck-up, snot-nosed, English, giant, twerp, scumbag, fuck-face, dickhead, asshole." Archie replied, "How very interesting. You're a true vulgarian, aren't you?" Otto shouts back, "You are the vulgarian, you fuck!" Otto's favorite put-down line was "Asshole." *See also* "You're stupid"

"Okay, Fatso, if it's killing you want, come on" - Burt Lancaster as Sgt. Milton Warden with broken bottle in hand tries to break up a barroom brawl started by sadistic Sgt. "Fatso" Judson (Ernest Borgnine) in the motion picture *From Here To Eternity* (1953). Fatso had taken a special interest in bullying Pvt. Angelo Maggio (Frank Sinatra), calling him a "wop" and reminding him, "Guys like you end up in the stockade sooner or later. Some day you'll walk in. I'll be waiting. I'll show you a couple of things." After Maggio is thrown in the stockade, he receives a vicious beating. Fellow solider Pvt. Robert E. Lee Prewitt (Montgomery Clift) finds Maggio dying, battered body and listens as Lee warns, "Prew, listen. Fatso done it, Prew. He liked to whack me in the gut. He asks me if it hurts and I spit at him like always—only yesterday it was bad. He hit me. He hit me...Watch out for Fatso."

"Okay! I'll talk!" - Jeff Cohen as Francis "Chunk" Cohen succumbs to pressure during an interrogation in the motion picture *The Goonies* (1985). In the film, the criminal Fratelli brothers Francis (Joe Pantoliano) and Jake (Robert Davi) are trying to find information that will lead them to a lost treasure. When they catch Chunk in their hideout, they growl, "Tell us everything. Everything!" Now frightened out of his mind, Chunk begins to spill his guts about everything he's done in his short life: "In third grade, I cheated on my history exam. In fourth grade, I stole my Uncle Max's toupee and I glued it on my face when I was Moses in my Hebrew School play. In fifth grade, I knocked my sister Edie down the stairs and I blamed it on the dog...When my mom sent me to the summer camp for fat kids and then they served lunch I got nuts and I pigged out and they kicked me out...But the worst thing I ever done—I mixed a pot of fake puke at home and then I went to this movie theater, hid the puke in my jacket, climbed up to the balcony and then, t-t-then, I made a noise like this: [sound of a person about to puke]—and then I dumped it over the side, all over the people in the audience. And then, this was horrible, all the people started getting sick and throwing up all over each other. I never felt so bad in my entire life."

"'Okay, Marlowe,' I said to myself, 'You're a tough guy. You've been slapped twice, choked, beaten silly with a gun, shot in the arm until you're as crazy as a couple of waltzing mice. Now let's see you do something really tough—like putting your pants on" - Dick Powell as hard-boiled private investigator Phillip Marlowe tries to summon enough strength to get dressed in the motion picture *Murder, My Sweet* (1945).

Old Barnacle, The - Pejorative nickname used by Martha the housekeeper (Reta Shaw) to describe Captain Gregg (Edward Mulhare), the deceased owner of Gull Cottage on the sitcom THE GHOST AND MRS. MUIR/NBC/ABC/1965-68. The ghost of Captain Gregg—who haunted the house—never revealed himself to Martha but she still formed a stern opinion of the Captain from his painted portrait that came with the cottage.

Old Lead Bottom - On the WWII military comedy MCHALE'S NAVY/ABC/1962-66 the rowdy crew of the PT Boat #73 stationed on the South Seas island of Taratupa nicknamed Captain Wallace B. Binghamton (Joe Flynn) "Old Lead Bottom" because he was constantly plotting (unsuccessfully) to get Lt. Cdr. Quinton McHale (Ernest Borgnine) and his con-artist crew members transferred from his command. Old Lead

Bottom favorite sayings: "What, What, What!", "Somebody up there, hates me!" and "Why me? Why me?"

"O'Neill, take a break. You don't have to be a prick every day of your life, you know" - Willem Dafoe as Sergeant Elias speaks to Sergeant O'Neill (John McGinley) in the Vietnam War movie *Platoon* (1986). In the opening narration Pvt. Chris Taylor (Charlie Sheen) comments, "Somebody once wrote. 'Hell is the impossibility of reason.' That's what this place feels like, hell. I hate it already, and it's only been a week."

"On my worst day I could beat the hell out of you!" - The defiant words of John Wayne as cattle drover Wil Andersen in the western film *The Cowboys* (1968). When a desperado called Long Hair (Bruce Dern) tries to rustle Andersen's cattle, Wil speaks his mind: "You look like the vermin' bitten son of a bitch you are." When Long Hair begins to taunt a young boy, Wil shouts, "We've seen what you can do to a boy. How are you when they come a little bigger?" "You're a pretty old man", replies Long Hair. "Yeh, thirty years older than you are. Had my back broke once, my hip twice and on my worst day I could eat the Hell out of you." Andersen started the fight with a punch to Long Hair's face. Unfortunately, the defeated desperado reaches for his gun and put five bullets into the man who had bested him. On his dying bed Wil says, "See the boys get home. Summer's over." After he dies, the young boys finish the cattle drive but not before dispatching all the rustlers, including Long Hair (he dangled upside down off his saddle as his horse dragged him and his broken leg through the brush and to his death). Note: On a segment of TNT production *Big Guns Talk: The Story of the Western* (1997) Bruce Dern remembered that just before he filmed the killing scene, actor John Wayne leaned into him and said, "Eww, they're (the American public) gonna hate you for what you about to do."

"One fucking word, and your head is everywhere" - Whoopi Goldberg as Eddie, a dying of brain cancer female robs people at gun point in the motion picture *Homer & Eddie* (1990).

"One in the head, one in the heart" - A master assassin's advice to a novice hit man in the motion picture *Angel's Dance* (1998), When Chicago mobster Uncle Vinnie (Joe Polito) offers a hit to a loyal thug (Kyle Chandler), he first sends him to California to train with a master assassin (James Belushi). The "Master" chooses a random victim named Angel as a practice target and advises his student, "When the time is right...one in the head, one in the heart, and if it's clean she won't feel a thing." The Master also shared his philosophy on killing: "I believe in reincarnation. Death and dying is part of the journey, part of the path to enlightenment. The type of people I hit, hell, they'll never achieve higher enlightenment in this life, anyway, so I just help 'em along to the next."

"One man can change the world with a bullet in the right place" - Malcolm McDowell as pupil Mick Travis leads a revolt at a British boarding school run by tyrants in the motion picture *If...* (1968).

"One more face-lift, you'll be able to blink your lips"- Rob Reiner as Dr. Morris Packman speaks to Elise Eliot Atchinson (Goldie Hawn) an ex-wife dumped for a newer model in the comedy motion picture *The First Wives Club* (1996).

"One of them is yellow, and the other one is white—but their souls are rotten" - Lawrence Grant as Reverend Carmichael explains the spiritual condition of Hue Fei (Anna May Wong) and Shanghai Lily (Marlene Dietrich) in the motion picture *Shanghai Express* (1932).

"One of these days, Alice...POW! right in the kisser!" - One of the mean-spirited catchphrases used by Jackie Gleason in his role of blustery bus driver Ralph Kramden on the sitcom THE HONEYMOONERS/CBS/1955-56. When Ralph didn't approve of something his wife, Alice (Audrey Meadows) said, he'd respond, "One of these days, Alice...POW! Right in the kisser!" or "BANG! ZOOM! Right to the Moon!" and "Alice, you're askin' for a knuckle sandwich." Alice however was no babe in the woods when it came to put-downs. Once after Ralph burned himself, he asked "Isn't there any lard around her. Alice's rejoinder: "Only about 300 pounds of it." Despite their bickering, both characters truly loved each other. At the end of each episode, Ralph apologizes for his behavior and says, "Baby, you're the greatest!" Some other insulting exchanges:

Episode "A Women's Work Is Never Done" 10/22/1955

Ralph: You're goin' to the moon, Alice. Right to the Moon!
Alice: Yeah, and you're just the blimp to take me!

Episode "Better Living through TV" 11/12/95

Ralph: You're askin' for it, Alice. You're really askin' for it!
and you're gonna get it, too! I don't know the exact minute,
but before this night is over, you're gonna get yours!
Alice: Why don't you shut up!
Ralph: You have just picked the exact minute!
Alice: Go ahead and hit me!
Ralph: You'd like that, Alice. You'd really like me to belt you, wouldn't you? Would you like a little belt, Alice? Would you like one?
Alice: What are you waitin' for?
Ralph: I wouldn't give you the satisfaction!

Episode "Hello, Mom" 12/3/1955

Trixie: Do you want anything else at the store?
Alice: You better get a pound of margarine, too.
Trixie: Okay, Alice.
Alice: [Ralph enters] Maybe you won't have to get the margarine, Trix.
Four hundred pounds of lard just walked in!
Ralph: You have just said the secret word, Alice. You have just won
your self a trip to the moon!

Episode "Unconventional Behavior" 5/12/56

Ralph: All Right, Norton. what could I do? I'm stuck with Alice,
Norton: Well! At least, Alice ain't no Trixie. Boy, what a personality that girl's got. She's grumblin' all the time. Believe me, if the Marx Brothers had a sister, she'd be it ...Complain-O!

Some "Lost Episodes" fat jokes

Ralph: I wear the pants around this house.
Alice: Believe me, your pants would fit around this house.

Ralph: Trixie, if you were only my size.
Trixie: If I was, I'd be the fat lady in the circus.

Ralph: All my life I wanted to be in sports...but I was a little too heavy to be a jockey.
Alice: A little too heavy? You're too fat to be a horse.

Ralph: I'm a hero, Alice. A hero. Do you know what a hero is?
Alice: Yeah:...it's a fat sandwich that's full of baloney.

"The only difference between you and the guy with the stocking over his head is you got a badge" - Matthew Laurance as street junkie Ronnie Ciello tells his cop brother, Daniel Ciello (Treat Williams) that he is no better than a crook in the motion picture *Prince of the City* (1981).

"The only good Indian is a dead Indian" - The politically incorrect sentiment in many TV and Movie westerns over the years. Actually, this racial slur is based on a statement of General Philip Sheridan uttered in 1869 that said, "The only good Indians I ever saw were dead." Note: In the science fiction film *Planet of the Apes* (1968), gorilla General Urko (James Gregory) declared, "The only good human...is a DEAD human." James Gregory as Ursus repeated the same sentiment in the sequel *Beneath the Planet of the Apes* (1970). *See also* "Doc, tag 'em and bag 'em"

"The only reason you're still living is because I never kissed you" - Charles Durning as Les who fell in love with a woman who turned out to be actor Michael Dorsey (Dustin Hoffman) posing incognito as a female named Dorothy Michaels to get an acting job on a soap opera in the motion picture *Tootsie* (1982).

"The only time a woman doesn't care to talk is when she's dead" - William Demarest as Constable Ed Kockenlocker responds to his daughter's reluctance to talk to him (she's pregnant) in the motion picture *The Miracle of Morgan's Creek* (1944).

"Our divorce was one of those tragedies that you read about in the papers. A trusting woman and a worthless man" - Cary Grant as Jerry Warriner in the motion picture *The Awful Truth* (1937).

"Our fathers are cowards" - The shameful admission of peasant farmers sons in the classic *The Magnificent Seven* (1960). When Mexican villagers hire seven gringo gunfighters to protect them from local bandits, the children of the village become infatuated with the glamour of being a fast draw. A group of boys adopt gunfighter Bernardo O'Reilly (Charles Bronson) and promise, "If you get killed, we take the rifle and avenge you…and we see to it there's always fresh flowers on your grave." They also admit, "We're ashamed to live here. Our fathers are cowards." Bernardo takes exception to their claim, smack one of the boys on the rump and says, "Don't you ever say that again about your fathers because they are not cowards. You think I'm brave because I carry a gun? Well, your fathers are much braver because they carry responsibility—for you, your brothers, your sisters, and your mothers. And this responsibility is like a big rock that weighs a ton. It bends and it twists them until finally it buries them under the ground. And there's nobody says they have to do this. They do it because they love you, and because they want to. I have never had this kind of courage. Running a farm, working like a mule every day with no guarantee anything will ever come of it. This is bravery."

"Out here, due process is a bullet" - Military sentiment of John Wayne as Colonle Mike Kirby, a Special Forces officer fighting during the Vietnam war in the motion picture *The Green Berets* (1968). His controversial response was prompted by George Beckworth, an American journalist in the field (David Janssen) who witnessed the execution of a Vietnamese soldier who betrayed his troops to the Viet Cong.

"Out of order? I'll show you out of order!" - The defiant cry of Al Pacino as blind veteran Lt. Colonel Frank Slade in the motion picture *Scent of a Woman* (1992). When college president Trask (James Rebhorn) unfairly pressures student Charlie Simms (Chris O'Donnell) to reveal the names of students involved in a prank, Lt. Colonel Slade steps up to his defense. When the president declares Pacino's comments out of order, he shouts, "Out of order, I'll show you out of order! You don't know what out of order is Mr. Trask! I'd show you but I'm too old, I'm too tired, and I'm too fuckin' blind. If I were the man I was five years ago I'd take a *FLAME-THROWER* to this place. Out of order, who the hell do you think you're talking to? I've been around you know? There was a time I could see. And I have seen, boys like these, younger than these, their arms torn out, their legs ripped off. But there isn't nothin' like the sight of an amputated spirit, there is no prosthetic for that. You think you're merely sending this splendid foot-soldier back home to Oregon with his tail between his legs but I say that you are executing his soul. And why? Because he's not a Baird man. Baird men, you hurt this boy, you're going to be Baird Bums, the lot of ya. And Harry, Jimmy, Trent, wherever you are out there, fuck you too."

Packy - Real-life family nickname of actress Sally Struthers who played Gloria, the scatter-brained daughter of blue-collar bigot Archie Bunker (Carroll O'Connor) on the sitcom ALL IN THE FAMILY/CBS/1971-83 and GLORIA/CBS/1982-83. When Sally was a child she was very chubby. Her sister decided to call her 'Packy'... short for "pachyderm." Note: In later years, Sally Struthers became spokesperson for a Christian Children's Fund charity. Unfortunately, she had gained considerable amount of weight since her days as Gloria Bunker and consequently she became the target of many TV comedians who implied that her weight gain was linked to her eating the food that was supposed to be sent to starving children in Africa. Sally Struthers's charity work was spoofed on the 1997 episode "Starving Marvin" on the Comedy Channel's animated series SOUTH PARK.

"Paul, at the store, can you buy another frying pan? I'm a little squeamish about using the one we use to kill people" - Mary Woronov as Mary Bland politely asks her husband Paul (Paul Bartel) if they could obtain a new cast iron frying pan in the black comedy motion picture *Eating Raoul* (1982). When the Blands accidentally kill a lecherous swinger whose wallet is filled with money, they hit upon a perfect way to supplement their meager incomes—lure swingers to their apartment, hit them over the head and steal their money. To dispose of their bodies, they engaged the services of a locksmith named Raoul (Robert Beltran) who sold the corpses to a dog food company. When Raoul is discovered stealing money from the Blands, he becomes a necessary ingredient for the movie's title.

Peeper, The - The college nickname of Cliff Murdock (Tom Poston) heard on the sitcom THE BOB NEWHART SHOW/CBS/1972-78. An old friend of psychologist Bob Hartley (Bob Newart) Cliff earned his malicious moniker by "peeping" through binoculars into the girl's campus dormitory. Cliff was also a practical joker and once put raw pieces of chicken in Bob's sock drawer (neck, wings, thighs, & gizzards). *See also* "Nature's Revenge on Peeping Toms"

"The pellet with the poison's in the flagon with the dragon; the vessel with the pestle has the brew that is true" - The confusing but deadly message delivered by Griselda (Mildred Natwick) to Hawkins (Danny Kaye) posing as Jachimo, the king of jesters and jester to the king in the motion picture *The Court Jester* (1956).

Penis Von Lesbian - The tongue-in-cheek nickname of actor Dick Van Dyke given to him by fellow actors Mary Tyler Moore, Morey Amsterdam and Rose Marie etc. while filming the now classic sitcom THE DICK VAN DYKE SHOW/CBS/1960-66. Of course, the name is a play on words with the actor's own name: "Dick" (Penis) "Van"

(Von) "Dyke" ("Dyke" being a slang name for a lesbian). *See also* "It was nothing like that, penis breath!"

"People should really learn to keep their hands to them self...Here's yours" - In the film *Stephen King's Sleepwalkers* (1992), teenager Charles Brady (Brian Krause) transfers to a new high school from a small town in Ohio. When a nasty school official discovers the boy's papers are forged, he tries to blackmail the boy by asking for sexual favors in return for his silence. What the man got back in return...was his hand, which Charles ripped off at the wrist after the man to gropes his body. Shocked, the man flees down the road crying, "I'm sorry." Charles then turns in to a demonic creature (a Sleepwalker), stalks the man and feasts on his fat body. Later in the film, Charles' mother (Alice Krige) rams a cooked ear of corn through the spine of a police officer, killing him. "No vegetables, No dessert. That's the rule," she quipped. Note: In the film *Maximum Overdrive* (1986) Laura Harrington as Brett tells a Bible salesman, "If you don't get your hand off my leg, you're going to be wiping your ass with a hook next time you take a dump!"

Perfect Fool, The - Comedian Ed Wynn, the recipient of one of the very first Emmy Awards in 1949 for "Best Live Show & Most Outstanding Live Personality was known nationally as "The Perfect Fool," a nickname derived from the title of a hit comedy, which he wrote in the 1920s.

"Pick it up or die looking at it" - Jock Mahoney as Brad Ellison speaks to a bearded cowpoke named Samuel Grypton (Edward C. Platt - the Chief on TV's GET SMART) in the western *The Last of the Fast Guns* (1958). With both of their guns on opposite sides of a table, and each man with a 50/50 chance of firing first, Ellison challenges Grypton to put up or shut up in a face-to-face draw down. Ellision wins the draw by wounding his opponent in the shoulder.

"Pick it up. Put it in. Die like a man" - Tossing one bullet to mangy cowpoke Kid Jarrett (James Russo), Cody Zamora (Madeline Stowe), a leather tough prostitute turned cowgirl choreographs a shoot-out on her own terms in the western movie *Bad Girls* (1994). Jarrett had abused Cody earlier in her life, and to add insult to injury, had robbed the bank where Cody deposited her life's savings.

Pig - Derogatory term used to describe a police officer or the capitalist power structure. The term "Pig" was first popularized by the radical Black Panther's group and later adopted by other radical groups, including student protesters during the 1960s and 1970s. According to publication *The Black Panther* (May 1967) "A Pig is an ill-natured beast who has no respect for law and order, a foul traducer who's usually found masquerading as a victim of an unprovoked attack." The use of the word "pig" can be found in numerous TV and movie scripts. A good example appears in the action adventure movie *Cobra* (1986) when Sylvester Stallone as police detective Marian Cobretti confronts a knife wielding psychotic killer who snarls, "Where are you, pig? I want your eyes, pig. I want them. Do you wanna go to hell? Huh? Huh, pig? Do you wanna go to hell with me? It doesn't matter does it. We are the hunters. We kill the weak so the strong survive. You can't stop the new world. Your filthy society will never get rid of people like us. It's breeding them. We are the future!" Cobretti cries, "No!

You're History!" Still goading Cobretti, the mad man continues, "You won't do it, pig. You won't shoot. Murder is against the law. You have to take me in...if...you...can. Even I have rights. Don't I, pig? Take me in. They'll say I am insane. Won't they? The court is civilized. Isn't it, pig?" To that, Cobretti coldly replies, "But I'm not. This is where the law stops...and I start." Note: In the film *Coneheads* (1993), the neighbor of Prymaat (Jane Curtin) says, "All men are pigs!" Prymaat responds, "Ah, pig: an omnivorous, domesticated, cloven hoof vertebrate that defecates the same place it consumes. "Exactly," agrees her neighbor. In the film *Strange Cargo* (1940) Joan Crawford as Julie says, "Remember this Pig, you're the one man in the world I can never get low enough to touch." ("Pig" was a reference to M'sieu Pig played by Peter Lorre). On the TV sitcom TAXI, immigrant garage mechanic Latka Gravis (Andy Kaufman) said, "My mother would rather I date a pig than a mountain girl." *See also* "Bite me, pig!" and "You're the disease and I'm the cure"

"Pinko" *See* "Red"

"Piss on them..." - In the motion picture *The Seduction of Joe Tynan* (1979) when Senator Birney, an aging politician (Melvyn Douglas) becomes angered when his constituents fail to support him for the Senate because he is too old, he shouts, "Piss on them for their self-satisfying talk about old age. They think that they ain't going to get old? Ha! They just have to wait a while, that's all. It don't take any talent to get old." Note: In the film *Convoy* (1978) Kris Kristofferson as a trucker with the handle "Rubber Duck" and a vendetta against an abusive sheriff offers this variation: "Piss on you, and piss on your law." *See also* "I wouldn't..."

"A plague on you!" - Richard Harris as English Bob in the western motion picture *Unforgiven* (1992). Brutalized by sadistic town sheriff "Little Bill" Daggett (Gene Hackman), English Bob admonishes his tormentors as he departs their fair town: "A plague on you! A plague on the whole stinking lot of ya, without morals or laws! And all you whores got no laws! You got no honor! It's no wonder you all emigrated to America, because they wouldn't have you in England! You're a lot of savages, that's what you all are. A bunch of bloody savages! A plague on you! I'll be back!"

"Please familiarize and observe the rules while in Fun World. No running, no jumping, no yelling, no cutting in line, no grumbling, no stealing. That means you. No breaking things and putting them back like nothing happened. No sad faces, bad attitudes, introspective moments, irritation at the mindless happiness of the masses, and no littering. Is that clear? Enjoy your stay" - Susan Silo as a Ticketlady explains the rules at an amusement park in the motion picture *Bebe's Kids* (1992). Note: In the film *Outside Providence (*1999) Timothy Crowe as Mr. Funderberk explains, "These are the rules, listen carefully: No smoking, no drinking, no drugs. No sex. No cheating. No lying, no gambling, no matches. Timothy Dunphy (Shawn Hatosy) interjects, "No shit!" Mr. Funderberk quickly points out "No swearing."

"Please put fifty thousand dollars into this bag and abt natural as I am pointing a gub" - The misspelled message on a holdup note presented by bumbling bank robber Virgil Starkwell (Woody Allen) to a confused bank teller in the motion picture *Take the Money and Run* (1969). The film's narrator Jackson Beck referred to one of Virgil's gang members as "A. D. Armstrong, wanted all over the country for arson, robbery, assault with intent to kill, and marrying a horse." He later informs the viewers, "Virgil complains and he is severely tortured. For several days he is locked in a sweatbox with an insurance salesman."

"Poor dope. He always wanted a pool. Well, in the end, he got himself a pool—only the price, turned out to be a little high" - William Holden as reporter Joe Gillis who befriends the troubled faded silent movie star Norma Desmond (Gloria Swanson) and gets himself murdered in the motion picture *Sunset Boulevard* (1950). The "poor dope" dialog is actually coming from the deceased body of Joe Gillis who is now floating face down in Desmond's swimming pool at the beginning of the movie. At end of the film, Joe says, "Well, this is where you came in, back at that pool again, the one I always wanted. It's dawn now and they must have photographed me a thousand times. Then they got a couple of pruning hooks from the garden and fished me out...ever so gently. Funny, how gentle people get with you once you're dead." When Joe initially tried to leave Norma, she threatens suicide. During one of those times, Joe yelled, "Oh, wake up, Norma, you'd be killing yourself to an empty house. The audience left twenty years ago." As Joe prepared to finally leave Norma's clutches, she says, "No one ever leaves a star. That's what makes one a star." After Norma kills Joe, the police and reporters arrive. As the now deranged Desmond is taken into custody, she slowly moves through the crowd of people she believes to be her adoring public and says, "And I promise you I'll never desert you again because after '*Salome*' we'll make another picture and another picture. This is my life. It always will be. There's nothing else. Just us and the cameras and those wonderful people out there in the dark. All right, Mr. De Mille, I'm ready for my close-up." Earlier in the film when Joe first recognized Norma, he said, "You used to be in silent pictures. You used to be big." Coming to her own defense, Norma countered, "I am big. It's the pictures that got small."

"Pop quiz, asshole. You have a hair trigger aimed at your head. What do you do? What do you do?" - Keanu Reeves as SWAT officer Jack Traven accidentally threatens Annie (Sandra Bullock) with a gun in the motion picture *Speed* (1994). Jack was actually looking for mad bomber Howard Payne (Dennis Hopper) who had previously told Jack, "Do not attempt to grow a brain." When Jack tried to dismantle a bomb placed under a speeding bus, a Hispanic passenger named Ortiz (Carlos Carrasco) compliments Jack's courage saying "You're not too bright, man, but you got some big, round, hairy cojones." Note: Other sample "Pop Quiz" phrases used in the film included Howard Payne, saying, "Pop quiz, Hotshot. There's a bomb on a bus. Once the bus goes 50 miles an hour, the bomb is armed. If it drops below 50, it blows up. What do you do? What do you do?" and Jeff Daniels as Jack's partner Harry Temple, saying, "All right, pop quiz. Airport. Gunman with one hostage. He's using her for cover; he's almost to a plane. You're a hundred feet away. Jack? Jack's answer, "Shoot the hostage."

Prince of Menace, The - The sinister nickname given to actor Vincent Price for his roles in such horror film classics as the 3-D thriller *House of Wax* (1953), *The Fly* (1958) *House on Haunted Hill* (1958) and a number of Edgar Allen Poe inspired films: *The House of Usher* (1960), *The Pit and the Pendulum* (1961); *The Raven* (1963), and *The Masque of the Red Death* (1964). Some of his memorable TV performances included the villainous Egghead on the fantasy BATMAN/ABC/1966-68; his regular role on the children's horror comedy program THE HILARIOUS HOUSE OF FRIGHTENSTEIN/SYN/1975; the mysterious Jason who escorted passengers through time on the fantasy series TIME EXPRESS/CBS/1979; and the host of the PBS anthology MYSTERY! (from 1982-89) which featured mystery stories (made mostly in England). Vincent Price died in 1993. *See also* "Nine Killed Her; Nine Shall Die!"

Prince of Pain, The - The neurotic nickname of comedian Richard Lewis. Fond of running his hand through his hair and wearing black clothing, his comic stand-up routine focused on tales of his personal anxieties and neuroses. Lewis frequented late night talk shows and starred in the situation comedies ANYTHING BUT LOVE/1989-92 and DADDY DEAREST/FOX/1993.

"Professional assassination is the highest form of public service" - Joel Grey as Chiun, an ancient Korean Sinanyu martial arts expert offers this bit of questionable wisdom to his new student Remo Williams (Fred Ward) in the motion picture *Remo Williams: The Adventure Begins* (1985)

"Professor Elwell, you're a little man..." - Finlay Currie as Shunderson, a former murderer who defends the reputation of physician-philosopher Dr. Noah Praetorius (Cary Grant) against the unfounded charges lodged by Professor Elwell (Hume Cronyn) in the motion picture *People Will Talk* (1951). Shunderson continues his defense: "It's not that you're short. You're little, in the mind and in the heart. Tonight, you tried to make a man little whose boots you couldn't touch if you stood on tip-toe on top of the highest mountain in the world. And, as it turned out, you're even littler than you were before." Elwell was trying to uncover some dirt on the doctor; Dirt which only existed in his envious little mind. Earlier in the film, Dr. Praetorius said, "Professor Elwell, you are the only man I know who can say 'malignant' the way other people say 'Bingo!'" Fellow colleague, Professor Barker (Walter Slezak) also said, "Elwell, you can use more words more unpleasantly than any irritating little pipsqueak I've ever known!"

Psycho Dad - On the sitcom MARRIED...WITH CHILDREN/FOX/1987-97 frustrated shoe salesman Al Bundy (Ed O'Neill) had little to be happy about in life. His only solace: his nudie magazines; the local nudie bar; and his favorite TV show "Psycho Dad" (played by Andrew Prine). Al especially enjoyed the show's rousing themes song ("Who's that riding in the sun/Who's the man with the itchy gun/Who's the man who kills for fun!/ Psycho Dad. Psycho Dad. Psycho Dad.") When Al's favorite show was scheduled for cancellation, he contacts a US senator to intervene. During the investigation, Senator Furman asks Al, "Is it not true that the lyrics to the 'Psycho Dad' theme song read: 'Killed his wife 'cause she weighed a ton'?" Frantic for an answer, Al cries, "But in Psycho Dad's defense, when he married her, she wasn't fat, your bigness." Sadly, Psycho Dad was canceled. When Al's nemesis Marcy Darcy (Amanda Bearce) heard the news, she chants a parody of the show's theme song, "Who's the guy who's show is done? / Who's TV hero's on the run / Who'll be watching VH-1? Loser Al. Loser Al. Loser Al." Dejected, poor Al Bundy retreats to the beautiful babes at the nudie bar and his fellow colleagues from NO MA'AM (National Organization of Men Against Amazonian Masterhood). For the feminine viewer, there was the spin-off series "Psycho Mom" whose theme song read: "Who's the gal who needs no man? Killed him dead with the frying pan/Did it 'cause he missed the can/Psycho Mom. Psycho Mom. She's Psycho Mom. ["Teacher's Pet" episode]

"Pucker up and kiss my ass!" - On episode #50 "Paperclip" of the fantasy drama THE X-FILES/FOX/1993-2002, FBI Assistant Director Walter Skinner (Mitch Pileggi) confronts the sinister Cigarette Smoking Man (William B. Davis) with a tape containing digitally encoded classified MJ documents ("Operation Paper Clip"). The documents detail the government's knowledge of UFO's and an unholy alliance bent on creating human-alien hybrids. Finally in the driver's seat, for a change, Skinner uses the tape as leverage to "bring these men to justice" and to get agents Mulder (David Duchovny) and Dana Scully (Gillian Anderson) reinstated. He then tells his chain-smoking nemesis to "Pucker and kiss my ass." Unfortunately, the CSM destroys the tape and tells Skinner "This is where you pucker and kiss MY ass!" Unshaken, at this turn of events, Skinner informs CSM that Albert Hosteen (Floyd Red Crow Westerman), a Navajo cryptologist who translated the original documents into the Navajo language, had memorized the tape's contents and related it to twenty other men under his tribe's narrative tradition. "So unless you kill every Navajo in four states," adds Skinner "that information is available with a simple phone call." At that, CSM is speechless. Skinner concludes his meeting with "Welcome to the wonderful world of high technology." The MJ documents were originally procured by a computer hacker called "The Thinker" who was later murdered—execution-style. *See also* "Kiss my ass!"

"Pusillanimous Polecat!" - Term of disapproval used by farmer George "Gramps" Miller (George Cleveland) when he gets irritated with someone on the rural family drama JEFF'S COLLIE/CBS/1954-57.

"Pussy, pussy, pussy!" - Politically incorrect reference to women used comically in the horror flick *From Dusk Till Dawn* (1996). Standing in front of roadside biker bar, Cheech Marin as vampire Chet Pussy, entices the rowdy bikers to sample the clientele: "Pussy, pussy, pussy! All pussy must go. At the 'Titty Twister' we're slashing pussy in half! This is a pussy blow out! Make us an offer on our vast selection of pussy! We got white pussy, black pussy, Spanish pussy, yellow pussy, hot pussy, cold pussy, wet pussy, tight pussy, big pussy, bloody pussy, fat pussy, hairy pussy, smelly pussy, velvet pussy, silk pussy, Naugahyde pussy, snappin' pussy, horse pussy, dog pussy, chicken pussy, fake pussy! If we don't have it, you don't want it!" *See also* "I could go on and on about his cock..."

Put 'em up! Put 'em up! - Bert Lahr as the Cowardly Lion challenges Dorothy Gale (Judy Garland) and her companions Scarecrow (Ray Bolger) and Tin Man (Jack Haley) to a fight in the motion picture *The Wizard of Oz* (1939). As Dorothy and her friends travel through a dark, creepy forest on their way to see the Wizard of Oz, they confront a growling lion. "Put 'em up! Put 'em up!" threatens the seemingly ferocious feline. To show his superiority, the lion agrees to fight Scarecrow and Tin Man at the same time and sweetens the pot, saying, "I'll fight you with one paw tied behind my back. I'll fight you standing on one foot. I'll fight you with my eyes closed." The lion calls the Tin Man a "shivering junkyard" and the Scarecrow "a lop-sided bag of hay." But when the lion tries to attack Dorothy's little dog, Toto, she smacks the nasty cat across his snout. Sobbing, the lion says, "You didn't have to go and hit me. Is my nose bleeding?" It was at that point that Dorothy realizes, "Why you're nothing but a great big coward." The lion admits his weakness and confesses, "I haven't any courage at all. I even scare myself." When the lion reached the Emerald City, he sings *If I were King of the Forest* in preparation for asking the Wizard of Oz for some courage. In the song, he states he would command fish and fowl with a "royal growl"; and if he were king he wouldn't be afraid of "not nobody, not no how." If provoked by a hippopotamus, he'd thrash it "from top to bottomus." If cornered by an elephant, he'd "wrap him in up cellophant." And if bothered by a brontosaurus, he'd show him "who was king of the forest."

"Put me down! You male chauvinistic pig ape!" - Jessica Lange as Dwan shouts at the 40-foot gorilla that plucks her off the ground in the motion picture *King Kong* (1976). When her insults ands struggling enrage the ape, she apologizes, "I didn't mean that! I swear I didn't. Sometimes I get too physical; it's a sign of insecurity, you know? Like when you knock down trees."

"Queen Cleopatra is widely read, well versed in the natural sciences and mathematics. She speaks seven languages proficiently. Were she not a woman, one would consider her to be an intellectual" - Andrew Keir as Agrippa relates the talents of Egypt's Queen Cleopatra to the conquering Roman General Julius Caesar (Rex Harrison) in the motion picture *Cleopatra* (1963). When Cleopatra (Elizabeth Taylor) addresses Julius Caesar as a "barbarian" he retaliates with "You're a descendent of generations of inbred, incestuous mental defectives—how dare you call anyone barbarian!"

"Racist? You dare call me racist? Well I say unto you, what does it matter the color of a man's skin when witnesses perjure themselves and prosecutors enlist the perjury; when a district attorney throws a man to the mob for political gain and men of the cloth, men of God, take the prime cut? Is that justice? Let me tell you what justice is. Justice is the law. And the law is man's feeble attempt to lay down the principles of decency. Decency! And decency isn't a deal, it's not a contract or a hustle or an angle! Decency...decency is what your grandmother taught you. It's in your bones! You go home now. Go home and be decent people. Be decent!" - Morgan Freeman as African-American Judge Leonard White in the motion picture *The Bonfire of the Vanities* (1990).

Rat Pack, The - The nickname assigned to showbiz greats Dean Martin, Sammy Davis Jr, Peter Lawford, Joey Bishop and their leader, Frank Sinatra. Their story is profiled in the book "Rat Pack Confidential: Frank, Dean, Sammy, Peter, Joey and the last Great Showbiz Party" written by Shawn Levy (Doubleday, 1997). The origin of the nickname came about when actress Lauren Bacall saw her husband Humphrey Bogart standing with Frank Sinatra and commented that they looked like a "Rat Pack." The HBO TV-Movie *The Rat Pack* (1998) starred Ray Liotta as Sinatra in the swinging Las Vegas days of the early 1960s.

"The reason people treat me like nothing is because I *am* nothing" - Patrick Swayze as Johnny Castle, a handsome Catskill Mts. resort dance instructor who falls victim to low self-esteem in the motion picture *Dirty Dancing* (1987). Johnny may feel that he's not much, but oh, the boy can dance!

Red - Slang term for "Communist." The term "Red Scare" refers to times in American History when fear of Communism reached a fever pitch as during 1919-1920 when US attorney general Mitchell Palmer arrested and deported hundreds after a bomb exploded at his home; or during the McCarthy Era when Joseph McCarthy, a junior senator from Wisconsin began a campaign to eradicate supposed Communist in the Federal Government. The 1953 play *The Crucible* by Arthur Miller equated the Communist "witch-hunts" of the 1950s with the Salem Witch Trials of 1692. A TV series that helped fan the flames of the Red Scare was the drama I LED THREE LIVES/SYN/1953-56 which began "This is the fantastically true story of Herbert A. Philbrick (Richard Carlson), who for nine frightening years did lead three lives - average citizen, member of the Communist Party, and counterspy for the FBI...the story is based on fact." The program was approved by J. Edgar Hoover and was most influential television for its time. A popular sentiment at the time stated, "I rather be dead then Red!" Other pejorative terms for Communists are "Commies" and "Pinko" (someone who sympathized with the Communists). Perhaps the most famous example of the "Communist witch-hunt" happened on September 12, 1953 when the *Los Angeles Express* newspaper broke the story of Lucille Ball's alleged association with communism with a front page banner headline in huge 4-inch red letters that proclaimed, "LUCILLE BALL NAMED RED." Their evidence was a Photostatted copy of a 1936 registration card on which Lucy indicated her intention to vote for the Communist Party candidate in the 1936 election. She had only registered to please her grandfather. When the news broke, the phone lines at Desilu Studios (Hollywood 9-5981) were jammed with inquiries. To help dispel public doubt, Desi Arnaz defended Lucy in a Friday night pre-show warm up of the audience.

> "Welcome to the first I LOVE LUCY show of the season," he began. "We are glad to have you back and we are glad to be back ourselves. But before we go on, I want to talk to you about something serious. Something very serious. You all know what it is. The papers have been full of it all day. Lucille Ball is no Communist! Lucy has never been a Communist. Not now and never will be. I was kicked out of Cuba because of Communism. We both despise the Communists for everything they stand for. Lucille Ball is one hundred percent American. She's as American as Barney Baruch and Ike Eisenhower. Tomorrow morning, the complete transcript of Lucille's testimony will be released to the papers and you can read it for yourself. Then, you will know this is all a pack of lies. Please ladies and gentlemen, don't believe every piece of bunk you read in today's papers. And now I want you to meet my wife, my favorite redhead, in fact, that's the only thing RED about her and even that's not legitimate."

As Desi finished, a devoted and supportive audience rose and cheered. Lucy sobbed. With her career on the line, Lucy appeared before the "Committee for Un-American Activities" who later exonerated her of all charges. The *Los Angeles Times* newspaper vindicated her with the banner headline "LUCILLE BALL NOT RED, REP. JACKSON DECLARES." Note: The motion picture *The Front* (1976) starring Woody Allen told the tale of a writer enlisted by blacklisted writers (accused of Communist affiliations) to put his name on their scripts. At one point in the film an angry man yells, "...you crawl in the gutter you Red bastard, you Commie son of a bitch!" And, in the film *Key Largo* (1948) when mobster Johnny Rocco (Edward G. Robinson) got deported, he complains, "After living in the U.S.A. for more that 30 years they called me an undesirable alien, me Johnny Rocco! Like, I was a dirty Red or something!" Other motion pictures using the term "Red" include *Red Dawn* (1984) starring Patrick Swayze about small town teenagers who become guerrilla fighters when the US is invaded by the Russians; *Red Kiss* (1986) starring Charlotte Valandrey as a Stalinist teenager coming of age in Paris of the 1950s; and *Red Heat* (1988) starring Arnold Schwarzenegger as a Soviet policeman who comes to Chicago to track down a drug dealer.

"Resistance is Futile" - Ominous statement made by an alien race known as the Borg when then attempt to assimilate the culture and technological components of a civilization on episodes of the science fiction adventure STAR TREK: THE NEXT GENERATION/SYN/1987-94 and STAR TREK: DEEP SPACE NINE/SYN/1993-99. The Borg resurfaced on the motion picture *Star Trek: First Contact* (1996) when they travel back in time to enslave the Earth; and on the science fiction series STAR TREK: VOYAGER/UPN/1995-2001 when they confronted the crew of the Spaceship Voyager while traveling through the Delta Quadrant. Note: In the film *Star Trek: First Contact* (1996) the Borg attacks a Federation ship, and says, "Lower your shields and surrender your ships. We will add your biological and technological distinctiveness to our own. Your culture will adapt to serve us. Resistance is futile. We are the Borg." Captain Jean Luc Picard (Patrick Stewart) enraged at the Borg says, "They invade our space, and we fall back. They assimilate entire worlds, and we fall back. Not again. The line must be drawn HERE. This far. NO farther. And I will make them pay for what they've done."

"Rick Von Slonecker is tall, rich, good looking, stupid, dishonest, conceited, a bully, liar, drunk and thief, an egomaniac, and probably psychotic. In short, highly attractive to women" - Christopher Eigeman as Nick Smith offers a personality appraisal of his friend, Rick (Will Kempe) in the motion picture *Metropolitan* (1990).

"Rommel, you magnificent bastard!" - Spoken by George C. Scott as WWII U.S. General Patton in the movie biography *Patton* (1970). As German General Rommel's 10th Panzer Division fell under a deadly barrage of American fire in North Africa, General Patton shouts, "Rommel, you magnificent bastard, I read your book." For a military leader, Patton was rather gruff and his vocabulary was often called into check. In the film, he called British General Montgomery "a Limy son of a bitch" and he told his troops that he was going to Berlin to "personally shoot" Hitler, whom he referred to as "that paper-hanging son of a bitch." Patton even slapped an American G. I. suffering from shell shock and declared, "The man was yellow. He should of been tried for cowardice and shot." The movie began with a rousing monologue as Patton stood in front of a huge American flag. He delivered these reassurances to his troops: "I want you to remember that no bastard ever won a war by dying for his country. He won it by making the other poor dumb bastards die for his country.... The Nazis are the enemy. Wade into them, Spill their blood. Shoot them in the belly. When you put your hand into a bunch of goo that a moment before was your best friend's face, you'll know what to do...I don't want to get any messages sayings that we are holding our position. We're not holding anything. Let the Hun do that. We are advancing constantly and we're not interested in holding onto anything except the enemy. We're going to hold onto him by the nose and we're going to kick him in the ass. We're going to kick the hell out of him all the time and we're gonna go through him like crap through a goose." Patton earned the nickname 'Blood and Guts'–with one soldier commenting, "Yeah, our blood, and his guts!"

"Russian roulette is a very different sort of amusement—which I could only wish your father had played continuously before he had you" - Rex Harrison as symphony conductor Sir Alfred de Carter clarifies his new bride Daphne's (Linda Darnell) confusion with a card game called "Russian Bank" in the motion picture *Unfaithfully Yours* (1948).

"Say hello to my little friend!" - Deadly invitation uttered by Al Pacino in the role of Cuban mobster Tony Montana in the film *Scarface* (1983). With his kingdom crumbling, a band of assassins enter Tony Montana's home to terminate him. Positioned inside of his upstairs room, Tony pulls out heavy weaponry and points it at the door. With no lack of bravado, he cries, "You wanna fuck with me? Okay. You wanna play rough? Okay. Say hello to my little friend!" Tony then fires a round that blows away the door and a number of killers on the other side. But, in the end, Tony's reign is over and he is shot and left floating in a fountain on the main floor of his home, despite his claims earlier in which he said, "I'm Tony Montana! You fuck with me, you fuckin' with the best!"

"Screw the procedure! I want somebody on the goddamn phone before I kill twenty million people" - Edward Jahnke as member of an underground nuclear headquarters who needs to solve a thermonuclear malfunction in the motion picture *Wargames* (1983).

"Screeew You!" - Avenging cry of Arnold Schwarzenegger as Doug Quaid in the sci-fi film *Total Recall* (1990). When Quaid discovers his mind has been altered, he travels to Mars and learns his alter ego was part of an elaborate plot to flush out the mutant leader of the Free Mars movement. Along the way, a mutant taxi driver named Benny (Mel Johnson, Jr.), who worked for the bad guys, consistently squealed on Quaid's activities. When Benny tries to kill Quaid with the ripping blades of a mining excavator, Doug rams a huge spinning drill bit through its cockpit door, screams, "Screeew you!" and tears Benny to pieces. Note: In the film *Straight Talk* (1992) Dolly Parton as radio talk show psychologist Shirley Kenyon is challenged to reveal her educational background by a snooty shrink. Pissed at his request, Shirley tells him she got her degree from "Screw U." *See also* "Consider that a divorce"

"Secret's in the sauce" - Revelation of an older woman in the motion picture *Fried Green Tomatoes* (1991). Jessica Tandy starred as Mrs. Threadgoode who waxed sentimental about her life in a small Alabama town to a younger female (Kathy Bates) who visited the Rose Hills nursing home. Over a period of visits, Mrs. Threadgoode unraveled a tale of two feisty females—Ruth Jamison (Mary-Louise Parker) and her best friend, Idgie (Mary Stuart Masterson)—who shared a special bond of love. When Ruth's abusive husband beat her, Idgie rescued her from his cruelness. The two women then opened a small eatery called The Whistle Stop Cafe. One night Ruth's disgruntled husband stole the baby boy that Ruth had delivered some time after leaving him. In taking the child, he attacked a black woman (Cicely Tyson) and slapped her to the ground with the barrel of the shotgun. The woman, however, revived, and wielding a stout frying pan banged the back of man's head and killed him. To cover up the act and thus save the black woman from the unfairness of the prejudiced southern courts, Idgie and friends disposed of the body. When a Georgia police detective arrived to investigate the man's disappearance, he stopped by the cafe and had himself a heapin' helpin of ribs. When he compliments the food, the waitress replied, "Secret's in the sauce, or so I'm told." The secret, of course, was that the wife-beating husband was the secret...and the sauce." *See also* "Face it girls, I'm older and I have more insurance"

"See these guys? Pete, Rizzo and Sammy B? They work all day and drink all night for 40 fucking years. Two weeks out of the year, they take a vacation and go to the Cape. What do they do? They drink all day, they drink all night. If we don't step it up, we're gonna wind up just like them" -Michael Rapaport as Paul Kirkwood tries to convince his buddy Kev (Max Perlich) that maybe they should get their life together during a high school reunion in the motion picture *Beautiful Girls* (1996). Unfortunately, after hearing Paul's mini-tirade, all Kev has to say is, "Cool!"

"See, you ain't nothing but a chickenshit pussy asshole who lives on the misery and suffering of others. And when it comes for you, you'll be crying like a baby" - Chuck Norris as Colonel Scot McCoy, a Special Forces soldier offers his opinion to Ramon Cota (Billy Drago) a despicable South American drug runner in the motion picture *Delta Force 2: The Colombian Connection* (1990). In the film, McCoy leads a brigade of skydiving commandoes to rescue hostages and exact revenge. Before the mission, General Taylor (John P. Ryan) briefs McCoy about his Colombian contact: "Let me tell you about your contact. Cota killed her husband in front of her, then he killed her baby and used the corpse to smuggle cocaine, then he raped her. I wouldn't mention any of this when you meet her–she's probably still a little touchy about it" Note: In the original film, *Delta Force* (1986), after Major Scott McCay takes out a Palestinian terrorist, he says, "Sleep tight, sucker." The terrorist was part of a plot to hijack a 707 aircraft jetliner on its way from Athens to New York City.

"Sell crazy somewhere else" - When a neighbor of a cranky romance novelist Melvin Udall (Jack Nicholson) knocks on his New York apartment door in the movie *As Good As It Gets* (1997) he matter-of-factly tells her to "Sell crazy somewhere else. We're all stocked up here." When a fan of his novels asks, "How do you write women so well?" He cattily responds, "I take a man. Then I take away all reason and accountability." *See also* "Never, never interrupt me"

"She has a shoulder that would make dry ice feel like a bed warmer" - Melvyn Douglas as Tice Collins reveals to fellow lawyer Harry Bertrand (Allyn Joslyn) his feelings about his "trial" three month marriage with insurance-company executive Ann Winters (Rosalind Russell) in the motion picture *This Thing Called Love* (1941). To stimulate Ann's interest in sex, Tice puts a statue of a Mexican fertility god in their living room. But, when that little experiment fails, Tice yells, "You're a fraud. You couldn't make spinach grow in the Garden of Eden.

"She's got a heart like a twelve-minute egg" - Michael J. Fox as drug-using New Yorker Jamie Conway in the motion picture *Bright Lights, Big City* (1988). Note: In the film *Ace in the Hole aka: The Big Carnival (*1951) Jan Sterling as Lorraine tells reporter

Charles Tatum (Kirk Douglas), "I've met some hard-boiled eggs in my time, but you, you're twenty minutes."

"She hates with her tongue as well as her eyes. She hates with everything. She's a real woman" - George Tobias as a French Legionnaire guard comments on desert Princess Mahla (Jody Lawrence) captured in the motion picture *Ten Tall Men* (1951).

"She is a beautiful woman. But when this trial is over, you will see her no differently than a gun, or a knife, or any other instrument used as a weapon. She's a killer, and the worst kind. A killer who disguised herself as a loving partner!" - Joe Mantegna as lawyer Robert Garrett talks about Rebecca Carlson (Madonna) accused of killing a man to inherit his millions in the motion picture *Body of Evidence* (1993).

"She is a lush, the lady...after she bends the elbow a few times, she begins to see things—rats, roaches, bats, you know...a sock in the kisser is the only thing that will bring her out of it." - Thomas Gomez as Curley, a gangster hoodlum poking fun at Gaye Dawn, the drunken mistress (Claire Trevor) of mob boss Johnny Rocco (Edward G. Robinson) in the motion picture *Key Largo (*1948).

"She's an American and you will sit here and listen to what she wants for Christmas or I will kill you" - Dennis Quaid, as hot-tempered union organizer Jack McGurn fights racism during WWII when a bigoted man in a Santa Claus suit refuses Jack's Japanese-American daughter the privilege of sitting in Santa's lap in the motion picture *Come See the Paradise* (1990).

"She's bad, bad to the bone. If ever there was an e-e-evil woman, she is one" - Louis Jourdan as valet Andre Latour expresses his distaste for his employer Maddalena Anna Paradine (Alida Valli) accused of poisoning her blind husband in the courtroom drama *The Paradine Case* (1947).

"She's so deliciously low, so horribly dirty" - Candid words of Professor Henry Higgins (Leslie Howard) in the motion picture *Pygmalion* (1939) based on the play by George Bernard Shaw. To win a bet wherein Higgins boasts he can take any person off the street and teach them to be sophisticated and refined, Higgins recruits Eliza Doolittle (Wendy Hiller) a flower peddler as his guinea pig, proclaiming, "I shall make a duchess of this draggle-tailed guttersnipe." Rex Harrison spoke the same lines to Audrey Hepburn as Eliza Doolittle in the movie remake *My Fair Lady* (1964). Higgins' opinion on the fair sex: "I'd prefer a new version of the Spanish Inquisition than to ever let a woman into my life." and "I'm very grateful she's a woman and so easy to forget." Not to be outdone, Eliza offered her own opinion of Higgins: "You oughta be stuffed with nails."

"She's so fat..." - Sexist remarks of detective Joe Hallenbeck (Bruce Willis) in the motion picture *The Last Boy Scout (*1991). When a thug in an alley (Badja Djola) asks Hallenbeck, "Do you want it in the chest or the head?" Joe quips, "Yeah that's what your wife says." The thug barks, "Hey, man, stop with the wife shit!" Joe continues, "Ask me how fat she is. Ask me." Playing along, the thug asks, "How fat is she?" Joe then taunts the crook: "She's so fat I had to roll her in flour and look for the wet spot. If you wanna fuck her, you gotta slap her thigh and ride the wave in! She's so fat, her high school picture was an aerial shot!" The thug was not amused but since Bruce Willis is the star of the movie, he didn't die for his effrontery.

"She learned life from Bugs Bunny" - In the motion picture *Network* (1976) William Holden plays television executive Max Schumacher who quips to his wife Louise (Beatrice Straight) about his mistress (Faye Dunaway), "I'm not sure she's capable of any real feeling. She's television generation. She learned life from Bugs Bunny."

"Shit, piss, fuck, cunt, cocksucker, motherfucker, and tits" (aka the 'Seven Dirty Words') - On October 30, 1973 radio station WBAI-FM broadcast a recording of comedian George Carlin over the public airwaves that featured the "seven dirty words you can never say on television" (i.e., shit, piss, fuck, cunt, cocksucker, motherfucker, and tits). These seven little words, however, were not appreciated by one New York City listener who complained that her young child had heard the supposedly indecent words. The FCC later ruled that the broadcast of the "seven dirty words" was in violation of its obscenity statutes. The FCC ruling was later overturned by the Court of Appeals in March of 1977 and but later reaffirmed by the Supreme Court in July, 1978 which stated that the FCC still had the power to ban what it considered to be "patently offensive" language (despite First Amendment considerations). In 1994, the Fox network actually promoted their April 24 episode of THE GEORGE CARLIN SHOW on which George Carlin as scruffy, pony-tailed New York cabbie George O'Grady utters a famous four-letter word ('Fuck') seven times after another taxi cuts him off. The words were bleeped, of course. Additionally, on episode No. 68 "The Non-Fat Yogurt" (11/4/93) on the sitcom SEINFELD/NBC/1990-98 the 'fuck' and 'shit' words were freely used in the script's dialogue, but again the audio track was bleeped. Note: Former lawyer, John Mortimer whose novels inspired the legal TV drama THE RUMPOLE OF THE BAILEY/THA/1978-88 was responsible for a landmark censorship case in his homeland of England. In 1960, Penguin Books published the unexpurgated edition of D. H. Lawrence's *Lady Chatterley's Lover* and was charged with publishing obscene literature. The book was ruled "literary" and although sexually descriptive, was not necessarily "prurient." The case changed the definition of obscenity and pornography in England at the time and is now required reading for those studying to become barristers in Great Britain. *See also* "Madonna on LETTERMAN"

"Shocking! Positively shocking!" - At the beginning of the spy thriller *Goldfinger* (1964) British agent James Bond (Sean Connery) starts to embrace a lovely flamenco dancer (Nadja Regin) but then sees the image of an approaching assassin (Alf Joint) reflected in her eyes. Whirling around, James lets the attractive but devious temptress take the full brunt of the assailant's billy club. Bond then ends the confrontation by throwing his attacker into a bubble-filled bathtub along with a fully charged electric heater. Staring down at the killer's limp, electrocuted body, James comments, "Shocking! Positively shocking!" and then changes into his dinner jacket.

Shoebootie - On an episode of the sitcom ALL IN THE FAMILY/CBS/1971-79 Archie Bunker (Carroll O'Connor) revealed that his childhood nickname was "Shoebootie." During the Depression, Archie's family didn't have enough money to buy him a proper new pair of shoes, so consequently, he had to wear one shoe and one bootie as makeshift footwear.

"Shoot straight, you bastards! Don't make a mess of it" - Final words spoken by Lt. Harry Morant (Edward Woodward) in the military drama *Breaker Morant* (1979). Lt. Morant and his fellow soldiers Lt. Peter Hancock (Bryan Brown) and Lt. George Wilson (Lewis Fitzgerald) were veterans of the Boer War. At the end of the war Lt. Morant was given an order by Captain Simon Hurst (Terence Donovan) to kill all prisoners. "No prisoners. The gentlemen's war is over." Unfortunately, one of the prisoners was the missionary son of a politically influential man who pressed the British Empire to conduct a trumped-up court martial. During the trial, Lt. Morant informs the court, "We were out in the veldt fighting the Boer the way he fought us. I'll tell you what rule we applied, sir. We applied rule 303. We caught them and we shot them under rule 303." At the conclusion of the trial, Lt. Morant is found not guilty but his two fellow soldiers are made scapegoats and sentenced to death. As Hancock and Fitzgerald sat strapped to chairs in the middle of field, a reluctant Morant instructs his firing squad "Shoot straight, you bastards. Don't make a mess of it."

Shorty - The nickname given to Eddie Munster (Butch Patrick) by his taunting schoolmates on episode No.19 "Eddie's Nickname" of the sitcom THE MUNSTERS/CBS/1964-66. To help Eddie, Grandpa Munster said, "You'll never have to cry again because someone called you Shorty. Your adoring Grandpa is gonna give you a magic potion that will make you grow six inches overnight. Maybe, seven. Once I gave it to a pirate friend of mine who was only five feet tall." "Did it work?," asked Eddie. "Ain't ya ever heard of Long John Silver?" Note: On episode No. 64 "Big Little Man" on the sitcom THE BRADY BUNCH/ABC/1969-74 Bobby Brady (Michael Lookinland) tries to exercise to make himself taller after Sam the Butcher calls him "Shrimpo." Bobby's self-esteem returns when he puts his "shortness" to positive use.

"Shut up, you American!" - The Grim Reaper chastises an American in the humorous motion picture *Monty Python's The Meaning of Life* (1983). The film features small comedy sketches dealing with all of the stages and trials of life. When Death, dressed in the traditional dark robe and hood arrives at a dinner party, it tells the guests they must follow him. When an American speaks, Death shouts, "Shut up, you American! You Americans, all you do is talk, and talk, and say 'let me tell you something' and 'I just wanna say'. Well, you're dead now, so shut up!" When a British guy speaks, Death shouts, "Be quiet! Englishmen, you're all so fucking pompous, and none of you have got any balls."

"Sic gorgiamus allos subjuctatos nunc" - Family credo of the Addams family carved on a tomb in a scene from the movie *The Addams Family: The Movie (1991),* an adaptation of the macabre sitcom THE ADDAMS FAMILY/ABC/1964-66. Translated from the Latin, the phrase reads: "We gladly feast on those who would subdue us."

"Sicilians were spawned by niggers" - Dennis Hopper as a gangster named Clifford Worley tells his Sicilian cohort Vincenzo Cocotti (Christopher Walken) about his family heritage in the motion picture *True Romance* (1993). Clifford continues his history lesson: "It's a fact. See, Sicilians have black blood pumpin' through their hearts. If you don't believe me you can look it up. Hundreds and hundreds of years ago, you see, the Moors conquered Sicily. And the Moors are niggers. So you see, way back then, Sicilians were like wops from northern Italy. They all had blonde hair and blue eyes, but uh, well, then the Moors moved in there, and uh, they changed the whole country. They did so much fuckin' with Sicilian women that they changed the whole bloodline forever. That's why blonde hair and blue eyes became black hair and dark skin. You know, it's absolutely amazing to me to think that to this day, hundreds of years later, that Sicilians still carry that nigger gene....Your ancestors are niggers. Yeah, and your great-great-great-great grandmother fucked a nigger, yeah, and she had a half nigger kid...Now, if that's a fact, tell me, am I lying? Cause you, you're part eggplant."

"Silence Whippersnapper!" - Frank Morgan as The Wizard of Oz chastises Kansas girl Dorothy Gale (Judy Garland) after she tells the Wizard that he should be ashamed for making the Cowardly Lion (Bert Lahr) faint in the motion picture *The Wizard of Oz* (1939). When Dorothy and her companions Scarecrow (Ray Bolger), Tin Man (Jack Haley) and the Cowardly Lion reach the Emerald City, they seek an audience with the "Great and Powerful Wizard of Oz." After the Wicked Witch of the West writes "Surrender Dorothy" in the sky, the Wizard offers to see them. Approaching the Wizard, whose appearance is masked in billowing flames and smoke, the travelers present their plea for help. The Tin Man (Jack Haley) requests a heart, but the Wizard bellows, "You dare come to me for a heart, do you? You clinking clanking collection of collisionous junk!" The Scarecrow asks for a brain, but the Wizard lashes out, "You billowing bale of bovine fodder." And, when the time comes for the Cowardly Lion to ask for courage, the scaredy cat faints under the strain.

"Silly Rabbit, Trix are for kids!" - Constant reminder delivered to a sleepy-eyed white rabbit that starred in a successful series of TV commercials for the General Mills breakfast cereal Trix since the 1960s. The commercials featured a rabbit who didn't like the conventional foods that rabbits ate. As he said in his black & white debut in 1961, "I'm a rabbit, and rabbits are supposed to like carrots. But I hate carrots. I like Trix!" The Rabbit's love for the "raspberry red, lemon yellow, orange orange" taste of Trix cereal forced him to dress in disguises of all sorts to beg, borrow or steal Trix from the neighborhood children. Unfortunately, all his work ended with the same negative reply, "Silly Rabbit, Trix are for Kids!" During the election year of 1976, a campaign was launched to see if the Rabbit should finally get some get Trix. Children wrote letters and voted 99% in favor of letting the rabbit eat his heart's desire. The Rabbit was awarded a whole bowl of Trix. However, when he asked for more, the kids said, "Wait till the next election." The ad campaign was created by the Dancer, Fitzgerald & Sample Advertising Agency. Russell Horton provided the voice of the Trix Rabbit.

Sir Limps-a-lot - Nickname and affectionate put-down of Chandler Bing (Matthew Perry), a data processing executive who is missing the little toe from his right foot on the sitcom FRIENDS/NBC/1994-2004. Chandler lost his toe during a Thanksgiving dinner when Monica Geller (Courtney Cox) accidentally dropped a large chopping knife onto the floor. The knife cut through Chandler's canvas shoe and severed his toe. He immediately went to the hospital to have it reconnected. Unfortunately, in the rush to get to the hospital, Monica mistakenly put a piece of a carrot in the bag of ice meant to preserve the toe. Consequently, Chandler's buddy, Ross Geller (David Schwimmer) dubbed him, Sir Limps-a-lot.

"Sit on it!" - Crude but to-the-point insult often heard on the 1950s based sitcom HAPPY DAYS/ABC/1974-84. For example "Sit on it, Ralph!" The 'it' on which one was to 'sit' was never identified (thankfully). When Rick Cronin, the president of Nick at Nite's TV Land was asked the trivia question "When Fonzie says, 'Sit on it!' What exactly is it?" he responded, "It's either a pepperoni pizza or a whoopie cushion, or perhaps a banana cream pie. Only Fonzie knows for sure and people are afraid to ask him."

"Six fuckin' car lengths! That's a hundred and six fuckin' feet, mister! If I had to stop suddenly, you woulda hit me! I want you to get a fuckin' driver's manual, and I want you to study that motherfucker! And I want you to obey the goddamn rules! Fifty-fuckin' thousand people were killed on the highway last year 'cause of fuckin' assholes like you! Tell me you're gonna get a manual!" - Robert Loggia as Mr. Eddy, a shady gangster who runs a tailgater off the highway, pulls out a large gun and menacingly waves his weapon in the man's face while shouting about the importance of highway safety in the David Lynch motion picture *Lost Highway* (1997).

Smartest Dumbbell in the History of Show Business, The - The pejorative nickname given to comedienne Gracie Allen for her scatterbrained housewife characterizations performed as part of her stage act in vaudeville, radio and television. She costarred with her husband George Burns on the sitcom THE GEORGE BURNS AND GRACIE ALLEN SHOW/CBS/1950-58. While the audience laughed at her apparent stupidity, Gracie actually believed she was extremely smart. Examples of her brainpower:

George: What's that?
Gracie: Electric cords. I had them shortened. This one's for the iron, this one's for the floor lamp.
George: Why did you shorten them?
Gracie: To save electricity.

(and)

George: What are you looking for in the Sears catalog?
Gracie: I'm looking for sweaters for cows.
George: Sweaters for cows?
Gracie: Yes, you know they must be very scarce. Fred told me that he had forty Holstein cows and only twenty two jerseys.

In the 1940s, Gracie bought some presents for her brother who was in the Army. Knowing how lazy her brother could be, she bought him a yo-yo. That way, when he rode a camel, its swaying motion would be able to move it up and down. When asked by her husband, George what she would get in case he goes to the Pacific Islands, Gracie says, "A knife and hatchet." However they weren't to be used for hacking through the jungle. "No!" she continued. "They grow bananas and coconuts there, don't they? Well, he likes banana splits with chopped nuts." Despite her acting stupid, Gracie was very sharp-witted. In 1939, she appeared on NBC's quiz show INFORMATION PLEASE and amazed the audience by answering a series of difficult questions along with her fellow panelists.

Smeg - Futuristic insult often used by space castaway Dave Lister (Craig Bierko) on the science fiction comedy RED DWARF/BBC/1988+. Some sample "smeg" quotes follow:

Lister:	Oh smeg! What the smegging smeg's he smegging done? He's smegging killed me" ("Bodyswap" episode)

Lister:	You see I try sir. I'm not an insubordinate man by nature. I try and respect and everything, but it's not easy because he's such a smeghead.
Rimmer:	Did you hear that sir? Lister, do you have any conception of the penalty for describing a superior technician as a smeghead?
Captain:	Oh Rimmer, you are such a smeghead. (*"The End" episode*)

"Smile when you say that!" *See* "When you call me that, Smile!"

"Smile, you son of a bitch!" - Suggestion made to a Great White shark at the conclusion of Steven Spielberg's famous fish film *Jaws* (1975). After a huge shark terrorizes the New England community of Amity Island, Chief Police Brody (Roy Scheider) sets to sea in a boat named *Orca* to hunt down the shark. In the film's climax, the shark rams the small craft, scuttles it and drags away the screaming body of Quint (Robert Shaw) a veteran shark hunter who earlier explained, "The thing about a shark, it's got lifeless eyes, black eyes, like a doll's eyes. When it comes at you it doesn't seem to be livin'... Until he bites you, and those black eyes roll over white." As "Jaws" made its last pass to collect another morsel of man, Brody fires his rifle into the mouth of the attacking shark and explodes an oxygen canister that he earlier crammed into its gaping maw. The resulting explosion tore the shark to pieces and made a marvelous meal for a horde of nearby seagulls that swooped in for the free eats. Brody and surviving shark expert, Hooper (Richard Dreyfuss) then slowly paddle their way back to the mainland. Note: The myth of the "exploding" oxygen tank was debunked on the Discovery Channel's science education series MYTHBUSTERS after multiple test shots (with various caliber projectiles) produced no exploding tanks. The tanks did, however, forcibly fly all over the place as the escaping gases propelled the damaged canisters this way and that.

"Snakes like you usually die of their own poison" - John Wayne as Chris Morrell spits venom at land grabber Sam Black (Yakima Canutt) in the western movie *'Neath the Arizona Skies* (1934).

"So, God was creating man, and his little assistant came up to him and he said: 'Hey, we've got all these bodies left, but we're right out of brains, we're right out of hearts and we're right out of vocal chords.' And God said: 'Fuck it! Sew 'em up anyway. Smack smiles on the faces and make them talk out of their arses.' And lo,

God created the Tory Party" - Stephen Tompkinson as Phil [posing as Mr. Chuckles] offers a hilarious political commentary in the motion picture *Brassed Off* (1996).

"So long, Sport" - Roy Scheider as Harry, a self-made, amoral businessman gives a final farewell to his blackmailer at the end of the motion picture *52 Pick-Up* (1986). Thinking he pulled off the perfect blackmail scheme, a cocky conman named Raimy (John Glover) takes his ransom money and the keys to his victims' car and attempts to leave the scene of the money drop. As he turns on the radio, the car doors automatically lock and a voice from the victim (Harry) proclaims, "Hi Allen, this is the first and the last 10 seconds of the rest of your life." Struggling to escape, the blackmailer shots a hole in the window but the car explodes. Glancing back with a splendid payback smirk on his face, Harry says, "So long, Sport." Earlier in the film, Raimy leered at Harry's wife (Ann Margaret) and said, "She's not bad. I wouldn't mind hurting her a little."

"So many people to kill, so little time" - Uma Thurman as the deadly villain Poison Ivy in the motion picture *Batman 4: Batman & Robin* (1997). After Poison Ivy dispatched Batman and Robin with her army of clinging vines, she glibly says, "Gotta go. So many people to kill, so little time." Poison Ivy worked in league with Mr. Freeze (Arnold Schwarzenegger) who planned to freeze Gotham City. ("Let them eat Ice"). While Batgirl (Alicia Silverstone) womped Ivy's botanical butt, Batman (George Clooney) thwarted Freeze's plan, saying, "Hey, Freeze, the heat is on."

"Some people are going to get hurt. Want to be first?"- Lee J. Cobb as Police Chief Robinson attempts to quell an angry lynch mob who wants John Waldron (Arthur Kennedy), a prisoner accused of murdering a minister in the motion picture *Boomarang* (1947).

"Somebody oughta belt you in the mouth..." - Spoken by John Wayne as George Washington McLintock, a wealthy cattle rancher in the rowdy western comedy movie *McLintock!* (1963). When G. W. McLintock hears that a father of a local girl (Leo Gordon) is about to hang an Indian suspected of kidnapping his daughter (who actually went on a horse ride with her beau) McLintock confronts the girl's father, takes the shotgun from his hand and confesses, "I haven't lost my temper in forty years, but pilgrim you caused a lot of trouble this morning and might of got somebody killed and somebody oughta belt you in the mouth, but I won't hitcha...I won't. [pauses] "The Hell I won't!" McLintock slugs the man in the face and knocks him down into a water-filled gully. A rip roaring fist fight ensues as dozens of people including McLintock and his wife (Maureen O'Hara) get knocked into the mud.

"Sometimes they both need a whip to put some sense in them. First you have to slip a bit in his mouth—and make him like it" - Barbara Stanwyck as Texan debutante Valentine "Val" Ransome alludes to horse training methods in an effort to explain how she controls her men in the motion picture *Breakfast for Two* (1937).

"A soul is nothing" - John Huston speaking his mind as Satan in the motion picture *The Devil and Daniel Webster* (1941). When New Hampshire farmer Jabez Stone (James Craig) says, "That's enough to make a man sell his soul to the Devil. And I would for about two cents!" Suddenly, the Devil appears and begins his sales pitch to buy the man's soul. "A soul is nothing. Can you see it? Smell it? Touch it? No. This soul, your soul, is nothing against seven years of good luck. You'll have money and all that money can buy." As Jabez agrees to the deal, the Devil offers up a contract and requests "a firm signature. One that will last till doomsday." Years later, the Devil comes for his property, but Stone recants and hires Daniel Webster (Edward Arnold) to defend him. Protecting his claim, the Devil expresses his importance. "Who has a better right? When the first wrong was done to the first Indian, I was there. When the first slave you put off from the Congo, I stood on the deck. Am I not still spoken of in every church in New England? It's true the North claims me for a Southerner and the South for a Northerner, but I'm neither. Tell the truth, Mr. Webster, though I don't like to boast of it, my name's older in the country than yours."

"The soul of a woman is darker than a back alley" - To set the mood for the beginning of the film noir parody *Fatal Instinct* (1993), Ned Ravine (Armand Assante) gives his opinion of the opposite sex in this opening voiceover. "Women are one of life's great mysteries. To some guys women are like a big jigsaw with pieces that just don't fit. I think the soul of a woman is darker than a back alley and more tangled than a telephone cord, and colder than an Eskimo pie in Anchorage, but those guys don't even have a clue. When you know women the way I do, you know exactly what makes them tick, what makes them hum, what makes them jiggle up and down when they walk. There are two kinds of women in the world and I've known them both. One will take you for a fast ride on a bumpy road with no seat belt, the other kind..." Suddenly, the voice of Ned's partner Arch (John Witherspoon) says, "Gee, knock off the chatter, will you, Ned?"

Soup Nazi - Pejorative nickname of a tyrannical New York City soup store operator on the classic episode "The Soup Nazi" from the sitcom SEINFELD/NBC/1990-98. Despite his sour demeanor, the Soup Nazi (Larry Thomas) made some of the best soup in the city and avid fans lined up around the block to wait for his savory concoctions. When ordering soups, the customer had to follow these strict procedures: 1) When you walk in, move immediately to the right; 2) Order your soup with no enthusiasm at all; 3) Put your money on the counter and move to the left; and 4) Take your soup and do not give any comments. Tip! Never push your luck and ask for bread. In the end, if the Soup Nazi is not pleased with the way you presented yourself at his soup counter he would yell, "No soup for YOU, Next!" And if you really irritated him he said, "No soup for YOU! Come back. One year. Next!" At the conclusion of the SEINFELD episode, Elaine Benes (Julia Louis-Dreyfus) who had been banned from the Soup Nazi's store, discovers a collection of hand-written soup recipes in the drawer of a piece of furniture formerly owned by the Soup Nazi. With recipes clutched in her hand, she triumphantly returns to the Soup Nazi's store and vows revenge by threatening to reveal his trade secrets to ZA VERLD! Soon after Elaine's visit, the Soup Nazi tells his customers that he is going to close his soup store and move to Argentina. Note: The real "Soup Nazi" (Ali "Al" Yeganeh) worked at the Soup Kitchen International at 8th Avenue and 55th Street 259A West 55 Street in New York City. He didn't appreciate the humor of the episode and threatened to sue the program if they used the character again. When Yeganeh learned the SEINFELD series was ending in 1998, he said, "it was the best gift America and the human race got this Christmas. The show really destroyed my personal life and my emotional and physical well being. Because of this show, customers think

I'm going to kill them and they panic." (*People Weekly* 1/12/98 p. 124) When David Letterman asked Yeganeh to appear on his 1998 show, he said, "to celebrate this clown going off the air, I was so happy he was leaving, I agreed to it."

"Soylent green is people!" - Charlton Heston as Detective Thorn reveals an awful truth in the sci-fi classic *Soylent Green* (1973). In the year 2222, food sources are scarce and Marshal Law has been declared all over the world. To satisfy the hunger of the citizenry, a new food source called soylent green (supposedly made from soybeans and lentils) is issued the people. Thorn, however, follows a corpse disposal truck to a factory and discovers the dead bodies are being processed into "soylent green" cubes. Escaping with the news, he flees back to the city and tries to report his findings to Hatcher, his supervisor (Brock Peters). The last line in the movie has Thorn (now shot and probably dying), pleading, "Soon they'll be breeding us like cattle! You've got to warn everyone and tell them! Soylent green is made of people! You can tell everybody, Listen to me, Hatcher, You've got to tell them! Soylent green is people!"

"Spearchucker" Jones - The nickname of Oliver Harmon Jones (played by Timothy Brown), an African-American football star turned doctor who was stationed at Mobile Army Surgical Hospital 4077th Division during the Korean War on the military sitcom M*A*S*H/CBS/1972-83. Spearchucker (played by Fred Williamson in the 1970 film M*A*S*H that inspired the series) hangs out with white surgeons Hawkeye Pierce and Trapper John. Spearchucker's character was written out of the show after the first season when the show's writers discovered that there were no black surgeons during the Korean Conflict. The "Spearchucker" nickname brings up associations with primitive spear-throwing people and as such denigrates the character's integrity as an educated, civilized man, although the nickname was probably meant to be "endearing" in regards to his fellow white officers.

"Spends a night in the box" - What happened to prisoners at Road Prison 36 for not following orders in the motion picture *Cool Hand Luke* (1967). When new prisoners enter the prison, Carr (Clifton James), the floor walker explains the rules: "Them clothes got laundry numbers on them...Any man forgets his number spends a night in the box. These here spoons you keep with you. Any man loses his spoon spends a night in the box. There's no playing grab-ass or fighting in the building...Any man playing grab-ass or fighting in the building spends a night in the box. First bell's at five minutes of eight when you will get in your bunk...Any man not in his bunk at eight spends the night in the box. There is no smoking in the prone position in bed...Any man caught smoking in the prone position in bed...spends a night in the box. You get two sheets...Any man turns in the wrong sheet spends a night in the box. No one'll sit in the bunks with dirty pants on. Any man with dirty pants on sitting on the bunks spends a night in the box. Any man don't bring back his empty pop bottle spends a night in the box. Any man loud talking spends a night in the box. You got questions, you come to me. I'm Carr, the floor walker. I'm responsible for order in here. Any man don't keep order spends a night in..." New prisoner Luke (Paul Newman) interjects, "the box." Carr continues, "I hope you ain't going to be a hard case." Luke just smiles and shakes his head. Luke is later mortally wounded after escapting from the road gang. His last words: (just before being shot in the neck) "What we have here is a failure to communicate."

"Splitting a little girl's throat is like cutting warm butter" - Vernon Wells as Bennett, a vile mercenary threatens to kill Jennie Matrix (Alyssa Milano), the kidnapped 11-year-old daughter of retired Special Forces leader John Matrix (Arnold Schwarzenegger) if he doesn't follow through on an assassination plan in the motion picture *Commando* (1985). When one kidnapper says, "Isn't that nice" when he hears that Matrix seems to be cooperating, Jennie spits back, "Not nearly as nice as watching him smash your face in." In the film's climax, John Matrix impales Bennett with a steam pipe and says, "Let off some steam, Bennett."

Spooky Mulder - On the fantasy drama THE X-FILES/FOX/1993-2002, David Duchovny appeared as Fox "Spooky" Mulder, a zealous, conspiracy obsessed FBI agent (trained in psychology at Oxford) who was assigned to investigate cases (aka "The X-Files") that bordered on the paranormal. His coworkers at the Quantico FBI Training Academy nicknamed Mulder "Spooky" because of his beliefs in unexplained phenomena (i.e. UFO's, etc.). Mulder refers to himself as "The FBI's Most Unwanted." In the film spin-off *The X-Files* (1998) Mulder shares the following to a bartender "I'm the key figure in an ongoing government charade, the plot to conceal the truth about the existence of extraterrestrials. It's a global conspiracy, actually, with key players in the highest levels of power that reaches down into the lives of every man, woman, and child on this planet, so, of course, no one believes me. I'm an annoyance to my superiors, a joke to my peers. They call me Spooky. Spooky Mulder, whose sister was abducted by aliens when he was just a kid and who now chases after little green men with a badge and a gun, shouting to the heavens or to anyone who will listen that the fix is in, that the sky is falling and when it hits it's gonna be the shit-storm of all time." *See also* "Cancer Man"

Spooky Old Alice - On the comedy variety program THE GEORGE GOBEL SHOW/NBC/CBS/1954-60, George Gobel, a small comedian with crew-cut hair referred to his wife on the series as "Spooky Old Alice." Lonesome George, as he was called, was very timid fellow who often had domestic confrontations with his much taller wife. Alice was the real-life name of George's wife, however on the show she was played by Jeff Donnell (1954-58) and later by Phyllis Avery (1958-59). The Alice sketches were dropped when the show moved to the CBS network. George's catchphrase was "Well, I'll be a dirty bird."

Spud - Pejorative nickname of Bud Bundy (David Faustino), given to him by his dim-witted but beautiful blond sister Kelly (Christina Applegate) on the dysfunctional family comedy MARRIED...WITH CHILDREN/FOX/1987-97. Kelly also referred to her brother Bud as Toad Boy. *See also* "The Dumbest Girl in America"

"Squeeeeeeal!" (like a pig) - Indecent proposal of perverted hillbilly in the classic outdoors thriller *Deliverance (*1972) about four Atlanta businessmen who take a weekend canoe trip. Pulling their canoe to the side of the river, two city dudes, Ed (Jon Voight) and Bobby (Ned Beatty) are confronted by a duo of backwoods hunters (played by Billy McKinney & Herbert "Cowboy" Coward). At gunpoint, the men force Ed and Bobby into the woods ("What we, uh, 're-quire' is that you get your goddamn asses up in them woods"). While Ed is tied to the tree, Bobby is forced to strip his clothes. One woodsman (McKinney) grabs at Bobby's body, molests him, and says, "You look just like a hog," and tells him to "Squeeeeeeeal" like a pig. Finishing with Bobby, he approaches Ed collared to the tree, undoes the belt around his neck and prepares to assist his toothless partner in further molestation. Luckily, Lewis (Burt Reynolds) one of the other four campers arrives, pulls out his bow and shoots Bobby's attacker through the back with a well placed arrow. As the toothless man retreats to the cover of the woods, the campers vote (three to one) to bury the evidence and move on. Resuming their river odyssey, Drew (Ronny Cox)—the only one who objected to keeping the killing a secret—is shot by a sniper (Coward) lurking atop the rock face along the river. With Drew dead, and Lewis' body battered and broken by the rapids, Ed climbs the rock face and dispatches the sniper with an arrow. The three survivors then bury their friend Drew and bid a fond farewell to the river after a few well-chosen words to a suspicious local sheriff (played by James Dickey, who wrote the book "Deliverance").

Squidhead - Dave Thomas, comedy veteran of SCTV NETWORK 90/NBC/1981-83 and THE DAVE THOMAS COMEDY SHOW/CBS/1990 was called "Squidhead" by his childhood schoolmates because he happened to have a head (7 3/4 XL) disproportionate to his body, a body which he figured was just a convenient vehicle for taking his head from place to place.

"Stay on your side of the street; that's what they have gutters for" - The harsh yet protective words of Jewish mother Kate (Blythe Danner) who objected to her sister Blanche's (Judith Ivey) Irish suitor, Andrew (Alan Weeks) in the motion picture *Brighton Beach Memoirs* (1986). Note: In the film Scarface (1932) C. Henry Gordon as police inspector Guarino insults mobster Tony Camonte (Paul Muni), saying, "Someday you're going to fall down in the gutter—right where the horses have been standing—right where you belong." And, in the film *Footlight Parade* (1933) Joan Blondell as Nan Prescott says to golddigger Vivian Rich (Claire Dodd), "As long as they have sidewalks, you've got a job."

"Steal from thy neighbor! Cheat thy neighbor! Kill thy Neighbor!" - J. Carroll Naish as Guiseppe, a captured Italian soldier explains the differences in ideology between his own Italian soldiers and those of Nazi Germany's in the motion picture *Sahara* (1943). He begins his rationale: "Italians are not like Germans—only the body wears the uniform and not the soul! Mussolini is not so clever like Hitler. He can dress his Italians up only to look like thieves, cheats, murderers. He cannot, like Hitler, make them feel like that. He cannot, like Hitler scrape from the conscience the knowledge that right is right and wrong is wrong, or dig holes in their heads to plant his own ten commandments: Steal from thy neighbor! Cheat thy neighbor! Kill thy Neighbor!"

"Stifle yourself!" - One of the more pleasant things that bigot Archie Bunker (Carroll O'Connor) said to his wife or family members when he got frustrated with them on episodes of ALL IN THE FAMILY/CBS/1971-83. *See also* "Dingbat" and "Meathead"

"Stringbean, if you so much as lay a hand on this automobile, I'm gonna jump down your throat and tap dance on your lungs" - Steve McQueen as turn-of-the-century handyman/chauffeur Boon Hoggenbeck warns Ned McCaslin (Rupert Crosse) of the consequences of tampering with his yellow 1905 Winton Flyer in the motion picture *The Reivers* (1969). Note: "Down your throat" seems to be the second most popular place to shove things when threatening a person (up your ass is the top choice). A few more throaty examples: In the film *Barb Wire* (1996) we hear a bad guy shout the venomous threat, "I will personally rip out your heart and stuff it back down your throat." and in the film *Attack! (1956)* platoon leader Lt. Costa (Jack Palance) threatens Captain Cooney (Eddie Albert) with this lovely sentiment, "I'll shove a grenade down your throat and pull the pin."

"Stink! Stank! Stunk!" - The three words that best describe the personality of Mr. Grinch (voice of Boris Karloff) on the classic Yule Tide cartoon THE GRINCH THAT STOLE CHRISTMAS. Based on a story by Dr. Seuss, this perennial holiday special featured Mr. Grinch, a grimacing curmudgeon who lives on the north side of Who-ville. After 53 years, the Grinch has finally had it with all the happiness and festivities of Christmas. As the Grinch says, "I must stop Christmas from coming!" His solution: Steal all the gifts, decorations and holiday food down in Who-ville. Why he even stole the candy canes from the fingers of sleeping children. That surely would make every one sad. But to the Grinch's surprise, his victims become the victors as they sang happy songs on Christmas day, despite the lack of material possessions. The animated special featured a wonderfully wicked song that begins, "You're a mean one Mr. Grinch." The song goes on to say that Mr. Grinch is as "cuddly as a cactus"; has "termites in his smile"; and that his "soul is an appalling dump heap, overflowing with the most disgraceful assortment of rubbish imaginable, mangled up in tangled up knots." *See also* "Humbug!"

Stinkerbelle – The childhood nickname of Frankie Reed (Julianne Phillips), the youngest of four sisters featured on the family drama SISTERS/NBC/1991-96. Her now grown sister Teddy Reed (Sela Ward) still continues to use the perjorative but affectionate moniker.

"Stuffy, huh? I'll give ya a little air" - James Cagney as psychopathic hoodlum Arthur Cody Jarrett talks to a snitch (Paul Guilfoyle) locked in the trunk of a car in the motion picture *White Heat* (1949). Of course, Cody kindly provides ventilation for the man by emptying his six-shooter into the truck and its occupant. When Cody realizes that one of his ambitious gang members Big Ed Somers (Steve Cochran) wants to be boss, he says, "Big Ed...great Big Ed. You know why they call him Big Ed? Cause he's got big ideas. One day, he's gonna get a big idea about me...and it's gonna be his last." At the film's conclusion, Cody is pursued by the police and takes refuge at the top of an oil refinery tank. Seeing no escape, the maniacal momma's boy cries, "Made it, Ma! Top of the world!" and fires his gun into the flammable fuel in the containment tank below his feet.

Sugarfoot - Name given to Tom Brewster (Will Hutchins), a young, naive lawyer who left the East in search of adventure on the 1860s western series SUGARFOOT/ABC/1957-61. A "sugarfoot" is a cowboy so inept that he was listed one class lower than a tenderfoot (a "Dude," a novice to frontier ways).

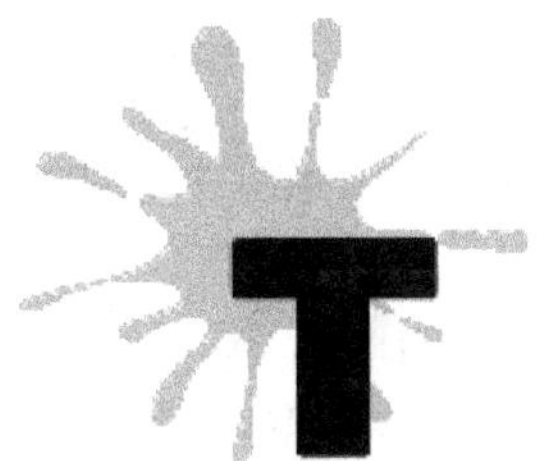

"Terminate with extreme prejudice" - Military order given to Captain Benjamin Willard (Martin Sheen) to seek out and destroy rouge Army officer Colonel Kurtz (Marlon Brando) living up river in the jungles of South East Asia in the motion picture *Apocalypse Now* (1979). Questioning the rational behind such orders, Willard says, "Charging a man with murder in this place (Vietnam) is like handing out speeding tickets at the Indy 500." Along his journey, Willard meets helicopter commander Lt. Colonel Kilgore (Robert Duvall) who says, "Let's bomb the shit out of them. These people never give up" and "I love the smell of napalm in the morning...Smells like—victory". By the film's end, Willard completes his mission. Kurtz's dying words: "The horror, the horror."

"*That* dress, you would wear to a hooker's wedding" - Gina De Angelis as Aunt Sofia pokes fun at one of the dresses worn by a wedding guest in the motion picture *Cousins* (1989).

"That squeaking, corpulent broad, I even hate the way she licks stamps" - Danny De Vito as Sam Stone creates a list of reasons why he should kill his wife, Barbara (Bette Midler) in the motion picture *Ruthless People* (1986). When Sam reveals a kidnapping plan to his close friend, Carol (Anita Morris), he confesses, "My only regret, Carol, is that the plan isn't more violent. As Barbara realizes her husband won't pay her full ransom, she screams, "I'm being marked down? I've been kidnapped by K Mart!"

"That's a goddamn lie! I never bought a congressman in my life! I rent 'em. It's cheaper." - Paul Newman as Louisiana Governor Earl Long lets the public know just how he really does business in the motion picture *Blaze* (1989).

"That's a Smith & Wesson, and you've had your six" - In the film *Dr. No* (1962) Sean Connery as secret agent James Bond investigates strange happenings in the Caribbean. When he gets too close, a Professor working for the sinister Dr. No enters Bonds bungalow, and shoots six shots into the bed he thinks is occupied by agent 007. Bond, however, gets the drop on the man, and queries him about his employer. While talking, the Professor surreptitiously reclaims his gun only to find he's expended all his ammunition. Bond, calmly says, "That's a Smith & Wesson, and you've had your six." Bond then shoots the man twice—once in the front and once in the back for good measure. *See also* "I think they were on their way to a funeral"

"That's faggot stuff" - Dustin Hoffman in the role of New York City street hustler Ratzo Rizzo educating Joe Buck (John Voight), a new gigolo in town that his cowboy hat and clothes will only attract a certain clientele in the motion picture *Midnight*

Cowboy (1969). When Joe complains, "You gonna tell me that John Wayne is a fag?" Rizzo answers, "I know enough to know that big dumb cowboy crap don't appeal to no one except every Jacky on Forty Second Street. Fag stuff. That's all it is. Fag stuff."

"That's not a knife. *That's* a knife" - Paul Hogan as Mick Dundee comparing knife blades in the film *Crocodile Dundee* (1986). When a New York City street punk pulls a knife on Mick "Crocodile" Dundee, a visitor from Australia's outback, Mick politely pulls out his own blade, and says, "That's not a knife. *That's* a knife. The incredible size of Mick's blade compared to the tiny one used by the mugger sent the hoodlum running away in panic.

"That's right, you're not a cocaine dealer, you're an importer—and your brother's not a scum-sucking pimp...he's a talent agent" - Charles Bronson as police detective Jack Murphy having an uncivil conversation with a drug dealer in the motion picture *Murphy's Law* (1986).

"Them Okies got no sense and no feelings. They ain't human. No, human being wouldn't live the way they do. A human being couldn't stand to be so miserable" - The words of a gas station attendant referring to the Joad family as they flee in their dilapidated truck from the poverty of the Dust Bowl of Oklahoma to the promise of California in the classic motion picture *The Grapes of Wrath* (1940).

"Then I'll get you there dead, boy" - Clint Eastwood as deputy marshal Jed Cooper in the western classic film *Hang 'em High* (1967). After taking a prisoner named Miller (Bruce Dern) into custody, the vengeful cowpoke tells Cooper, "You ain't never gonna get me back to town alive, boy" Unfazed by the threat, Jed simply answers, "Then I'll get you there dead, boy."

"Then the man they call Judas Escariot went to the chief priests, and asked, 'How much will you pay me to betray him to you?' They paid him thirty pieces of silver, and from that moment, he began to look out for a way to betray him" - David Haskell as Judas in the Christian bible-inspired musical *Godspell* (1973).

"There are two kinds of woman: high maintenance and low maintenance. You're the worst kind. You're high maintenance but you think you're low maintenance." - Billy Crystal as Harry Burns analyzes his friend Sally Allbright (Meg Ryan) in the motion picture *When Harry Met Sally* (1989). In the film, Harry's friend, Marie (Carrie Fisher) describes the type of woman he enjoys as "Thin, pretty, big tits...your basic nightmare."

"There are two things I don't like about you—your face. So how about shutting both of them" - Hugo Weaving as lip-synching drag queen Tick/Mitzi in the motion picture *The Adventures of Priscilla, Queen of the Desert* (1994). Fellow drag queen/transsexual Bernadette (Terence Stamp) also offers his/her own biting put-down: "One more push and I'm gonna smack his face so hard he'll have to stick his toothbrush up his ass to clean his teeth." Note: In the film *The Presidio* (1988), Jack Warden as retired Sgt. Major Ross "Top" Maclure tells his diamond smuggler crony, "I'll shove your head up your ass and you'll be talking out of your armpits!"

"There's a law against hitting actresses. Legally, they're considered women" - Sam Levene as Ben Melnick in the motion picture *Kathy O'* (1958).

"There's no question of honor, sir, between an American officer and Cochise" - Henry Fonda as frontier cavalry officer Lt. Colonel Owen Thursday in the motion picture *Fort Apache* (1948). Thursday also referred to Apache Indian chief Cochise (Miguel Inclan) as a "breechclouted savage, an illiterate uncivilized murderer and a treaty breaker."

"There's nothing more toxic or deadly than a human child. A single touch could kill you. Leave a door open, and one can walk right into this factory; right into the monster world" - James Coburn as Henry J. Waternoose, the ruthless director of Monsters Inc, that harvests the screams of little children to power Monstroplis, a netherworld city of boogey men and misshapen creatures in the motion picture *Monsters, Inc* (2001) Upon learning just how dangerous children could be, a monster trainee shouts, "I won't go into a kid's room. You can't make me!"

"There'll be no locks or bolts between us, Mary Kate—except those in your own mercenary little heart" - John Wayne as Sean Thornton speaks to his wife, Mary Kate Danaher (Maureen O'Sullivan) on their honeymoon night in the motion picture *The Quiet Man* (1952). When Mary Kate gets married, she is entitled to a dowry from her blustery brother Will Danaher (Victor McLaughlin). Sean, who is not on speaking terms with Will, tells Mary Kate to forget her money. When Mary Kate insists on getting what is owed her, she says, "I'll wear your ring, I'll cook, and I'll wash, and I'll keep the land. But that is all. Until I've got my dowry safe about me, I'm no married woman. I'm the servant I've always been, without anything of my own." Mary Kate then runs to her bedroom and locks the door. Sean breaks the door down, picks her up, throws her on the bed, and just when she thinks he is going to force himself on her, Sean leaves the room, but not before chastising her with his "locks or bolts" speech.

"They cast a spell on you, you know, the Jews. When you work closely with them, like I do, you see this. They have this power. It's like a virus. Some of my men are infected with this virus. They should be pitied, not punished. They should receive treatment because this is as real as typhus. I see it all the time. It's a matter of money? Hmm?" - Ralph Fiennes as German administrator Amon Goeth in the WWII motion picture *Schindler's List (*1993).

"They just shoot a bullet in their head, and then retract it. It's just BOOM-shht-BOOM-shht" - Paul A. Partain as wheelchair-bound Franklin Hardesty explains how livestock are killed at a slaughter house in the horror film *Texas Chain Saw Massacre* (1974). Disgusted at the story, Franklin's sister Sally (Marilyn Burns) says, "Franklin, I like meat, please change the subject!" This cult film is extremely vile. It follows the tale the Hardesty's and three other teenager friends who investigate the desecration of Sally's grandfather's cemetery (bodies have been stolen). Along the way, they encounter a family of backwoods cannibals and a sicko named Leatherface who hunts his prey with chainsaws, sledgehammers and assorted cutlery. *The Texas Chain Saw Massacre 2* (1986); *Leatherface: Texas Chain Saw Massacre III* (1990); and *The Return of the Texas Chainsaw Massacre* (1994) sequels produced such memorable phrases as "Peel that pig and slice him thick."; "I'm gonna service you real good babe"; and "You have one choice, boy: sex or the saw! Sex is, well, nobody knows. But the saw, the saw is family!" Note In the film *Hollywood Chainsaw Hookers* (1988) Jay Richardson as private eye Jack Chandler says, "I'd stumbled into the middle of an evil, insidious cult of chainsaw worshipping maniacs. I had to wonder if we'd let our religious freedom go too far in this country, or maybe our immigration laws were just too lax."

"They're animals..." - In the motion picture *The Godfather* (1972) a group of 1940s mobsters discuss the possibility of getting into the illegal drug trade. Mafia Don Vito Corleone (Marlon Brando) is against the idea (although gambling, liquor and prostitution were acceptable). In deference to Don Corleone, one of the mobsters recognizes the dangers of drugs but consoles him by saying, he would only sell to the "dark people, the coloreds...They're animals anyway. So let them lose their souls." Note: In the film *The Elephant Man* (1980) John Merrick (John Hurt), who suffered a physical disability that made him look frightening to others, explodes after years of insults, "I am not an animal! I am a human being! I am a man!"

"They're going to have to upDATE my file" - On the spy adventure LA FEMME NIKITA/USA/1997-2001 Peta Wilson plays Nikita (Code name: Josephine), a young woman reluctantly recruited as an assassin for a covert anti-terrorist group called Section One. While on assignment, Nikita faces down a terrorist who tries to convince Nikita that she can't pull the trigger because he has read her file and knows she doesn't have what it takes to kill someone in cold blood. Nikita replies, "They're going to have to upDATE my file" and wastes the bad guy.

"They couldn't find a fart in a rain barrel" - Charles Durning as Murphy, a 1920s Chicago newspaperman refers to incompetent prison guards in the motion picture *The Front Page* (1974). Note: In the film *Lucky Lady* (1975) Liza Minnelli as Claire says, "Gee, it's so quiet in here you could hear a fish fart."

"**They *FUCK YOU* at the drive-thru, okay? They *FUCK YOU* at the drive-thru! They know you're gonna be miles away before you find out you got fucked! They know you're not gonna turn around and go back, they don't care. So who gets fucked? Ol' Leo Getz! Okay, sure! I don't give a fuck! I'm not eating this tuna, okay?"** - Joe Pesci as small time crook Leo Getz complains about the irritations of life in the motion picture *Lethal Weapon 2 (*1989). In the sequel *Lethal Weapon 3 (1992)* Getz shouts, "They *FUCK YOU* at the hospital, OK? They *FUCK YOU* at the hospital! First they drug you, then, they *FUCK YOU!* And then along comes the insurance company and *FUCKS YOU* some more!" And again in *Lethal Weapon 4* (1998) Leo grumbles, "They *FUCK YOU* with cell phones! That's what it is! They're fuckin' you with the cell phone! They love it when you get cut off! Y'know why, huh? You know why? 'Cause when you call back—which they know you're gonna do!—they charge you for that fuckin' first minute again at that high rate!...They fuck ya, they fuck ya, they fuck ya!"

"They used me as you would use a woman" - Sal Mineo as Dov Landau, a survivor of the Nazi concentration camps admits the unthinkable abuse he lived through during the Holocaust days in the motion picture *Exodus* (1960).

"They were all disloyal, I wanted to run the ship properly...They fought me at every turn" - Humphrey Bogart as paranoid Captain Philip Francis Queeg makes mutinous accusations about his crew of the minesweeper *USS Caine* in the motion picture *The Caine Mutiny* (1954). To show proof of their guilt, Queeg proclaims "Aha, the strawberries, that's where I had them. They laughed at me. But I proved beyond a shadow of a doubt and with geometric logic that a duplicate key to the wardroom icebox did exist. I'd have produced that key if they didn't pull the Caine out of action." Of course, with such rambling testimony, crew members Lt. Steve Maryk (Van Johnson) and Ensign Willie Keith (Robert Francis) were found innocent of mutiny charges. After the trial, however, defense attorney Lt. Barney Greenwald (José Ferrer) accused Lt. Tom Keefer (Fred MacMurray) for his part in the whole mutiny mess. "I want to drink a toast to you, Mr. Keefer. From the beginning, you hated the Navy. You thought up the whole idea, and you kept your shirts all starched and clean. Steve Maryk will be remembered as a mutineer—but you! You'll publish a novel, you'll make a million bucks, you'll marry a big movie star, and, for the rest of your life, you'll have to live with your conscience, if you have any. Now, here's to the real author of the "The Caine Mutiny." Here's to you, Mr. Keefer. Greenwald then tossed champagne into Keefer's face and challenged him to step outside and be pummeled.

"They will dissect you! And they will kill you! In that order!" - David Watson as chimpanzee scientist Dr. Cornelius advises humans in the motion picture *Beneath the Planet of the Apes* (1970).

"They will fail at whatever they try" - The family curse of the Bundy family on the sitcom MARRIED...WITH CHILDREN/FOX/1987-97. The curse complemented the family credo, "If your gonna lose, lose big."

"They will say that I have shed innocent blood. What's blood for, if not for shedding?" - Tony Todd as Candyman, a sinister urban legend come to life with a killing hook for a hand in the horror film *Candyman* (1992). According to the film, "If you look in the mirror and say his name 5 times He'll appear behind you, breathing down your neck."

Thief of Bad Gags, The – The nickname given to comedian Milton Berle by influential Broadway columnist, Walter Winchell for allegedly pirating material from other comedians. Defending himself, Milton Berle quipped, "Not true. I never stole a joke in my life. I only find them before they're lost." Note: Reportedly, Jackie Gleason used to hire two ushers at Loew's Metropolitan Theater to copy down and supply him with materials taken from such well known vaudeville comedians as Milton Berle and Eddie Garr (Teri Garr's father).

"Think of all the people you've had ten percent of. Almost enough to make you a complete person" - Smack-in-the-face put-down spoken by a Svengali-like Hollywood film director (Peter Finch) to a theatrical agent (Milton Selzer) in the motion picture *The Legend of Lylah Clare* (1968).

"This hospital will kill no quadriplegic before their time" - Richard Dreyfus as paralyzed sculptor with a death wish making a really bad joke with his physician (Christine Lahti) in the motion picture black comedy *Whose Life Is It Anyway* (1981). Note: The "before their time" crack is inspired by a classic Ernest and Julio Gallo Wine TV commercial wherein actor Orson Welles says, "We will serve no wine before its time."

"This is hell, and I'm going to give you the guided tour" - Deadly greeting of Donald Sutherland as sadistic prison warden Drumgoole arranges for a prisoner named Frank Leone (Sylvester Stallone) with only six-month left on his sentence to be transferred to a hell-hole with intentions of making his life miserable in the motion picture *Lock Up* (1989). Drumgoole plans to get even with Leone for a prior public humiliation. Note: In the film *Shawshank Redemption* (1994) Warden Norton (Bob Gunton) concludes his meeting with a fresh batch of inmates saying, "Put your trust in the Lord....your ass belongs to me. Welcome to Shawshank."

"This is the happiest moment of my life. Is there anything I can do to make you sicker?" - Mary Astor as Alberta Marlow taunts Richard Lomas Leland (Humphrey Bogart) after she he had a little too much to drink in the WWII adventure film *Across the Pacific* (1943).

"This place is bullshit, man. I hate the fucking place...If the gooks had half a brain, they'd be fighting to get out of this stinkhole instead of keeping it" - Sean Penn as Sgt. Maserve, an off-the wall American soldier fighting in the jungles of Vietnam and hating every minute of his tour of duty in the motion picture *Casualties of War* (1989).

"This town seems to be perfect for me. I never saw a place where there are so few brains and so many guns!" - Burt Reynolds as an American inspector called "The Sheriff" in the motion picture *Crazy Six* (1998).

"This trip sucks!" - John Leguizamo as drag queen Miss Chi Chi Rodriguez in the motion picture *To Wong Foo, Thanks for Everything, Julie Newmar (1995).* After Vida Boheme (Patrick Swayze) and Noxeema Jackson (Wesley Snipes) win a major New York drag contest and a trip to Hollywood, they invite an inexperienced 'drag princess' named Chi Chi to accompany them on the trip in a beat-up Cadillac. Along the way, Chi Chi's nerves get frazzled and he/she looses it: "I didn't ask to come on this trip, did I? No, I don't think so! Did I ask you to be making me over and jump all kinds of hoops like some circus poodle? No, I don't think so! Do I want to go to jail because of some cop killer? No, I don't think so! So as soon as we get to the next town, I am jumping on the first man and riding him all the way to New York City and away from you two puckered up, stuck up putas 'cause this trip sucks! It sucks!"

"Three billion human lives ended on August 29th, 1997. The survivors of the nuclear fire called the war Judgment Day. They lived only to face a new nightmare: the war against the machines" - Linda Hamilton as Sarah Connor explains the realities of a terrible future in the motion picture *Terminator 2: Judgment Day* (1991). She continues, "The computer which controlled the machines, Skynet, sent two Terminators back through time. Their mission: to destroy the leader of the human resistance, John Connor, my son. The first Terminator was sent to strike at me in the year 1984. It failed. The second was set to strike at John himself when he was still a child. As before, the resistance was able to send a lone warrior, a protector for John. It was just a question of which one of them would reach him first." *See also* "Hasta la vista, baby" and "You're terminated, fucker"

"'Til I ran up against you, Nazi was just a word in the newspaper to me. Now it's another way to spell cockroach" - Alan Ladd as Lucky Jordan, a cynical gambler turned soldier in the motion picture *Lucky Jordan* (1942).

"The time has come to punish ALL God's little children!" - Part of a rousing speech given to an army of penguins in the action adventure film *Batman Returns* (1992). In preparation of destroying Gotham city, the arch-villain Penguin (Danny DeVito) addresses his tuxedo-clad troops: "My dear penguins, we stand upon a great threshold! It's alright to be scared; most of you won't be coming back. But, thanks to Batman, the time has come to punish ALL of God's children! 1st, 2nd, 3rd AND 4th-born! Why be biased? Male and female! Hell, the sexes are equal with their erogenous zones BLOWN SKY HIGH! FORWARD MARCH! THE LIBERATION OF GOTHAM HAS BEGUN! Penguin's reason for blowing up Gotham City?: "They wouldn't put me on a pedestal, so I'm layin' 'em on a slab."

Toad Boy - *See* "Spud"

"Tokyo lies in burning ruins" - Part of a news broadcast narrated by American foreign correspondent Steve Martin (Raymond Burr) in the Japanese science fiction *Gojira* (1954) [released in America as *Godzilla* in 1956]. As a 400-foot prehistoric reptile with radioactive breath is revived due to nuclear testing, it begins to ravage the Japanese coastline. Reporter Martin reports on the damage: "My name is Steve Martin, I'm a correspondent for *United World News*. I was headed for an assignment in Cairo when I stopped off in Tokyo for a social call. But it turned out to be a visit to a living hell from another world. Here in Tokyo, time has been turned back 2 million years. Tokyo lies in burning ruins. The dead litter the streets...the dying hole up in the shattered remains of once-great structures. No nuclear weapon could have caused more destruction or taken a greater toll—though a nuclear bomb would perhaps have been a quicker, more merciful end than the ravages of GODZILLA!"

"Tom Jones. Of whom the opinion of all was that he was born to be hanged" - Message in the beginning of the motion picture *Tom Jones* (1963) which predicts the future of newly born child Tom Jones, who grows up to be a womanizing Lothario played by Albert Finney.

"The torture of the bells. It never stops. You will be frantically thirsty. You will be unspeakably foul. But there you will lie, day after day, until you tell..." - Boris Karloff as Asian madman Dr. Fu Manchu places his captive Sir Lionel Barton (Lawrence Grant) underneath a bell-like torture device to get him to reveal secrets of the tomb of Genghis Khan in the motion picture *The Mask of Fu Manchu* (1932).

"Tough Shit!" - To the point put-down made by Steven Seagal as EPA agent Jack Taggert investigates toxic waste dumping in rural Kentucky in the motion picture *Fire Down Below* (1997). When a group of hillbilly thugs surround Seagal at the loading dock, he tells them they do not intimidate him and that he's going to continue his investigation. He concludes, "And if you don't like it. Tough Shit!" As the thugs attack, Seagal quickly lays waste to them using some stylish martial arts moves and a sturdy piece of 2x4 lumber. Another of Jack's put-downs: "If your daddy knew exactly how stupid you were, he'd trade you in for a pet monkey."

Ugly Betty - The title of the 2006 ABC sitcom starring America Ferrera as Betty Suarez, a slightly plump plain-Jane from Queens who gets hired as the assistant to Daniel Meade, the new editor of *Mode* magazine, the bible of the fashion industry. Betty was hired by publisher Bradford Meade because he hoped Betty's unsophisticated looks would keep his womanizing ("Player") son focused on his new job, of which he knew very little. At first, Betty, with her braces and dark-rimmed glasses, finds it hard fitting in, but her indomitable spirit and bright ideas help her survive in the superficial world of high fashion and inevitably support her boss, Daniel who is in a constant battle to prove his worth to his father and his more experienced coworker Diva fashionista Wilmelmina Slater who wants Daniel to fail so she can get his job. The series is based on "Yo Soy Betty, la Fea," ("I am Betty, the Ugly") the groundbreaking Colombian telenovela produced by RCN (1999 to 2001) and starring Ana María Onozco as Beatriz Aurora "Betty" Pinzón Solano. *See also* "Coyote Ugly" and "You sure is ugly!"

Ugly John - The nickname of Captain John Black (John Orchard), an anesthesiologist stationed in Korea during the 1950s at the 4077th Mobile Army Surgical Hospital during the first season of the military sitcom M*A*S*H/CBS/1972-83. In the movie M*A*S*H (1970), Ugly John was played by Carl Gottlieb. *See also* "Spearchucker Jones"

Ugly Naked Guy - Nudist neighbor of roommates Monica Geller (Courtney Cox) and Rachel Green (Jennifer Aniston) introduced on the episode "The One with the Sonogram at the End" (9/29/1994) on the twenty something sitcom FRIENDS/NBC/1994-2004. The Ugly Naked Guy lived in a nearby apartment and could, on occasion, be spotted through the window by Monica & Rachel's friends on their visits to their apartment. When across the hall friend Chandler Bing (Matthew Perry) said, "Ugly Naked Guy's got a Thighmaster," the others cried, "Eeaach!" Other observations from the window reveal, "Ugly Naked Guy's laying kitchen tile"; "Ugly Naked Guy's lit a bunch of candles;" and "Ugly Naked Guy's got gravity boots." Note: On the comedy program IN LIVING COLOR comedian Jamie Foxx created a character called Wanda the Ugly Woman. Wanda was so ugly (truly an insult to the eyes) that men shivered in their shoes as she approached them. UglyWanda greets each potential date with the catchphrase, "I'm gonna rock your world!"

"Unclean beast! Get thee down! Be thou consumed by the fires that made thee!" - Ian McDiarmid as Brother Jacopus addresses a fire breathing dragon in the Dark Ages fantasy film *Dragonslayer* (1981).

Undateable, The - On the sitcom AMEN/NBC/1986-91 Thelma Frye (Anna Maria Horsford), the hulking and opinionated daughter of Deacon Frye was called the "Undateable" when she attended West Holmes High School. Thelma later married Minister Reuben Gregory (Clifton Davis) in February of 1990. *See also* "Barky"

"Up your nose with a rubber hose!" - Insult used by Brooklyn high school student Vinnie Barbarino (John Travolta), a member of the Sweathogs on the sitcom WELCOME BACK, KOTTER/ABC/1975-79. The insult varied according to what body part he chose to assault, as in "Off my case potato face!" Another example of Vinnie's put-downs: [to the Principal] "Well you little snow capped leprechaun; it looks like somebody played Danny Boy on your face with an ugly stick."

"Up yours nigger!" - The not-so-nice greeting of an elderly frontier woman to the new black town sheriff (Cleavon Little) in the bawdy western comedy *Blazing Saddles* (1974). Walking the streets of his new town, Sheriff Bart casually says, "Morning ma'am! And isn't it a lovely morning." The woman crudely quips "Up yours nigger!" To appease Bart's wounded pride, Jim, 'The Waco Kid' (Gene Wilder) explains "What did you expect. 'Welcome Sonny. Make yourself at home. Marry my daughter.' You gotta understand that these are just simple farmers. These are people of the land, the common clay of the New West. You know...morons." Later, the same old lady, who snubbed the sheriff, gives him a fresh baked apple pie for defending the town from outlaws but advises, "Of course, you'll have the good taste not to mention that I spoke to you." *Blazing Saddles* wreaks of raunchy, off-color lines and antics, including "punching out a horse, bean-eating cowboys farting around a campfire; and American Indians with Jewish accents. Some memorable lines: "You use your tongue prettier than a $20 whore"; "All right. We'll give some land to the niggers and the chinks. But we don't want the Irish"; "You spare the women? NAW, We rape the shit out of them at the number 6 Dance later on...marvelous!"; "We can't afford to lose any horses. Send over a couple o'niggers"; Piss ant prairie punk"; "Little bastard shot me in the ass"; "Excuse me while I whip this out" (the racial inferences of large black body parts); and "Tell me, is it true how zey say zat you people are gifted? It's twue! It's twue! It's twue!" Note: Comedian Richard Pryor contributed his screen writing talents to this Mel Brooks film.

"Very stupid to kill the only servant in the house. Now we don't even know where to find the marmalade" - Judith Anderson as Emily Brent callously comments on a domestic's death in *And Then There Were None* (1945).

"Victims? Don't be melodramatic, Holly. Look down there. Would you really feel any pity if one of those dots stopped moving—forever? If I said you could have twenty thousand pounds for every dot that stops, would you really, old man, tell me to keep my money—without hesitation? Or would you calculate how many dots you could afford to spare? Free of income tax, old man. Free of income tax. It's the only way to save nowadays." - Orson Welles as the nefarious Harry Lime entices his friend Holly Martins (Joseph Cotten) with a ghastly proposition after Harry asks, "Have you ever visited the children's hospital? Have you seen any of your victims?" in the motion picture *The Third Man* (1949).

"The villagers have laid siege to the castle and are crying out for blood, blood, blood!" - Basil Rathbone as crazed scientist Baron Wolf von Frankenstein comments on the angry villagers who object to him resurrecting the unholy experiments of his father Heinrich von Frankenstein in the horror motion picture *Son of Frankenstein* (1939). Pressuring the Professor to assist in finding a killer roaming the countryside, a one-armed police inspector (Lionel Atwill) insists "There's a monster a foot, and you know it! He's in your control! By heaven! I think you're a worse fiend than your father! Where is the monster?...I'll stay by your side until you confess. And, if you don't, I'll feed you to the villagers like the Romans fed the Christians to the lions."

"Waiter, will you serve the nuts? I mean, will you serve the guests the nuts?" - Myrna Loy as Nora Charles makes a Freudian slip of the tongue about her dinner party guests in the motion picture *The Thin Man* (1934).

"Wake up. Time to die" - Deadly greeting in the science fiction film *Blade Runner* (1982) as rouge android Leon (Brion James) gets the drop on android hunter Deckard (Harrison Ford) who was authorized to track down and decommission mutinous androids from space. Note: In the film *His Kind of Woman* (1951) Raymond Burr as gun-totting gangster Nick Ferraro says, "Wake up, little boy. I want you to see it coming" to Dan Milner (Robert Mitchum) who passed out after being violently whipped with a belt.

"We're intellectual opposites. I'm intellectual and you're opposite" - Mae West as dance-hall girl Cleo Borden puts down gigolo Ivan Valadov (Ivan Lebendeff) in the motion picture *Goin' to Town* (1935).

"We're not vermin. We're not creeps. And we're not pests. We're Borrowers....A Borrower is quiet, conscientious, and inconspicuous. We don't steal; we borrow....We may be small but heaven help anyone who thinks he might squish us" - Jim Broadbent as Pod Clock, a four-inch high humanlike creature who lives under the floorboards with his other friends in the motion picture *The Borrowers* (1997) based on Mary Norton's novel.

"We're not worthy" - Self-deprecating pronouncement of Mike Myers and Dana Carvey as teenagers Wayne Campbell and Garth Algar on comedy skits from NBC's SATURDAY NIGHT LIVE. Every time Wayne and Garth were in the presence of greatness, such as being introduced to the rock group Aerosmith, they fell prostrate to the ground, bowed in appreciation and chanted, "We're not worthy!" When not worshipping their rock idols, Wayne and Garth hosted 'Wayne's World,' a Channel 10 cable access program produced every Friday night at 10:30 P.M. from the basement of Wayne's home in Aurora, Illinois. Their private language called 'Waynespeak' included such phrases as

- **And monkeys might fly out of my butt** - meaning like "that" could really happen
- **Fished In** - meaning that you took the bait-hook line and sinker–this phrase is accompanied by placing your hands aside your head to simulate a fish's flapping gills caught in the net

- **I think I'm gonna hurl** – meaning like that makes me sick, man. The phrase "blow chunks" was also popular
- **NOT!** - used at the end of a statement of fact to negate or refute it
- **You're pail, you're bucket** – meaning "You are bad. You are awful"
- **Take a pill** – meaning relax, unwind
- **Schwing!!** – meaning a female is attractive (the word was accompanied by a slight thrusting of the pelvis).

Special mention goes to two of "Waynespeak" words..."Swing" and "Not!" According to an article in *Entertainment Weekly*, "If all the teenage boys in the United States SCHWUNG! at once, the Earth would tilt three degrees of its axis, resulting in full global warming and causing untold ecological damage." The origin of Wayne's "NOT!" response dates back to a 1978 SATURDAY NIGHT LIVE "Nerds" sketch in which Steve Martin as Chaz the Spaz told Gilda Radner's Lisa Loopner, "That's a fabulous science fair project...NOT!" Inspired by the "NOT!" craze blustery host of PBS's THE MCLAUGHLIN GROUP John McLaughlin greeted panelist Fred Barnes with a friendly "Welcome back, Fred...NOT!" The Wayne's World skits spawned the motion pictures *Wayne's World* (1992) and *Wayne's World 2* (1993).

"We are the Judean People's Front crack suicide squad! Suicide squad, attack! [they all stab themselves] That showed 'em, huh?" - Suicide Squad leader instructs his fanatical follower in this biblical spoof set in the Roman occupied state of Jerusalem in the motion picture *Life of Brian* (1979).

"*We're* the lunatics!!" - In the film *The 'burbs* (1989) Tom Hanks as Ray Peterson becomes obsessed with watching the Klopeks, his strange new next-door neighbors whom he suspects are murderers (they actually are). After a few days of snooping, Ray says, "Remember what you were saying about people in the 'burbs, Art? People like Skip? People who mow their lawns forty-eight hundred times, and then SNAP? Well, that US!! It's not them. That's us! WE'RE the ones who are vaulting over the fences, and peeking into people's windows! WE'RE the ones throwing garbage in the streets, and lighting fires! WE'RE the ones who're acting suspicious and paranoid, Art. WE'RE the lunatics!! It's not them!! It's us." During the investigation, Art Weingartner (Rick Ducommun) jokingly remarks, "I want to kill everyone, Satan is good. Satan is our pal" Another neighbor Mark Rumsfield (Bruce Dern) frustrated with local dogs crapping on his lawn screams, "That piece of scum-barking rat of yours has just taken his last dump on my lawn. I find one more—just one—and I'm going to catch him and staple his ass shut!"

"We are the wretched refuse. We're the underdogs" - In the film *Stripes* (1981) Bill Murray appears as John Winger, a reluctant soldier given the responsibility of improving and organizing a gaggle of goofy grunts. In a speech meant to inspire, Winger addresses his troops: "We're all very different people. We're not Watusi, we're not Spartans, We're Americans, with a capital A. Do you know what that means? Do You? That means that our forefathers were kicked out of every decent country in the world. We are the wretched refuse. We're underdogs. We're mutts. Here's proof [touching a soldier's nose] His nose is cold. But there's no animal that's more faithful, that's more loyal, that's more lovable than the mutt. Who saw *Old Yeller*? Who cried when Old Yeller got shot at the end? I cried my eyes out. So we're all dog faces. We're all very, very different. But there is one thing that we all have in common: we were all stupid enough to enlist in the army."

"We came. We saw. We kicked its ass!" - The triumphant exhortation of Bill Murphy as Dr. Peter Venjkman in the horror comedy film *Ghostbusters* (1984) after he and his team of Ghostbusters, Dr. Ray Stantz (Dan Aykroyd) and Dr. Egon Spengler (Harold Ramis) successfully capture a slimy green Class-Five free roaming vapor on the 12th floor of a posh New York Hotel. Later in the film, the Ghostbuster take on a Sumerian gatekeeper god named Zuul, a minion of a God named Gozer who has possessed the body of Dana Barrett (Siquorney Weaver). As he hunkers down for a fight, Dr. Venkman barks, "All right, this chick is TOAST! Let's show this prehistoric bitch how we do things downtown." In the film's climax, the boys battle a 100-foot Stay Puft Marshmallow man who attacks the city. When it destroys a local religious building Dr. Venkman vows, "NOBODY steps on a church in my town." Venkman's catchphrase curse word is "Mother Pus Bucket" One of the hazards of the job was getting hit with green gobs of ectoplasmic goo. When attacked, the Ghostbusters cried, "I've been slimed!"

"We deal in lead, my friend" - Remark made by Steve McQueen as a gun-for-hire named Vin in the classic western *The Magnificent Seven* (1960). In the film, a group of seven gringo gunslingers are hired to protect a small Mexican village against marauding bandits. Eli Wallach as Calvero, the leader of the bandits revealed his philosophy about plundering the villagers to head gunfighter Chris Adams (Yul Brynner) by saying, "If God didn't want them sheared, he wouldn't have made them sheep!" The film was a remake of the Japanese film *The Seven Samurai* (1954) directed by Akira Kurosawa. *See also* "What do you think of farmers"

"We don't murder, we kill" - Lee Marvin as a gruff WWII sergeant educating his subordinate Pvt. Griff (Mark Hamill) on the differences between killing and murder as the U.S. Army First Infantry Division does battle in the motion picture *The Big Red One* (1980). Note: In the film *84 Charlie Mopic* (1989) Christopher Burton as Hammer explains to a group of soldiers in Vietnam, "Mercenaries kill for money, sadists kill for fun, paratroopers kill for both." And, in the film *Hamburger Hill* (1987) Michael A. Nickles as Galvan says, "We're Airborne. We don't start fights; we *finish* 'em!"

"We don't surrender! You hear that, New York? We don't quit" - Defiant cry of Jack Lemmon as George Kellerman in the comedy motion picture *The Out of Towners* (1970). After visiting New York City, George and his wife, Gwen Kellerman (Sandy Dennis) are inflicted with a plague of problems (being mugged, among other things). At the film's conclusion, the beaten but not defeated George Kellerman screams, "We don't surrender! You hear that, New York? We don't quit. Now, how do you like that? You go ahead, and you can rob me, and starve me, and break my teeth, and my wife's ankles! I'm not leaving! You're just a city! Well, I'm a person, and persons are stronger than cities! This is George Kellerman talking! And you're not getting away with anything! I got all your names and your addresses!"

"We got us another crazy nigger here with a gun" - Keith David as unstable Vietnam veteran Louis Fedders in the movie *Men at Work* (1990). Confronted by "Pizza Man" (Dean Cameron), Louis lays it on the line and says, "Yeah cop. I know you man! I know what you're thinkin'. You're thinkin' we got us another crazy nigger here with a gun. Well let me tell you somethin'. Human life means very little to me at this point in time. You see, I thrive on misery. In the jungle, misery's all ya got but things are different back here in the world or so they seem. Nobody wants to talk about pain and suffering. Everybody wants everything to be nice, and civil. Well okay then! Let's be nice. Let's be civil. And let's drop those guns before I pull this trigger and change the way you feel about me."

"We have ways of making men talk" - Douglas Dumbrille as Indian tyrant Mohammad Khan threatening vile torture to captured members of a British Bengal Lancers division if they don't cooperate in the motion picture *The Lives of a Bengal Lancer* (1935). This now classic veiled-threat has since been turned into the phrase "Vee have vays" when spoken by the many Nazi villains portrayed on the silver screen and TV. Note: In the film *The Mask of Fu Manchu* (1932) Lewis Stone as Scotland Yard Inspector Nayland Smith recalls the evil of Asian madman Fu Manchu (Boris Karloff) who said, "In the East they have ways of shattering the strongest courage."

"We shall bomb Germany..." - The beginning of a defiant speech delivered by the narrator of the motion picture *Flying Fortress* (1942). The full narration states: "We shall bomb Germany by day, as well as by night, in every increasing measure, casting upon them month by month a heavier discharge of bombs and making the German people taste and gulp each month a sharper dose of the miseries they have showered upon mankind. Once underway, our attack will be relentless. We will smash Cologne, Essen, Emden, Bremerhaven, Kiel, Danzig, building with increasing fury towards the day when we shall visit upon Berlin itself the complete destruction to which our preliminary raids have been but a prelude, that great day when we will strike with devastation and unconquerable strength at the detested enemy of all the free people of the earth."

"We train young men to drop fire on people. But their commanders won't allow them to write 'fuck' on their airplanes because it's obscene!" - Marlon Brando as rouge Army officer Colonel Walter E. Kurtz living in Vietnam expresses an ironic military sentiment in the motion picture *Apocalypse Now* (1979).

"We were just informed by the U.S. Marshal's Office that Doctor Richard Kimble is alive and well and living in the city of Chicago. Now you all know in what high regard I hold the scumbag. So I am personally donating a bottle of twelve-year-old Scotch to whoever puts the collar on this quack" - Ron Dean as police Detective Kelly adding an incentive for catching fugitive Dr. Richard Kimble (Harrison Ford) in the motion picture *The Fugitive* (1993).

"We'll hang Bertram Cates from a sour apple tree / we'll hang Bertram Cates from a sour apple tree / we'll hang Bertram Cates from a sour apple tree / We'll hang Henry Drummond from a sour apple tree, our God is marching on." - Chanting townsfolk of Hillsboro, Tennessee picket outside of the county jail to sing their dissatisfaction for a young man named Bertram Cates who dared teach evolution in their school in the motion picture *Inherit the Wind* (1960). Colonel Henry Drummond (Spencer Tracy) who was hired to defend Cates defiantly tells the court, "If you take a law like evolution and you make it a crime to teach it in the public schools, tomorrow you can make it a crime to teach it in the private schools? And tomorrow you may make it a crime to read about it. And soon you may ban books and newspapers. And then you may turn Catholic against Protestant, and Protestant against Protestant, and try to foist your own religion upon the mind of man. If you can do one, you can do the other. Because fanaticism and ignorance is forever busy, and needs feeding. And soon, your Honor, with banners flying and with drums beating we'll be marching backward, BACKWARD, through the glorious ages of that Sixteenth Century when bigots burned the man who dared bring enlightenment and intelligence to the human mind!" Note: The film is based on the 1925 Scopes Trial (aka the "Scopes Monkey Trial") about John Scopes, a high school teacher from Dayton, Tennessee who was arrested for violating the Butler Act that forbad teaching evolution in schools. In the trial, Clarance Darrow quoted Proverbs, chapter 11, verse 29, "He that troubleth his own house shall inherit the wind and the fool shall be servant to the wise of heart."

"We'll tear your soul apart" - Promise of a demon called a Cenobite in Wes Craven's horror flick *Hellraiser* (1987). When a young woman named Kirsty (Ashley Laurence) experiments with a mystical puzzle box, it accidentally opens a doorway to another dimension. "You solved the box. We came. Now, you must come with us," announces a hideous demon (Doug Bradley) whose head is pricked with pins. The box in question "opens doors...doors to the pleasure of Heaven or Hell." As the girl screams for mercy, she confesses she knows that her Uncle Frank (Sean Chapman) who initially summoned the demons, had escaped their domain and that she would exchange his recapture for her release. Their leader (Pinhead) agrees but tells her if she is lying they will "Tear her soul part." In the meantime, Uncle Frank has killed his brother, Larry (Andrew Robinson), and his unfaithful wife, Julia (Clare Higgins) who aided in Frank's resurrection from the dead. In the end, the Cenobites materialize, tear into Frank's flesh with grappling hooks and drag him back to the torments of their netherworld. Turning next to the girl, Pinhead ominously confides, "We have such sights to show you." Luckily, Kirsty manipulates the puzzle box correctly and sends Pinhead back to his world as she screams, "Go to Hell!" The box is reclaimed by a demon (disguised as a vagrant) and placed for sale in a market place for the next unsuspecting victim to discover its secret. The words "What's your pleasure?" are spoken by a salesman just as the film ends. In the sequel *Hellbound: Hellraiser II* (1988) when the girl (now in a psychiatric unit) sees a vision of her father and the message "I am in Hell. Help me!", she enters the kingdom of the Cenobites to rescue him. The film opens with Pinhead sighing, "Ah, the suffering, the sweet, sweet suffering", and later continues, "We have eternity to know your flesh"; and "Your suffering will be legendary, even in hell." Note In the film *Evil Dead II* (1997) a demon yells, "I'll swallow your soul! I'll swallow your soul!" The hero of the movie Ash (Bruce Campbell) points a shotgun at the demon's head and proclaims, "Swallow this!" *See also* "I am...Pain!"

"Wealthy people are hated and resented. Look what's written on the Statue of Liberty. Does it say 'send me your rich?' No, it says 'send me your poor.' We're not even welcome in our own country" - Tony Randall as ad agency boss Peter

Ramsey rants about the economic classes with fellow ad exec Jerry Webster (Rock Hudson) in the motion picture *Lover Come Back* (1961).

"Welcome to earth" [Bam!] - When downed pilot Capt. Steven Hiller (Will Smith) runs across a crashed alien spacecraft in the motion picture *Independence Day* (1996) he inspects the wreckage for signs of life and discovers an ugly and still quite frisky alien who attacks him. Hiller extends the alien a similar greeting, "Welcome to earth" and then punches the alien's lights out. As Hiller drags the alien's body across the desert, he complains, "Y'know, this was supposed to be my weekend off, but noooo. You got me out here draggin' your heavy ass through the burnin' desert with your dreadlocks stickin' out the back of my parachute. You gotta come down here with an attitude, actin' all big and bad...and what the hell is that smell? I could've been at a barbecue! But I ain't mad." Later, in the film, U.S. President Thomas J. Whitmore (Bill Pullman) connects with one of alien's minds and says, "I saw...his thoughts. I saw what they're planning to do. They're like locusts. They travel from planet to planet, their whole civilization. After they've consumed every natural resource, they move on. And we're next. Nuke 'em. Nuke the bastards."

"Welcome to hell, Blofeld!" - Deadly eulogy delivered by secret agent James Bond (Sean Connery) in the motion picture *Diamonds Are Forever (1971)*. At the beginning of the film, secret agent 007 travels the globe tracking down the sinister leader of SPECTRE. When he does, Bond slides (whom he thinks is) Blofeld (Charles Grey) into a bubbling vat of hot mud accompanied by the phrase "Welcome to hell, Blofeld!" Of course, like all good villains, Blofeld escapes to wreak more havoc in later sequels. In an earlier film *You Only Live Twice* (1967) Donald Pleasence as Blofeld says, "Allow me to introduce myself. I am Ernst Stavro Bloefeld. They told me you were assassinated in Hong Kong. You only live twice, Mr. Bond." The Blofeld character inspired the nefarious Dr. Evil (Mick Myers) in the espionage spoof *Austin Powers: International Man of Mystery* (1997). Note: On episode #21 "The Carpathian Caper Affair" of the spy adventure THE GIRL FROM U.N.C.L.E/NBC/1966-67 nefarious THRUSH agent Mother Magda (Ann Sothern) plummets into a scalding pot of borsch. Mr. Waverly (Leo G. Carroll) the head of U.N.C.L.E. who was imprisoned in a metal cage above the bubbling mess offered this tongue-in-cheek observation: "You can't deny it. Magda puts her heart and soul into her soap." *See also* "Bond Women"

"Welcome to slavery" - Unfriendly announcement delivered by a vampire in the horror flick *From Dusk Till Dawn* (1996). After two bank robbing brothers Seth and Richard Gecko (George Clooney & Quentin Tarantino) successfully elude the Texas authorities, they commandeer a motor home (with family onboard) and flee across the border with their loot. Arriving in Mexico, they rendezvous at a seedy biker nightspot only to discover that most of the clientele are actually vampires. As one of the dancers hisses, "Dinner is served," another known as the Satanico Pandemonium (Selma Heyak) attacks Richard. Trying to protect his brother, Seth accidentally kills Richard with a shot meant for the vampire. Knocking Seth to the floor, Satanico snarls, "I'm not gonna drain you completely. You're gonna turn for me, you'll be my slave. You'll live for me. You'll eat bugs because I order it. Because I don't think you're worthy of human blood, you'll feed on the blood of stray dogs. You'll be my foot stool. And at my command, you'll lick the dog shit from my boot heel. Since you'll be my dog, your new name will be 'Spot.'

Welcome to slavery." Not wanting any part of her plan, Seth replies, "No thanks, I've already had a wife" and then shoots down a chandelier which impales the evil bloodsucker. Now trapped inside this bar from hell, our wayward travelers chop, dice, slice, and puree their way through an army of vampires until the sun rises.

"Well, as long as I got a foot, I'll kick booze. And, as long as I got a fist, I'll punch it. And, as long as I got a tooth, I'll bite it. And when I'm old and gray and toothless and bootless, I'll gum it till I go to heaven and booze goes to hell" - Burt Lancaster as bible-thumping preacher Elmer Gantry poetically puts-down the scourges of alcoholism to a congregation of believers in the motion picture *Elmer Gantry* (1960).

"Well, go ahead and kill everybody" - Joe Pesci as Joey La Motta yells at his self-destructive prizefighter brother Jake LaMotta (Robert De Niro) for being overweight in the motion picture *Raging Bull* (1980). His full tirade: "Well, go ahead and kill everybody. You're a tough guy, go kill people. Kill Vickie, kill Salvy, kill Tommy Como, kill me while you're at it. What do I care? You're killing yourself the way you eat, you fat fuck, look at ya." Earlier, Joey told Jake, "Just get down to 155 pounds, you fat bastard."

"Well, he always did have an inflated opinion of himself" - James Bond (Roger Moore) delivers a tongue-in-cheek remark after he crams an inflation device into the mouth of a drug dealer Kenanga, aka Mr. Big (Yaphet Kotto) which causes him to inflate and explode in the motion picture *Live and Let Die* (1973). Earlier, Kenanga instructed his employee: "Tee-Hee, on Solitaire's first wrong answer, you will sever the little finger of Mr. Bond's left hand. On the next wrong answer, you will move on to more...*vital* parts of his anatomy."

"Well, here's another nice mess you've gotten me into" - Oliver Hardy reciting his classic catchphrase to his comic partner Stan Laurel after they climb onto the roof in the rain trying to escape their wives in the motion picture *The Sons of the Desert* (1933). The word "nice" or "fine" is interchangeable. Oliver Hardy is usually fiddling with his tie or banging Laurel over the head with his hat while he says his signature put-down.

"Well, I've never really killed anyone before, but that's what I'm shooting for" - Don McKellar as Russel, a serial killer wanna-be in the motion picture *Roadkill* (1989). In the film, Ramona (Valerie Buhagiar) travels across Canada in a taxicab to retrieve members of a band so they don't miss their next tour gig. Along the way, she meets a variety of interesting characters, including Russell, a killer in the making. When Ramona asks Russell if he really is a serial killer he answers, "I've never really killed anyone before, but that's what I'm shooting for. That's my ambition. I know it's a hard profession, and it's a competitive field and getting tougher every year. You have to kill about 20 people now before you're taken seriously. But let's face it, what other options do I have? There's not a lot of opportunities up here for social mobility. I mean you can either become a hockey player or take up a life of crime. And I have weak ankles, so there you go."

"Well, of course Aunt March prefers Amy over me. Why shouldn't she? I'm ugly and awkward and I always say the wrong things. I fly around throwing away perfectly good marriage proposals. I love our home, but I'm just so dreadful and I can't stand being here! I'm sorry, I'm sorry Marmee. There's just something really wrong with me. I want to change, but I—I can't. And I just know I'll never fit in anywhere" - Winona Ryder as Jo March confesses her inadequacies to Marmee March (Susan Sarandon) in the classic retelling of Louisa May Alcott's novel *Little Women* (1994).

"Well, they say a man who has to buy a big car like that is trying to compensate for smaller genitals." - Robin Williams as Daniel Hilliard speaks to his ex-wife's new handsome boyfriend Stuart 'Stu' Dunmeyer (Pierce Brosnan) about his expensive Mercedes in the motion picture *Mrs. Doubtfire* (1993). A jealous Daniel (dressed incognito as Mrs. Euphegenia Doubtfire) had just torn off the car's hood ornament in anger and coyly said, "Can you help me with something, I found this outside."

"Well, what do you think? Is she totally bananas or merely slightly off center?" - Anne Bancroft as Mother Superior Miriam Ruth elicits a response from psychiatrist Dr. Martha Livingston (Jane Fonda) on whether young nun Sister Agnes (Meg Tilly)—who mysteriously gave birth and then killed her child—is actually mentally competent in the motion picture *Agnes of God* (1985).

"Well why don't we harpoon Charles straight through the head, drag him back to the apartment, and hit him with a hammer until he agrees to come back?" - Imaginary childhood friend Fred suggests possibilities to his now grown childhood friend Elizabeth (Phoebe Cates) on how to get her boyfriend (Tim Matheson) back in the fantasy film *Drop Dead Fred* (1991). When Elizabeth asks, "Harpoon him through the head? That won't work, Fred", Fred replies, "Why not? How many times have you tried it?"

"What a dump!" - Bette Davis as Rosa Moline expresses her utter contempt for her small Midwestern home in the motion picture *Beyond the Forest* (1949). To keep herself busy, Rosa treats her husband (Joseph Cotten) abominably, kills an old man, and plunges down a mountainside to end an unwanted pregnancy. Note: The line "What a dump!" was later used by author Edward Albee in his 1962 New York stage play *Who's Afraid of Virginia Woolf?* In the 1966 film adaptation starring Elizabeth Taylor and Richard Burton, Taylor as Martha berates her weakling husband George for not knowing the Bette Davis movie from whence came the famous line "What a dump!"

"What a pity your manners don't match your looks, Your Highness" - Errol Flynn as the legendary Sherwood forest outlaw Robin Hood chastising the lovely Maid Marian (Olivia De Havilland) in the motion picture *The Adventures of Robin Hood* (1938).

"What a shame we haven't a scalpel with us. I'd make a slight incision to convince you" - Jennifer Jones as Han Suyin, a Eurasian physician jokingly threatens Korean war correspondent Mark Elliot (William Holden) for not believing she is a doctor in the motion picture *Love is a Many Thing* (1955).

"What are you gonna do? Kill me? Everybody dies" - John Garfield as prizefighter Charley Davis talks to his crooked manager after winning a fight he was supposed to lose in the motion picture *Body and Soul* (1947).

"What'chu talkin' 'bout, Willis?" - Cocky comeback of Arnold Jackson (Gary Coleman), an adopted black youth living in a Park Avenue apartment with his older brother Willis (Todd Bridges) on the situation comedy DIFF'RENT STROKES/NBC/ABC/1978-86.

"What do I want to do? I want to blow a hole in your head and donate your organs to science, but I've got a few questions first" - Charlie Sheen as astronomer Zane Ziminiski talks to an outer space alien bent on destroying the world's atmosphere in the sci-fi film *The Arrival* (1996).

"What do you know about love? What could you possibly know about love. You know, I'm sick and tired of men using love as if it's some disease you just catch. Love should have brought your ass home last night" - Halle Berry as Angela in the motion picture *Boomerang* (1992).

"What do you think of farmers? You think they're saints? Hah! They're foxy beasts! - Toshirô Mifune as Kikuchiyo in the motion picture *Seven Samurai,* aka *Shichinin no samurai* (1954). Kikuchiyo continues: "They say, 'We've got no rice, we've no wheat. We've got nothing!' But they have! They have everything! Dig under the floors! Or search the barns! You'll find plenty! Beans, salt, rice, cake! Look in the valleys, they've got hidden warehouses! They pose as saints but are full of lies! If they smell a battle, they hunt the defeated! They're nothing but stingy, greedy, blubbering, foxy, and mean! God damn it all! But then who made them such beasts? You did! You samurai did it! You burn their villages! Destroy their farms! Steal their food! Force them to labor! Take their women! And kill them if they resist! So what should farmers do?" *See also* "We deal in lead, my friend"

"What do you want from me? You want me to tell you to stay, hmm? Is that what you're looking for? You want me to get down on my knees and beg you to save the Baker Boys from doom? Forget it, sweetheart. We survived for 15 years before you strutted onto the scene. Fifteen years. Two seconds, you're bawling like a baby. You shouldn't be wearing a dress; you should be wearing a diaper." - Jeff Bridges as Jack Baker a professional musician who plays piano lounges in small clubs with his brother Frank (Beau Bridges) lets loose a volley of venom at the act's new singer Susie Diamond (Michelle Pfeiffer) in the motion picture *The Baker Boys* (1989)

"What fucking kind of human being am I, if my own mother wants me dead?" - James Gandolfini as Anthony "Tony"Soprano, Sr., a "fat fucking crook from New Jersey" with a dysfunctional family on the crime drama THE SOPRANOS/HBO/1999-2007. Frustrated at his life, Anthony said, "I'm like King Midas in reverse. Everything I touch turns to shit." To resolve some of his daily strife, Tony sets up regular visits to Prozac-prescribing psychiatrist Dr. Jennifer Melfi (Lorraine Bracco) to talk over problems relating to his widowed mother, Livia; his long-suffering wife, Carmela; his spoiled kids Meadow and Anthony Jr., as well as his mobster activities. Tony once offered this old world adage to sum up his mobster philosophy: "There's an old Italian saying: you fuck up once, you lose two teeth." But when required, Tony killed ("Whacked") errant mobsters or friends who got out of line. Tony's wife, Carmela (Edie Falco) who was aware of Tony's criminal background, hopes her husband will become a better person, but she knows her cheating, philandering spouse, too well, and acknowledges, "What's different between you and me is that you're going to hell when you die!" When Carmela caught her son, Tony Jr. smoking pot at his confirmation party, she shouts, "Act like a good Catholic for fifteen fucking minutes. Is that so much to ask?"

"What he did to Shakespeare, we are doing now to Poland" - Sig Rumann as Nazi officer Colonel Ehrhardt refers to the acting ability of Polish actor Joseph Tura (Jack Benny) as he performed in a stage play of "Hamlet" in the motion picture *To Be or Not To Be* (1942).

"What he'll do is hit you on the head, and you'll wake up with an asshole the size of the Lincoln Tunnel" - Linda Fiorentino as Carla advises Louden Swain (Matthew Modine) about the flaws in his fantasy about getting ahead by helping a millionaire fix his flat tire in the motion picture *Vision Quest* (1985). Note: In the film *The Opposite of Sex* (1998) Johnny Galecki as Jason confesses. "If I save one kid from getting butt-fucked, from having his ass totally reamed until it looks like the Lincoln Tunnel and he can't stand up for three weeks, then maybe all of this is worth...something. Teachers everywhere have to learn that no means no...at least until we've dropped out."

"What in the hell are you doing with that lawn mower blade? ...I aim to kill you with it. Mmm" - Red-neck Doyle Hargraves (Dwight Yoakam) asks Karl Childers (Billy Bob Thornton), a poignant question and Karl obliges with an answer in the motion picture *Sling Blade* (1996). In the film, Karl, a man hospitalized since the age of 12 for the murder of his mother and her lover is released from a psychiatric facility and returns to his childhood hometown. There, he befriends a young boy named Frank (Lucas Black). Frank's Mom, Linda (Natalie Canerday) has the misfortune of having Doyle as a boyfriend. He dislikes the fact that Karl is allowed to hang out at her house and complains, "Hey is this the kind of retard that drools and rubs shit in his hair and all that, 'cause I'm gonna have a hard time eatin' round that kind of thing now. Just like I am with antique furniture and midgets. You know that, I can't so much as drink a damn glass of water around a midget or a piece of antique furniture." Doyle also told Linda in no uncertain terms, "If you even think about leaving me, Linda, I told you: I'm gonna kill you deader than a door nail." Unfortunately for Doyle, Karl tires of Doyle's abusive behavior, kills him, and then phones the police. Stoically, Karl reports, "Yes, Ma'am, I've killed Doyle Hargraves with a lawnmower blade. Yes, ma'am, I'm right sure of it. I hit him two good whacks in the head with it. That second one just plum near cut his head in two...It's a lil' ol' white house on the corner of Vine Street and some other street. There's a pick-up truck out front that says "Doyle Hargraves Construction" on it. Doyle said, besides sending the police, you might wanna send an ambulance or a Hearst. I'll be sitting here, waiting on ye."

"What's the point of teaching if kids don't care about education?" - Glenn Ford as Richard Dadier, a high school teacher angrily asks his former college professor about the apathy of the American student in the motion picture *The Blackboard Jungle* (1955). He continues, "You were my professor in college. You should have taught me how to stop a fight in a classroom, how to deal with an I.Q. of 66. If I'm going to be a lion tamer, I should teach with a chair and a whip."

"What's the point they're all the same, some stupid killer stalking some big breasted girl who can't act and is always running up the stairs when she should be running out the front door, it's insulting" - Neve Campbell as teenager Sydney Prescott expresses her dissatisfaction with the plotlines and women actors that appear in the "typical" horror film in the motion picture *Scream* (1996).

"What's the use, baby? I'm a bum. She saw right through me like an X-ray machine. There's no place in the world for a guy like me" - William Holden as drifter Hal Carter who concedes to female acquaintance Madge Owens (Kim Novak) that a personal critique from a local schoolteacher, Rosemary Sydney (Rosalind Russell) might be right on target in the motion picture *Picnic* (1955). Earlier, Sydney had told Carter, "You'll end you life in the gutter, and it'll serve you right. The gutter's where you come from, and the gutter's where you belong."

"What the fuck is wrong with all y'all? Selling drugs to each other, 'cause ya damn sure ain't selling them in Beverly Hills. Killing yourselves, and for what? Make ya feel like a man? Or does it make ya dick hard? Punk motherfuckers" - Denzel Washington as Nick Styles, an LAPD cop (turned assistant district attorney) tries to get the "Just say No" message across to some street hoodlums in the motion picture *Ricochet* (1991).

"What the hell is this, a piano bar or a Nazi work camp? I'm singing my heart out for bupkus, peanuts. I'm eating dog food and you can't even give me fifty dollars you already owe me?! [Harry gives her the money.] Oh, Harry, you're an angel. If you're mother hadn't been such a bitch, we could've shared something important" - Bette Midler as struggling entertainer CC Bloom asks for an advance on her salary from her boss Harry (Robert Blum) in the motion picture *Beaches* (1988).

"What you lookin' at? You all a bunch of fuckin' assholes." - Al Pacino as Cuban Mobster Tony Montana in the film *Scarface* (1983), Montana continues his lecture: "You know why? You don't have the guts to be what you wanna be? You need people like me. You need people like me so you can point your fuckin' fingers and say, 'That's the bad guy.' So, what that make you? Good? You're not good. You just know how to hide, how to lie. Me, I don't have that problem. Me, I always tell the truth. Even when I lie. So say good night to the bad guy! Come on. The last time you gonna see a bad guy like this again, let me tell you. Come on. Make way for the bad guy. There's a bad guy comin' through! Better get outta his way!" *See also* "Say hello to my little friend!"

"When a man gets a hard on, you know where the blood comes from, right? His head and his feet. So A—he's stupid and B—he can't run" - Isaiah Washington as Savon Garrison in the motion picture *Love Jones* (1997).

"When I come home from a long day in Hell, there's nothing I'd rather reach for than a fire-brewed bottle of Styx Beer. Made from the filthiest waters from our own River Styx. Styx Beer is a third more toxic than any other regular beer. The worst beer—the filthiest beer—the deadliest beer. It's Styx Beer!" - Michael Waxman as a "Beer Pitchman" in hell rattles off the slogan for Styx Beer in the motion picture *Highway to Hell* (1992).

"When I dress for a date with you, it will be a suit of armor and brass knuckles" - Barbara Stanwyck as stripper Dixie Daisy expresses her preferred dating etiquette when going out with guys with busy fingers in the motion picture *Lady of Burlesque* (1943).

"When I see five weirdoes stabbing a guy in broad daylight, I shoot the bastards. That's my policy" - Leslie Nielsen as Lt. Frank Drebin speaks to the Mayor of Los Angeles (Nancy Marchand) in the motion picture *The Naked Gun: From the Files of Police Squad!* (1988). Unfortunately the Mayor informs Drebin, "That was a Shakespeare in the Park production, you moron! You killed five actors! Good ones!"

"When I want your opinion, I'll beat it out of you." - Chuck Norris as Eddie Cusack, a tough, honest Chicago cop who has to contend with waring factions of Mafia mobsters and Colombian drug dealers in the motion picture *Code of Silence* (1985). During a chance meeting on the street, Luis Camacho, a Colombian drug dealer says to Cusack, "One day, I would like to give you a gift of a Colombian neck-tie....It's very special. You slit the throat, pull out the tongue and on you, (Camacho laughs), it would look beautiful. Unperturbed and with a smirk on his face, Cusack replies, Why don't you give it to me right now?"

"When I was a kid, I killed gophers for money. Then I killed Indians and Spaniards for money. Now I just kill for money" - Macdonald Carey as gunfighter Bus Crow in the western film *Outlaw Territory* (1953). Crow's personal thoughts on killing a man: "Nobody really cares if a man's cut down from the front or the back... as long as he deserves killin'."

"When the Grey Hair is dead, Magua will eat his heart. Before he dies, Magua will put his children under the knife, so the Grey Hair will know his seed is wiped out forever" - Wes Studi as Magua in the motion picture *The Last of the Mohicans* (1992).

"When ya pull a gun, kill a man." - Walter Brennan as Old Man Clanton educates his grown sons in the ways of the Old West in the motion picture *My Darling Clementine (*1946). When Old Man Clanton kills the brother of town sheriff Wyatt Earp (Henry Fonda), he tells Earp, "We'll be waiting for you, Marshal at the O.K. Corral." After Wyatt, assisted by Doc Holiday (Victor Mature) turns the tide and kills all of Clanton's sons, Wyatt tells Clanton, "I ain't gonna kill you. I hope you live a hundred years, feel just a little what my pa is going to feel. Now get out o' town. Start wanderin'."

"When you call me that, smile!" - Famous line from Owen Wister's 1902 western novel "The Virginian" when the book's antagonist Trampas insults the Virginian who coolly responds, "When you call me that, Smile!" The book inspired the 1929 film *The Virginian* starring Gary Cooper; a 1946 remake starring Joel McCrea and the TV series

THE VIRGINIAN/CBS/1962-71 starring James Drury as the Virginian and Doug McClure as Trampas, the headstrong assistant foreman. In the film versions of the novel, the phrase was rewritten to "If you want to call me that, smile!" Note: In the film *Block-Heads* (1938) James Finlayson as Mr. Finn insults Oliver Hardy, saying, "I'm talking to you, you big overstuffed pollywog!" Hardy replies, "You smile when you call me that!" And, in the film *Call me Madam* (1953) Ethel Merman as US Ambassador Sally Adams says, "When you call me madam, smile."

"When you're slapped, you'll take it and like it" - Humphrey Bogart as tough guy private eye Sam Spade hitting the face of Joel Cairo (Peter Lorre) in the motion picture *The Maltese Falcon* (1941). Note: Years later in the film *Code of Silence* (1985) Chuck Norris as Chicago police detective Eddie Cusack utters a similarly mean remark, "When I want your opinion, I'll beat it out of you."

"When your husband makes love to you, it's my face he sees!" - Rebecca De Mornay as home wrecker Peyton Flanders just before killing the lady of the house in the motion picture *The Hand That Rocks the Cradle* (1992). In the film, De Mornay plays Peyton Flanders whose gynecologist husband is accused of sexual misconduct with his patients and consequently he commits suicide. When Peyton has a miscarriage and loses her baby, she seeks revenge on Claire Bartel (Annabella Sciorra), one of the women whose sexual claims had forced her husband to kill himself. Hiring on as the family's nanny, Peyton tells Claire that her husband was murdered and, "They never caught who did it. But I firmly believe, what goes around comes around." Peyton then slowly works her way into the family's good graces with plans of making the house, the husband and the children hers. And, killing Claire wasn't going to be a problem. When the family's handyman Solomon (Ernie Hudson) suspects Peyton's motives, she calls him a "retard" and gets him fired.

"Where the hell did you get him: Psychos-R-Us?" - Ed O'Ross as Mendez, a gangster questions 'The General' (Mitchell Ryan) about his squirrelly assassin Joshua (Gary Busey) who just burned his hand under the flame of a cigarette lighter to prove his loyalty in the motion picture *Lethal Weapon* (1987). Note: In the film *Just One of the Guys* (1985) Joyce Hyser as Terry, a pretty high school senior says, "With my help he's come a long way. He's stopped buying his clothes at Nerds-R-Us."

"Who do you think you're talkin' to, that first wife of yours out in Montana?" - Jean Harlow as social climber Kitty Packard puts her husband Dan (Wallace Berry) in his place in the motion picture *Dinner at Eight* (1933). She continues, "The poor mealy-faced thing with her flat chest that didn't have enough nerve to talk up to ya', washin' out your greasy overalls and cooking and slavin' in some mining shack? No wonder she died. Ya' big wind bag!"

"Who ever heard of a Jewish cop? Everyone knows you gotta be Irish to get ahead on the force" - Eileen Heckart as Mrs. Brummel yells at her police detective son, Morris "Mo" Brummel (George Segal) in the motion picture *No Way to Treat a Lady* (1968). Note. In the film *Pressure Point* (1962) a racist expressed a similar slur to Sidney Poitier when he inferred "Who ever heard of a Negro psychiatrist anyway? Don't you people have enough problems? Boy you must be a real masochist."

"Who says I'm dumb?" - When Corporal Randolph Agarn (Larry Storch) from the sitcom F TROOP/ABC/1965-67 unwittingly gives Sgt. Morgan O'Rourke (Forrest Tucker) a solution to a problem, he tells Agarn, "I don't know why people say you're dumb." Agarn would quickly snatch off his hat and ask, "Who says I'm Dumb?" The reruns of the program are still popular and Larry Storch often heard fans yell out, "Who says I'm dumb", wherever he traveled.

"Who sent that young man out to kill Germans?...And who sent my boys? And your boy—and your two boys?...We gave them bullets and gas and bayonets? We—the fathers!" - Impassioned denouncement of war fervently delivered by a German father (Lionel Barrymore) to fellow villagers soon after the First World War in the motion picture *Broken Lullaby* (1931). He continues his rant: "Here on the other side. We're too old to fight, but we're not too old to hate. We're responsible. When thousands of other men's sons were killed, we call it victory, and celebrate with beer. And when thousands of other men's sons were killed, they called it victory and celebrated with wine. Fathers!...drunk to the death of sons. My heart isn't with you any longer old men. My heart's with the young, dead and living...everywhere, anywhere."

"Who shall defile the temples of the ancient gods, a cruel and violent fate shall be his fate, and never shall his soul rest until eternity. Such is the curse of Amon-Ra, king of all the gods" - Eduardo Ciannelli as the High Priest of Karnach reciting a curse that directs the vengeful actions of Kharis (Tom Tyler), a reincarnated mummy in the motion picture *The Mummy* (1940).

"Who'd want to put a contract on me?" - Roger Moore as British secret agent James Bond pleads ignorance in the motion picture *The Man with the Golden Gun* (1974). "M" (Bernard Lee) answers Bond's question with "Humiliated chefs! Outraged tailors! Jealous husbands! The list is endless!"

"Why, Ada here never...never spoke a word to me for the first ten years we was married. Heh! Them was the happiest ten years of my life" - Charley Grapewin as shiftless hillbilly Jeeter Lester referring to his wife, Ada (Elizabeth Patterson) in the motion picture *Tobacco Road* (1941).

"Why are you so happy? Did you run over a small child?" - Olympia Dukakis as Clairee Belcher sports with her close friend Ouiser Boudreaux (Shirley MacLaine) in the motion picture *Steel Magnolias* (1989). In the tradition of the gossip in all of us, Clairee says, "Don't have anything nice to say about some one? Come sit by me." (variation of Alice Roosevelt Longworth's immortal line, "If you have something bad to say about somebody...sit down right here beside me."

"Why, I'll murder ya!" - Popular phrase used by Moe Howard while smacking the hell out of his other stooge partners (Curly, Larry & Shemp) in a series of black and white *The Three Stooges* comedy shorts produced in Hollywood from the 1930-50s. Some other zany quips: "I'll squeeze the cider out of your Adam's apple" —Moe to Curly in *Disorder in the Court* (1936); "Remind me to kill you later. I'll make a note of that" —Moe to Curly in *Cash and Carry* (1937); You know, if I wasn't so weak from hunger, I'd bash your brains out—if you *had* brains" —Moe to Curly in *Oily to Bed, Oily to Rise*

(1939); "I'll knock your head right down to your socks" —Moe in *Spook Louder* (1943); "I'll tear your tonsils out and tie them around your neck for a bow tie"—Moe in *If a Body Meets a Body* (1945); "Are you sure this will be in competent hands?" Soitanly, we're all incompetent." —Man to Curly in *Slippery Silks* (1936); and "What kind of fool do you take me for?"..."Why, is there more than one kind?" —Man to Curly in *Saved by the Be*lle (1939). *See also* "Moronica for Morons"

"Why didn't you starve first?" - Humphrey Bogart as gangster Baby Face Martin shocked by his former girlfriend in the motion picture *Dead End* (1937). When Martin meets former neighborhood friend Francey (Claire Trevor) they both quickly discover what path each chose in life. Disgusted that Francey was now a prostitute, Baby Face grimacing says, "Why didn't you starve first? Coming to her own defense, she condemns Martin's role as a gangster and says, "Why didn't you?

"Why don't you whistle for your broomstick?!" - Dennis Farina as Dan De Mora insults his ex-wife, Lily Leonard (Bette Midler) in the comedy film *That Old Feeling* (1997). When Dan and Lily meet after 14 years at their daughter's wedding, old hostilities surface and they begin to bad mouth each other in the parking lot. "You're a witch...Why don't you whistle for your broomstick", cries Dan to his agitated ex. When Lilly yells, "Oh, well, at least I was faithful", Dan counters, "Yeah, you were faithful like a Kennedy was faithful!" Surprisingly, all the passion from this encounter re-ignites their love for each other and they run off together on a romantic adventure.

"Why, he's so mean he'd shut off the air in a baby's incubator, just to watch the little sucker squirm" - Clark Gable as San Francisco gambling hall boss Blackie Norton insulting statement about process server Sheriff Jim (Edgar Kennedy) in the motion picture *San Francisco* (1936).

"Why, I committed murder to get you!" - Betty Davis as Marie Roark admits to her lawyer husband Johnny Ramirez (Paul Muni) that she killed her own husband Charlie (Eugene Paulette) so she could marry Johnny in the motion picture *Bordertown* (1935). Leading up to her startling admission, Marie confesses, "If it weren't for me you'd still be rolling drunks at the Silver Slipper, I made you rich. I put those swell clothes on your back. Now, just because you got your neck washed, you think you're a gentleman. No one can make you that. You're riffraff, and so am I. You belong to me, and you'll stay with me. You bet your going to stay with me because I'm holding on to you." Note: In the film *They Drive by Night* (1940) Ida Lupino as Lana Carlsen (who killed her husband to get a new lover) says, "You're not marrying that cheap, redhead...you're mine and I'm hanging on to you...I committed murder to get you."

"Why would two men—who like each other—want to beat each other to a pulp?...They can't have babies" - Yasmine Bleeth as Pepper Upper questions and gets an answer from Alice Briggs (JoBeth Williams) in the motion picture *It Came From the Sky* (1999).

"Why you monstrous mechanized misguided moron" - One of the many insults slung by Dr. Zachary Smith (Jonathan Harris) at the robot guardian (Bob May) stationed onboard the spacecraft *Jupiter II* on the science fiction series LOST IN

SPACE/CBS/1965-68. Dr. Smith also called the Robot a "Booby," a "Bucket of Bolts," a "Disreputable Thunderhead," a "Pot-Bellied Pumpkin," and a "Tin-Plated Tattletale."

"Why, you overgrown, dime-a-dozen wiseacre pig-puss! Who made your clothes? Or did you grow 'em yourself?" - Betty Grable as motor-mouthed burlesque queen Ruby Summers trashes Andy Clark's (Victor Mature) fashion sense in the motion picture *Wabash Avenue* (1950).

"Why, your type's as old as history" - Gary Cooper as vagrant Long John Willoughby/John Doe in the motion picture *Meet John Doe* (1941). Recruited by a newspaper as a poster boy for a new altruistic political movement (The John Doe Club), Long John does battle with greedy fascist tycoon D. B. Norton (Edward Arnold) who wants to quell the rising tide of the John Doe movement. "What the American people need is an iron hand," cries Norton. Disagreeing, John vents, "Why, your type as old as history—if you can't lay your dirty fingers on a decent idea and twist it and stuff it in your own pockets, you slap it down. Like dogs, if you can't eat something, you bury it."

"Will someone get this walking carpet out of my way?" - What rebel Princess Leia (Carrie Fisher) said about the towering Wookie co-pilot known as Chewbacca (Peter Mayhew) while escaping the Death Star in the science fiction film *Star Wars* (1977). When captured by the Empire's henchman and presented to Governor Moff Tarkin (Peter Cushing) Leia snarls, "Governor Tarkin, I should've expected to find you holding Vader's leash. I recognized your foul stench when I was brought on board." Tarkin replies, "Charming to the last." Leia later called Han Solo (Harrison Ford) a "Laser Brain" and "Why, you stuck up, half-witted, scruffy-looking nerf-herder!" in the sequel *The Empire Strikes Back* (1980).

"Wipe that smile off your puss or I'll knock your teeth through the top of your head" - Humphrey Bogart as Sgt. Joe Gunn threatens a captured Nazi pilot with bodily harm for calling black Sudenese Sgt. Tambul (Rex Ingram) a 'nigger' in the motion picture *Sahara* (1941).

"With this scum, you gotta take the law into your own hands. You don't just book these guys, you kill 'em" - Strother Martin offers his personal opinion on how to handle criminals in the motion picture *Love and Bullets* (1979).

"Without the gun I'm nothing, and I never had anything before I got one" - Frank Sinatra as paid assassin John Baron boasts to his hostages that his best friend in the world is his six-shooter in the motion picture *Suddenly* (1954). Baron continues his gun lesson: "First time I got one in my hands and killed a man I got some self-respect. I was somebody. Without the gun you would never have spit on me. You would never have even noticed me. But because of the gun, you'll remember me as long as you live."

Women (TV Character sentiments) - Besides being slapped, killed, raped and generally abused or ignored, the female of the species has been put-down on a variety of television shows. The following are just a few nostalgic nuggets of classic TV abuse: "Women. Can't live with 'em, pass the beer nuts." —George Wendt as Norm on CHEERS; "What kind of a woman are you? You seduced me, you lied to me, you nearly got me killed. You shamelessly manipulated not only me but the station, the news media and the entire city of Seattle. What do you have to say for yourself? Bebe [coyly]: "Aren't you glad I'm on your side?"—FRASIER; "If women are so smart, why do they dance backwards?" —Jack Lord as Steve McGarrett, HAWAII FIVE-O; "When it comes to compliments, women are ravenous blood-sucking monsters, always wantin' more...more...more! And if you give it to them, you'll get plenty in return!" "Like what?" asks Bart. "I'll tell you when you're older"—Homer to son Bart, THE SIMPSONS; and "Women are the enemy, and we treat them accordingly. The key is to never let them get the upper hand. If she says she doesn't see you enough, threaten to see her even less. If she wants more gifts, take back the ones you've already given her."—Armin Shimerman as Quark from STAR TREK: DEEP SPACE NINE.

"Women are strange little beasts. You can beat them like dogs; you can beat them until your arms ache—and they still love you. Of course, it's an absurd illusion that they have souls" - George Sanders as painter Charles Strickland states his twisted view of womanhood in the motion picture *The Moon and Sixpence (*1942). Note: In the film *Private Lives* (1931) Robert Montgomery as Elyot Chase offers this abusive thought: "Certain women should be struck regularly, like gongs" *See also* "All dames are all alike"

"A word with me? How about a word for me? Or better yet, how about a word for you? Let's see, a word for Tyrone Capulet. Boofball. Dickbag. Peon. Freak. Cocksucker. Shithead, ratcatcher, geek. Loser, anus, fruitcake, lunk, fiddlefucker, dweeb, feeb. Cunt. Assfuck; ah, that one's close to the mark. How 'bout guinea, schmuck, or pussyfart?" - Valentine Miele as Murray Martini reacts to Tyrone Capulet's (Patrick Connor) request to have a "word" with him in the motion picture *Tromeo and Juliet* (1996).

World's Greatest Liar, The - Given to overstatement, character Fibber McGee of FIBBER MCGEE AND MOLLY/NBC/1959-60 was known affectionately as "The World's Greatest Liar." Fibber McGee first appeared on the radio comedy FIBBER MCGEE AND MOLLY that ran from 1935 through 1952 and starred Jim Fibber as Fibber and Marian Driscoll Jordon as Molly. The TV version starred Bob Sweeney and Cathy Lewis. Note: Another great spinner of tales was Captain Horatio K. Huffenpuff (he received a trophy for being the "World's Greatest Liar") who commanded the bridge of the Leakin' Lena on the cartoon adventure THE BEANY AND CECIL SHOW/ABC/1963-67. The program also featured a villain named Dishonest John whose catchphrase was "Nya, ha, ha, Tis' I Dishonest John!"

"Would somebody *PLEASE* shoot this guy?" - Robert Patrick as Rome, a diamond thief pursued by a US Marine whose wife has been kidnapped by Rome and his cronies in the motion picture *The Marine* (2006). When fellow thief Morgan (Anthony Ray Parker) responds, "What does it look like we're doing? Rome replies, "Missing!" As police set chase to the thieves, Morgan confesses, "Cops! I hate cops! That and rock candy."

Wussy Wagon, The - An oversized red wagon filled with a group of socially inept businessman that first appeared on skits during the late night talk show LATE NIGHT WITH CONAN O'BRIEN/NBC/1993+. As the occupants of the Wussy Wagon (six frightened briefcase-carrying men dressed in grey business suits) were pulled through the streets of New York City, they cried, moaned, clutched each other in panic and basically looked terrified as they encountered all of the strange sites and sounds of the Big Apple. On occasion, the Wussy Wagon pulled onto the show's sound stage and directed one of the show's guests to get on board.

"Yak-da-veh!" - Derogatory remark meaning "Kiss my ass!" used by European immigrant garage mechanic Latka Gravas (Andy Kaufman) on the sitcom TAXI/ABC/NBC/1978-83.

"Yeah, alright you primitive screwheads, listen up" - The words of Ash (Bruce Campbell), a hardware store employee accidentally transported in time to the medieval days of King Arthur in the fantasy film *Army of Darkness* (1993). As Ash speaks to a crowd of awed bystanders, he directs their attention to his strange devices (a chainsaw, '73 Olds and a shotgun) and says "See this? THIS is my BOOMSTICK! It's a 12-gauge, double-barreled Remington; S-MART's top of the line. You can find this in the sporting goods department. That's right! This sweet baby was made in Grand Rapids, Michigan. Retails for about $109.95. It's got a walnut stock, cobalt blue steel, and a hair trigger. That's right! Shop smart. Shop S-MART. *YOU GOT THAT*?"

"Yes, Angel, I'm going to send you over" - Humphrey Bogart as hard-boiled private eye Sam Spade tells Brigid O'Shaughnessy (Mary Astor) she's going to jail for killing his partner Miles Archer (Jerome Cowan) in the motion picture *The Maltese Falcon* (1941). To clarify his position, Sam continues, "The chances are you'll get off with life. That means if you're a good girl, you'll be out in twenty years. I'll be waiting for you. If they hang you, I'll always remember you." When Brigid can't understand how Sam could let her "take the fall" for murder, Sam explains, "Listen. This won't do any good. You'll never understand me, but I'll try once and then give it up. When a man's partner's killed he's supposed to do something about it. It doesn't make any difference what you thought of him. He was your partner and you're supposed to do something about it."

"Yes, I killed him. And I'm glad I tell you. Glad, glad, glad!" - In the film *The Letter* (1940) Bette Davis stars as Leslie Crosbie, the respectable wife of a Malaysian rubber plantation owner. After Leslie murdered her lover who wanted to leave her, she claims self-defense based on unwanted sexual advances. In a tear jerking performance in front of the court, Leslie slyly acts the hysterical victim to convince her peers of her innocence.

"Yes, I understand—but I don't agree with killing helpless men!" - Karl Michael Vogler as Otto Heideman speaks to General Count Von Klugerman (James Mason) in the WWI aviation adventure film *The Blue Max* (1966). Klugerman objects and says, "Otto, this is 1918—things have changed. Unrestricted submarine warfare, bombing of civilians, poison gas. Ask your wife—she's a nurse. Ask Elfi about the mustard gas casualties." Disgusted, Otto asks "So you approve of this kind of ruthlessness!" Klugerman concludes, "We fight to win, Otto."

"Yippie-Ki-Yay, Motherfucker!" - The avenging words of police officer John McClane (Bruce Willis) in the action adventure *Die Hard 2* (1988). When terrorists take Dulles International hostage on Christmas, off-duty police officer John McClain (Bruce Willis) jumps in to thwart their plans. At the film's conclusion, as the terrorist commandeer a jet plane, McClane manages to cause a spill in the plane's fuel tanks, pulls out his lighter, ignites the trail of jet fuel and remarks, "Yippie-Ki-yay Motherfucker" as a sudden rush of flames engulfs the plane and explodes it. McClane then let's out a primal (Bye-bye scum suckers) scream of delight. The TV version dubbed the phrase "Mother Fucker" with "Mr. Falcon." In the first *Die Hard* film (1988) terrorist Hans Gruber (Alan Rickman) meets John and says [talking over the radio], "Just another American who saw too many movies as a child? Another orphan of a bankrupt culture who thinks he's John Wayne? Rambo? Marshall Dillon?...Do you really think you have a chance against us, Mister Cowboy?" John replies, "Yippee-ki-yay, motherfucker!"

"Yo dude! You obviously in the wrong hood. This is my dominion, and it's a drug free zone. You understand? Now I'm feelin' generous today. So I'm gonna let you get your sorry vanilla booty out of here before we be usin' your eyeballs as hockey pucks!" - Brandon Quintin Adams as Jesse Hall offers sound advice to a lost soul in the motion picture *The Mighty Ducks* (1992).

"You're a crook! You're a cheat and a swindler! How could you do a thing like this, raise up a little boy's hopes and then dash all his dreams to pieces? You're an inhuman monster!" - Jack Albertson as Grandpa Joe yells at Mr. Wonka (Gene Wilder) after his grandson Charlie Bucket (Peter Ostrum) is denied a wonderful prize in the movie *Willie Wonka and the Chocolate Factory* (1971). When Charlie wins the right to visit Mr. Wonka chocolate factory, he signs an agreement not to touch, eat or drink any items not sanctioned by Mr. Wonka. During their tour, however, Grandpa Joe tempts Charlie into drinking a solution that makes them belch and float into the air. For this infraction, Willie was unceremoniously asked to leave the factory. Before he leaves, Charlie returns a piece of experimental candy (the everlasting gob stopper) that he could have sold to Wonka's competitors. For this act of honesty Charlie is made the new owner of the chocolate factory.

"You're a drunk and a bad lawyer" - Brad Renfro as streetwise kid Mark Sway in motion picture *The Client* (1994). After witnessing a suicide of a prominent Louisiana lawyer connected to the Mafia and accidentally learning the location of the body of a murdered Senator, Mark realizes he needs a lawyer. But, when he discovers his new attorney, Reggie Love (Susan Sarandon) has been sober for three years, Mark quips, "Yeah right, that's what all the drunks say, how they're gonna get sober and all. They even say they love you but they don't. And then they come home wasted and beat on you and your mother so bad that you gotta hit 'em in the face with a baseball bat!" "You're talkin' about your daddy aren't you?" inquires Reggie Love. "Yeah, well, I got rid of him. When me and my mom went into court our divorce lawyer sucked as usual, so I went up there and told the judge myself about all the beatin's, about how he made us sleep in the street. And that's when my father became my ex-father, and now I got you, and you're a drunk and a bad lawyer too! So now I'm gettin' rid of you, you're fired, okay?" Note: In the film *Good Will Hunting* (1997) Robin Williams as Sean, a washed-up shrink, recalls his childhood, "My father was an alcoholic. Mean fuckin' drunk. He'd come home hammered, lookin' to whale on somebody. So, I had to provoke him so he wouldn't go after my mother and little brother. Interesting nights were when he wore his rings."

"You're a fuckin' criminal" - Robert De Niro as bounty hunter Jack Walsh in the film *Midnight Run* (1988). Frustrated with bail jumper Jonathan Mardukas (Charles Grodin), Jack lets loose with his opinion of his prisoner: "You're a fuckin' criminal, and you deserve to go where you're goin' and I'm gonna take you there. I hear any more shit outta you I'm gonna fuckin' bust your head, and I'm gonna put you back in that fuckin' hole, and I'm gonna stick your head in a fuckin' toilet bowl and I'm gonna make it stay there." When Jonathan complains of suffering from aerophobia, acrophobia and claustrophobia, Jack says, "If you don't cooperate you'll also suffer from fistophobia!"

"You're a fuckin' secretary, Fuck you!" - Pissed at the way he's been treated in the film *Glengarry Glen Ross* (1992) Jack Lemmon as real estate man Shelley Levene takes out his frustrations, screaming, "What the hell are you? You're a fuckin' secretary! Fuck you! That's my message to ya. Fuck you and you can kiss my ass and if you don't like it baby, I'm going across the street to Jerry Graff, period, fuck you."

"You're a joke—a dirty joke, from one end of the town to the other!" - Laurence Harvey as married socialite Weston Liggett berates his high-class prostitute Gloria Wandrous (Elizabeth Taylor) who wants to go straight in the motion picture *Butterfield 8* (1960).

"You're a low down Yankee liar" - Alan Ladd's famous put-down of Jack Palance in the classic western film *Shane* (1953). In the final scene of the movie, a wandering gunfighter named Shane (Alan Ladd) faces down and kills a ruthless gunfighter named Jack Wilson (Jack Palance) who was harassing a group of homesteaders to leave their land. To get Wilson to draw his gun Shane says, "You're a low down Yankee liar." That statement referred to an earlier scene in the film, when Jack Wilson goaded a proud but drunken ex-confederate farmer (Elisha Cook, Jr.) into a gun fight. To get the farmer to draw his weapon, Wilson insulted the man's southern heritage by saying that General Lee and Stonewall Jackson were all trash. When the farmer replied, "You're a low down lyin' Yankee" Wilson answered with the challenge, "Prove it" and then shot the farmer dead.

"You're a smart boy, and I know how to deal with smart boys" - James Cagney as Captain Morton in the motion picture *Mister Roberts* (1955). Resentful of "college" educated boys, Morton, who rose through the ranks from seaman, was constantly at odds with his second-in-command Lt. Doug Roberts (Henry Fonda). Not as rigid as the Captain, Mr. Roberts was a favorite of the crew. He often pushed for shore leave for the men and once in a fit of anger threw the Captain's prized potted palm tree overboard. Later, when Roberts is transferred into combat (and reported killed), Ensign Frank Thurlowe Pulver (Jack Lemmon) marches up to Morton's quarters in the spirit of Mr.

Roberts and barks, "Captain, it is I, Ensign Pulver, and I just threw your stinking palm tree overboard. Now, what's all this crud about no movie tonight?" The Palm Tree was "The Admiral John J. Finchley award for delivering more toothpaste and toilet paper than any other Navy cargo ship in the safe area of the Pacific."

"You're a smart-mouth, stupid ass, swamp-running nigger...that's all you'll ever be" - Morgan Freeman as black Sergeant Major John Rawlins puts errant black Private Trip (Denzel Washington) in his place before a major battle in the civil war motion picture *Glory* (1989).

"You're a social disease" - In the film *The General Died at Dawn* (1936) mercenary O'Hara (Gary Cooper) lashes out his disapproval of evil Asian warlord General Yang (Akim Tamiroff) and says, "You're a social disease. I don't like your disposition. I don't like your friends. I don't like your politics, and I don't like your hat. Your faithful denizens may stick to you but you're still a small noise at the end of a parade."

"You are a total nutcase, completely deranged, delusional, paranoid. Your thought process is all fucked up. Your information train is jammed, man!" - Brad Pitt as Jeffrey Goines, the insane son of a famous scientist who is incarcerated in a psychiatric facility in the movie *Twelve Monkeys* (1995). Jeffrey is talking with James Cole (Bruce Willis) a time traveler from A.D. 2035 who traveled back in time to 1990 to prevent Jeffrey from activating a lethal virus that would wipe out five billion people in 1996.

"You're a very nosy fellow, kitty cat. Huh? You know what happens to nosy fellows? Huh? No? Wanna guess? Huh? No? Okay. They lose their noses" - Jack Nicholson as 1930s Los Angeles detective Jake Gites gets warned to mind his own business by a man with a knife (Roman Polanski) in the film-noir motion picture *Chinatown* (1974). Later, a guy named Loach (Richard Bakalyan) asks, "What happened to your nose, Gittes? Somebody slammed a bedroom window on it? Jack replies, "Nope. Your wife got excited. She crossed her legs a little too quick. You understand what I mean, pal?"

"You're a warped frustrated old man...!" - Angry put-down heard every Christmas during the annual viewing of the classic Yuletide film *It's a Wonderful Life* (1946) starring James Stewart as George Bailey, the loan officer at Bailey Saving & Loan. When 'Old Man' Potter (Lionel Barrymore), the richest man in the town of Bedford Falls, tries to seduce George with a lucrative offer to come work for him in an attempt to weaken Bailey's Savings and Loan, (the only place in town not under Potter's total control) George jumps up from his chair and shouts, "Your a warped frustrated old man...You sit around and spin your little web and you think the whole world revolves around you and your money. Well it doesn't, Mr. Potter. In the whole vast configuration of things, I'd say you were nothing but a scurvy little spider..."

"You're a yellow belly Jap lover!" - Spoken by Ernest Borgnine as Coley Trimble in the motion picture *Bad Day at Black Rock (*1955). In the film, Spencer Tracy plays John J. Macreedy, a WWII disabled veteran with an injured arm who travels to a tiny desert town of Black Rock to give a medal to a Japanese farmer named Kimoko (Kimoko's dead son earned the medal in Italy saving the life of Tracy's character). Unfortunately,

Macreedy discovers that town roughnecks murdered Kimoko. One of them, Coley Trimble angered at John for digging up skeletons in the town's closet shouts, "You're a yellow belly Jap Lover!" and "I'm half horse and half alligator. Mess with me, I'll kick a lung out of you." When Coley attacks John, he defends himself with a well placed karate chop to the neck and a few other tosses and punches. Later, the leader of the conspiracy, Reno Smith (Robert Ryan) lures MacReedy into the desert to kill him. John thwarts the attempt by using a bomb made from rags and gasoline from a nearby jeep. The movie was based on the story "Bad Time at Hondo" by Howard Breslin.

"You're a worthless piece of slime" - James Cagney as police commissioner Rheinlander Waldo compares the worth of a new million-dollar library with the worth of bigoted fire chief Willie Conklin (Kenneth McMillan) in the motion picture *Ragtime* (1981). Waldo is also referred to as "a piece of shit." *See also* "We came, we saw, we kicked its ass"

"You're acting like a shit today" - Jean-Hugues Anglade as Zorg the writer insults his mistress Betty (Beatrice Dalle) in the motion picture *Betty Blue* (1986).

"You're afraid of emotion. You keep your heart in a steel safe" - Lucille Ball as Kathleen, the secretary and girlfriend of moody private eye Bradford Galt (Mark Stevens) shouts displeasure at her boss's inability to get emotionally involved in the motion picture *The Dark Corner* (1946). Note: In the film *The Long Goodbye* (1973), Marty Augustine (Mark Rydell) tells private investigator (Elliot Gould), "You keep your heart in an ashcan." And, in the film *Bordertown* (1935) Bette Davis remarks, "I think you must have an adding machine for a heart" to her indifferent Mexican lawyer, Johnny Ramirez (Paul Muni).

"You're all going to die" - Charles Dutton as Dillon in the science fiction film *Alien 3* (1992). Faced with the realization that a marauding alien creature will probably kill everyone on Fiorina 161 prison planet, Dillon barks, "You're all going to die. The only question is how you check out. Do you wanna go on your feet? Or down on your fuckin' knees...beggin'? Well I ain't much for begging! Nobody ever gave me nothing! So I say FUCK that thing! Let's fight it!"

"You're all I thought about for six months. They threw me in a jail filled with rejects from the communicable disease ward. Every wacko, drippy, open-sored low-life was in that joint, all of them wanting to hire on as my proctologist" - Danny DeVito as a small-time crook named Ralph talks to the people who got him incarcerated in the motion picture *The Jewel of the Nile* (1985).

"You're an incredible flake" - Critical appraisal of pool hustler Eddie Felson (Paul Newman) in the motion picture *The Color of Money* (1986). When veteran pool player Eddie Felson meets up-and-coming pool hustler Vincent Lauria (Tom Cruise), he sizes up his competition, saying, "You are a natural character. You're an incredible flake. See, guys spend half their lives trying to invent something like that." At first, Eddie tells Vincent, "You couldn't find big time if you had a road map," but later Eddie offers Vincent this counsel: "You got to have two things to win. You got to have brains, and you got to have balls. Now, you've got too much of one, and not enough of the other."

"You are beautiful when I beat you" - Giancarlo Giannini as Gennarini, a Communist castaway shares a desert island with a beautiful wealthy woman named Raffaella (Mariangela Melato) in the Italian motion picture *Swept Away...by an usual destiny in the blue sea of August* (1974). Note: In the film *The Mad Miss Manton* (1938) newspaper editor Peter Ames (Henry Fonda) threatens heiress Melsa Manton (Barbara Stanwyck), saying, "You're a nasty creature, aren't you. But, in time, I'll beat it out of you."

"You're both gonna take a beating till someone uses that phone. That means one of you's gonna take a beating for nothing. I don't care which one it is. We'll start with you" - Humphrey Bogart as Harry "Steve Morgan, a partner on a boat-for-hire on the island of Martingue during World War II who intimidates Captain Renard (Dan Seymour) and Lieutenant Coyo (Sheldon Leonard) into making a phone call in the motion picture *To Have and Have Not* (1944).

"You're chicken, you've got no guts" - George Peppard as writer Paul Varjak confronts jet-setting escort Holly Golightly (Audrey Hepburn) in the classic motion picture *Breakfast at Tiffany's* (1961). His full critique: "You know what's wrong with you, Miss Whoever-you-are? You're chicken, you've got no guts. You're afraid to stick out your chin and say, Okay, life's a fact, people do fall in love, people do belong to each other, because that's the only chance anybody's got for real happiness. You call yourself a free spirit, a 'wild thing,' and you're terrified somebody's gonna stick you in a cage. Well baby, you're already in that cage. You built it yourself. And it's not bounded in the west by Tulip, Texas or in the east by Somali-land. It's wherever you go. Because no matter where you run, you just end up running into yourself."

"You're dangerous and unwholesome and children should not be exposed to you" - Criticism thrust upon eccentric Edinburgh school teacher Miss Jean Brodie (Maggie Smith) by an upset student (Pamela Franklin) in the motion picture *The Prime of Miss Jean Brodie* (1969). Miss Jean Brodie teaching philosophy states: "Give me a girl at an impressionable age and she is mine for life. I am dedicated to you in your prime...you little girls must be on the alert to recognize the prime at whatever time it might occur and live it to the full."

"You're dead. D. E. D. Dead" - John Leguizamo as Clown, a blue-faced demon with a vile sense of humor out to start Armageddon between heaven and hell in the fantasy motion picture *Spawn* (1997). Clown liked to use twisted versions of famous movie lines, for example "Every time someone farts, a demon gets his wings. [farts twice] Oh, twins!" (*It's a Wonderful Life*); and "I love the smell of burnt asphalt in the morning." (*Apocalypse Now*).

"You're dead Porter. Nobody fucks with my family. You hear me? You're a dead man." - Kris Kristofferson as Bronson threatens a small time crook in the motion picture *Payback* (1999). Porter (Mel Gibson) kidnaps Bronson's son, Johnny as collateral so he can retrieve his share of a $140,000 robbery he did a few years. Porter was betrayed by his partner and his wife who shot him twice in the back and left him for dead. Porter survived and now, he only wants $70,000 but no one wants to pay. As

Bronson negotiates with Porter, he says, "Tell me where John is and I'll finish you quick. I promise you won't have to find out what your left ball tastes like."

"You're dead son. Go get yourself buried" - Burt Lancaster as ruthless columnist J. J. Hunsecker expresses his anger for publicity agent Sidney Falco (Tony Curtis) in the motion picture *Sweet Smell of Success* (1962). Hunsecker also tells Sidney, "I'd hate to take a bite out of you. You're a cookie full of arsenic."

"You're despicable! ('desthpicable')" - The spitty insult of Warner Brother's cartoon character Daffy Duck when he gets frustrated with his adversaries.

"**You are fined one credit for a violation of the Verbal Morality Statute"** - Futuristic computer informs psychotic criminal Simon Phoenix (Wesley Snipes) that he has violated a "no cursing" law in the motion picture *The Demolition Man* (1993). In the film, Simon had been placed into cryogenic storage for crimes against the state. However, he is released in the future by an ambitious businessman and given the task of disrupting a now very complacent, stable society. As Simon asks a computer booth about a gun, it responds: "Gun. Noun. Portable firearm. This device was widely utilized in the urban wars of the late twentieth century. Referred to as a pistol, a piece." Interrupting, Simon says, "Look I don't need a history lesson! C'mon, HAL, where are the god damn guns?" The Moral Statute Machine' then interjects" You are fined one credit for a violation of the Verbal Morality Statute". Simon Phoenix replies, What? Fuck you!" The Moral Statute Machine answers, "Your repeated violation of the Verbal Morality Statute has caused me to notify the San Angeles Police Department. Please remain where you are for your reprimand." Simon says, "Yeah, right" and flees the fast approaching police. Simon's nemesis, John Spartan (Sylvester Stallone) who was released from cryogenic storage to find and capture Simon, discovers that the future society doesn't use toilet paper and tells a machine on the wall, "Thanks a lot you shit-brained, fuck-faced, ball breaking, duck fucking pain in the ass." The Moral Statute Machine in his apartment tells him, "John Spartan, you are fined five credits for repeated violations of the Verbal Morality Statute." John uses the violation tickets issued from the machine to better use. At the film's conclusion, John Spartan activates a cryogenic device, freezes Simon Phoenix and shatters his frozen body into a million pieces.

"You're fired!" - This phrase–dreaded by employees everywhere–has been used successfully in a number of motion pictures. In the sci-fi film *Robocop* (1987) Peter Weller plays a futuristic cyborg known as Robocop whose internal prime directives were tampered with to prevent the RoboCop unit from harming specific personnel—namely, the evil corporate executive Richard "Dick" Jones (Ronnie Cox). However, when company Chairman (Dan O'Herlihy) tells the executive "You're fired!" Robocop was free to "terminate" the executive from his employment responsibilities (he drops him out of a high-rise). In the action adventure yarn *True Lies* (1994) when a terrorist from the Crimson Jihad jumps off a building onto a hovering jet fighter plane to kill super spy Harry Tasker (Arnold Schwarzenegger), he slips off the wing and gets hung up in a missile. Thinking quickly, Tasker activates the missile, pushes a button and says, "Your fired!" The missile takes off with the terrorist dangling from it, flies through an opening in the building, exits on the other side, and blows to hell a helicopter filled with other terrorists. And, in the sci-fi film *Independence Day* (1996), Bill Pullman as President Thomas J. Whitmore says, "The only mistake I ever made was to appoint a sniveling little weasel like you Secretary of Defense. However, that is a mistake, I am happy to say, that I don't have to live with. Mr. Nimzicki (James Rebhorn)...you're fired!" In the film, *Edtv* (1999) Rob Reiner as TV executive Whitaker threatens, "One more word out of you, Cynthia, and you're fired." Producer Cynthia Topping (Ellen DeGeneres) responds, "Oh, and which word would that be? Asshole? Shithead?" Note: The phrase "You're Fired" became the popular mantra of American businessman and billionaire Donald Trump when he starred in the 2004 NBC TV series THE APPRENTICE, a reality-TV based show in which contestants competed for a job as an apprentice to "The Donald." As Mr. Trump culled the ranks of those competing for the job of apprentice, he told the unlucky ones, "You're Fired."

"You're full of beans and so's your old man!" - School yard argument between two young boys – Schwartz (R. D. Robb) and Flick (Scott Schwartz) – about whether or not a person's tongue will freeze to a cold metal object in the Yuletide film A *Christmas Story* (1983). Schwartz's Dad said a person's tongue would stick to a cold surface while Flick's Dad said it couldn't happen. When Schwartz tossed out a "double dog dare" and then "triple dog dare" Flick touches the tip of his tongue against the flagpole and is sorely surprised to discover it grips tightly. Flick cries out for help but all his classmates upon hearing the schoolyard bell, flee back to class and leave poor Flick standing alone in the snow waving his arms and frantically shouting for help. Finally extricated from the pole by members of both the fire and police departments, Flick returns to his classroom with bandaged tongue while his teacher Miss Shields gives his classmate's a good tongue lashing for goading Flick into trying the silly stunt.

"You're going to love it here, Doc. You can drive drunk and get anybody killed for fifty bucks" - James Wood as sleazeball photojournalist Richard Boyle praises the benefits of El Salvador to newcomer Dr. Rock (James Belushi) in the motion picture *Salvador* (1986).

"You're gonna look real funny sucking my dick with no teeth" - Sadistic prison Captain Hadley (Clancy Brown) talks to newcomer Andrew Dufresne (Tim Robbins) in the motion picture *The Shawshank Redemption* (1994). Later, when the prisoners began to shout vulgarities at the new inmates, Hadley enters shouting, "What the Christ is this happy horseshit? One prisoner yells, "Hey, he took the Lord's name in vain! I'm tellin' the warden!" Hadley replies, "You'll be tellin' the warden about my baton up your ass!" When a new fat prisoner cries, "I'm not supposed to be here! I want to go home! I want my ma!", a wisecracking prisoner says, "Yeah, I had your momma, she wasn't that great!" A few days later, a group of prisoners try to sexually assault Andy Dufresne and a creep named Boggs tells Andy, "Now, I'm gonna open my fly and you're gonna swallow what I give ya. And when you swallow mine you gonna swallow Rooster's cause ya done broke his nose and I think he oughta have something to show for it. Andy threatens, "Anything you put in my mouth you're gonna lose." Boggs continues his taunt, "Naw, you don't understand. You do that and I'll put all eight inches of steel in your ear." Unperturbed, Andy says, "All right. But you should know that sudden serious brain injury causes the victim to bite down hard. In fact, I hear the bite reflex is so strong they have to pry the victims jaws open with a crow bar." Concerned, Boggs asks,

"Where do you get this shit?" Andy replies, "I read it. You know how to read, you ignorant fuck?" With that, Boggs and his other cronies beat Andy within an inch of his life. In retaliation, the prison guards beat Boggs, crippled him and transfer him to another facility where what the prisoners hear, he drinks all his meals through a straw.

"You're gonna look silly eating corn on the cob without teeth" - Charles Napier as Tucker McElroy suggests possibilities to ex-con Joliet Jake (John Belushi) in the cult comedy film *The Blues Brothers* (1980).

"You're greedy, unfeeling, inept, indifferent, self-inflating and unconscionably profitable. Aside from that, I have nothing against you. I'm sure you play a helluva game of golf" - George C. Scott as Dr. Herbert Bock expresses his opinion of fellow colleague Dr. Welbeck (Richard Dysart) in the medical drama *The Hospital* (1971).

"You're just dog shit" - 'Dirty' Harry Callahan (Clint Eastwood) offers his opinion to a street thug in the thriller *Sudden Impact* (1983). Harry's full put-down: "Look, punk, to me, you're just dog shit. A lot of things can happen to dog shit. It can get stepped on and squashed, or it can just dry up and blow away. So remember that when the dog shits ya!"

"You're just walking around to save funeral expenses" - Valerie Perrine as Charlotta analyzes near-derelict Sonny Steele (Robert Redford) in the motion picture *The Electric Horseman* (1979).

"You're like wet sand in my underwear" - Rosie Perez as waitress Cindy gives a gritty putdown in the motion picture *Untamed Heart* (1993).

"You're lower than a caterpillar with fallen arches" - Lou Costello as vacuum cleaner salesman vents his anger in the motion picture *Little Giant* (1946).

"You're madness, Diana. Virile madness" - Heated critique of UBS network executive Max Schumacher (William Holden) directed at coworker/mistress Diana Christensen (Faye Dunaway) in the film *Network* (1976). His full comment: "War, murder, death—all the same to you as bottles of beer, and the daily business of life is a corrupt comedy. You even shatter the sensation of time and space into split seconds, instant replays. You're madness, Diana. Virile madness, and everything you touch dies with you. But not me. Not as long as I can feel pleasure and pain...and love."

"You're my best buddy and I love you—and if you get accepted and I don't, I hope you rot in hell" - Arye Gross as Gordon Bloomfield shows a little bit too much competitive spirit as he and his friend Mark Watson (C. Thomas Howell) open their letters to see whether they got accepted to Harvard Law School in the motion picture *Soul Man* (1986).

"You're my designated fuck" - Linda Fiorentino as conniver Bridget Gregory (aka Wendy Kroy) summarizes her relationship with Mike Swale (Peter Berg) in the motion picture *The Last Seduction* (1994). Curious, Mike asks, "What if I don't want to be?" Bridget calmly says, "Then I'll designate someone else." While having sex inside of a parked car, Mike asks Bridget, "I'm trying to figure out whether you're a total fucking bitch or not." As she straddles Mike's body, Bridget pounds on the interior roof of the vehicle and confesses in no uncertain terms, "I am a total fucking bitch."

"You're not gonna have a very long life, Stevie. You're like a rat in a box, without any holes. But they're gonna make a hole for you...six by three, filled with quicklime." - Richard Boone as Lt. Ed Cornell advises thug Steve Christopher (Elliott Reid) in the motion picture *Vicki (*1953).

"You're not too smart, are you? I like that in a man" - Kathleen Turner as the sultry blond Matty Walker, a clever con woman who flaunts her sexual wares in front of libidinous Florida lawyer, Ned Racine (William Hurt) in the motion picture *Body Heat* (1981). When Ned asks, "What do you like? Lazy, Ugly. Horny. I got them all." Mattie replies, "You don't look lazy." After a steamy romp under the sheets, Matty convinces Ned to kill her wealthy but abusive husband (Richard Crenna). In the end, Ned gets framed for murder while Matty sits on a tropical isle sipping cool drinks and laughing her ass off at the stupidity of men (well, at least Ned). Note: In the film *It's My Party* (1996) Bronson Pinchot as a gay man named Monty says, "You're not too bright. I like that in a man."

"You're not worth killing, but if you come at me again I'll put a window through your head" - Richard Farnsworth as real-life train robber Bill Miner warns a tough guy to back off in the motion picture *The Grey Fox* (1982).

"You are nothing! If you were in my toilet I wouldn't bother flushing it. My bathmat means more to me than you!" - Kevin Spacey as big-time movie producer Buddy Ackerman belittles an associate in the motion picture *Swimming with Sharks* (1994).

"You are one dumb son of a bitch, bringing a knife to a gunfight" - Mark Collie as Harry Heck, a bad guy who thinks he has the upper hand in the motion picture *The Punisher* (2004). In the film, G-Man Frank Castle (called "the finest solider, the finest undercover cop, the finest man" by his colleagues) forsakes justice for punishment as he vows vendetta against Howard Saint (John Travolta), the man responsible for the death of his wife and family. When one of Saint's henchmen pursues him, Frank's car crashes and flips over. As he crawls from beneath the wrecked vehicle, he sees Harry Heck standing over him with a gun. As a defense, Frank pulls out a switch blade and challenges Frank who chastises him for being so stupid to think that his knife is any good against a gun. Suddenly, to Heck's surprise, the knife blade launches from its hilt and jams itself into Harry's neck, slashing his carotid artery. At the conclusion of the film, Frank kills an army of mercenaries, shoots Howard Saint in a face-to face draw down and then shackles his leg to a limousine which drags Saint's body slowly through a parking lot and finally explodes. As a warning, Frank Castle left these words of wisdom: "In certain extreme situations, the law is inadequate. In order to shame its inadequacy, it is necessary to act outside the law. To pursue–natural justice. This is not vengeance. Revenge is not a valid motive, it's an emotional response. No, not vengeance...Punishment" and "Those who do evil to others–the killers, the rapists, psychos, sadists–you will come to know me well. Frank Castle is dead. Call me: The Punisher."

"You're out of order" - Al Pacino as outraged lawyer Arthur Kirkland in the motion picture *And Justice for All* (1979). When a corrupt judge (Jack Warden) is charged with rape, Arthur Kirkland must defend him. Unfortunately, Kirkland and the judge have an adversarial history. When Kirkland was told he was out of order he shouts, "YOU'RE out of order! YOU'RE out of order! THE WHOLE TRIAL is out of order! THEY'RE out of order! That man, that sick, crazy, depraved man, raped and beat that woman there, and he'd like to do it again! It's just a show! It's a show! It's "Let's Make A Deal"! "Let's Make A Deal"! Hey Frank, you wanna "Make A Deal"? I got an insane judge who likes to beat the shit out of women! Whaddya wanna gimme Frank, 3 weeks probation?" In his opening statement Arthur screams, "You, you son of a bitch, you! You're supposed to stand for somethin'! You're supposed to protect people! But instead you rape and murder them! [dragged off by court baliffs] You killed McCullough! (a former client) You killed him! Hold it! Hold it! I just completed my opening statement!"

"You're out of your mind!" - Christian Slater as Captain Riley Hale puts-down a demented Air Force pilot in the military thriller *Broken Arrow* (1995). In the film, crazed Air Force pilot Vic Deakins (John Travolta) steals two nuclear bombs and threatens to detonate them on the fault line near Los Angeles unless he is handsomely compensated. When fellow pilot Riley Hale seeks to stop Deakins from detonating the bombs, he confronts his former buddy and says, "You're out of your mind!" To which Vic quips, "Yeah, ain't it cool."

"You're really starting to annoy me. I think I'm gonna have to shoot you in a minute or two" - Robert Cicchini as John, a corrupt Los Angeles cop in the motion picture *Cool Crime* (1999).

"You are rich. You are white. So you will not do time. Which is why they call the song the 'America the Beautiful'" - The ugly racial slur spoken by a lawyer as he counsels his guilty client on the premiere episode of the adventure VENGEANCE UNLIMITED/ABC/1998. Mr. Chapel (Michael Madsen), a mysterious vigilante, doesn't feel the same way, however, and puts the man through the hoops until he is killed in a shoot-out with a crooked crony. Earlier, Mr. Chapel informed his client, "People will think that innocent and not guilty are the same thing. People who treat justice like some sort of business. Well, I've got my own business. It's called Vengeance Unlimited."

"You're right, you shouldn't have been deported, you should have been exterminated" - Lionel Barrymore as wheel-chair-bound James Temple denounces gangster Johnny Rocco (Edward G. Robinson) who got thrown out of the country for being a Communist in the motion picture *Key Largo* (1948).

"You're sick, you're filthy and you smell bad" - The Bim! Bam! Boom! put-down of a housewife (Lynne Adams) speaking to the ghost of a murderer (Wings Hauser) in the motion picture *The Carpenters* (1989).

"You're short. Your belly-button sticks out. And your a terrible burden on your mother" - Bill Murray as Dr. Peter Venkman talking to Baby Oscar , the newborn baby boy of Dana Barrett (Sigourney Weaver) in the motion picture *Ghostbusters II* (1989). Although it may sound insulting, this cutesy put-down is just gushing with tenderness. When Peter first hears the baby is called Oscar, he laments, "Oh no, they named you after a weiner."

"You are smug, Mr. Darnay, when you ask why people drink, but I'll tell you. So they can stand their fellow men better. After a few bottles, I might even like you." - Ronald Colman as carefree lawyer Sidney Carton speaks to Charles Darnay (Donald Woods) in the motion picture *A Tale of Two Cities* (1935).

"You're so cheap, you're wholesale" - Annette Benning as leggy starlet Virginia Hill offers her opinion to Las Vegas gangster Benjamin "Bugsy" Siegel in the motion picture *Bugsy* (1991). When Virginia met Bugsy while visiting a movie set, she shared these sparkling thoughts: "Most of the time you're just another good-looking, sweet-talking, charm-oozing, fuck-happy fella with nothing to offer but some dialog. Dialogue is cheap in Hollywood...Why don't you go outside and jerk yourself a milk shake." Note: In the film *Mildred Pierce* (1945) mother Mildred Pierce (Joan Crawford) tells her spoiled daughter, Veda (Ann Blyth), "I think I'm really seeing you for the first time in my life—and you're cheap and horrible."

"You're so damn smart!" - Rod Steiger as white Police Chief Bill Gillespie in the motion picture *In the Heat of the Night* (1967). After Gillespie meets new black detective Virgil Tibbs (Sidney—"They call *Mr.* Tibbs"—Poitier) the chief's small town sensibilities clash with Tibb's big city outlook on law enforcement. In a mini-tirade Gillespie explodes, "You're so damn smart! You're smarter than any white man. You're just going to stay here and show us all. You got such a big head that you could never live with yourself unless you could put us all to shame."

"You're so dumb you wouldn't know rabbit turds from Rice Krispies" - Robert Easton as Wisconsin-ite Dan Kester in the sci-fi film *The Giant Spider Invasion* (1975).

"You're soft, you're soppy, you're unruly, you're undisciplined—and I never saw anything look so wonderful in my whole life. Thank you all" - Dean Jagger as retired army General Waverly reviews his former troops who traveled to a Vermont Inn during the Christmas season to visit their favorite WWII commander in the motion picture *White Christmas* (1954).

"You're stupid!" - Angry statement directed at Kevin Kline in the movie *A Fish Called Wanda* (1988). In the film, Jamie Lee Curtis calls her macho boyfriend Otto (Kevin Kline) "Stupid!" When he shouts, "Don't call me stupid!" Jamie Lee replies, "Oh right. To call YOU stupid would be an insult to stupid people! I've known sheep who could outwit you. I've worn dresses with higher IQs, but you think you're an intellectual, don't you, ape?" Note: In the film *Yours, Mine and Ours* (1968) Frank Beardsley (Henry Fonda) says, "I don't quite understand. Am I being stupid? to Helen North (Lucille Ball). She responds, "No, you're being a man, which is sometimes the same thing." On the TV series CHEERS/NBC/1982-93 Sam Malone (Ted Danson) & Diane Chambers

(Shelley Long) were always arguing with each other and calling each other names. Here's a sample:

Diane: Sam, that's the stupidest thing I ever heard.
Sam: I thought you weren't going to call me stupid now that we're being intimate.

Diane: No, I said I wasn't going to call you stupid *while* we were being intimate.

"You're terminated, fucker!" - Linda Hamilton as Sarah Connors puts the final squeeze on a futuristic killing machine ("The Terminator") as she activates a hydraulic press to crush the remains of its twisted yet still deadly skeleton in the sci-fi classic *The Terminator* (1984). In the film, Sarah is targeted by a murderous cyborg because she will give birth to a child who will lead a resistance movement in the future that challenges a tyrannical government. To save Sarah, the Resistance sent back a human named Kyle Reese (Michael Biehn) who provides Sarah with this explanation of the deadliness of the Terminator: "Listen! And understand! That terminator is out there. It can't be bargained with! It can't be reasoned with! It doesn't feel pity, or remorse, or fear. And it absolutely will not stop, ever, until you are dead!" Under police interrogation Kyle reveals, "You still don't get it, do you? He'll find her. That's what he does. That's all he does! You can't stop him! He'll wade through you, reach down her throat, and pull her fucking heart out! Note: In the film *Terminator 3: Rise of the Machines* (2003), Arnold Schwarzenegger as Terminator T-101 sticks an explosive device into the mouth of a female terminator called T-X (or Terminatrix) and says, "You are Terminated!" *See also* "Hasta la vista, baby!" and "I'll be back!"

"You're the best looking mountain trash I've seen in a long while. I'll be seeing you around" - Kevin Tighe as Hickey, a 1920s coal company detective offers a West Virginia coal miner's widow Bridey Mae (Nancy Mette) an off-color compliment in the motion picture *Matewan* (1987).

"You're the disease...and I'm the cure!" - Deadly diagnosis delivered by Sylvester Stallone in the action adventure *Cobra* (1986). In the film, Stallone plays police detective Marion Cobretti, the member of the "Zombie Squad" who is a specialist at dirty jobs that nobody else wants. When a member of a fanatical group takes a woman hostage, Cobretti discreetly dispatches the maniac with a knife but not before saying, "You're the disease...and I'm the cure." Later when an army of crazed extremists stalk a woman (Brigette Nielsen) who witnessed a murder, Cobretti becomes her protector. Battling it out in a steel mill with the group's meanest motherfucker, Cobretti declares, "This is where the law ends...and I begin." At the conclusion of a vicious hand-to-hand combat, Cobretti lifts up the bad guy and impales him on a huge conveyor belt hook that carries the criminal's body into a blast furnace.

"You're the lowest thing on a newspaper, a picture snatcher, stealing pictures from folks who are so down in the mouth they can't fight back—just a thug doing the same thing you always did" - Patricia Ellis as Patricia Nolan shouts at cocky ex-con turned reporter Danny Kean (James Cagney) for his low-handed methods used to get photographs (he snaps a shot of an electric chair execution) in the motion picture *Picture Snatcher* (1933). Note: Speaking of electric chairs, in the movie *The Bad Seed* (1956) Henry Jones as Leroy the handyman taunts eight-year-old murderess Rhoda Penmark (Patty McCormick) with the delightful reassurance, "They got a little blue chair for little boys and a little pink one for little girls." Rhoda didn't get the electric chair but she did get hit with a bolt of lightning that smoked her mean little ass in the film's finale.

"You are the most unattractive man I have ever met in my entire life" - Honest appraisal of Daryl Van Horne (Jack Nicholson), a mysterious wealthy suitor in the comedy horror film *The Witches of Eastwick* (1987). When Van Horne visits the small New England town of Eastwick, he makes sexual advances at Alexandra "Alex" Medford (Cher). Unhappy with such conduct, Alex rejects him with the following monologue: "I will try to be as direct and honest with you as I possibly can. I think, no, I am positive, that you are the most unattractive man I have ever met in my entire life. You know, in the short time that we have been together you have demonstrated every loathsome characteristic of the male personality and even discovered a few new ones. You are physically repulsive, intellectually retarded, you're morally reprehensible, vulgar, insensitive, selfish, stupid. You have no taste, a lousy sense of humor and you smell. You're not even interesting enough to make me sick." An additional observation: "I hope his dick is bigger than his I.Q." Alex (and two other women in town) soon fall under Van Horne's spell (the Devil in disguise) and, in the end, bear him children. Note: In the film *The Lady Vanishes* (1938) Margaret Lockwood as Iris Henderson tells her annoying hotel neighbor Gilbert (Michael Redgrave), "You're the most contemptible person I've ever met in all my life" Gilbert confesses, "I'm about as popular as a dose of strychnine. He then admits to Iris, "Confidentially, I think you're a bit of a stinker, too." *See also* "Coyote Ugly"

"You're too stupid to even be a good bigot." - Scott Colomby as Brian Schwartz reprimands friend Tim (Cyril O'Reilly) when he incorrectly pronounces the racial slur "kike" in the low budget comedy *Porky's* (1981).

"You're unsophisticated, ignorant and totally lacking in social grace" - Joely Richardson as Princess Anna of Finland evaluates King Ralph (John Goodman), the new monarch of England as potential husband material in the motion picture *King Ralph* (1991). Despite her objections, Anna consoled her self with the fact that Ralph had a "nice buttocks" and that he could "strap her to the throne chair with a string of pearls."

"You're useless, Beatrice!" - The abusive banter of Vincent D'Onofrio as Edgar, a redneck husband complains to his wife, Beatrice (Siobhan Fallon) in the motion picture *Men in Black* (1997). "I go out, I work my butt off to make a living, all I want is to come home to a nice clean house with a nice fat steak on the table, but instead I get this. It looks like poison. Don't you take that away, I'm eating that, damn it! It is poison, isn't it? I swear to God I would not be surprised if it was, the way you skulk around here like a dog that's been hit too much or ain't been hit enough, I can't make up my mind. You're useless, Beatrice! The only thing that pulls its weight around here is my goddamn truck!" (Just then a UFO crashes into the truck)

"You're yellow. I never saw you pick on anything who wasn't old and sick" - Charlton Heston as bookmaker Danny Haley confronts Augie, a demented killer (Jack Webb) with his cowardly ways in the motion picture *Dark City* (1950).

"You are wrong...breath!" - On THE TONIGHT SHOW STARRING JOHNNY CARSON/NBC/1962-92, host Johnny Carson occasionally read excerpts from books or magazine articles as an introduction to a comedy skit. When Carson finished reading this information, his sidekick Ed McMahon shouted, "Everything you wanted to know about...is in that book (or article). Johnny Carson answered, "You are Wrong!" and interjected an insult. The following are examples of the insulting put-downs Carson called McMahon during these skits.

- You are wrong Ozone Killer Breath!
- You are wrong Derelict Denture Breath!
- You are wrong Rabbit Test Breath!
- You are wrong Barracuda Breath!
- You are wrong Mail-Fraud Breath!
- You are wrong Manifold Breath!
- You are wrong Disinfectant Breath!
- You are wrong Rancid Chittlin Breath!

In addition, Johnny Carson often kidded Ed McMahon (aka "Mr Budweiser") about his alleged drinking lifestyle—once referring to him as "Sea Lush" during a pirate sketch.

"You bastard! Drop dead!" - Richard Dawson as Damon Killian shows utter contempt for one his contestants in the motion picture *The Running Man* (1987). In the film, Damon Killian hosts a futuristic audience participation capital punishment game show called "The Running Man" One of Killian's contestants is Ben Richards, an ex-cop framed for the massacre of innocent people. Killian proceeds to strap Richards into a sled and send him sliding into an arena filled with "stalkers" who hunt down and kill the game show participants. But Killian escapes the killing grounds and takes over the game show. Fearful of his own safety, Killian pleads, "This is television, that's all it is. It has nothing to do with people; it's to do with ratings! For fifty years, we've told them what to eat, what to drink, what to wear...for Christ's sake, Ben, don't you understand? Americans love television. They wean their kids on it. Listen. They love game shows, they love wrestling, they love sports and violence. So what do we do? We give 'em 'what they want!' We're number one, Ben, that's all that counts, believe me. I've been in the business for thirty years." Tired of listening to Killian's rant, Ben Richards says, "Well, I may not have been in show business for as long as you have. But I'm a quick learner. And right now, I'm going to give the audience what 'I' think they want." Then Richards straps Killian into a sled and sends him in to same arena that kills off his contestants. Before leaving, Killian shouts, "You bastard! Drop Dead!" To which, Richard replies, "I don't do requests!" Note: Earlier in the film, the game show needs a new contestant and we hear an elderly woman say, "I can pick anyone I choose. And I choose...Ben Richards. That boy is one mean motherfucker." *See also* "How 'bout a light!"

"You bastards!" *See* "Oh my God, they killed Kenny!"

"You bastards! You vicious, heartless bastards!" - Mungo the Cook expresses his opinion in the Monty Python inspired motion picture *And Now for Something Completely Different* (1971). Mungo continues, "Look what you've done to him! He's worked his fingers to the bone to make this place what it is, and you come in with your petty feeble quibbling and you grind him into the dirt, this fine, honorable man, whose boots you are not worthy to kiss! Oh... it makes me mad... [Slams cleaver into the table] Mad! Stark, stirring... MAD!" Note: The film is a compilation of the best skits from their 'Monty Python's Flying Circus' series produced for the BBC.

"You believe in Jesus?...Well, you're gonna meet him" - In the film *Death Wish II* (1982) architect Paul Kersey (Charles Bronson) hunts down the street hoodlums who savagely raped/killed his wife and raped his daughter. Along the way, the thugs kill his daughter by impaling her onto the spikes of a metal fence. When Paul finally corners one of the crooks (who's wearing a crucifix around his neck), he says, "You believe in Jesus?" The thug answers, "Yes, I do." And Kersey concludes, "Well you're gonna meet him" and shoots the punk dead.

"You bet your ass, mamma! I'm a big bad bulldyke and my tongue has been places you don't even know you've got and it's great" - Catherine Carlin as a gay biker letting a fellow 'cycle slut' know that she's proud to be a lesbian in the motion picture *Chopper Chicks in Zombietown* (1991).

"You bums forgotten how to kill people?" - Al Pacino as gangster Big Boy Caprice in the film *Dick Tracy* (1990) rebukes his henchmen for failing to kill police detective Dick Tracy (Warren Beatty). Perturbed Big Boy shouts, "All right, that's enough. I want Tracy dead. What's the matter, you bums forgotten how to kill people? Have you no sense of pride in what you do? No sense of duty, no sense of destiny? I'm looking for generals; what have I got? Foot soldiers! I want Dick Tracy dead!"

"You butcher one more patient, and law or no law—I'll find you. I'll put a bullet in the back of your head, and I'll drop your body in the East River. And I'll go home—and I'll sleep sweetly" - Kirk Douglas as New York City police detective Jim Macleod warns an abortionist (George Macready) to retire from his dirty little career or face the consequences in the motion picture *The Detective Story* (1951).

"You cad, you dirty swine! I never cared for you, not once! I was always makin' a fool of ya! Ya bored me stiff; I hated ya! It made me SICK when I had to let ya kiss me. I only did it because ya begged me, ya hounded me and drove me crazy! And after ya kissed me, I always used to wipe my mouth! WIPE MY MOUTH!" - Betty Davis as illiterate waitress Mildred Rogers breaks off her relationship with med student Philip Carey (Leslie Howard) in the motion picture *Of Human Bondage* (1934). Mildred also uttered the phrase "Good riddance to bad rubbish." *See also* "What a dump"

"You can die or you can die happy" - Theresa Russell as Catherine Peterson, a 'black widow' murderess (she kills her husbands for their money) invites a crooked Chinese detective named Shin (James Hong) to choose which kind of death he wants: a bullet to the brain or an overdose of heroin in the motion picture *Black Widow* (1987).

"You can get it doggy-style or you can get it laying on your side. Those are your only choices. This is my house and I get to say. Got it?" - Robert De Niro as alcoholic garage mechanic Dwight Hansen tells his new wife, Caroline (Ellen Barkin) what she can expect from their sex life in the motion picture *This Boy's Life* (1993).

"You can kiss my ass" - In the motion picture *The Big Score* (1981) a blonde prostitute (Katherine Welch) asks, "Say baby, lookin' for some action?" to black Chicago narcotics cop Frank Hooks (Fred Williamson). When he responds, "I don't think they got a needle big enough to kill the shit you got" the insulted hooker yells, "Well, you can kiss my ass!"

"You can kiss my ass, Pal!" - The parting comment of Dr. Donald Westphall (Ed Flanders) on the episode "Moon for the Misbegotten" (9/30/1987) on the medical drama ST. ELSEWHERE/NBC/1982-88. Frustrated with the new hospital owners, Dr. Westphall drops his pants, moons the new administrator Dr. John Gideon (Ronny Cox) and says his now classic put-down, "You can kiss my ass, Pal!" Note: Late night talk show host Arsenio Hall also took the opportunity to berate his bosses (his producers at Paramount Studios) on THE ARSENIO HALL SHOW/SYN/1989-94 when he told his employers to "kiss my black ass!" *See also* "Kiss my ass!" and "Pucker up and kiss my ass!"

"You can take your Bunker Hills and your bloodlines and stuff a codfish with 'em. And then you know what you can do with the codfish" - Jean Harlow as Lola, a goodhearted dumb blond movie star who gets angry with a stuck up Bostonian Gifford Middleton (Franchot Tone) in the motion picture *Bombshell* (1933). Note: In the film *Ride the Pink Horse (1947)* Robert Montgomery as blackmailer Blackie Gagin described a woman he didn't like, by saying "She had a dead fish where her heart oughta be...A dead fish...with a bit of perfume on it."

"You can't handle the truth!" - The angry put-down of Jack Nicholson as Marine Colonel Nathan R. Jessep in the motion picture *A Few Good Men* (1994). In the film, Colonel Jessep is responsible for approving the hazing cover-up of a recruit named William Santiago who accidentally died. At the trial investigation, Jessep takes the stand and when pressured by a Navy attorney Lieutenant Daniel Kaffee (Tom Cruise) to give the truth about the recruit's death, Jessep yells, "You can't handle the truth! Son, we live in a world that has walls, and those walls have to be guarded by men with guns. Who's gonna do it? You? You, Lieutenant Weinberg? I have a greater responsibility than you can possibly fathom. You weep for Santiago and you curse the marines. You have that luxury. You have the luxury of not knowing what I know: that Santiago's death, while tragic, probably saved lives. And my existence, while grotesque and incomprehensible to you, saves lives. You don't want the truth because, deep down in places you don't talk about at parties, you want me on that wall; you need me on that wall. We use words like honor, code, loyalty. We use these words as the backbone of a life spent defending something. You use them as a punch line. I have neither the time nor the inclination to explain myself to a man who rises and sleeps under the blanket of the very freedom that I provide and then questions the manner in which I provide it. I would rather you just said 'thank you' and went on your way. Otherwise I suggest you pick up a weapon and stand at post. Either way, I don't give a damn what you think you are entitled to." Kaffee persists, "Did you order the code red?" "Your damn right I did!", admits Jessep. After the M.Ps hold Jessep for criminal charges, he shouts, "I'm being charged with a crime?" [Jessep lunges at Kaffee] "I'm gonna rip the eyes out of your head. You give me your dead skull. You messed with the wrong Marine...You friggin' people. You have no idea how to defend a nation. All you did was weaken a country. That's all you did. You put people's lives in danger. Sweet dreams, son." "Don't call me son," replies, Kaffee. "I'm a lawyer and an officer in the United States Navy and you're under arrest, you son of a bitch. The witness is excused."

"You can't shot an unarmed man..." - In the western adventure *A Man Alone* (1955) Ray Milland played Wes Steele, a man falsely accused of murder. When Steele confronts his accuser, the man (Raymond Burr) drops his guns and says, "You can't shoot an unarmed man." Steele answers, "No, but I can sure beat you to death." Note: In the anti-western film *Unforgiven* (1992) the town sheriff Little Bill Daggett cries, "You just shot an unarmed man!" The killer William Munny (Clint Eastwood), a former outlaw come out of retirement replies, "He should have armed himself if he's gonna decorate his saloon with my friend." And, in the film *Out for Justice (1991)* when a murdering creep asks, "You gonna shoot an unarmed man?" to pissed off cop (Steven Seagal), the cop answers, "No, you know what I'm gonna do?" and then throws the guy out a window to his death.

"You computerized half-breed!" - William Shatner as starship Captain James T. Kirk insulting his Vulcan First Officer Mr. Spock (Leonard Nimoy) in episode #25 "This Side of Paradise" on the science fiction series STAR TREK/NBC/1966-69. After alien spores on planet Omicron Ceti III take control of the minds of the crew of the starship *Enterprise*, Captain Kirk discovers that strong negative or aggressive emotions destroy the spore's euphoric grip on its host. To bring Mr. Spock back to his senses, Kirk needed to get him angry. As Spock transports back onto the *Enterprise,* Kirk taunts, "You computerized half-breed." Always the logical one, Spock corrects Kirk. "The term half-breed is somewhat applicable, but computerized is inaccurate. A machine can be computerized, not a man." Continuing his taunts Kirk says, "What makes you think your a man...Your an overgrown jackrabbit. An elf with a hyperactive thyroid." When Spock says he doesn't understand his attitude, Kirk yells, "Of course, you don't understand...You don't have the brains to understand. All you have is printed circuits." As Spock tries to ignore the mean-spirited remarks, Kirk continues his harangue. "What can you expect from a simpering devil-eared freak whose father was a computer and whose mother's an encyclopedia." While Spock calmly interjects that his mother was a teacher, and his father was an ambassador, Kirk insists, "Your father was a computer, like his son. An Ambassador from a planet of traitors. The Vulcan never lived who had an ounce of integrity. You're a traitor from a race of traitors. Disloyal to the core. Rotten like the rest of your sub-human race." Kirk's abusive statements were now having the desired effect as Spock says, "Captain, don't." But Kirk pounds the final nail into his coffin by saying, "And you've got the gall to make love to that girl (Jill Ireland)...Does she know what she's getting, Spock? A carcass full of memory banks who should be squatting on a mushroom instead of passing himself off as a man. You belong in a circus, Spock. Not a starship. Right next to the dog-faced boy!" Finally enraged, Spock attacks the Captain but luckily just about the time Kirk's life was to be compromised by Spock's immense Vulcan strength, the spores which had taken over his mind are destroyed by his internal anger.

"You cross me, I'll personally grease the pole that slides you into a tub of shit" - Chicago cop Eddie Jillette (Richard Gere) speaks to New Orleans cajun cop Lt. Hall (Bruce McGill) while investigating the murder of his partner in the film noir thriller *No Mercy* (1986).

"You didn't blink an eye when you killed him, you were perfect" - Ron Silver as Eugene Hunt, a psychopathic killer infatuated with a rookie New York City police officer in the motion picture *Blue Steel* (1990). When Eugene sees officer Megan Turner (Jamie Lee Curtis) shoot a thief at a convenience store, he gets stimulated at her intense focus, and concentration. After killing Megan's fellow detective, Eugene forces Megan to kill him in a sort of morbid "oh baby, shot that bullet through me" scenario.

"You dirty rat!" - The legendary insult allegedly spoken by film actor James Cagney. Actually, the quote is a variation on a line he said in the movie *Taxi (*1932). In the film, Cagney played cab driver Matt Nolan, whose brother was killed by a taxi syndicate's hit man. When Matt corners his brother's murderer in a locked room, he yells, "Come out and take it, you dirty, yellow-bellied rat, or I'll give it to you through the door." Note: In the film *Blonde Crazy* (1931) James Cagney as cocky con man Bert Harris says, "Mmm, that dirty, double-crossin' rat!" Additionally, Cagney starred in *Each Dawn I Die* (1939) as a reporter framed for manslaughter, but it was actor Ed Pawley as a convict named Dale who shouts, "Listen, you dirty rats in there!" The "You dirty rat!" phrase has been a staple of nightclub impressionists for years, especially the phrase, "You dirty rat! You're the guy that killed my brother." *See also* "Feed Me! Feed me!"

"You dirty nigger, get up and walk!" - Jeff Corey as a psychiatrist getting down and dirty with Moss (James Edwards), a black soldier whose paralysis is linked to a deep trauma associated with racism in the motion picture *Home of the Brave* (1949).

"You don't live with me, you live among the remnants of dead people. You sift through the detritus, you read the terrain, you search for signs of passing, for the scent of your prey...and then you hunt them down. That's the only thing you're committed to. The rest is the mess you leave as you pass through" - Diane Verona as Justine Hanna speaks to her police detective husband Vincent (Al Pacino) in the motion picture *Heat* (1995). When Vincent criticizes Diane, she retaliates, "I may be stoned on grass and Prozac, but you've been walking through my life dead." Aware of his inability to satisfy his wife, Vincent confesses to a crook, "My life's a disaster zone. I got a stepdaughter who's all fucked up because her real father is this large type asshole. I got a wife who I'm passing on the down slope of a marriage, my third, because I spend all my time chasing guys like you around the corner."

"You forgot your fortune cookie. It says: 'you're shit out of luck'" - Clint Eastwood as police detective 'Dirty' Harry Callahan forecasts the demise of a street hood right before he shoots him in the motion picture *The Dead Pool* (1988).

"You got any contraceptives?...No, but I gotta a magazine with Whoppi Goldberg on the cover" - Amanda Bierce as Marcy Darcy asks her next-door neighbor Al Bundy (Ed O'Neill) for sexual aides on a 1993 Christmas episode of the Fox network sitcom MARRIED...WITH CHILDREN.

"You got heart, but you fight like a goddamn ape" - Burgess Meredith as fight trainer Mickey tries to knock some sense into up-and-coming boxer Rocky Balboa (Sylvester Stallone) in the motion picture *Rocky* (1976). In the sequel, *Rocky II* (1979) Rocky says, "I'm a fighter, not too good, but that's what I do."

"You gotta snap some collars" - Tough guy advice from Bishop (Tupac Shakur) in the motion picture *Juice* (1992). Talking to three of his homey friends living in a Harlem ghetto, Bishop shares his philosophy on success: "You gotta snap some collars and let them motherfuckers know you here to take them out anytime you feel like it! You gotta get the ground beneath your feet, partner, get the wind behind your back and go out in a blaze if you got to! Otherwise, you ain't shit! You might as well be dead your damn self!"

"You guys think you're above the law. Well, you ain't above mine." - In the motion picture *Above the Law* (1988) Steven Seagal plays Nico Toscani, a former Special Forces soldier turned Chicago policeman. When Nico discovers a plot to kill a congressman, he is warned off by an old "Company" friend who is involved in the conspiracy. But Nico refuses to be part of his treachery and says, "Whenever you have a group of individuals beyond any investigations, who can manipulate the press, the judges, members of Congress—you are always going to have those who are above the law...Not one CIA agent has ever been accused, much less tried of any crime. You guys think you're above the law. Well, you're not above mine." In the ensuing hours, Nico is captured by a vicious and quit psychotic doctor (Henry Silva) who gives Nico an overdose of heroin. Fighting back, Nico breaks loose from his bindings and kills everyone in the room. Note: In the film *The Siege* (1998) Bruce Willis as General William Deveraux, says, "The CIA didn't know the Berlin Wall was falling until the bricks started hitting them in the face."

"You have a good mind, a pretty face, and a disciplined body that does what you tell it. You have everything it takes to make a lovely woman except the one essential—an understanding heart. Without it, you might just as well be made of bronze" - John Halliday as Seth Lord councils his haughty, high-strung daughter Tracy (Katherine Hepburn) in the motion picture *The Philadelphia Story* (1940). Cary Grant as C. K. Dexter Haven, Tracy's playboy ex-husband also offers this advice: "You'll never be a first class human being or a first class woman until you've learned to have some regard for human frailty."

"You've gained seven pounds. If you want to put something in your mouth, try a gun" - The insensitive suggestion from a "talking" scale addressing its inventor, Joe (Richard Dreyfuss) in the motion picture *The Buddy System* (1984).

"You've tricked and fooled your readers for years. You've tortured us all with surprise endings that made no sense. You've introduced characters in the last five pages that were never in the book before. You've withheld clues and information that made it impossible for us to guess who did it. But now, the tables are turned. Millions of angry mystery readers are now getting their revenge. When the world learns I've outsmarted you, they'll be selling your $1.95 books for twelve cents." - Truman Capote as the revenge-filled Lionel Twain in the murder mystery spoof *Murder by Death* (1976).

"You've pulled over the wrong black man" - Glenn Plummer as Jeriko One, a popular rap star in the motion picture *Strange Days* (1995). Pulled over by crooked cops, Jeriko protests, "You know what? You've pulled over the wrong black man, Officer *Steckler!* I'm the 800-pound gorilla in your mist, fucker! I make more money in a day than you make in a whole year! And my lawyer loves sending sorryass Aryan RoboCop fuckers like you to jail!...You're gonna be in my next song. It's called 'RoboSteckler.' It's about a cop who met his worst nightmare: a nigga with enough political juice to squash your ass like a stinkbug! You gonna be famous, fucker!" Unfortunately, Jericho's bravado bought him a bullet to the brain. The execution was caught on video and truth over the matter became the fodder for the conclusion of the film when the Police Commissioner saw the tape and arrested the cops.

"You have sunk lower that frog shit on the bottom of a New Jersey scum swamp" - Michael Douglas as soon-to-be divorced Oliver Rose speaks to his soon-to-be ex-wife Barbara (Kathleen Turner) in the dark comedy film *War of the Roses* (1989). Barbara's feelings about Oliver were equally putrid because as she told Oliver, "When I watch you eat, when I see you asleep, whenever I look at you lately I just want to smash your face in." *See also* "I'm pond scum"

"You have the money for me by Christmas Eve, or Christmas morning you'll find your head in a Christmas stocking." - Fred Clark as gangster Moose Moran intimidates a racetrack gambler (Bob Hope) into a prompt payment schedule in the motion picture *The Lemon Drop Kid* (1951).

"You have the right to remain silent, so shut the fuck up!" - While struggling to cuff a suspect in the film *Lethal Weapon 4* (1998), police detective Lee Butters (Chris Rock) says, "You have the right to remain silent, so shut the fuck up! You have the right to get an attorney. If you can't afford one, we'll get you the dumbest goddamn lawyer we've got. If you get Johnnie Cochrane, I'll kill ya!" In the first *Lethal Weapon* (1987) undercover cop Matrin Riggs (Mel Gibson) lampoons the Miranda Rights by advising a knocked out criminal, "You have the right to remain unconscious. Anything you say...ain't gonna be much!" Note: In the film *Running Scared* (1986) Billy Crystal as Chicago cop Danny Costanzo points his gun at a Hispanic crook and says, "Habla Smith & Wesson. You have the right to be...dead. You have the right to a coroner." In the film *Psycho Cop Returns* (1993) Officer Joe Vickers (Robert R. Shafer) says, "You have the right to remain dead. Anything you say can and will be considered very strange because you're dead. You have the right to an attorney, but it won't do you any good because you're dead. Do you understand these rights that have just been read to you? Are you even listening? It would be a lot easier if you were a little more cooperative!" And, on the episode "Switched at Birth" (10/8/94) of the science fiction sitcom WEIRD SCIENCE bully older brother Chett (Lee Tergesen) advises teenager Gary Wallace (John Mallory Asher), "You have the right to beg for mercy. You have the right to a speedy butt-kick. My fists can and will be used against you. If you choose to scream, your scream will not be heard above the sound of my laughter." *See also* "How 'bout a light?"

"You have to learn to talk like a Mexican. Tell me it's a hot day" - In the film *El Norte* (1983) a concerned friend tries to teach Enrique Xuncax (David Villalpando) how to pass as a Mexican so he can successfully cross the border. However, when Enrique repeats the phrase, "It's a hot day", his friend says, "No! You won't make it two miles past the border. 'It's a *fucking* hot day." Mexicans are always saying fuck. Fuck this, fuck that. Now try it again."

"You hideous yellow monster, do you mean to destroy us all?" - Karen Morley as Sheila Barton questions the evil intentions of Asian madman Dr. Fu Manchu (Boris Karloff) in the motion picture *The Mask of Fu Manchu* (1932).

"You hoodlums don't own these streets, and I've had all the roughhouse I'm gonna put up with around here. If you want to kill each other, kill each other, but you ain't gonna do it on my beat" - Simon Oakland as police Lieutenant Schrank yells at members of the Jets and the Sharks, two street gangs in the motion picture *West Side Story* (1961).

"You imbecile!" - Angry words of Joel Cairo (Peter Lorre) as he screams at Kasper Gutman, the Fatman (Sidney Greenstreet) in the motion picture *The Maltese Falcon* (1941). When Cairo discovers that a supposedly rare and valuable black bird statuette is actually a fake, he lambastes his oversized partner, "You! It's you who bungled it! You and your stupid attempt to buy it! Kemedov found out how valuable it was, no wonder we had such an easy time stealing it. You...you imbecile! You bloated idiot! You stupid fat-head, you!" Earlier, in an effort to obtain the Maltese Falcon, Cairo told private eye Sam Spade (Humphrey Bogart), "I am not a violent man. Mr. Spade, but if you do not give me that black bird, I shall be compelled to murder you without mercy."

"You keep looking at me, you'll see me kill you" - Tony Epper as a hoodlum threatens race car driver Alex Furlong (Emilio Estevez) for looking at him during his dinner in the motion picture *Freejack* (1992). Note: In the film An *Officer and a Gentleman* (1982) Lou Gossett as tough drill Sgt. Emil Foley shouts to a recruit, "Don't you eyeball me, boy! Use your peripheral vision!"

"You kill a few people, they call you a murderer. You kill a million and you're a conqueror. Go figure" - John Lithgow as mercenary Erik Qualen in the motion picture *Cliffhanger* (1993). At the film's climax, Qualen is killed when his helicopter slides off the face of a cliff and explodes in the rocks below. Note: In the film *Monsieur Verdoux*

(1947) Charlie Chaplin as convicted woman killer Henri Verdoux says, “Wars, conflict—it’s all business. One murder makes a villain; millions, a hero. Numbers sanctify!” And, in the film *Masculin, féminin* (1966) Jean-Pierre Léaud as Paul says, “Kill a man and you’re a murderer. Kill thousands and you’re a conqueror. Kill everyone and you’re a god.”

“You killed him, why lie?” - Humphrey Bogart as tough WWII veteran Rip Murdock accuses Coral Chandler (Lizabeth Scott) of killing her former lover and his wartime buddy Johnny Drake (William Prince) in the motion picture *Dead Reckoning* (1947). His entire accusation reads: “Go ahead, put Christmas in your eyes and keep your voice low. Tell me about paradise and all the things I’m missing. I haven’t had a good laugh since before Johnny was murdered...I’m not the type that tears do anything to...Maybe the trouble is my name isn’t Johnny and I never taught college anywhere. Like looking at a doll cry and taking the rap for a murder she committed...do you think I fell for a murder she committed...Do you think I fell for that fancy tripe you gave me? It’s not a new story, baby...You killed him, Why lie?”

“You know, Alfeaus, the problem with polygamy is that when you've had 27 wives and 56 children, one's just bound to turn out as dirt-stupid and pig-ugly as you” - Tom Berringer as Miles Utley explains the drawbacks of Mormonism multiple marriage to Alfeaus Young (Daniel Quinn) in the made for TV motion picture *The Avenging Angel* (1995).

“You know, considering you’re a crook and a horror, you’re really nice company” - Shirley Jones as Linda Cabot offers up a kind sentiment about corrupt waterfront union racketeer Jake Maclllaney (James Cagney) in the motion picture *Never Steal Anything Small* (1958).

“You know, I had you pegged right from the jump. Just a spoiled brat of a rich father. The only way you get anything is to buy it, isn’t it? You're in a jam and all you can think of is your money. It never fails, does it? Ever hear of the word humility? No, you wouldn’t. I guess it would never occur to you to just say, ‘Please mister, I’m in trouble, will you help me?’ No, that would bring you down off your high horse for a minute. Well, let me tell you something, maybe it will take a load off your mind. You don’t have to worry about me. I’m not interested in your money or your problem. You, King Westley, your father. You’re all a lot of hooey to me!” - Clark Gable as Peter Warne, an out-of-work reporter in need of a juicy story who hooks up with Ellie Andrews (Claudette Colbert), a socialite on the run from her father in the motion picture *It Happened One Night* (1934).

“You know, I’ve been thinking. Women ought to come capsule-size, about four inches high. When a man goes out for an evening, he just puts her in his pocket and takes her along with him, and that way, he knows exactly where she is” - Humphrey Bogart as Rip Murdock, a tough WWII veteran tells his companion Coral Chandler (Lisabeth Scott) his outrageously politically incorrect fantasy about women in the motion picture *Dead Reckoning* (1947). Rip continues his fantasy: “When he gets to his favorite restaurant, he puts her on the table and lets her run among the coffee cups while he swaps a few lies with his pals. And when he wants her full-sized and beautiful he just waves his hand and she becomes full-sized and beautiful...And if she starts to interrupt, he just shrinks her back to pocket-size and puts her away."

"You know, Steve, You're not very hard to figure, only at times. Sometimes I know exactly what you're going to say—most of the time. The other times...The other times you're just a stinker" - Lauren Bacall as Marie 'Slim' Browning analyzes Harry 'Steve' Morgan (Humphrey Bogart) in the motion picture *To Have and Have Not* (1944). Steve also notices something about Marie, namely, "That slap in the face you took...Well, you hardly blinked an eye. It takes a lot of practice to be able to do that."

"You know what I do with squealers?" - Richard Widmark as psychopathic gangster Tommy Udo talks to a disabled woman in the motion picture *Kiss of Death* (1947). Visiting the upstairs apartment of wheel-chair-bound Ma Rizzo (Mildred Dunnock), Tommy inquires, "I'm askin' ya, where's that squealin' son of yours? [weird giggle] You think a squealer can get away from me? Huh? [crazy laugh] You know what I do to squealers? I let 'em have it in the belly, so they can roll around for a long time thinkin' it over. You're worse than him, tellin' me he's comin' back? Ya lyin' old hag!" Tommy wheels Ma Rizzo to the top of the staircase and shoves her down a flight of steps. Note: Richard Widmark's ghastly giggle inspired comedian Frank Gorshin to create a similar nefarious laugh for his criminal persona The Joker on the 1960s ABC series BATMAN. In the film *Little Caesar* (1930), Edward G. Robinson as gangster Caesar Enrico Bardello warns, "If anyone turns yellow and squeals, my gun's gonna speak its piece." And in the motion picture *Dead End* (1937) street kid Spit (Leo Gorcey) betrays his fellow street thugs by squealing about the gang's illegal actions. Angered at such disloyalty, thug Milty (Bernard Punsley) expresses his displeasure and says, "I pity the guy who snitched." *See also* "The kid who tells on another kid is a dead kid"

"You know what they say: 'To save the world, you have to push a few old ladies down the stairs'" - Richard Sanders as nerdish college student Bernard Bernoulli after he pushes Edna (Peggy Roberts-Hope) down the stairs in the animated sci-fi adventure *Day of the Tentacle* (1993).

"You know what wakes me up in the middle of the night covered in a cold sweat? Knowing that you aren't any worse than anyone else in your whole screwed up generation - J. E. Freeman as Victor, Sr. in the motion picture *Go* (1999). Victor continues his observation: "In the old days, you know how you got to the top? Huh? By being better than the guy ahead of you. How do you people get to the top? By being so fucking incompetent, that the guy ahead of you can't do his job, so he falls on his ass and congratulations, you are now on top. And now the top is down here, it used to be up here...and you don't even know the fucking difference."

"You know what you are? You're an ass-half. It takes two of you to make an ass-hole" - Robin Williams as aggressive car salesman Joey O'Brien in the motion picture *Cadillac Man* (1990). When Joey tries to make a date with a coworker, she shoots him down by saying, "Oh, I'd like that, Joey, but I think I'd rather eat worms and die." Joey responds, "Hey, you know my worm doesn't have a hook." Another time, Joey tells a guy not to lie to him because he would end up "doing a little East River snorkeling."

"You know where you can bury your hatchet? Now get your bony ass out of my sight" - Melanie Griffith as ambitious secretary Tess McGill who finally had enough of her back-stabbing, idea-stealing corporate boss Katherine Parker (Sigourney Weaver) in the motion picture *Working Girl* (1988).

"*YOU LIAR!* You know what I'm going to do about this...Absolutely nothing, because if I go to court, it'll just drain eight hours of my life I'll never get back, and you'll probably stiff me anyway. So I'm just going to moan and complain like some impotent jerk, and take it up the tailpipe" - Jim Carrey as attorney Fletcher Reede expresses his true feelings to a motor pool guy who scratched his car in the motion picture *Liar Liar* (1997). Fletcher was forced to tell the truth for 24 hours because his young son made an honesty wish—that came true.

"You like this ring? You want to keep the hand this ring is on? If I see or hear or smell you anywhere near my gorillas, you'll be writing with your other hand and I'll have a new ashtray" - Sigourney Weaver as environmentalist and gorilla expert Dian Fossey threatens a poacher in the motion picture *Gorillas in the Mist* (1988).

"You little tramp" - The frank opinion of jealous wife, Jane Barton (Gene Tierney) who corners golddigger Maggie Williams (Carol Lynley) in the ladies room for making moves on her husband, Paul (Brian Keith) in the motion picture *The Pleasure Seeke*rs (1964). Before Jane slaps Maggie in the face, she asks, "What's the goal sweetie, a nasty little love nest? That's all you get, if that. No cold-eyed, calculating little viper's going to do me out of a thing. Those wide, wide blue eyes turned on him like red-hot pokers. It makes me sick! He doesn't give a damn about you...you little tramp." Note: In the film *My Best Friend's Girl* (1983) Micky the disc jockey (Michel Coluche) asks, "How can you be such a tramp?" to Vivane (Isabelle Huppert). She replies, "I've had a lot of practice, I was lucky enough to start very young, so it becomes second nature."

"You look like you just got banged by the dick of doom!" - Smart-mouthed remark made by Brian Austin Green as Metal Louie when he first meets a teenager named Kid (C. Thomas Howell) in the motion picture *Kid* (1991).

"You make me sick with your heroics" - William Holden as alleged American officer Shears in the motion picture *The Bridge on the River Kwai* (1957). Escaping from a Japanese prison compound, Shears is taken to a British hospital in Ceylon but is blackmailed into returning on a mission to destroy a bridge that the Japanese are building over the River Kwai. Not thrilled with having to return to the Burma Jungles, Shears explodes at British Major Warden (Jack Hawkins): "You make me sick with your heroics. There's a stench of death about you. You carry it in your pack like the plague. Explosives and L-pills—they go well together, don't they? And with you it's just one thing or the other: destroy a bridge or destroy yourself. This is just a game, this war! You and Colonel Nicholson, you're two of a kind, crazy with courage. For what? How to die like a gentleman? How to die by the rules? When the only important thing is how to live like a human being."

"You miserable bitch!" - Spoken by the beautiful Krystle Jennings (Linda Evans) to Alexis Carrington (Joan Collins) in the now famous cat fight that climaxed in the mansion pool on an episode of the prime time soap DYNASTY/ABC/1981-89. Note: The fight scene was actually shot in the two-foot deep lily pond on the grounds of the Arden Villa, a 20,000 square-foot mansion located at 1145 Arden Road in Pasadena, California.

"You miserable slug! You think you can talk your way out of this? You betrayed me!" - Surly remark of a spurned mystery woman (Carrie Fisher) who stalked her former lover Jake Blues (John Belushi) in the nutty comedy film *The Blues Brothers* (1980). After bombing his apartment and other assaults, she corners Jake in a tunnel sporting heavy-duty firearms. Confronted with almost certain death, Jake cries, "No, I didn't. Honest. I ran out of gas! I had a flat tire! I didn't have enough money for cab fare! My tux didn't come back from the cleaners! An old friend came in from out of town! Someone stole my car! There was an earthquake! A terrible flood! Locusts! It wasn't my Fault I SWEAR TO GOD!!!"

"You murdering little sneak, I can smell your hate. It's no different from your love" - Charles Bickford as a great painter (gone blind) having an intense lover's spat with his petulant wife (Joan Bennett) in the motion picture *The Woman on the Beach* (1947).

"You no good tramp. You dog. You dirty yellow dog, you! Don't call me Mom. You ain't no son of mine. Go away, and leave us alone. Stay away, leave us alone to die, but leave us alone" - Marjorie Main as Mrs. Martin, the mother of gangster Baby Face Martin (Humphrey Bogart) who cuts the umbilical cord to her affections for her criminal son when he returns home to his old neighborhood in the motion picture *Dead End* (1937).

"You old fish-eyed fool!" *See* "Dummy!"

"You ought to kill him merely because he is an actor" - In the film *The Seventh Seal* (1956), the wife of The Smith (Åke Fridell) runs away with an actor. Upon hearing his story, friend Jof (Nils Poppe) says, "The actor! Now I understand. There are too many of them, so even if he hasn't done anything in particular, you ought to kill him merely because he's an actor."

"You peroxide kissing bug...I'll pull that blond hair by its black roots. Put 'em up" - Ginger Rogers as Edwina Fulton threatens bombshell Lois Laurel (Marilyn Monroe) in the motion picture *Monkey Business* (1952).

"You perverted hypocrite square bastard" - Jane Fonda as New York City prostitute Bree Daniels sizes up the sexual proclivities of John Klute (Donald Sutherland) an investigator working on a missing person case in the motion picture *Klute* (1971). Bree begins, "Klute, tell, what's you're bag?" and continues her probing with, "Are you a talker, or a button man or a doubler, or maybe you like very young—children—or get your chest walked around with high heel shoes, or have us watch you tinkle. Or—You want to wear women's clothes or you get off ripping things—you perverted hypocrite square bastard."

"You pissy little bitch!" - On an episode of the police drama NYPD BLUE/ABC/1993-2005 the gritty, alcoholic Detective Andy Sipowicz was displeased with female assistant district attorney Sylvia Costas (Sharon Lawrence). Grabbing his crotch, he matter-of-factly says, "You pissy little bitch." Despite this rather rude first encounter, Andy and Sylvia later married. Other frequently used Andy-isms included "Dickhead" and "Asshole."

"You poke me one more time, I'm gonna have to redefine your face" - Danny DeVito as aluminum-siding salesman Ernest Tilley discusses plastic surgery options with fellow salesman Bill "BB" Babowsky (Richard Dreyfuss) in the motion picture *Tin Men* (1987).

"You poor slob! You're all alone" - At the end of the legal drama *Inherit the Wind, (1960)* Spencer Tracy as lawyer Henry Drummond (who defended a case of a science teacher accused of the crime of teaching evolution) is approached by reporter E. K. Hornbeck (Gene Kelly) to chat about the losing verdict of the trial. Earlier in the trial Hornbeck revealed, "It is the duty of a newspaper to comfort the afflicted and afflict the comfortable. I do hateful things for which people love me and I do loveable things for which they hate me. I'm admired for my detestability." As they part, Drummond asks Hornbeck, "What touches you? What warms you? Every man has a dream. What do you dream about? What—what do you need? You don't need anything do you? People love an idea just to cling to them. You poor slob! You're all alone. When you go to your grave, there won't be anybody to pull the grass up over your head. Nobody to mourn you. Nobody to give a damn. You're all alone." Hornbeck answers, "You're wrong, Henry. You'll be there. You're the type. Who else would defend my right to be lonely?"

"You put a greased, naked woman on all fours, with a dog collar around her neck, and a leash, and a man's arm extended out up to here, holding onto a leash and pushing a black glove in her face to sniff it. You don't find that offensive?" - Fran Drescher as Bobbi Flekman speaks to Tony Hendra (Ian Faith) in the motion picture parody of the rock music scene *This Is Spinal Tap* (1984).

"You ready to be fucked man?...Let me tell you something pendejo, you pull any of your crazy shit with us, you flash your piece out on the lanes, I'll take it away from you and stick it up your ass and pull the fucking trigger 'till it goes click....Nobody fucks with the Jesus" - John Turturro as Jesus speaking to "Dude" Lobowski (Jeff Bridges) in the motion picture *The Big Lebowski* (1998).

"You robbed me!" - The voice of Ray Walston as Applegate (The Devil) crying foul in the motion picture *Damn Yankees* (1958). In the film, Joe Boyd (Robert Shafer) a frustrated Washington Senators fan innocently says he'd sell his soul if only their baseball club could get a good hitter to compete against the Yankees and win the division pennant. Taking advantage of the moment, the Devil, in the guise of a man called Applegate, suddenly appears and transforms the middle-aged fan into a young baseball player (Tab Hunter as Joe Hardy) who becomes the Senators' newest and best hitter. Unfortunately, for the Devil, Joe finagles his way out of his contract and gets to return to his wife and children. The last words in the film are those of Applegate screaming, "Listen to me, you wife-loving louse. You belong to me. You sold me your soul. You can't run out on me like this. Ya thief. Ya crook. You robbed me. That's what you did. You robbed me. You robbed me!"

"You said don't shoot him, right? Well I didn't; I strangled him. If you didn't want me to kill him, why did you leave me alone with him?" - Don Cheadle as Mouse, a genial psychopath in a bowler hat assists 1940s Los Angeles private eye Easy Rawlins (Denzel Washington) in the motion picture *Devil in a Blue Dress* (1995).

"You should've let him kill me, 'cause I'm gonna kill you'"- John Wayne as cattle drover Tom Dunson in the motion picture *Red River* (1948). When Mathew Garth (Montgomery Clift) decides to no longer take orders from Dunson (who raised him), he goes against Tom's plans to drive cattle to Abilene. As Matt leaves, Tom screams, "You should've let him kill me, 'cause I'm gonna kill you...I don't know when, but I'll catch up. Ever time you turn around, expect to see me. 'Cause one time you'll turn around and I'll be there...and I'm gonna kill you, Matt." When next they meet, Tom and Matt engage in a rough and tumble fistfight, but then realize they're family and go home together.

"You show me a happy homosexual and I'll show you a gay corpse" - Kenneth Nelson as Michael, a Catholic-raised gay man talking at a birthday party who uses a variation of the old "only good Indian is a dead Indian" adage to express how hard it is for a gay man to find happiness in a society that resents homosexuals in the motion picture *The Boys in the Band* (1970). Fellow partygoer Alan (Peter White) tells Michael, "You are a sad and pathetic man, Michael. You are a homosexual and you don't want to be, but there's nothing you can do to change it. Not all your prayers to your God. Not all the analysis your money can buy in the years you have left to live. You may one day be able to know a heterosexual life. If you want it desperately enough. If you pursue it with fervor with which you annihilate. But you will always be homosexual as well, Michael. Always, Until the day you die."

"You snot-looking, scrotum-cheek, donkey breath - Kathleen Wilhoite as Arabella McGee, a rowdy 14-year-old street punk sasses a Los Angeles police detective (Charles Bronson) in the motion picture *Murphy's Law* (1986).

"You sound like one of them old war movies. A regular Hitler" - Sidney Poitier as black handyman Homer Smith in motion picture *Lilies of the Field (*1963). When Homer Smith's car overheats, he pulls into a small settlement to ask for some water. Little did he know that he would be volunteered by a bunch of German-speaking nuns to build a chapel. After a few days, Homer gets tired of being ordered around and complains to Mother Maria (Lilia Skala), "You know that stuff you wear? You think it's a uniform that makes you some kind of cop, or something, laying down the law. Throwing your weight around. You sound like one of them old war movies. A regular Hitler."

"You stink! You stink with corruption. You're worse than a murderer. You're a grave robber" - Arthur Kennedy as crippled Connie Kelly condemns his unscrupulous boxer brother Midge Kelly (Kirk Douglas) for seducing his ex-wife Emma Bryce (Ruth Roman) and then preventing Connie from marrying her in the motion picture *Champion* (1949).

"You suffer from a common feminine delusion" - The critical opinion of Waldo Lydecker (Clifton Webb) a cynical columnist in the motion picture *Laura* (1944). When Laura Hunt (Gene Tierney) interrupts Waldo during his dinner, he takes exception to the intrusion and spouts, "Young woman, either you have been raised in some incredible rustic community where good manners are unknown, or you suffer from the common feminine delusion that the mere fact of being a woman exempts you from the rules of civilized conduct. Possibly both."

"You sure is ugly!" - Insulting observation from the Academy Award winning motion picture *The Color Purple* (1985). In the film, Whoopi Goldberg plays Celie Johnson, a lonely black woman trapped in an abusive relationship with her cruel husband, Albert (Danny Glover). When Shug Avery (Margaret Avery) first sees Celie, she cruelly says, "You sure is ugly." As the story progresses, Celie gains self confidence. When her husband says, "You're black, you're poor, you're ugly, you're a woman, You're nothing at all!" Celie renounces him and shouts, "I'm poor, black, I may even be ugly, but, dear God, I'm here. I'm here....It's time for me to get away from you. And end your creation. And your dead body be just the welcome mat I need." Note: In the film *The Toast of New York (*1937) Cary Grant as Wall Street broker Nick Boyd asks beautiful but vain socialite Fleurique (Thelma Leeds), "Did anyone ever call you ugly?" "No." she asserts. "You're ugly!" says Grant. "Why, I think I hate you!" the belittled woman replies. In the film *For Richer of Poorer* (1997) Kirstie Alley as Caroline Sexton says to her husband Brad (Tim Allen), "I can do ugly! I did *YOU* for the last ten years!" And in the horror flick *Seed of Chucky* (2004) a supernaturally-possessed doll named Chucky says, "It looks like the kid fell off the ugly tree and hit every branch on the way down."

"You talkin' to me?" - Ominous words of Robert De Niro in Martin Scorsese's motion picture *Taxi Driver* (1976) about Travis Bickle, a disturbed New York City cab driver whose obsession with low-lifes and street scum pushes him over the edge. The most famous scene from the film finds De Niro standing in front a mirror, loaded-down with four firearms and hell bent for leather intent on assassinating a Senator. Looking at his reflection, the tormented cabby points a gun and says, "You talkin' to me? You talkin' to me? You talkin' to me? Then who the hell else are you talkin' to? You talkin' to me? Well I'm the only one here. Who do you think you're talking to? Oh yeah? Huh? Ok." Note: The motion picture *Back to the Future III* (1990) mimicked this scene as Michael J. Fox, a time-traveling teenager named Marty McFly practices his fast-draw for an upcoming gunfight in front of a mirror. Pointing his peacemaker at his reflection, Marty says, "You talkin' to me. You talkin' to me. Go ahead, make my day." In the movie *Hacker* (1995) a computer hacker punk about to hassle an FBI agent whips out a floppy disk, looks into the mirror and says, "Talkin' to me?" *See also* "Go Ahead, Make My Day"

"You tell me where he is, and I'll kill you quick. You can die without ever finding out what your left ball tastes like" - Kris Kristofferson as Bronson in the motion picture *Payback (*1999).

"You think beautiful girls are going to be in style forever! I should say not! Any day now they're going to be over! Finished! Then it'll be my turn!" - Barbara Streisand as Jewish Ziegfield Follies comedienne Fanny Brice puts her personal looks into perspective in the motion picture *Funny Girl* (1968).

"You think they can swim?" - In the espionage thriller *The Mackintosh Man* (1973) thugs pursue an ex-convict named Reardon (Paul Newman) and his female compatriot Mrs. Smith (Dominique Sanda) along the rough coastal roads of Ireland. In a fast and slippery car chase, Newman out-maneuvers the bad guys and forces their white Mercedes Benz off a cliff into the murky surf below. Peering down the rocky precipice, Sanda asks, "You think they can swim?" Newman replies, "I hardly think that matters." Note: In the film *The Addams Family (1991)* when two people are blown from the Addams' mansion into an open grave in the family's cemetery, Pugsley asks, "Are they dead?" His sister Wednesday replies, "Does it matter?"

"You think this man is the enemy? Huh? This is a worker! Any union keeps this man out ain't a union, it's a goddam club! They got you fightin' white against colored, native against foreign, hollow against hollow, when you know there ain't but two sides in this world—them that work and them that don't. You work, they don't. That's all you get to know about the enemy" - Chris Cooper as labor union organizer Joe Kenehan shakes up the status quo in 1920s Mingo County, West Virginia in the motion picture *Matewan* (1987). *See also* "Nobody fucks with the union"

"You think you're too good for me? Nobody's too good for me. Anybody thinks they're too good for me I make sure I knock 'em over sometime" - Marlon Brando as motorcycle gang leader Johnny in the motion picture *The Wild Ones* (1953). When a women in a bar asks, "Hey, Johnny, what are you rebelling against?" Johnny replies, "What've you got?" The film's opening title read: "This is a shocking story. It could never take place in most American towns—but it did in this one. It is a public challenge not to let it happen again." ("again" being a biker gang taking over a town).

"You thought wrong, dude!" - In the motion picture *Back to the Future III* (1990) Michael J. Fox as teenager Marty McFly travels back to the year 1885 to rescue scientist inventor, Emmett "Doc" Brown. While there, he meets a frontier outlaw named Buford Tannen who challenges Marty to a gunfight. When Marty drops his gun into the dirt and says, "I thought we could settle this like men" Buford Tannen says, "You thought wrong, dude" and shoots Marty in cold blood. As Buford nears his fallen victim, Marty opens his eyes, slams him with an iron stove cover hidden under his poncho that deflected Buford's bullet and begins to pelt Buford with punches until he falls face down into cart load of manure. Marty then travels back into the future of 1985 to find Buford Tannen's descendant Biff Tannen (originally a bully in an alternate timeline) has become a cowering, butt-kissing wimp. *See also* "Chicken"

"You two-timing bastard! I hope your prostate falls out!" - Jada Pinkett as Peaches Jordon shouts at her television set while watching her favorite soap opera in the motion picture in *A Low down Dirty Shame* (1994).

"You very bad man!" - On a classic episode of the sitcom SEINFELD/NBC/1990-98 well-meaning comedian Jerry Seinfeld gets an East Indian immigrant deported when he mislays the man's citizenship application papers. Swearing vengeance, Babu Bhatt (Brian George) cries, "You bad man, you very bad man!" Note: In the classic film *The Wizard of Oz (*1939) Dorothy's dog, Toto pulls back a curtain to reveal the "Great and Powerful Oz." Dorothy chastises the alleged Wizard for deceiving her, and says, "Oh, you're a very bad man!" The Wizard replies, "Oh, no my dear, I...I'm a very good man—I'm just a very bad wizard."

"You want a job? I got a job for you—fix up this goddamn pigsty!" - Jack Nicholson as Jonathan Fuerst who's pissed at his live-in lover, Bobbie (Ann-Margret) for not taking any initiative in the motion picture *Carnal Knowledge* (1971) He continues his tirade: "Listen, you've got a pretty good salary for testing out that bed all day. You want another fifty a week? Try vacuuming. You want an extra hundred. Try making the bed. Try opening the windows! That's why you can hardly stand up. This goddamn place smells like a coffin."

"You want to get Capone? Here's how you get him. He pulls a knife, you pull a gun. He sends one of yours to the hospital, you send one of his to the morgue. That's the Chicago way and that's how you get Capone" - Sean Connery as James Malone speaks to US Treasury agent Eliot Ness (Kevin Costner) in the motion picture *The Untouchables* (1987). When Capone (Robert De Niro) hears of a second raid on his criminal empire he tells his henchmen, "I want you to find that fancy boy Eliot Ness. I want him dead. I want his family dead. I want his house burned to the ground. I want to go there in the middle of the night; I want to piss on his ashes." Note: The television series THE UNTOUCHABLES/ABC/1959-63 (which inspired the 1987 feature film) told the story of Bruce Gordon as Frank Nitti, an Italian-American mobster who took over the reigns of the Chicago underworld when Al Capone was arrested on tax evasion in the early 1930s. Although the program was quite popular with the general public, the use of Italian characters in criminal roles aroused the wrath of the Italian-American League to Combat Defamation. Their group threatened to boycott advertisers over their concerns. On March 17, 1961, the pressure group settled the matter with ABC. The network agreed there would be no more fictitious hoodlums with Italian names and more emphasis was to be given concerning the great contributions made by Italian Americans.

"You want to play games, I can play games" - The beginning line in a tirade towards a female talent scout delivered by stand up comedian Steven Gold (Tom Hanks) in the film *Punchline* (1988). Steven's entire put-down reads: "You want to play games, I can play games. I can play ventriloquist with my underwear. I can play darts while maintaining an erection. I can gargle dish water and fart 'O Canada' at the same time. I can play the piano without being popular. I once had this dream I was dancing on a street corner with a jackhammer up my ass. Now let's see. It's either a sex dream or I need more fiber in my diet. If any of this is turning you on, just let me know." *See also* "I want to play a game"

"You watch your mouth, buddy" - The parking lot eulogy delivered to would-be rapist in the chick flick *Thelma and Louise* (1991). After partying at the Silver Bullet honky tonk, Thelma Dickerson (Geena Davis) walks into a parking lot with a man named Harland (Timothy Carhart). As Thelma refuses his advances, he says, "I'm not gonna hurt you" and then proceeds to slap her around and rape her. Out of the dark, Thelma's best friend Louise Sawyer (Susan Sarandon) jams a .38mm pistol into the man's face. "You let her go now or I am gonna splatter your ugly face all over this nice car." Walking away, Louise advises, "In the future when a woman's crying like that, she isn't having any fun." Instead of taking her council, Harland cries, "Bitch" and starts to say "Suck my..." Before he can finish, Louise fires her gun, and kills the creep. As she stands over his lifeless body, Louise snarls, "You watch your mouth, buddy." Believing the police wouldn't understand, ("You shoot off a guy's head with his pants down, believe me, Texas ain't the place you want to get caught.") Thelma and Louise elude the authorities and head for Mexico. Thelma later confides to Louise, "I am not sorry that son of a bitch is dead. I am just sorry it was you who did it instead of me." Later, a salacious trucker propositions the girls and they signal him to pull off the road. Instead of giving him a good time, the man is asked to apologize for his rude behavior. "You say your sorry or I'm gonna make you sorry," insists Louise. When he refuses, both Thelma and Louise produce handguns and shoot up his tanker truck, igniting the fuel and blowing it to smithereens. As the girls drive away hooting and a hollering, the trucker screams, "You're bitches from hell. You're gonna pay for this!" At the film's conclusion, the two women are cornered at a precipice of the Grand Canyon by an army of police vehicles. "Let's not get caught. Let's keep going" pleads Thelma. ("Certain words and phrases just keep drifting through my mind, things like, incarceration, cavity search, death by electrocution, life in prison, shit like that, know what I'm sayin', so do I want to come out alive?"). With a kiss and a hug, Louise says goodbye to Thelma and then accelerates their powder blue Thunderbird convertible off the cliff. As they plummet to oblivion, Thelma and Louise clasp hands in a final act of solidarity.

"You were a pretty little thing. Not that looks are important—not even for a woman. You don't look at the mantelpiece when you poke the fire" - Roger Livesey as Billy Rice offers a backhanded complimented in the motion picture *The Entertainer* (1960).

"You were gonna ask me for money? Who the hell do you think you're dealing with?" - In the motion picture *Midnight Cowboy* (1969) a naive male street hooker (John Voight) attempts to get paid for the sexual services that he just performed on an older woman named Cass (Sylvia Miles). Unfortunately, she is angered at the thought of having to "pay for it" and begins to scream, "What the hell do you think you're dealing with, some old slut on 42nd Street? In case you didn't happen to notice it, you big Texas longhorn, I'm one hellavah gorgeous chick!"

"You will be doomed to a living hell...a hunger...wild animal gnawing hunger! You will starve for an eternity!...You shall be Blacula, a living fiend doomed to never know that sweet blood which will become your only desire" - Charles Macaulay as

Count Dracula places a curse on an African Prince (William Marshall) visiting 1790s Transylvania in the motion picture *Blacula* (1972).

"You will learn one day, Great King, that there are but three things that men respect: the lash that descends; the yoke that breaks; and the sword that slays. By the power and terror of these, you may conquer the earth." - Conrad Veidt as Jaffar, the evil advisor tutors Persian ruler Ahmad (John Justin) in the fantasy motion picture *The Thief of Bagdad (*1940).

"You will look at what I have done and say, 'Of course—why not— they are all animals. They have slaughtered each other for centuries.' But the truth is, I'm not a monster. I'm a human man—I'm just like you, whether you like it or not" - Marcel Lures as terrorist Dusan Gavrich explains his rationale [on a taped message] for wanting to explode nuclear devices in the motion picture *The Peacemaker* (1997). Continuing his reasoning, Dusan says, "For years, we have tried to live together, until a war was waged on us, on all of us, a war waged by our own leaders. And who supplied the Serb cluster bombs, the Croatian tanks, the Muslim artillery shells that killed our sons and daughters? It was the governments of the West who drew the boundaries of our countries—sometimes in ink, sometimes in blood—the blood of our people. And now you dispatch your peacekeepers to write our destiny again. We can never accept this peace that leaves us with nothing but pain—pain the peacemakers must be made to feel. Their wives, their children, their houses and churches. So now you know, now you must understand. Leave us to find our own destiny. May God have mercy on us all."

"You'll never be big time because you're small time in your heart" - Judy Garland as Jo Hayden talks to her vaudeville partner Harry Palmer (Gene Kelly) in the motion picture *For Me and My Gal* (1942).

"You'll regret this for the rest of your life—both seconds of it" - Sylvester Stallone as police Sgt. John Spartan (recently unfrozen in the year 2032) threatens a bad guy in the motion picture *Demolition Man* (1993). Wesley Snipes played Spartan's nemesis Simon Phoenix. When he was unfrozen from a cryogenic prison, Simon says, "I'm sorry to say that the world has turned into a pussy-whipped, Brady Bunch version of itself, run by a bunch of robed sissies." *See also* "You are fined one credit..."

"*You'll* shoot your eye out! *You'll* shoot your eye out!" - In the film *A Christmas Story* (1983) Peter Billingsley plays a young boy named Ralphie who wants a Red Ryder BB rifle for Christmas. Unfortunately, at every turn, he hears his mother's warn, "You'll shoot your eye out." In school, Ralphie writes a "What I want for Christmas" theme paper but even his teacher Miss Shields (Tedde Moore) is against him. On the bottom of his graded paper, Ralphie finds the message, "P.S. You'll shoot your eye out." And to make matters worse, the Santa Claus at the local department store is also part of the conspiracy to keep Ralphie from getting his gun. Finally, Christmas comes, and low and behold, Ralphie's dad gives him his Red Ryder BB gun. Rushing outside into the backyard, Ralphie shoots his gun, but the BB ricochets and hits Ralphie glasses, shattering his lens ("Oh my god, I shot my eye out!"). Astonished, Ralphie thinks quickly, starts crying and then blames his accident on a huge icicle that allegedly fell off the roof. His mother commiserates, "Ralphie, you're lucky it didn't cut your eye! Those icicles have been known to kill people." *See also* "Oh, Fuck!"

"You would bore the leggings off a village idiot" - The callous observation of Rowan Atkinson as Richard the IV's younger son Prince Edmund, Duke of Edinburgh, a sniveling coward who calls himself the "Black Adder" in the British produced comedy THE BLACK ADDER (1983). While giving the moronic Lord Percy, Duke of Northumberland (Tim McInnerny) a tongue lashing, Edmund says, "Because Percy, far from being a fit consort for a prince of the realm, you would bore the leggings off a village idiot. You ride a horse rather less well than another horse would. Your brain would make a grain of sand look large and ungainly. And the part of you that can't be mentioned, I'm reliably informed by women around the court, wouldn't even be mentioned even if it could. If you put on a floppy hat and a velvet cod-piece, you might get by as a fool. But since you wouldn't know a joke if it leapt up and gave you a haircut, I sincerely doubt it. THAT is why you are dismissed from my service. [pause] Oh, and Baldrick. (Tony Robinson)...You're out, too."

"You'd make your crippled grandmother do a fan dance" - Jean Harlow as Gladys Benton accuses her fiancé newspaper editor Warren Haggerty (Spencer Tracy) of being uncaring in the motion picture *Libeled Lady* (1936).

"You wouldn't like me when I'm angry" - What Dr. David Banner (Bill Bixby) said to anyone who was on the verge of hurting or upsetting him on the sci-fi adventure THE INCREDIBLE HULK/CBS/1978-82. A victim of an overexposure of Gamma radiation, David Banner's body now mutates into a muscular green monster named the Hulk whenever anything angers him. Searching for a cure for his predicament, Dr. Banner wanders incognito across the USA and woe to anyone who gets in his way.

"You! You're the elevator killer! Merv Griffin!" - Steve Martin as Dr. Michael Hfuhruhurr discovers that pop singer and talk show host Merv Griffin is a serial killer in the motion picture *The Man with Two Brains (*1983). When asked "Why?" he took up killing, Merv Griffin says, "I don't know. I've always just loved to kill. I really enjoyed it. But then I got famous, and - it's just too hard for me. And so many witnesses. I mean, *everybody* recognized me. I couldn't even work anymore. I'd hear, 'Who's that lurking over there? Isn't that Merv Griffin?' So I came to Europe to kill. And it's really worked out very well for me."

"Your Dad wants to dump you, he wants you to marry a Korean prince. The Koreans love beating their wives! At least nine times per day. A wife is shared among 6 to 7 brothers. 9 times 6 equals 63, so you'll be beaten 63 times per day!" - Carol 'Do Do' Cheng as Snow White in the Chinese motion picture *Holy Weapon* aka *Wu xia qi gong zhu* (1993).

"Your love affair with yourself has reached heroic proportions. It doesn't seem to leave much room for me. Are you sure you can get along without somebody to help you admire yourself?" - Joan Crawford as Louise Howell Graham puts cold-hearted lady killer David Sutton (Van Heflin) through his paces in the motion picture *Possessed* (1947).

"Your Mama!" - In the motion picture *White Men Can't Jump* (1992) Woody Harrelson as Billy Hoyle and Wesley Snipes as Sidney Deane supplement their income by hustling basketball players on the inner city courts of Los Angeles. Part of their on-court banter includes spitting out "Your Mama" jokes to unsettle their opponents. Some classic "Your Mama" put-downs include:

- "Your Mama's so old she drove chariots in high school"
- "Your mama's so fat that she fell and broke her leg and gravy poured out!"
- "I told your Mama to act her age and the bitch dropped dead!"
- "Your mother's teeth so yellow she can butter a whole loaf of bread"
- "Your Mama's so stupid it takes her two hours to watch SIXTY MINUTES."

The film's script is also cleverly peppered with other assorted colorful insults and putdowns. When Wesley Snipes gets mad at one of his friends, he says, "Shut your anorexic, malnutrition, tapeworm aten overdosed Dick Gregory Bahamian diet drinking ass up!" When Woody Harrelson is called an "Opie Taylor" by a black basketball player, he shouts back, "Opie Taylor! Opie Taylor! Hey, I got your Opie, you big bad Gomer Pyle goofey-eyed son of a bitch!" Woody's put-down is countered with, "Take your ass back to Mayberry and tell Aunt Bee she BETTER have my bean pies or I'm a kick her ass." The ultimate put-down in the movie is when Wesley Snipes tells Woody Harrelson, "White Men Can't Jump" after he fails to perform a slam-dunk shot. Note: In the motion picture *The Nutty Professor* (1996) Eddie Murphy plays Dr. Sherman Klump whose slender alter ego Buddy Love plays dueling "Your Mama" jokes with a loudmouthed nightclub comedian named Reggie Warrington (David Chappelle). Reggie begins his put-down of Buddy Love with, "It's time to attack black. Time for Reggie to lay into your mama." He continues, "Your Mama's so fat she went to Sizzler and the bitch got a group discount." Buddy Love counters, "Your Mama's so fat the bitch needs a Thomas Guide to find her asshole." On a roll, Buddy continues, "Your Mama's so fat after sex I rolled over twice and I'm still on the bitch...she's so fat she fell into the Grand Canyon and got stuck...she's so fat she gets her toenails painted at Earl Scheib." Driving the nail into Reggie's comic coffin, Buddy love concludes, "She's so fat her blood type is Rocky Road...She's so fat, her belt size is Equator." The TV comedy show IN LIVING COLOR/FOX/1990-94 spoofed the "Your Mama" phenomenon when they featured a game show called "The Dirty Dozen" where the contestants are encouraged to "Dis" the other contestant's mothers by answering such categories as Your Mama's so 'hairy,' 'so old,' and 'so ugly.' Examples of their responses include:

- "Your Mama's so ugly that she has to trick or treat over the phone"
- "She so hairy Bigfoot takes a picture of her"
- "She's so fat that when she bunji jumps, the bitch goes straight to hell!"
- "Your Mama's teeth are so yellow when she yawns, traffic slows down!"
- "Your Mama's gums are so black she can spit chocolate milk
- "Your Mama's so fat that when God said, 'Let there be light,' he told your Mama to 'Get your butt out of the way."

Special competition rounds included a mystery guest section of the show, where the lead contestant had 60 seconds to provoke the mystery guest into violence; and the wheel of insults filled with assorted "Your Mama" categories. In either segment, the person with the best put-downs won a car. On a classic comedy sketch entitled "Samurai Hotel" on NBC's SATURDAY NIGHT LIVE John Belushi plays a Samurai Warrior who dueled with another bellhop (Richard Pryor) over who was going to carry the guest's bag. The words "Your mama-san!" are heard in between grunts. In the film *Bebe's Kids* (1992) Dorothea (Myra J.) and Robin Harris (Faizon Love) shot off a volley of "Your Mama" put-downs including, "Your Mama's so old, she was there the first day of slavery."; "Your Mama's so old, she older than your grandmama."; "Your Mama's so fat, she on both sides of the family."; "Your Mama's so dumb, she thought a quarterback was a refund."; "Your Mama's so dumb, they told her it was chilly outside, she went and got a bowl."; and "Your Mama's so country, she got in an elevator, thought it was a mobile home" In 2006, the MTV network broadcast a show called YO MOMMA featuring Wilmer Valderrama as he criss-crossed the country in search of America's best trash-talkers.

"Your small minds are muscle-bound with suspicion. That's because the only exercise you ever get is jumping to conclusions." - Danny Kaye as the daydreaming Walter Mitty rebukes his family and friends in the motion picture *The Secret Life of Walter Mitty* (1947).

"Your mother sucks cocks in hell, Karras!" - The voice of Mercedes McCambridge as the demon who possesses the body of twelve-year-old Regan MacNeil (Linda Blair) in the motion picture *Exorcist* (1973). As the demon takes over the girl's body, it bellows, "Keep away! The sow is mine!" When Max von Sydow as Father Merrin prepares to exorcise the demon, with the help of his assistant Father Karras (Jason Miller), he instructs, "Especially important is the warning to avoid conversations with the demon. We may ask what is relevant, but anything beyond that is dangerous. He is a liar; The demon is a liar. He will lie to confuse us, but he will also mix lies with the truth to attack us." The demon taunts Father Karras by imitating the voice of his deceased mother and proclaiming, "Your mother sucks cock in hell, Karras!" The *Exorcist* and its sequels *Exorcist II: The Heretic* (1977) and *Exorcist III* (1990) were adapted from the William Peter Blatty's best-selling novel "The Exorcist."

"Your mother's uglier than Hazel" - Childhood insult directed at George Costanza (Jason Alexander), a balding, perennial loser featured on the situation comedy SEINFELD/NBC/1990-98. The "Hazel" taunt refers to the homely housekeeper Hzel Burke (Shirley Booth) on the sitcom HAZEL/NBC/CBS/1961-66. George revealed this childhood memory while talking to a female stranger (actually a thief) with whom he thought he was going to have sex. George was handcuffed to a hotel room bed at the time. Estelle Harris played George's mother Estelle.

"Your mouthwash ain't making it" - In the motion picture *The Enforcer* (1976) when Captain McKay (Bradford Dillman) bullies Inspector 'Dirty' Harry Callahan (Clint Eastwood) Callahan inquires, "May I say something...Your mouthwash ain't making it." In the sequel 'Dirty Harry' film *Sudden Impact* (1983) Bradford Dillman tells Harry, "You're a walking, friggin' combat zone. Your ideas don't fit anymore." Harry counters with "You're a legend in your own mind!" And in the sequel *The Dead Pool* Harry asks

his supervisor, “Do you have any children, Lieutenant? When the man answers, “No”, Harry says, “Lucky for them.”

"A zombie has no will of his own" - Richard Carlson as Jeff Montgomery explains the undead in the motion picture *The Ghost Breakers* (1940). He continues, "You see them sometimes walking around blindly with dead eyes, following orders, not knowing what they do, not caring." His colleague Larry Lawrence (Bob Hope) quips, "You mean like Democrats." Note: On a 1989 episode of THE SIMPSONS Bartholomew "Bart" Jo-Jo Simpson (Nancy Cartwright) says, "Oh my God! The dead have risen and are voting Republican!"

THE END

APPENDIX

Top Ten TV & Movie Lists

Top Ten "All-Time" Classic Action Movie Paybacks

You're the disease...and I'm the cure.	*Cobra*
Yippee-Ki-Yay, Motherfucker!	*Die Hard 2*
You killed my wife. Fuck you and die!	*Hard to Kill*
It's just been revoked!	*Lethal Weapon 2*
You're fired!	*Robocop*
You're a low down Yankee liar.	*Shane*
Go ahead, make my day.	*Sudden Impact*
You're terminated, fucker!	*Terminator*
Hasta la vista, Baby!	*Terminator 2*
Consider that a divorce!	*Total Recall*

Top Ten "All-Time" Classic Movie Put-downs

What a dump!	*Beyond the Forest*
Humbug!	*Christmas Carol*
You sure is ugly!	*Color Purple*
Frankly, my dear, I don't give a damn!	*Gone With the Wind*
You Imbecile! You bloated idiot!	*Maltese Falcon*
You're a low down Yankee Liar!	*Shane*
I don't need to show you no stinkin; badges	*Treasure of the Sierra Madre*
When you call me that, smile	*The Virginian*
I'll mow ya down!	Charlie McCarthy
You dirty rat!	James Cagney

Top Ten Foul "Animal" Put-down Phrases

I feel like a country dog in the city. If I stand still, they screw me. If I run, they bite my ass.	*Best Little Whorehouse in Texas*
Cross me and you're snail food	*City Heat*
At least he's not a book burner, you Nazi cow!	*Field of Dreams*
He an unlovely combination of a son of a bitch and a rat's knackers	*High Spirits*
Put me down! You male chauvinistic pig ape!	*King Kong*
Alligators have the right idea. They eat their young	*Mildred Pierce*
Snakes like you usually die of their own poison	*'Neath Arizona Skies*
Get your stinking paws off me, you damn dirty ape!	*Planet of the Apes*
Are you gonna bark all day, little dog, or are you gonna bite?	*Reservoir Dogs*
You're just dog shit	*Sudden Impact*

Top Ten "Foul" Bits of Movie Wisdom

You'll shoot your eye out!	A *Christmas Story*
We don't murder, we kill	*The Big Red One*
If you ain't a cowboy, you ain't shit.	*Fool for Love*
Mama says 'Stupid is as stupid does'.	*Forrest Gump*
Never trust a man with pinched nostrils and thin lips.	H*unchback of Notre Dame*
Man's got to know his limitations.	*Magnum Force*
Kill, then love When you have known that, you have known ecstasy.	*Most Dangerous Game*
Never give a sucker an even break.	*Poppy*
Steal from thy neighbor, Cheat thy neighbor, Kill thy neighbor.	*Sahara*
Greed is good.	*Wall Street*

Top Ten Foul "Food" Phrases in Movies

She's got a heart like a twelve-minute egg	*Bright Lights, Big City*
Paul, do you think you could buy another frying pan? I get little squeamish about cooking in the one we use to kill people	*Eating Raoul*
He was so crooked, he could eat soup with a corkscrew	*The Grifters*
Get your big, fat extra-crispy-bucket-of-chicken, two-liter-Pepsi-Cola drinking ass out of bed	*Heart Condition*
I could peel you like a pear and God himself would call it justice.	*The Lion in Winter*
Feed me! Feed me!	*Little Shop of Horrors*
He'll have you skewed, tattooed and served with an apple in your mouth	*Nate and Hayes*
A Census taker once tried to test me. I ate his liver with some fava beans and a nice Chianti.	*Silence of the Lambs*
I drink to your safe return in English ale. I wish that it were English blood.	*The Vikings*
Are you eating a tomato or is that your nose?	*You Can't Cheat an Honest Man*

Top Ten "Foul" Movie Greetings

Hello. My name is Inigo Montoya. You killed my father. Prepare to die	*The Princess Bride*
Dr. Kervorkian, I presume?	*Absolute Power*
Hi, I'm Chucky. Wanna Play?	*Child's Play*
Welcome to hell, Blofeld.	*Diamonds Are Forever*
Say hello to my little friend!	*Scarface*
Welcome to Slavery.	*From Dusk till Dawn*
Welcome to Earth! [Bam]	*Independence Day*
This is hell, and I'm going to give you the guided tour	*Lock up*
Heerrreee's Johnny!	*The Shining*
Glad to meet you, kid. You're a real horse's ass	*The Sting*

Top Ten "Foul" Requests of Movie Characters

Get away from her you bitch!	*Aliens*
Terminate with extreme prejudice.	*Apocalypse Now*
Don't call me babe!	*Barb Wire*
Grant me revenge!	*Conan the Barbarian*
Squeal...like a pig!	*Deliverance*
I want you to hold it between your knees .	*Five Easy Pieces*
Smile, you son of bitch!	*Jaws*
Don't fuck with me fellas, this ain't my first time at the rodeo	*Mommie Dearest*
Get your stinking paws off me, you damn dirty ape	*Planet of the Apes*
Get a Life!	*Sliver*
Go ahead, make my day.	*Sudden impact*

Top Ten James Bond Put-downs & Paybacks

Welcome to hell, Blofeld!	*Diamonds are Forever*
Shocking! Positively shocking!	*Dr. No*
You've had your six!	*Dr. No*
Yes, she's had her kicks.	*From Russia with Love*
All those feathers and he still can't fly	*A View to a Kill*
No more foreplay!	*Goldeneye*
Oh, he blew a fuse.	*Goldfinger*
He just dropped in for a quick bite.	*Spy Who Loved Me*
I think he got the point.	*Thunderball*
I never miss!	*World Is Not Enough*

Top Ten "Mean" Movie Questions

Do I feel lucky? Well, do you punk?	*Dirty Harry*
You know what I do to squealers?	*Kiss of Death*
Where the hell did you get him: Psychos-R-Us?	*Lethal Weapon*
Guess where you get the first one?	*Never Say Never Again*
Have you considered drowning?	*Pat—the Movie*
Do I ice her? Do I marry her? Which of dese?	*Prizzi's Honor*
Is that a nose or did a bus park on your face?	*Roxanne*
You talkin' to me?	*Taxi Driver*
How do you like your stake, bitch?	*Vampires*
How about a little fire, scarecrow?	*Wizard of Oz*

Top Ten Most "Cruel" Movie Phrases

Gotta go. So many people to kill, so little time.	*Batman 4*
I'll turn your balls into earrings.	*City Slickers*
Nothing like a strangulation to get the circulation going.	*Child's Play 3*
When I want your opinion, I'll beat it out of you.	*Code of Silence*
I'll torture you so slowly you'll think it's a career	*Hudson Hawk*
Freeze, hombre, or I'll be wearing your asshole for a garter.	*Lust in the Dust*
When you're slapped, you'll take it and like it.	*Maltese Falcon*
I'll crucify him...real bad.	*Rocky III*
He's so mean he'd shut off the air in a baby's incubator, just to watch the little sucker squirm.	*San Francisco*
You are beautiful when I beat you.	*Swept Away*

Top Ten "Most Disgusting" Phrases in Movie History

The hospital will kill no quadriplegic before their time	*Whose Life Is It Anyway*
I only raped her once	*Catch-22*
Splitting a little girl's throat is like cutting warm butter	*Commando*
Your mother sucks cock in hell, Karrras!	*The Exorcist*
Squeal! (like a pig)	Deliverance
It takes a lot of Critters to make Farmer Vincent Fritters	*Motel Hell*
Beat 'em or burn 'em	*Night of the Living Dead*
[Farts] There, my colon is clean. My colon is squeaky clean!	*Nutty Professor*
Soylent Green is People!	*Soylent Green*
You have one choice, boy: sex or the saw!	*Texas Chain Saw Massacre 2*

Top Ten Movie Threats

You fuck with me; I'll send you a love letter! (a bullet)	*Blue Velvet*
I'll make him an offer he can't refuse.	*The Godfather*
I'm gonna take you to the bank, Senator Trent —the blood bank.	*Hard to Kill*
Then I'll get you there dead, boy.	*Hang 'em High*
We'll tear your soul apart.	*Hellraiser*
I'm gonna get that gun of mine and I'm gonna change you from a rooster to a hen with one shot.	*Nine to Five*
You should of let him kill me, 'cause I'm gonna kill you!	*Red River*
Look out, Hitler! The Niggers is coming to get your ass!	*A Soldier's Story*
I'll be back!	*Terminator*
I'll get you, my pretty, and your little dog, too!	*Wizard of Oz*

Top Ten - Pejorative TV Character Nicknames - The Men

Meathead	*All in the Family*
Cheapest Man in the World	*The Jack Benny Show*
Ferret-face	*M*A*S*H*
Old Lead Bottom	*McHale's Navy*
Old Fish-eyed Fool	*Sanford and Son*
Girly-Man	*Saturday Night Live*
Soup Nazi	*Seinfeld*
The Thief of Bad Gags	*Texaco Theatre (Milton Berle)*
Cancer Man	*X-Files*
Spooky Mulder	*X-Files*

Top Ten - Pejorative TV Character Nicknames - The Women

Dinghy	*Alice*
Dingbat	*All in the Family*
The Undateable	*Amen*
Backseat Becky	*Cheers*
Nature's Revenge on Peeping Toms	*Duffy's Tavern*
Smartest Dumbbell in the History of Show Business	*Burns &* Allen Show
Spooky Old Alice	*George Gobel Show*
Hot Lips	*M*A*S*H*
Chicken Legs	*Married with Children*
Dumbest Girl in America	*Married with Children*

Top Ten Politically Incorrect Movie Phrases

That's faggot stuff	*Midnight Cowboy*
You're a yellow belly Jap lover	*Bad Day at Black Rock*
Up yours Nigger!	*Blazing Saddles*
Oh, You English. You're so fucking superior, aren't you?	*A Fish Called Wanda*
The only good human is a dead human	*Planet of the Apes*
You hideous yellow monster, do you mean to destroy us all?	*Mask of Fu Manchu*
It's shite being Scottish	*Trainspotting*
I hate the British	*Bridge on River Kwai*
Shut up, you American	*Monty Python's The Meaning of Life*
In Japan, men come first; women come second	*You Only Live Twice*

Top Ten TV Character Put-downs & Paybacks

Exterminate! Exterminate!	*Dr. Who*
Bite Me, Pig	*Drew Carey Show*
You miserable bitch	*Dynasty*
Sit on it!	*Happy Days*
Homey don't play that!	*In Living Color*
For me to "Poop" on!	*Late Night with Conan O'Brien*
I hate spunk!	*Mary Tyler Moore*
You pissy little bitch	*NYPD Blue*
Jane, you ignorant slut!	*Saturday Night Live*
Oh my God! They killed Kenny!	*South Park*
Up your nose with a rubber hose	*Welcome Back, Kotter*

ABOUT THE AUTHOR

Born in Philadelphia, Jerome Alphonse Holst received his undergraduate degree in Art History from Temple University. He later earned graduate degrees in Library Science from California State University in Fullerton and the University of Kentucky in Lexington.

The author is also the webmaster of TV ACRES, a huge archive of television facts that chronicles TV programs from the 1940s to the present (www.tvacres.com).

Mr. Holst currently lives in Northeast Ohio and works as a medical librarian. Besides TV and movies, the author likes to collect memorabilia about elves and fairies in the popular culture.

INDEX

The index for *The Encyclopedia of TV and Movie Insults* features an alphabetical list of TV programs and movies. The TV programs are displayed in CAPITAL LETTERS; the movies are *lower case italics.*

And don't forget to visit TVACRES.COM

TV ACRES is a huge archive of TV program facts, arranged by subject. Our mission: To provide an easy-to-use, on-line guide that quickly finds information about the characters, places and things that appeared on television programs broadcast from the 1940s to the present (during prime time and Saturday mornings). Check it out!

***USA Today* - Hot Site of the Week & *Yahoo Picks* – Editor's Choice**

Bookmark this great site – http://www.tvacres.com

www.ingramcontent.com/pod-product-compliance
Lightning Source LLC
LaVergne TN
LVHW061220100826
845148LV00004B/808

* 9 7 8 0 9 7 9 4 1 3 3 0 8 *